F
128.5
.W22
W34

Walsh, George
Gentlemen Jimmy Walker

DATE DUE

#47-0108 Peel Off Pressure Sensitive

GENTLEMAN JIMMY WALKER

GENTLEMAN JIMMY WALKER

Mayor of the Jazz Age

GEORGE WALSH

Foreword by Robert Moses

PRAEGER PUBLISHERS
New York • Washington

Published in the United States of America in 1974
by Praeger Publishers, Inc.
111 Fourth Avenue, New York, N.Y. 10003

© 1974 by Praeger Publishers, Inc.
All rights reserved

Library of Congress Cataloging in Publication Data

Walsh, George   1931–
  Gentleman Jimmy Walker, mayor of the jazz age.

  Bibliography: p.
  1. Walker, James John, 1881–1946.   I. Title.
F128.5.W22W34   974.7′1′040924   [B]   74-7897
ISBN 0-275-50840-4

Printed in the United States of America

To Joan, Grail, and Simon

CONTENTS

FOREWORD

by Robert Moses

This is the age of revivals, when readers and viewers, tired of violence, pornography, and psychedelic freaks, turn back to half-forgotten heroes who never had their due but seem to have perennial appeal. This is not trick stuff like breathing life into mummies or fashioning a new image. And so it is that Mayor Walker is at last to have a first-rate biographer.

"Manners maketh man" is the inscription on the gateway of New College, Oxford. Manners, my eye! Our hostile, well-mannered gentry on Long Island had manners, but I can never forget that Jimmy Walker gave us the city water-supply easements in Nassau County, which became the backbone of the Long Island State Park system and the means of access to Jones Beach and the finest oceanfront park in the world. Jimmy did not say he would give the subject profound and prayerful consideration and refer it to a committee. He did it. By the same token, I cannot forget the snide, sideline eunuchs and bitches who impeded and belittled our Jones Beach and other projects. The conclusion seems inescapable that only those with an instinct for the jugular can build complex public works in a great metropolis. Manners make good inscriptions on college gateways, but they do not build Jones Beaches.

The denouement, the payoff at the end of the Walker incumbency at City Hall, was the Seabury investigation. Apart from the legal issues, the battle of Seabury versus Walker, which finished Jimmy politically if not otherwise, was high drama. It was a conflict of personalities. The judge was austere, not to say frigid, and little under-stood or liked by the hoi polloi. He was wrapped in the seamless garment of unchallengeable, old-family Episcopalian respectability beyond the pales and ghettos which surround exiles and newcomers yearning to breathe free. (The Judge's protégé was the sainted Fiorello LaGuardia, an Episcopal recruit with some Old Testament background, who was buried from the Cathedral of St. John the Divine.) When grim old Dean Swift strode the streets of Dublin near his Cathedral, plain people solemnly and respectfully doffed their hats. So it was with Judge Seabury, but the first sight of Jimmy Walker invited an anticipatory grin. He was like Scaramouche, born with the gift of laughter and a sense that the world is mad, but also the cause of mirth and gaiety in others. He struck sparks off dull metal. It's a great gift which has little to do with the higher moralities.

The passing of Judge Seabury reminded me of the much-quoted obit of Cardinal Wolsey in Shakespeare's *Henry VIII*. The great prel-ate and Chancellor was depicted as lofty and sour to them that loved him not, but to those men that sought him he was sweet as summer. The eulogy ended with the supreme tribute, that Woolsey had died fearing God. Jimmy Walker was as sweet as summer to everyone and also died humbly.

There was little public understanding of the relations between Al Smith and Walker. When it came to the business of government, Smith was a serious man dedicated to the job, and he disliked Walker's flippancy and irresponsibility. He didn't like Jimmy's fancy, tight-fitting duds, although he affected a brown derby himself. Smith had not backed Jimmy for Mayor. He was for the Senior Wagner. The leaders wanted Jimmy.

Seabury never associated Smith with Walker. He disliked Smith largely because he thought Smith had prevented him from becoming President. Don't ask me how he figured this out because he never had a ghost of a chance at the White House. William Church Osborn, another aristocratic New York Democrat, had the same illusion. The *ex post facto* reasoning of those who fall short of the highest office is impossible to fathom.

Walker was no typical New York lawyer. He was a sort of British-style barrister whose anxious solicitors prepared briefs that he never saw until he came bounding into court—late—for trial. He drove his partners nuts, but he usually won their cases.

Jimmy was the extrovert, the spontaneous eccentric, the sidewalk favorite, the beloved clown, the idol of those who seek companion-ship and mercy above and beyond justice. Jimmy had genuine charm, not charisma. Charm is what that quaint Scotch philosopher James M. Barrie said gives a person a sort of bloom. If you have it you don't need anything else. If you don't, it doesn't matter what else you have. Jimmy had his two Charlies, Kerrigan and Hand, the knights of the Kerry Ring and the Glad Hand, who protected him from the press and the elements. They were not at all like those formidable, growling German shepherd dogs, Haldeman and Erlichman. Judge Seabury had neither a Boswell nor a Cerberus. His privacy was safe from invasion by the common folk.

Governor Smith used to tell us about a freak Republican Assemblyman from Manhattan who was disliked by his own party. He was a member of the City Committee, but they even froze him out of the Committee room between sessions. This was his only club, and he had to sit outside with the pageboys. He went to Governor Smith, then Democratic minority leader, for help; Smith asked the Speaker to let him in; and the Speaker did. Subsequently this assemblyman was appointed a magistrate by Mayor Mitchel. A case came before him involving bookmaking by a little clerk in a little newsshop in Boss Foley's district. The Boss asked Smith to intervene. Smith said, "No problem, I know the Magistrate." So Smith walked into the Magistrate's office unannounced. The Magistrate, becoming very magisterial, said, "You have no right to come into my chambers. Your client will receive substantial justice." Smith exploded and went to the D.A., who promptly dropped the prosecution. When Smith became Governor, one of our instructions was to give troublesome critics "substantial justice." We all knew what that meant. It was just about the worst thing that could happen to you. Jimmy Walker never asked for substantial justice. He wanted small favors for his people.

Mayor LaGuardia once said that he was loyal to principles, not to people. That was a horrifying remark, and I am sure the sainted Fiorello never meant and later regretted it. Jimmy Walker was always for people as against principles. Is not that the philosophy of the rank and file who, in our dog-eat-dog civilization, ask for friendship, not nobility?

In a strange way I admired both Walker and Seabury. Without venturing into the intricacies of conflict of interest, I thought they both had integrity—integrity of very different kinds, but integrity nevertheless. The Judge was the remote Civic Conscience of the Community. Jimmy was the frank, candid Celtic champion of the unpredictable, backsliding, and forward-looking immigrant masses. In the vast limbo where law and logic do not always prevail the Jimmy Walkers live and move and have their being.

In ethical terms the Judge represented Reform, the Higher Strategy, and the Eternal Verities in what seemed to the unregenerate a somewhat unattractive form. Jimmy Walker as Mayor was not much concerned with such considerations. He figured that reform is periodic, short-lived, and in a way contrary to nature; that the waves of excessive virtue recede, having perhaps washed away some litter. To the extent that he had himself been on an occasional spree and lacking in serious purpose, he knew that finally there remained Confession, Repentence, Forgiveness, and underneath it all the Everlasting Arms.

When the music stopped and the party was over, Jimmy had a curious, almost winsome humility. Perhaps his significance lies in being what all sophisticated, urban, frivolous folk admired in the jazz age and would like to revive. In these grim days of violence and skepticism, the wags of New York chuckle over the carefree consulship of Walker and entertain their grandchildren with tall tales of our Riviera that prove that the town, if not governable, is irrepressible.

I always like to recall the Inner Circle City Hall reporters' dinner shortly after Jimmy died. There were no orations. As the old quatrain ran:

> A noise arose in the orchestra
> As the leader drew across
> The intestines of the agile cat
> The tail of the noble horse.

The first violin rose and, exhorting the strings to their utmost tenderness, played Jimmy's song, written in his Tin Pan Alley days: "Will You Love Me in December as You Do in May?" There was not a dry eye in the Astor.

ACKNOWLEDGMENTS

For their time and interest in helping me discern the character of James J. Walker, I wish to thank the late Charles Lockwood, Laurette Dunn, Robert Moses, George Jessel, James A. Farley, Ed Sullivan, Robert Newman, Paul O'Dwyer, Lois Long Fox, the late Paul Schoenstein, Morris Ernst, Luke Burke, and James McNally.

I am similarly indebted, for their courtesy and cooperation, to Sylvia Hilton, Helen Ruskell, Joan Auger, and Rita Atterton of the New York Society Library; to John Carey of the New York Public Library; and also to staff members of the newspaper division of the New York Public Library and of the Kilroe Collection of Tammaniana at Columbia University.

Lastly, my thanks to editor William Weatherby for helping develop the book's structure, editor Gladys Topkis for her ever sensible guidance on content, and literary agent Sterling Lord for furthering the over-all project.

GENTLEMAN JIMMY WALKER

PROLOGUE

"Let me carve the pig," said Cet.

"You're not the man to carve," said Eogan, rising to his feet.

"I know you," answered Cet.

"How so?" asked Eogan.

"You threw a spear at me that I caught with my shield. I hurled it back at you and pierced your eye. The men of Ireland see you with one eye. I cut the other out of your head." So Eogan sat down.

"You are not to carve the pig," said Muinremor, rising in turn.

"Your people were the last I bloodied my spears in, Muinremor," said Cet. "It hasn't been three days since I took the heads of three of your warriors and the head of your eldest son." So Muinremor sat himself down.

"The carving is not for you," declared a stalwart warrior named Menn.

"And what are herdsmen's sons doing competing with me?" said Cet. "I cut the heel from your father so that he went from me a cripple. What's the cripple's son doing, challenging me?" So Menn sat down.

But when Cet took knife in hand and was about to begin the carving, Conall Cernach came into the great hall.

"It's good the food is ready," said Conall. "Who is doing the carving?"

"Cet mac Magach," he was told.

"Get up from the pig, Cet," said Conall.

"Will you make me?" said Cet.

"I swear by my people's gods," said Conall, "that since I took a spear in my hands I was never a day without killing a Connachtman, and I never slept a night without a Connachtman's head under my knee."

"You're a better hero than I am, Conall," Cet admitted. "But if my brother Anluan were here, he would give you a contest."

"He is here," said Conall, taking Anluan's head from his belt. He hit Cet in the chest with it and blood spilled from its lips. Then Conall went up to the pig and began carving.

—Irish legend

In the summer of 1925, the Irish politicians of the Democratic Party who dominated Tammany Hall and the affairs of the city of New York were setting about the freshest carving of the mayoralty. Most were nowhere near so sanguinary as their Celtic ancestors, the opportunities of office having cooled their blood while swelling their bank balances, but almost all were men who kept their own counsel, were loyal to their word, and firmly believed the Irish were born to rule.

So it happened that, on July 2, George W. Olvany, the newly elected head of Tammany, received a delegation of some 500 noisy citizens urging him to support James J. Walker, the Democratic leader of the state senate in Albany, for the mayoralty. The group entered the Wigwam on Fourteenth Street, "Win With Walker" buttons on every lapel, while bands blared the tune "Tammany, Tammany . . . Swamp 'em, Swamp 'em . . . Get the wampum . . . Taammanee!" The crowd hushed while its spokesman, former New York Secretary of State Bainbridge Colby, made its feelings clear to Olvany.

"No office carries a greater opportunity for service or carries greater responsibilities than that of Mayor of New York City," said Colby. "We want ability in that office, not only good intentions. We do not want a self-seeker or a self-exploiter in the Mayor's chair. We want a Mayor of mental girth commensurate with the problems incidental to that growth."

When Colby spoke the name Walker, the audience—which included members of such organizations as the Friars, the Grand Street Boys' Association, the Jewish Theatrical Alliance, the Music Publishers' Association, and the Motion Picture Producers' Chamber of Commerce—broke into cheering that lasted a full minute. "He knows the city in all its moods," Colby said of Walker. "He knows its big and good heart and the fervor with which it lives. He is a New Yorker of New York."

Olvany's acknowledgment of Walker's candidacy was, predictably, noncommittal. "I have known him since he was a little boy," he intoned. "His father was Alderman of my district. [Senator Walker's] progress has been continuous and marvelous. I cannot designate him or anyone else for that nomination. But I can communicate to the Executive Committee of Tammany Hall that you favor his nomination. It will give me great pleasure to do so." With that the delegation, which was heavily weighted with show-business personalities, took its leave.

Indeed, James J. Walker himself seemed less a politician than a showman. Among the burly Tammany leaders, his slim, straight-figure was a study in contrasts. (At five foot eight inches, Walker seldom weighed more than 130 pounds.) Amid their severe black suits and derby hats, his tastes dictated fitted double-breasteds and wide-brimmed fedoras. Among impassive faces, his was the ready smile. Amid careful silences and laconic phrases, his was the voice that crackled with wit and charm. Walker had served for sixteen years in Albany, in both the Assembly and the Senate. His forte was the give-and-take of debate, the quick-read school of legislation. "A legislator," Walker would say, "is like an actor thrown on the stage without any lines." He was involved, particularly in his later years in the Senate, with much legislation, but his function was to push through bills, not to conceive them. The latter task, more often than not, was the province of Democratic Governor Alfred E. Smith. The few bills Walker interested himself in more deeply reflected his enthusiasms: He saw to it that New Yorkers could watch professional baseball on Sunday, and he played a key role in the legalization of professional boxing. A former song writer (hadn't he written the lyrics to the popular tune "Will You Love Me in December as You Do in May?") and a determined sentimentalist, Walker liked good theater, good fun, good parties. He enjoyed show-business people, and they warmed to him as one of their own. But popularity alone does not ensure a candidate's success or even his nomination. To understand Walker's emergence into the mayoral arena, we must examine the political background of New York City at the time and the loyalties, resentments, and alliances of the various Democratic chieftains.

John F. Hylan, the incumbent mayor of New York in 1925, was nearing the end of his second four-year term. Called "Red Mike" by his constituents, both for his carroty hair and for his irascible nature, Hylan could not have been more unlike Walker. To many people it seemed that he had devoted his entire stay in City Hall to fulminating against the "traction interests," as the owners and operators of the city's transit lines were then known. Faced with any municipal problem, he resorted to an impassioned defense of the five-cent fare or, in a crisis, shouted, "Get an injunction!" The federal courts denied these legal stratagems with humorless regularity, dismissing lawsuit after lawsuit.

Hylan, who was reared on a farm in the Catskill Mountains, came to Brooklyn in his late teens. (Although the Catskills are within a hundred miles of the city, New Yorkers tend to regard those who have lived there, however briefly, as rustics; Hylan never quite overcame this liabilty.) In Brooklyn, the young émigré attended law school by night and worked as a motorman on the elevated lines by day. He was fired from his job for "rounding a curb too quickly," and in later years this may have accounted for his antipathy to the traction magnates. Eventually Hylan began the practice of law, joined a Brooklyn Democratic club, and by 1906 was prominent enough in politics to be named to magistrates' court. In 1914, he was advanced to a judgeship in Brooklyn's county court, where the strapping six-footer, who neither smoked nor drank, began to be cultivated by the powerful Hearst press. So scrupulously was his every remark on a public matter reported that the non-Hearst papers, in classic self-defense, were forced to give him similar coverage. As a thinker, Hylan was a heavy breather, but he was quick to take up popular causes like the five-cent fare, and he developed a sizable following. In 1917, when the rumor circulated that William Randolph Hearst, making one of his periodic forays into politics, was interested in the Democratic nomination for mayor, the anti-Hearst legions in Tammany Hall were so desperate to block the wealthy publisher that they agreed to consider Hylan, his puppet, in his place.

The Tammany leader who preceded Olvany, the oracular Charles Francis Murphy, met with the white-haired, cherubic John H. McCooey, his Brooklyn counterpart.

"Is Hylan a man we can trust and do business with?" said the Irish boss of Manhattan to the Irish boss of Brooklyn.

"He certainly is," said McCooey. "Do you want to meet him?"

"No," answered Murphy, who, as we shall see, had his reasons for not wanting to be too closely identified with any friend of Hearst's. "I want you to ram him down my throat."

Charles F. Murphy was the most successful and, despite certain financial irregularities, the most enlightened leader Tammany ever had. Before his twenty-two-year rule was over, he groomed for public office such exemplary men as Governor Alfred E. Smith, Senator Robert F. Wagner, Surrogate James A. Foley, and "Boss" Edward J. Flynn of the Bronx. (There were even those who maintained that, had Murphy lived a few years longer, he would have been able to curb and guide the prodigal Mayor James J. Walker.) Yet Murphy dominated the political scene not by fiat but by persuasion, the giving and withholding of favors, the calm weighing of pros and cons. And so in 1917 Murphy was willing to accept Hearst's man; he saw that by giving the nomination to Hylan, a Brooklynite, he could, at one and the same time, seemingly accommodate the publisher and strengthen his alliance with McCooey. (Except in those rare instances when Fusion fervor swept the city, the Democratic nomination was tantamount to election.) McCooey and Hylan had been friends for years, ever since young McCooey was a post-office employee and motorman Hylan would regularly step up to the window to send for money orders for the support of his mother; Brooklyn would get out the vote for such a dutiful son.

Murphy realized that he would need strong allies to head off, or at least control, Hearst's political ambitions. Because of the millions of people his newspapers influenced, and because of the financing he could bring to a campaign, the publisher was a formidable opponent.

The Murphy-Hearst rivalry was a hate-love relationship of long standing. Back in 1905, Hearst had decided to run for mayor of New York on his own ticket, in defiance of both the Tammany machine and the Republican opposition. It was a most bitter campaign. Murphy and his cohorts, taking advantage of Hearst's early concern with the rights of working men to organize, pictured him as an anarchist; they hung banners showing a likeness of Hearst with a red flag and underneath the picture the legend "Under Which Flag Do You Vote?" And because one of the Hearst papers, the New York *Journal,* had published a humorous quatrain by Ambrose Bierce shortly before President McKinley's assassination that tastelessly suggested McKinley might deserve a bullet in the breast, Hearst was characterized as having "incited" the murder. In turn, the Hearst press ran cartoons depicting Murphy as a stripe-suited felon, and an inspired Hearst supporter composed a campaign song, to the tune of "Everybody Works But Father," that went:

> Everybody woiks but Moiphy;
> He only rakes in the dough. . . .

That this accusation was not without merit is demonstrated by the fact that Murphy, when he died in 1924, left a net estate of almost

$2,000,000, even though his Tammany post was unsalaried. (Through a brief stint as one of four dock commissioners—the only municipal office he ever held—Murphy learned how to use his political connections to the full; he formed a contracting firm that leased piers from the city at advantageous rentals, then released them to commercial interests for whatever the maritime traffic would bare.)

When the last vote was counted in the 1905 election, and undoubtedly recounted in many of the Tammany-controlled districts, it was clear how close Hearst had come to besting the machine. Out of 590,500 votes cast, he had lost, to Tammany's George B. McClellan, by a mere 3,500. Despite the animosities that had been aroused, Murphy the very next year took cognizance of Hearst's popularity and got him the Democratic nomination for governor. If the publisher ran independently, Murphy felt, he would split the Democratic vote and ensure the election of a Republican. Hearst had solid voter appeal, particularly because of his support of labor and his attacks on the monopolistic trusts. But foot-dragging by some unforgiving Tammany leaders and worse, an attack by innuendo on Hearst's less-than-puritanical private life by President Theodore Roosevelt's Secretary of State Elihu Root, who was dispatched to New York at the last moment to sling some genteel mud, narrowly gave the Republicans the governorship. Hearst would impatiently wait for another electoral opportunity.

In 1917, then, Tammany found itself once again in uneasy alliance with Hearst, backing Hylan for mayor. Alfred E. Smith, then sheriff of New York after twelve years in the legislature, was Murphy's top-ranking protégé and Hearst's wariest adversary. To sidetrack the publisher from himself running for mayor, Smith swallowed the slow-witted Hylan. Murphy made the placebo more meaningful to Smith by putting him on the ticket to run for the presidency of the board of aldermen and by implicitly promising him the gubernatorial nomination the following year.

Smith's resentment of Hearst was grounded in the loyalty that most Irish politicians of the day felt for the men who had given them their start. Thomas F. Foley, the leader of Al's home district on the Lower East Side, was Smith's mentor. Al could not forget that in 1907, a decade before, Hearst had entered a candidate against Foley in a sheriff's election, even though "Big Tom," who knew every man, woman, and child in his district by their first names, was obviously unbeatable. Against so popular a candidate as Foley, all the Hearst forces could do was hurl the basest of insults. Foley won the contest easily, but he smarted under these slurs on his character as only a church-going Irishman could. Like most Tammany district leaders, Foley was a saloonkeeper as well, and his "store" was a natural gathering place for his supporters. Over many a glass of beer, Smith would hear Hearst assigned to eternal damnation for his effrontery.

With Tammany and Hearst behind him, Hylan's election in 1917 was all but assured. His opponent was the antimachine Fusion candidate, Mayor John Purroy Mitchel, who was seeking a second term, a reward reformers in New York do not ordinarily receive. During the campaign, Hylan was virtually ignored. Instead, Hearst bore the brunt of Mitchel's charges; because the Hearst press had adopted an anti-British stance and was demanding that America not join with Britain and France in the war against Germany, the publisher was labeled "the spokesman of the Kaiser." When Mitchel did mention Hylan's name, it was in attacking "Hearst, Hylan and the Hohenzollerns." The jingoism was unavailing. When the votes were in, "Red Mike" Hylan had amassed an impressive plurality of 147,000.

As the Democrats met in Saratoga in 1918 to name a gubernatorial candidate, old rivalries and loyalties came to the fore. During the first year of Hylan's administration, Smith and Hearst had been on almost amicable terms. It was even given about that the Smith children had been invited to play at Hearst's Riverside Drive mansion. At the convention, however, the inevitable chill descended; both men hoped to get Murphy's backing for the governorship. Ostensibly, the Tammany leader remained neutral, repeating his refrain, "The convention will decide," to newsmen and confidants alike. "Most of the troubles of the world could be avoided," Murphy told Walker, then in the state senate, "if men opened their minds instead of their mouths." In truth, Murphy probably weighed the two candidacies until the last moment. On the one hand was his respect and affection for Smith; on the other, Hearst's enormous wealth and influence. In the end, it was Smith who won the nod. Perhaps even the inscrutable Murphy was influenced by ancient ties of Celtic blood. Perhaps he feared an anti-Tammany uprising among upstate Democrats and felt Smith's integrity might stifle it. Or perhaps he simply realized that many of Tammany's leaders, angry at Hearst for past indignities, would not get out the vote if he were the candidate. As the Democratic standard-bearer, Smith that fall easily defeated the Republican incumbent, Governor Charles Whitman.

Hearst's chagrin over his dismissal by the Irish politicians at Saratoga must have been monumental. Within a year his papers focused on an issue calculated to embarrass Smith in turn. The Republican-controlled legislature, conscious of the upstate influence of the dairy industry, had given regulatory power over milk production to a board answerable only to the lawmakers; the governor could not give orders to this board or remove its members from office. Knowing this, the Hearst press hit hard at various milk impurities and at overpricing, and demanded that Smith take action. Of course, he could do nothing. As the weeks went on, the attacks grew in violence, to the extent of implying that the governor, by not acting on the milk situation, was permitting the babies of the poor to die. Besides the political implications, this charge was all the more galling to Smith because, as a product of the slums himself, he knew how greatly the poor were penalized by bad and costly milk. His patience in the face of the attacks reached its limit when his ailing mother, who had learned of the charges, supposedly murmured from her sickbed, "My son did not kill those babies."

On October 29, 1919, Smith stepped out alone on the stage of Carnegie Hall. Labeling Hearst the "greatest living enemy of the people whose cause he pretends to espouse," the governor had challenged his accuser to public debate. Hearst had declined. Now Smith was at Carnegie Hall anyway, putting his case before the electorate. His ruddy face crimson, his nasal voice harsh and cracking, he emphasized his lack of authority over the milk trust and assailed the motives of his rival in unequivocal terms, asking that, "we may be rid of this pestilence that walks in the dark." By the next morning, all thinking New Yorkers knew the charges against Smith to be baseless.

Incredibly, Hearst's influence, and his ability to keep Hylan in office, persisted. In large part, this was because Smith, despite a progressive record as governor, lost his bid for re-election in 1920. Though he ran 1,000,000 votes ahead of the Democratic national ticket, it was not enough. The conservative swell that swept the country after World War I carried Warren Gamaliel Harding and Calvin Coolidge to the White House and sent Smith home from Albany. Out of office, he found his ability to shape events considerably diminished. The next year, Hylan, as willing as ever to share patronage with Tammany, was renominated and re-elected.

At Syracuse in 1922, another chapter began in the Smith-Hearst confrontation. The Democrats were meeting to name both a governor and a senator, and, while Murphy maintained his usual knowing silence, other men were taking sides. Mayor Hylan arrived at the convention site escorted, appropriately enough, by Hearst's personal attorney. Lined up with Hylan and Hearst was Brooklyn's McCooey. Down in the baroque lobby of the Onondega Hotel, delegates strove to learn how they might be on the winning side; whispering became the normal tone of conversation, even when asking for a match. The Hearst-Hylan-McCooey supporters were confident, the Smith men strangely timid. Gradually the word spread: Hearst has the governor's nomination nailed down . . . Murphy knows Smith will go along. So sweeping was the Hearst camp's confidence that it announced its man would welcome Smith's nomination as senator on the same ticket.

On the evening of September 28, the delegates became aware that Smith was not behaving like a Tammany Brave. He was staying in his suite, swearing that he would never join Hearst in any political race. Al was so mad, some sources claimed, that he spat whenever he mentioned the publisher's name.

In truth, Smith was taking a shrewd risk. He knew the convention felt it needed Hearst to ensure victory in the election, yet he sensed that this was his chance to outgrow Tammany, to lead rather than compromise. He sensed, too, that Murphy's traditional silence, perhaps by design, would ultimately work to Hearst's disadvantage.

All that night, the delegates wrestled, not with their consciences, but with their ambitions. The initial shock of the realization that Smith was standing on principle had passed, and their early chagrin had turned to fear. Hearst could never win without Smith on the ticket, the politicians began to realize. Yet Smith well might win alone. The next day, September 29, the tiny band of Smith supporters saw that their numbers had grown enormously; the dazed Hearst forces could do nothing to stop the mass desertions from their ranks. Charles S. Hand, reporting for the New York *World*, would write:

> The whole anti-Smith combine collapsed this afternoon. First, Hearst quit cold. He wired his managers to withdraw his name. Second, Hylan packed up his duds and beat it to New York on the first train. Third, the whole Hearst outfit evacuated the town in the wake of Mayor Hylan, leaving Smith the boss of the works. . . .

Smith quite handily captured the governorship that fall. Two years later, after narrowly failing to get the presidential nomination, he ran again for governor and was the only statewide candidate to win for the Democrats. (Coolidge, running on his own after Harding's death, carried even New York for the Republicans.) Smith's control of Tammany was now complete. He revealed as much at the 1924 Democratic National Convention when, after being rejected by the delegates in his presidential bid, he assured them that he, and therefore all Democrats in his state, would work for the election of the nominee, John W. Davis. "For I," Smith said, "am the leader of the Democracy of New York."

Twelve months later, he would demonstrate his power by forcing Tammany to turn down Mayor Hylan, Hearst's man, for a third term. Smith's choice for the mayorality, a fáteful one, ultimately would be State Senator James J. Walker.

≋≋≋

William H. Walker, father of the mayor-to-be, came to the United States from County Kilkenny, Ireland, in 1857. He was eighteen years old, all but penniless, and knew only the carpenter's trade. But he was affable, hard-working, and, most important, Irish. In a city dominated by a changing Tammany Hall, these qualities would ensure him at least a degree of success. The great immigrations of the 1840s had swollen New York's population to almost 1,000,000 persons, a quarter of them Irish. Tammany's leaders, up to this time native American Protestants, were willing, in exchange for votes, to do all they could for the newcomers.

A patriotic society whose rituals and titles were pseudo-Indian, Tammany sprang up after the Revolutionary War in various northern cities. It took its name from Tamanend, an Indian chief who had told his warriors: "Stand together and support each other, and you will be a mountain. . . ." The New York branch, the only one to have a long life, was founded in 1786. At its meetings, it used Indian terms like *wigwam* (for meeting hall), *brave* (for member), *sachem* (for tribal elder). Today we may regard such ritualizing as forced, but in the eighteenth century it was quite in keeping with the passionate mood of the electorate. From the beginning, the membership of New York's Tammany (its motto: "Freedom Our Rock") was largely composed of "have-nots," although its leadership came from the upper classes. In sum, its politics were Jeffersonian rather than Hamiltonian. By 1798, Tammany had been taken over by Aaron Burr, who molded it into an egalitarian battering-ram. The society's support of the plebian Andrew Jackson in his successful 1828 and 1832 Presidential campaigns made it New York's principal political group; it stood for reforms benefiting the common man—calling for democratic suffrage and abolition of imprisonment for debt. By the mid-nineteenth century, when William Walker arrived in America, Tammany was beginning to absorb the Irish immigrants, although it originally had banned Irishmen and Catholics from membership. About this time, the tiger became the society's symbol.

Tammany's chief was then Fernando Wood, a dignified brigand so adept at using inside information to sell land to the city at inflated prices that an awestruck William Marcy Tweed remarked, "I never went to get a corner lot that I didn't find that Wood had got in ahead of me." Within a few years, Boss Tweed succeeded Wood. By the time Tweed and his notorious colleagues were exposed, in 1871, they had looted the city of $200,000,000.

William Walker's first two decades in America were years of transition for Tammany. Both Wood and Tweed were Protestants; now the immigrant Irish-Catholics were demanding the leadership for one of their own. Tammany bowed to the challenge and named John Kelly, a long-time member of the organization, a second generation Irish-American, and a Catholic, to the post. Kelly, called "Honest John" for the no-nonsense manner in which he had amassed $800,000 during six years in the unsalaried job of Sheriff of New York County, moved into the leadership with great vigor. In 1880 he even elected the city's first Irish-Catholic mayor, William R. Grace, whose business career had progressed from singing in saloons to ownership of the Grace Shipping Line.

Kelly's greatest political contribution, however, was the firming up of Tammany's power structure. He did this, roughly speaking, by carving the city into districts, thirty-three in his day, and making sure that a man retained the district leadership only if he got out the vote. In return, the subchiefs elected the over-all Tammany leader, had direct access to him, and were given a voice in all patronage matters that might concern them. How did the system work in practice? Let one of Kelly's district leaders, the legendary George Washington Plunkitt, tell us, almost as if he were still sitting on the bootblack stand at the New York County Courthouse, where he used to receive his unschooled constitutents:

On Getting Out the Vote: I hear of a young feller that's proud of his voice, thinks he can sing fine. I ask him to come around to Washington Hall and join our Glee Club. He comes and sings, and he's a follower of Plunkitt for life. . . . Then there's the feller that likes rowing on the river, the young feller that makes a name as a waltzer on his block, the young feller that's handy with his dukes—I rope them all in by givin' them opportunities to show themselves off. I don't trouble with political arguments. I just study human nature and act accordin'.

As for the older voters, I reach them, too. No, I don't send them campaign literature. That's rot. . . . What tells in holdin' your grip on your district is to go right down among the poor families and help them in the different ways they need help. . . . If there's a fire in Ninth, Tenth or Eleventh Avenue, for example, any hour of the day or night, I'm usually there with some of my election district captains as soon as the fire engines. If a family is burned out I don't ask whether they are

Republicans or Democrats. . . . I just get quarters for them, buy clothes for them . . . and fix them up till they get things runnin' again.

On Loyalty: The politicians who make a lastin' success in politics are the men who are always loyal to their friends, even up to the gate of State prison, if necessary; men who keep their promises and never lie.

On Knowing Your Constituents: Every district leader is fitted to the district he runs and wouldn't exactly fit any other distict. That's the reason Tammany never makes the mistake the Fusion outfit always makes of sendin' men into the districts who don't know the people, and have no sympathy with their peculiarities. We don't put a silk stocking on the Bowery. . . .

On Honest Graft: My party's in power in the city, and it's goin' to undertake a lot of public improvements. Well, I'm tipped off, say, that they're going to lay a new park at a certain place.

I see my opportunity and I take it. I go to that place and I buy up all the land I can in the neighborhood. Then the board of this or that makes its plan public, and there is a rush to get my land, which nobody cared particular for before.

Ain't it perfectly honest to charge a good price and make a profit on my investment and foresight? Of course, it is. Well, that's honest graft.

During the 1860s and 1870s, while Tammany was broadening its base and accepting the Irish, William Walker had settled in Greenwich Village, an enclave of twisting, tree-lined streets on the West Side of Lower Manhattan. There he began to prosper, first as a builder and then as a lumberyard owner. The city was bustling but compact; Manhattan Island in these years grew from 800,000 to over 1,000,000 residents; yet Forty-second Street was so far north of the population center it might as well have been in Westchester; the Bronx could have been Nova Scotia. But do not think the times idyllic: the immigrants were presenting a crime problem, and one out of ten New Yorkers had a police record. A respectable, middle-class citizen would not think of strolling after dark along the streets of the Lower East Side, infested as they were with Irish toughs. The New York *Times* would shake its head at the "masses of human beings in this city—few of them native to American soil—whom it seems almost hopeless to attempt to elevate." And *Leslie's Illustrated Weekly* would complain that "prison has no terror" for the city's criminals and would advocate that law-enforcement officials "go for the cat-o'-nine-tails . . . judiciously applied."

In a sense, Tammany's weaknesses and strengths were simply a reflection of New York's. The city was brawling, uncomfortable, and avaricious, yet alive, vibrant, and eager to improve itself. There were fearsome fights in the Bowery, to the east of William Walker's Village enclave, as a result of wars between rival gangs (the "Bowery Boys" and the "Dead Rabbits") for the control of petty rackets. But the preservation of Central Park, a sylvan retreat for future generations of New Yorkers, was also being planned and executed. During the Civil War, the immigrants, many of whom were unwilling to fight for the Union while the rich could buy their way out of service, staged bloody draft riots in Lower Manhattan; they burned down a colored orphanage, killed and manhandled Negroes, and razed the homes of abolitionists. Then these same immigrants subscribed the money to complete the towering Gothic spires of St. Patrick's Cathedral on Fifth Avenue. The *Evening Post,* in an 1867 editorial, would describe New York as "the most inconveniently arranged commercial city in the world. Its wharfs are badly built, unsafe and without shelter; its streets are badly paved, dirty and necessarily overcrowded; its warehouses are at a distance from the ships, and for the most part without proper labor-saving machinery; its laborers are badly lodged." At the same time, the politicians, though in many instances corrupt, were civic-minded enough to authorize a metropolitan fire department and a board of health, and private citizens founded the American Museum of Natural History and the Metropolitan Museum of Art.

In 1870 and 1871, the Irish quarreled among themselves—over religion, of course. Orangemen battled Catholic immigrants in a series of manic encounters that made the streets decidedly unsafe, and an impressive list of casualties was amassed. On the credit side, Thomas Nast's political cartoons in *Harper's Weekly* aroused the electorate against Boss Tweed's thievery, and the Sixth Avenue Elevated Railroad began operation, from Rector Street to Central Park, as did the Third Avenue El, from South Ferry to Forty-second Street. Most of the Irish, however, still despaired of finding decent housing; they were forced to occupy evil tenements, with narrow, dank "air" shafts and dark, windowless interior rooms.

Toward the end of the 1870s, William Walker met Ellen Ida Roon, the daughter of a saloonkeeper, and decided to take a wife. Perhaps "met" is misleading. Ellen's father, James Roon, was a stiff-backed, puritanical man who believed the sexes should be kept apart. There was no ladies' entrance to his West Twelfth Street establishment, nor were females even allowed to send their children into the place with empty beer buckets for refilling. Roon carried this professional sternness over to his own women folk, making sure his five daughters saw as few young men as possible. (He allowed his four sons more socializing—including the privilege of rising to serve the six o'clock mass.) Gentlemen callers were not welcome in the Roon home, and he would take care that the shades to the front-parlor windows were drawn every Sunday lest his daughters be able to wave at male acquaintances out for a stroll in the Village streets.

William Walker took notice of the auburn-haired Ellen at services at St. Joseph's, the neighborhood church. There was always time for pleasantries after mass, and gradually a friendship developed. Despite her father's rigidity, Ellen had managed to remain a friendly, outgoing girl, and Walker found her charming. Through a mutual friend, he even gained admission to the Roon home, being allowed to pay a formal call on New Year's Day. Ellen must have found life with father a series of vexations. Mr. Roon, who disapproved of jewelry, once tried to snatch a pair of earrings from her. Ellen was spirited enough to hang onto one of them, and thereafter, whenever she was having her photo taken, she would turn her head so that the single earring showed. Stymied in their efforts to see more of each other, Ellen and Walker took direct action. With the aid of Mrs. Roon, a graying eminence in the affair, and without Mr. Roon's knowledge, they went off to the parish next door to St. Joseph's and were married. (The other four Roon daughters remained unmarried; they lived at home and were a comfort to the old gentleman in his declining years.)

The Walkers raised four children. First born was William, Jr. Next came James John Walker, who was born on June 19, 1881, baptized at St. Joseph's, and named for Ellen's favorite brother, James Roon, Jr. William Walker chose to ignore the fact that the boy's maternal grandfather bore the same name. "We are not calling our baby after a certain hard-headed party," he said, "but in honor of the boy's good-natured Uncle Jim." Then came a third boy, George, and later a girl, Anna, whom the family called Nan. All the children but Nan were born in a flat at 110 Leroy Street. In 1886, William Walker moved his family to a spacious, three-story brick house at 6 St. Luke's Place, for which he paid $17,000 in cash; it was here that James Walker would eventually bring his own wife, and here he would make his home for four decades.

When James Walker was born, three men were already living who would most affect his public life. Around Twentieth Street on the Lower East Side, the so-called Gas House District, Charles Francis Murphy, then twenty-three, had already become well known. He was a tough, plate-blocking catcher for his Sylvan Social Club's base-ball team, rowed stroke for Sylvan's crew, and was solidifying his political base by opening a saloon. Further downtown on the East

Side, Alfred E. Smith, a boy of eight, was playing tag and selling newspapers under the huge towers of the Brooklyn Bridge, which was still under construction. As an adult, he would remember the thrill of traversing the bridge, before the pedestrian way was completed, on an open, narrow catwalk. (Perhaps we should admit here, quickly, that Smith, who came to be the best-known Irishman of his time, was not a pure-blooded Irishman at all but a mixture of Italian, German, English, and Irish strains.) Near Fourteenth Street, in the rectory of the Church of the Annunciation, Samuel Seabury, also eight years old, lived with his father, the Reverend William Seabury. An Episcopal blue blood whose lineage went back to the Puritan landings, young Seabury came from a family (its motto: "Hold to the Most High") that had little tolerance for the weaknesses of public officials. As the man who would spearhead the investigation of the James J. Walker administration in the early 1930s, Seabury would be relentless.

It was in 1886, the year of the move to St. Luke's Place, that William Walker entered politics, running successfully for alderman from the Village's old Ninth Ward. As a carpenter, he had often worked with John R. Voorhis, a master stair-builder by trade. They had become friends, and Voorhis, a veteran politician, had sponsored Walker for membership in Tammany Hall. Now the fifty-seven-year-old Voorhis, who held the post of police commissioner, was instrumental in getting organization backing for Walker, which was tantamount to election. (Voorhis, incidentally, would live until 102 and become a Tammany sachem; all his adult life he drank straight whiskey, smoked dark cigars, and, what was most unusual for a Tammany man, bought his suits at Brooks Brothers.) William Walker would serve four terms as adlerman, be elected to the State Assembly (the 1892–93 term), and would close out his political career as Manhattan's superintendent of public buildings. Perhaps his most notable achievement was sponsoring the city's first recreation piers. A bandstand, lighting, swings for children, and benches for adults converted unused docks, during the hot summers, into cool nighttime retreats.

In 1894 Richard Croker, the Tammany leader who replaced "Honest John" Kelly, was forced into temporary exile in England when the Lexow Committee, headed by State Senator Clarence Lexow, uncovered evidence of widespread police corruption. That same year, William Walker was elected, on an anti-Croker ticket, for his last aldermanic term.

Croker returned to New York in 1897, bluffed his way back into control of Tammany, and ran Robert A. Van Wyck for the mayoralty.

Van Wyck became the first mayor of Greater New York, formed by the consolidation of several counties into five boroughs. By 1900, however, another investigating committee, this one headed by Assemblyman Robert Mazet, mounted a second attack on Croker. Helping the Mazet Committee was the New York *Journal's* revelation that Croker, Van Wyck, and Dock Commissioner Charles F. Murphy were the powers behind an ice company that had been given exclusive rights to use the city's docks. This meant that the company could charge for ice as much as it wished. More Mazet Committee revelations followed, and in 1901 Croker again sailed abroad. His exile was quite comfortable: a stately manor house in England, a castle in Ireland, a racing stable that in 1907 produced a winner of the famed Epsom Derby. Twenty-one years after leaving New York, Croker died at the age of seventy-nine, leaving an estate of $5,000,000.

Emboldened by Croker's second departure from Manhattan, William Walker in 1902 ran against the remnants of the Croker machine, attempting to win the Democratic leadership of his district. This time he failed. A short while later, Charles Francis Murphy, who had survived the ice-company exposé anl succeeded Croker in the pantheon of Tammany leaders, saw to it that Walker's anti-Croker efforts were rewarded. Manhattan Borough President Jacob Cantor named Walker superintendent of public buildings.

James J. Walker, meanwhile, was growing up in St. Luke's Place, attending St. Joseph's Parochial School. By all testimony, young Jimmy was an alert, well-liked boy. Perhaps he was a bit too frivolous in his approach to authority; the St. Joseph's pastor called him "Jimmie Talker." But the Irish have a saying that "merry-hearted boys make the best of old men," and his parents were not particularly disturbed by the nickname. After St. Joseph's, Jim went a few blocks uptown to St. Francis Xavier, a Jesuit preparatory school located on West Sixteenth Street. There he wrestled with Latin and geometry, but not too rigorously, and he did not distinguish himself academically. In 1898, at age seventeen, he indicated where his true talents might lie. His father, campaigning (unsuccessfully, as it turned out) for the aldermancy, was ill, and Jim was called upon to make a speech outlining the local issues and how William Walker would handle them. Since Jim did not know the local issues, he instinctively fastened on a theme guaranteed to lift the hearts of his audience. "And the day will come," he declaimed, "when you and I and every good Irishman can go back to that green isle of ours and sit upon its shores at the blue ocean and sing 'Home Sweet Home.' " The enraptured voters, who had no intention of going back to the famine they had fled, cheered lustily.

William Walker, who had already placed his eldest son in medical school, was determined that Jim would become a lawyer. And so, in 1902, after a brief stay at La Salle Business College, young Walker found himself attending New York Law School. His heart, however, was in song writing. The year before, while playing the piano at a St. Joseph's vaudeville night, Jim had met a team of song-and-dance performers named Higginson and Connolly. Encouraged by them, he hurriedly wrote a song he called "Mary Cook" and rushed to their hotel, where he enthusiastically sang it unaccompanied. When Jim was finished, he waited for the reaction. "To tell you the truth, kid," one of the vaudevillians said, "I don't know whether it's good or bad. You've got a terrible voice." Later, after hearing "Mary Cook" on the piano, Higginson and Connolly bought it, and Walker's show-business career was launched.

Despite the running debate about Jim's future, the Walker home was a happy one. His sister, Nan, would look back and say, "At the family table we had one laugh after another until the meal was finished. My brothers rarely missed a lunch. . . . In the afternoon, the Walker house seemed like a rendezvous. I rarely got back from school without running into a houseful of people being entertained."

While still in law school, Jim met a vivacious young singer named Janet Allen, who had come to New York from Chicago, where her father was a newspaperman. Walker and a fellow law student, Harry Carey (who later became a Hollywood actor, playing a succession of cowboy roles), devised a vaudeville skit for Miss Allen in which she was cast as Phoebe Snow, a woman enamored of the Erie Lackawanna Railroad because its locomotives, using only high-grade anthracite coal, did not soil her dresses with their soot. ("My gown stays white from morn till night/Upon the road of anthracite," was Phoebe's—and the Lackawanna's—boast.) Though the skit was not well received by a demanding audience in Yonkers, New York, Miss Allen bore no grudges. In 1905, when Jim had left law school behind to work as a lyric writer for a music publishing firm, they resumed their acquaintance. The five-foot, ninety-five-pound Janet was a chorus girl and understudy to the leading lady in *The Duke of Duluth*, a musical George Broadhurst was attempting to stage. Walker was called in to write additional songs for the show, in the hope that it would survive its New York run. He turned out three numbers, including a typically romantic effort, "I Like Your Way ("I like you the best/For you're not like the rest/I like your way"). *The Duke of Duluth* did not do well, and "Allie," as Jim called her, drifted back into vaudeville. But her frienlship with Walker was ripening. Their world was a new-born Broadway, a magical place peopled by showmen, pretty girls, and song-pluggers. In restaurants like Reisenweber's and Rector's, where ten dollars would buy them a sumptuous champagne supper, the couple chatted with such celebrities as George M. Cohan and such "unknowns" as Irving Berlin. It was Allie who introduced Jim to Ernest Ball, the composer who in 1905 wrote the music for Walker's most successful song:

Now in the summer of life, sweetheart,
You say you love but me,
Gladly I'll give my heart to you,
Throbbing with ecstasy.

But last night I saw, while a-dreaming,
The future, old and gray,
And I wondered if you'll love me then, dear,
Just as you do today.

Will you love me in December as you do in May?
Will you love me in the same old-fashioned way?
When my hair has turned to gray,
Will you kiss me then and say,
That you love me in December as you did in May?

"I'll never forget the night Ernie Ball ran his fingers over the keyboard, plucking the tune he was improvising, note by note," Walker would say afterward. "He finally swept both hands over the keys, and I knew a hit had been born. I clasped Ernie around his shoulders." The blatantly sentimental ballad sold several hundred thousand copies of sheet music and earned each of its authors royalties in excess of $10,000—big money in those days. Already a dudish dresser, Jim immediately went out and bought three custom-made suits, four pairs of shoes, a dozen silk shirts, three fedoras, and a walking stick. (The last affectation he left for safekeeping in a Broadway cigar store; he knew a cane would not be well received by his father.) "It's a burning desire, this song writing," Jim confessed. "You know, a song about a boy and a girl? Just to hear a piano or a band play the tune, or a pretty girl say the words that came from your heart. . . ."

For Walker, during these years at least, Janet Allen was the pretty girl, and in various vaudeville halls around New York, she sang many of his songs—innocent lyrics like "There's Music in the Rustle of a Skirt," "Kiss All the Girls for Me," and "After They Gather the Hay." Theirs would be a protracted courtship, for they would not marry until 1912. It was not that Allie was not accepted by Jim's family;

despite her vaudeville background, she was always basically a home-body, and this naturally endeared her to the conservative William Walker. But Jim was one of those peripatetic men who find it almost impossible to settle down. Though he never came close to duplicating the success of "Will You Love Me in December as You Do in May?" he tried to hang on in show business.

By 1909, it was apparent even to Walker that he would have to seek a new career. His song writing talents, never better than third-rate, were seldom in demand. Moreover, his father had suffered a severe political reverse. Caught in the feud between Tammany's Charles Murphy and Mayor George B. McClellan, who had turned against Murphy because of his support of William Randolph Hearst's unsuccessful race for governor in 1906, William Walker was removed as superintendent of public buildings. (Mr. Walker, as we shall call him to avoid confusion, was actually removed by his immediate chief, Manhattan Borough President John F. Ahearn, who was him-self under state investigation and was seeking a scapegoat; he was replaced, ironically, by his old friend John Voorhis, and Ahearn's strategem did not succeed, as his own subsequent dismissal bore out.) Considering the fact that the public buildings post was tradi-tionally a boondoggle, Mr. Walker may have been roughly treated. He was accused, not of incompetence, but of having allowed the pay-ment without contract of $888,728, of which sum at least a third repre-sented excessive profits to builders, who then kicked back the over-payments to Tammany Hall. On top of this political setback, Mr. Walker's lumberyard burned down. His youngest son, George, staring at the embers, then and there decided on his future career: the in-surance business.

With William, Jr., in medicine and George highly motivated, Mr. Walker, much as he loved to hear Jim play "Sweet Genevieve" on the piano at St. Luke's Place, increased the pressure on his third son to pass his bar examinations and get into politics. Jim would not be ready to pass his exams for some years, but he did have a natural bent for politics. Smiling and affable, an excellent speaker with the gift of quick-wittedness, he had already attracted the attention of Charles W. Culkin, then head of the Village's Fifth Assembly Dis-trict—which now included the Ninth Ward—and at thirty-two the youngest district leader in the city. (In 1925, when Walker was elected to his first term as mayor, Culkin would be elected Sheriff of New York County.)

Charles Culkin felt that the present assemblyman from his district, John Eagleton, had been in Albany long enough; this was the attitude of many leaders, who believed that a couple of terms in office were sufficient to help a man build his career and that he should then step aside to make way for others. Knowing this, Jim's uncle James Roon brought his nephew to see Culkin about the assembly nomination. The district leader had his reservations about Jim's elegant dress ("You might be an ornament among the upstate farmers"), but he decided to back Walker. "Jim, I've heard you speak," he said, "and if you really settle down to it I think you'll go places in politics."

Culkin's words were prophetic. Walker would remain continuously in elective office from 1909 until that fateful day in September 1932, when he resigned the mayoralty.

Munificently bankrolled by one thousand dollars of Culkin's money, Walker plunged into the campaign against Eagleton. There were two major ways to reach the voters. One was to tour the saloons. Walker would enter an establishment, amid waving, shouting, and backslapping, and announce that the drinks were on him. The only ability required was judging whether a two-dollar bill would buy the house or whether five dollars was necessary. Walker's tendency was to overspend, with the result that Culkin had to come through with a second thousand dollars. The other strategem involved street-corner speechifying; the candidate would mount a platform, shuck his hat and coat as Irish protocol required, no matter how cold the weather, and do his best to elicit cheers and silence hecklers. Here Walker was even more effective. His poise was that of an actor, and audiences were most impressed. Billed on posters as "The Young Man's Candidate,,' Walker won an easy victory. He and Janet Allen celebrated by becoming formally engaged.

At Albany in 1910, when Walker joined the legislature, Charles Evans Hughes, a Republican of great rectitude who had achieved national prominence by exposing New York insurance-company frauds, was in the governor's mansion. Yet three of Walker's Democratic confreres, Tammany men though they might be, would also make distinguished names for themselves. Alfred E. Smith, then thirty-seven, was already an assemblyman to be noticed, and it had been with considerable pleasure that William Walker accepted Smith's offer to watch over Jim. "Billy," Al said, "you had better let me take that young fellow and tip him off at Albany." With Smith in the legislature were the liberal Robert F. Wagner, who would become a state supreme court justice and a long-time U.S. senator, and the industrious

James A. Foley (Charles Murphy's son-in-law), who would follow
Wagner as the Democratic leader of the senate and become a respected judge in New York's surrogate court. Walker profited from
contact with all these men, but it was Smith with whom he worked
most closely during his upstate years. Yet Smith, while he could be
charmed by Walker, recognized the flaws in his character. When
Smith decided in 1925 to dump Hylan, Walker was his third choice
for the mayoralty; previously, the governor offered the nomination to
Foley and to Wagner.

Alfred E. Smith grew up, as we have seen, on the Lower East
Side, in the shadows of the Brooklyn Bridge. He was raised a devout
Catholic and always remained one, practicing a stern morality regarding the sanctity of the home. His parish was St. James, where
his mother sent him each Sunday and most weekdays, starched and
scrubbed, to serve as an altar boy. Smith's father died when he was
twelve, and the youngster hustled his way through a succession of
hard and menial jobs: errand boy, laborer, factory worker, fish ped-
dler. Like Walker, Smith was fascinated by the theater; he often
gained parts in amateur productions staged by the St. James Lyceum
Company, which rehearsed in the church's basement. (His most
noteworthy role was that of a politician—the Honorable Bardwell
Sloate, long-winded and blustering hero of *The Mighty Dollar*, a
farce perennially popular among Irish-American audiences of the
times.) Though Smith's schooling had been meager, he had a rough-
hewn gift for elocution. In 1894, before he was twenty-one, Smith
delivered his first political speech. He stood up in his local clubhouse to denounce Richard Croker's order from Tammany Hall that
Smith's district, the Fourth, should throw out its congressman and
replace him with Croker's choice. The gesture proved futile: Smith
and the other incensed Democrats in the district not only lost the
congressional contest but indirectly helped to elect Republican William L. Strong, running as a Fusionist, to the mayoralty. Nonetheless, Smith's oratory established him as something of a comer. Within
a year, a friendly politician got him a job as a subpoena server; the
position, which paid almost $1,000 a year, elevated Smith from the
laboring class and firmly established his interests in politics. He
would keep this city job for nine years, until he was sent to the
assembly.

By 1900 Smith had married, and he and his wife, Katie, were on
their way to raising five children. He had long been friendly with
the aforementioned Tim Foley, the burly saloonkeeper who ran
Smith's district. As Foley's influence increased, so did Smith's for-

tunes. In 1903, when Foley wanted to send a man to the assembly, he had only to say, "Dig up Al, and ready him up," and the untutored elocutionist was as good as elected.

At first, Smith disliked the legislature. To someone of his parochial background, it seemed cold, aloof, alien. But Smith had the capacity to grow. He learned parliamentary techniques, observed the benefits of compromise, explored ways to make the lot of New York's poor more bearable. In turn, Tammany boss Charles Murphy began to show Smith the signs that tell a politician's peers he has been specially anointed. When Smith was in the city, the two would meet for lunch in Murphy's private dining room at Delmonico's; at the state capital, choice legislative assignments began to come Smith's way. By the end of the decade, when James J. Walker arrived in Albany, Smith's promise to take Mr. Walker's boy in hand was one of sure significance.

Most of the Tammany Hall men in the legislature, of course, were far less commendable than Smith. Perhaps the most powerful of these was "Big Tim" Sullivan, the "clear-skinned, fair-faced" boss of the Bowery and its northernmost adjunct, Times Square's so-called Tenderloin District. Just the year before Walker took office, Sullivan had been attacked in *McClure's* magazine by George Kibbe Turner, who described the St. Patrick's Day dance held annually in the "Big Feller's" honor thusly:

> That night . . . the streets of the Tenderloin lie vacant of its women; the eyes of the city detective force are focused on the great dancing-hall stuffed to the doors with painted women and lean-faced men. . . .
>
> The "Big Feller" smiles gayly upon the frail congregation below him—the tenth short-lived generation of prostitutes he had seen at gatherings like this since, almost twenty years ago, he started his first Five Points assembly—he himself as fresh now as then. In the rear of the box a judge of the General Sessions court sits modestly, decently, hat in hand. In the welter on the slippery floor, another city judge . . . leads through the happy mazes of the grand march a thousand pimps and thieves and prostitutes, to the blatant crying of the band:
>
> "Sullivan, Sullivan, a damned fine Irishman!"

This acid portrait understandably drew an angry answer. When Sullivan appeared before an overflow audience at Miner's Bowery Follies, he did not deny that he was many times a millionaire, despite his modest $1,500-a-year salary as a state senator. He attributed his worth to his part-ownership of a chain of New York theaters. (Sullivan might also have mentioned that prize fights could take place throughout the state only under his auspices, and at considerable profit to himself.) "I am worth something," he said, "and there is no reason why I shouldn't be. I'm an average downtown boy, with a good, clear head, and it's always clear, for I don't drink or smoke. But I haven't changed my residence since I got my money, and I ain't going to. I was born among you, and I'm going to die among you." Sullivan told his listeners he "was born in poverty, one of six children, four boys and two girls. The boys used to sleep in a three-quarters bed, not big enough for two, and the girls in a shake-down on the floor. . . . And our mother used to sing to us at night and maybe it would be next day before we would think that she had been singing but that she had gone to bed without anything to eat. . . . That is the kind of mothers that bore us down here. . . . The thieves we have down here ain't thieves from choice, they are thieves from necessity and necessity don't know any law. . . ."

While in the state senate, Sullivan sponsored only two bills of any significance. One resulted in Columbus Day being made a legal holiday, to the joy of his Italian constituents. The other bill resulted in the Sullivan Law, which made it a felony to carry a handgun without a license. This greatly cheered the Irish policemen, who were then able to keep the Italian gangsters (and their Jewish and Irish counterparts) under control by "planting" guns on miscreants and arresting them for carrying concealed weapons; the more cerebral of the mobsters retaliated by having their suit pockets sewn up and hiring aides to tote their revolvers.

At one point, Sullivan thought he would interrupt his service in the state legislature by allowing himself to be elected to Congress. "Say," he opined, "those guys that bag the Washington graft get famous and get to be the main squeeze at the White House if their gang is in, don't they? . . . That ain't a bad lay." He went to Washington for a term but soon grew disillusioned. "There's nothing in this Congressman business," he said. "The people down there use 'em as hitchin'-posts. Every time they see a Congressman on the street they tie their horses to him." Sullivan's attitude in this regard paralleled that of Richard Croker, who, when asked to make a deserving young man clerk of New York County, replied: "That job requires brains and experience. He'll have to be satisfied with being a Congressman."

Sullivan returned to the state senate and the Tenderloin, where he tightened his hold on the district's shady activities. In 1912, just about the time the murder of a loquacious gambler named Herman Rosenthal would be used by newspaperman Herbert Bayard Swope to focus public scrutiny on the ties among gangsters, policemen, and gamblers, Big Tim would go insane, suffering from delusions of persecution. Shortly thereafter he died mysteriously, under the wheels of a freight train, after eluding the private guards who had been hired to keep him confined to his Williamsbridge estate in the north Bronx.

~~~

Both Smith and Sullivan grew up fatherless, in the depressing tenements of the poor. Afterward, when they established their careers, they represented the best and the worst that Tammany could produce. Both men possessed keen intellects and forceful personalities, both were shrewd and demanding, both dominated those with whom they came in contact. Their backgrounds had tempered them. James J. Walker, unlike Smith and Sullivan, had been reared in relative affluence. His was a comfortable home, he had received considerable schooling, had even been allowed the indulgence of a fling at song writing. Walker's strength derived from his likability. Jimmy was a regular fellow, a charming companion; he made one laugh. "It takes only one or two reasons for me to like a man," he once said, "but it takes a hundred for me to dislike him." Such a philosophy can be endearing. Smith would attack political matters, assiduously wrestling with their implications; Sullivan would put a hammerlock on patronage and vice; Walker would content himself with verbal parries. Smith worked hard at politics, Sullivan worked hard at being corrupt. But Jimmy? He made his way effortlessly.

Great changes had been taking place in the city of New York in the two decades before the twenty-eight-year-old Walker made his 1910 debut in the legislature. Besides the Brooklyn Bridge, two more massive structures linking Lower Manhattan to Brooklyn—the Williamsburg and the Manhattan—had been completed and opened. So had the Queensborough Bridge at Fifty-ninth Street, joining midtown Manhattan and Queens. On the West Side, the Hudson Tunnel now connected New York with New Jersey. From the Battery, one could see the Statue of Liberty, the gift of the French people, firmly implanted on Bedloes Island. A new Madison Square Garden, that sweaty setting for sports events and political rallies, was raised on the block bounded by Madison and Fourth Avenues, and by Twenty-sixth and Twenty-seventh streets. (It would be demolished during Walker's campaign year of 1925 and moved to Eighth Avenue between Forty-ninth and Fiftieth streets.) The luxurious Waldorf Astoria Hotel welcomed guests on Fifth Avenue between Thirty-third and Thirty-fourth streets. Electric lighting was commonplace, and the city possessed the largest and most efficient telephone service in the world. Trustees of various private libraries had agreed to consolidate their corporations into the New York Public Library; its new home was nearing completion, on the site of the old Croton

Reservoir, at Fifth Avenue and Forty-second Street. The automobile had made its appearance; by 1907 the last horse cars were taken off Fifth Avenue and replaced by motor buses. Wireless telegraphy came into existence between New York and London, the West Side subway was opened (from City Hall to One Hundred Forty-fifth Street), and Wilbur Wright made the first flight over New York Harbor. By 1910, the population of New York was 4,785,000, with 2,330,000 people on Manhattan Island and 1,642,000 others in Brooklyn.

Despite these evidences of growth and sophistication, slums were everywhere. Three-quarters of the city's population lived in squalid tenements. In Manhattan, perhaps the worst of these were along Big Tim Sullivan's Bowery, an all-embracing term for the Irish area, south of Fourteenth Street, along Third Avenue. To the east of the Bowery was the Lower East Side, a melting pot of nationalities but particularly Eastern European Jews; to the west was Little Italy and Chinatown. (Russian, Italian, German, and Austrian immigrants all formed large New York ethnic groups—in some cases as sizable as the Irish. But Irishmen controlled Tammany Hall, perhaps because, as a Tammany leader was to explain years later, "the Irish are natural leaders," perhaps because they had the advantage of knowing the language.) North of Fourteenth Street along Third Avenue one passed through Charles Murphy's Gas House District to the Upper East Side. Here the slums on Third, Second, and First avenues were not quite so vile, and the tenements, because they had janitors and front doors that could be locked to keep out strangers, were called "flats." (The mansions of the rich on Fifth Avenue, facing the park, formed a thin granite line that resolutely turned its back on the masses.) The Upper East Side ended around Eighty-sixth Street, in the German enclave of Yorkville. On Manhattan's West Side, making allowances for the peaceful Greenwich Village area where Walker was reared, the signs of poverty were equally obvious. Hell's Kitchen, where the sons of Irish mothers more often than not grew up to be convicts, priests, or prize-fighters, extended from Twenty-third to Fortieth streets, from Seventh Avenue to the Hudson River. In all these areas, Tammany's district leaders exchanged favors for votes and often made the votes pay interest in their own bank accounts a thousand-fold. As for the Tenderloin, where Big Tim had extended his sway, it was located in the heart of Manhattan, from Thirty-fourth to Forty-eighth streets, from Fifth to Ninth avenues; studded with theaters, fashionable restaurants and hotels, the Tenderloin was an upper-class version of the Bowery, its gambling and prostitution for patrons who could afford the best.

The five years that Walker served in the assembly were uneventful save for the fact that they sharpened his speaking style. He introduced more than 150 bills, but they were of a routine nature and were for the most part given to him by his political betters for perfunctory handling. In the midst of this limbo, however, Walker attained two personal milestones. In 1912 he was married to Janet Allen, who had given up her Christian Science religion to adopt the Catholic faith, and that same year he passed his State Bar Examinations.

He was two hours late for his wedding, establishing a reputation for tardiness that persisted all his life. On April 11, 1912, Allie, who had lost her singing voice and must have been fearful of losing her man, stood nervously waiting in an anteroom at St. Joseph's Church. When Walker finally appeared, his excuse was comic. The best man, on his way with the wedding ring to pick Walker up at St. Luke's Place, had encountered some horse-drawn fire engines. A fire buff, he supposedly changed direction and pursued them, completely forgeting the ceremony. What could I do? Walker asked Allie. I had to wait, didn't I? His bride accepted the story. It was not what Walker said, quite often, but how he said it that charmed his listeners. As Allie came down the aisle, clad in white satin and carrying a bouquet of lilies of the valley, the organist mingled the strains of "Here Comes the Bride" with "Will You Love Me in December as You Do in May?" The honeymoon took place in Atlantic City, then the St. Tropez of New York's Irish, amid stiff sea breezes, boardwalk chairs, and the smell of salt-water taffy. When they returned to Manhattan, the newlyweds took up residence on the third floor of the William Walker house at 6 St. Luke's Place.

Walker's admittance to the bar was timely, for he needed a law practice to supplement his legislative salary. His expensive tastes were already evident in Albany, and he had run up quite a bill at the Ten Eyck Hotel, where almost all the lawmakers stayed. His suite was usually filled with men and women eating, drinking, and making phone calls. Walker would pick up the tab. His own imbibing seems to have been impressive. Still, the evidence indicates that, while Walker could carouse, he was far from being a drunkard. His favorite drink was champagne or Black Velvet—champagne mixed with Guinness. Al Smith looked askance at this partying and held up to Walker the examples of Robert F. Wagner and James A. Foley. The young assemblyman turned aside the criticism with smiles and jokes.

Like most of New York's political Irish, Walker and Smith saw each other socially as well as professionally. Smith's daughter Emily, then twelve, recalled years later that on Sunday evenings her home usually was crowded with visitors, and among them often were the newlywed Walkers. Jim would sit at the piano and play everyone's favorite tunes; he was forever improvising as well, and one night he dedicated a song to young Miss Smith, which went in part:

> Meet me after school
> Down by the swimming pool.

"I wish I remembered more of that song," Emily Smith reminisced. "It was not great music, I know. And Jimmy Walker, though he had much innate ability, was in no sense a great man. Both he and that little song, however, had something bright and attractive about them, and I have never forgotten the schoolgirl thrill I felt that evening. . . ."

In early 1913, Walker's abilities as a speaker and debater attracted the attention of Charles F. Murphy, who sent word that he wanted Walker to attend him in his home on East Seventeenth Street. This was a sign of esteem, for Mr. Murphy customarily saw only his friends at home, receiving everyone else in his Tammany Hall office. The Tammany leader was one of two men in New York who were seldom called anything but "Mr." (the other being John McGraw, the hardnosed manager of the New York Giants), even by men who knew them well. Walker called on Murphy, who told him he was being considered for the state senate.

"I am greatly flattered," said Walker.

"I flatter nobody," said Murphy. "And I advise you to treat flattery as you would abuse. Pay no attention to either."

With that, Murphy told Walker to keep the prospective nomination confidential and walked him to the door. As his visitor was leaving, Murphy added a final comment. "You seem to have many friends on Broadway and in the sports world," he said. "Tammany Hall long has neglected these interesting people. I believe you are making us popular there."

Leaving Murphy's townhouse that night, Walker knew he would be nominated and elected to the state senate the following year. Mr. Murphy had as much as said so.

Charles Francis Murphy, as we have seen, used his athletic prowess to win popularity and his saloonkeeping to win votes. By 1890, he was the owner of four "handsome cafés," as the *Tammany Times* put it, and two years later, at the age of thirty-four, was the leader of the Gas House District. Noted equally for his stinginess with words and his largesse with charities, he then held court for his constituents under a lamp post on a Second Avenue street corner where, weather permitting, he arrived each evening about nine o'clock. In 1898, after Boss Croker saw his man Robert A. Van Wyck elected mayor, Murphy was rewarded for getting out the vote by being named one of four dock commissioners. Huge sums were being spent to improve the piers, and numerous companies were vying for their use; there was money—honest graft and otherwise—to be made. Within a couple of years, the new dock commissioner became a millionaire. Murphy was the treasurer of the commission, J. Sergeant Cram its president. Cram, one of those wealthy patrician types who occasionally wandered into the abattoir of Democratic politics, struck up a friendship with Murphy. He taught him the quiet pleasures to be derived from wearing a dress suit, introduced him to the game of golf, and influenced his table manners.

Nobody knows how often Murphy dressed up formally, but golf became a passion for him second only to politics. He bought an estate at Good Ground, Long Island, where he built a nine-hole golf course. And when Murphy succeeded Croker as Tammany's leader, after the latter's self-imposed exile in 1901, the table manners came in handy at Delmonico's, where Murphy enjoyed lunch daily in a private salon the newspapers called "The Scarlet Room of Mystery." There was red damask on the walls, a thick red rug on the floor, red plush on the chairs; Mr. Murphy would sit at the head of a mahogany table, its legs footed with carved tiger's paws in honor of the legendary Tammany Tiger. Writing about "The Scarlet Room," the *Evening Post* declared, "Nearly every important financier in the city is said to have entered at one time or another."

The biggest thorn in Murphy's paw during the early years of his regency was "Bill" Devery, who desired the leadership for himself. He had been removed from the police department, where he was deputy commissioner when not consorting with pimps, gamblers, and assorted criminals, by the reform-minded Seth Low administration that swept Van Wyck out of the mayoralty. Now, in 1903, Murphy was trying to elect George B. McClellan as mayor, and Devery thought the way to gain the Tammany leadership was by blocking his efforts. This he did by attacking and lampooning Murphy rather than McClellan. "He's goin' through the bluff of being decent," said Devery of Murphy to seemingly appreciative crowds, "but look at his record in the old Dock Board. Does that look as if he's dyin' for his feller man? What's more," said Devery, "since Charlie Murphy has got to running with J. Sergeant Cram, he's turned up his trousers at the bottom, and he's wearing glasses. One of these days . . . when you go to ask him for a job it'll be, 'Ah really cawn't do it, old chappie, don't you know.'" Murphy dampened Devery's high spirits by allying himself with Big Tim Sullivan, who himself had close ties to gangs run by "Monk" Eastman and Paul Kelly, each of whom controlled over a thousand thugs. In return for political protection, Big Tim expected his associates to reason with the opposition on election days. This in 1903 Monk Eastman dutifully did, cracking more than a few heads around the polling places, and McClellan won, preserving Murphy's leadership. Devery retired to Far Rockaway, Long Island, where he spent his declining years poring over scrapbooks of press clippings, all carefully cross-indexed.

In 1905 Murphy ran McClellan for mayor again (the term then being only two years). This time the Tammany leader's opposition came, as has been described, from William Randolph Hearst, whose Municipal Ownership League, quite popular among the workers, advocated public ownership of utilities and transit lines. Hearst lost to McClellan, but his support was so impressive that the next year Murphy ran him, as we have seen, for governor against Republican Charles Evans Hughes. Even though Tammany support of Hearst was predictably lukewarm (the publisher losing to Hughes), Murphy's pragmatism angered McClellan. The mayor proceeded to feed "inside" information to a state committee investigating Murphy's borough presidents, including John F. Ahearn of Manhattan. And so we come full circle—back to the Walker family. For it was Ahearn's desperate attempt to save his own job that led him to remove William H. Walker, his superintendent of public buildings, from office. Charles Murphy may have felt guilt about his part in the sacrifice of a faithful party worker; at any rate, he would later take an avuncular interest in William Walker's son.

Despite Hearst's defeat, or perhaps because of it, Murphy in 1906 solidified his leadership. He struck up an alliance with the Brooklyn Democrats (whose slogan had been "The Tiger Must Not Cross the Bridge") and came to an understanding with the less numerous New York Republicans (so that, in exchange for guaranteed patronage, they did not campaign particularly hard). In this way, Murphy came to be the single most powerful influence in the state—the first Tammany leader since Martin Van Buren in the 1830s to stretch the tiger's claws toward Albany and Washington. Murphy's plans, of course, were occasionally interfered with. In 1909 he would elect Judge William J. Gaynor as mayor and totally underestimate his character and integrity; luckily for Murphy, an assassin's bullet would impair Gaynor sufficiently so that he could mount no lasting threat to the machine. And in 1910, a young state senator named Franklin Delano Roosevelt would lead a small group of reform Democrats to block the nomination of "Blue-eyed Billy" Sheehan, Murphy's

choice for U.S. senator. (Senators were then chosen by a majority of
the legislature.) This minor setback worked out for Murphy, too,
for James A. O'Gorman, the compromise candidate, was even more
Murphy's man; moreover, the judgeship O'Gorman vacated could
be filled, with mathematical tidiness, by his own son-in-law. So,
throughout the state, Murphy's grasp on the organization grew
stronger and stronger.

James J. Walker took his place in the state senate in 1915. His
nomination and election in the previous fall had gone according to
plan; Murphy and Tammany had seen to that. In the upper chamber,
Walker was as well received as he had been in the assembly. He was
pleasant to be with, knew how to tell a joke, impressed everyone
with his parliamentary give-and-take. The only clouds in Walker's
perennially sunny world were the death of his father in 1916, and
then of his mother in 1918. He was passionately attached to both;
like so many Irishmen, he thought of his parents' marriage as something ideal, something truly sacred.

In his own married life, the fledgling state senator practiced no
such idealism. If he was fascinated by Broadway, he was dazzled
by its showgirls, those nubile creatures who hoofed gallantly in the
chorus or posed provocatively on-stage—waiting for just one break
but willing to settle for just one supper invitation. The girls, in turn,
were just as impressed with the young, handsome legislator, whose
slim physique and clean-cut features made him almost unique among
the politicians of his day. As for Allie, she had used marriage (and
perhaps Jim's infidelities) as an excuse to give up on herself; overweight and matronly, she bore little resemblance to the sprightly
vaudevillian he had married. Yet the only liaison of any duration
that Walker made during these pre-mayoral years involved Yvonne
Shelton, a singer-dancer of mercurial temperament whom he met in
1917. They were introduced at a cocktail party by Mayor John Purroy Mitchel, who had not let the fact that he had been elected on a reform ticket curb his fondness for uninhibited young ladies. (After losing to Hylan in the 1917 election, the adventuresome Mitchel, though
overage for the war, joined the army air service; tragically, he later
fell from a training plane to his death.)

Vonnie was appearing in the annual Ziegfeld Follies, which that
year featured the comics W. C. Fields and Fannie Brice. The Follies
that year also offered the lariat-twirling and astute comment of Will

Rogers ("Congress is so strange . . . A man gets up to speak and says nothing . . . Nobody listens . . . Then everybody disagrees"), and it marked the debut of Eddie Cantor, whose singing of "That's the Kind of Baby for Me" earned him a dozen encores an evening. Walker and the tiny Vonnie made a private, third-floor dining room in Leone's their regular meeting place, and they were often joined there by stars of the Follies. Like Jim, Vonnie was warm, impulsive, quick with a smile. They were much alike in their frantic search for excitement, and their relationship would last several years.

By the 1918–19 session of the legislature, Walker was deeply involved with the passage of bills to legalize professional baseball on Sundays and professional boxing at any time. The baseball controversy arose when John McGraw's Giants attempted to play an exhibition game on a Sunday in August for the benefit of needy families of World War I servicemen. The Catholic Church, reflecting the enthusiasms of its immigrant parishioners, gave the event tacit approval, sending the well-known Monsignor John J. Lavelle to toss out the first ball. To evade the ban on Sunday professional sport, the price charged for the tickets supposedly was for the band concert preceding the contest, and admission to the game was free. This strategem did not hoodwink the New York Sabbath Society, which had the effrontery to have McGraw arrested and hauled into court. When the charges came before Judge Francis X. McQuade (who years later acknowledged having been treasurer of the New York Giants), he dismissed the case. "Playing baseball on the first day of the week, when not amounting to a serious interruption of the repose and religious liberty of the community, is not a violation," thundered McQuade.

Knowing that the smaller New York communities were largely against permitting Sunday baseball and the cities were for it, Walker introduced a bill allowing each community to make its own decision on the issue. In this way, he felt, he would attract the largest number of legislators to his cause, since even men representing small towns would be able to explain to their blue-stocking constituents that ball playing was a local option. The bill soon became law.

Shortly afterward, Walker began pressing to legalize boxing. He came up with a plan that called essentially for a troika of unsalaried boxing commissioners, appointed by the governor, who would oversee prize fighting throughout the state; moreover, everyone connected with the sport—from promoters to managers to boxers to referees—would be approved and licensed. With this kind of supervision, Walker felt, the chance of "fixes" would be greatly lessened.

There were many supporters of the Walker boxing bill, and perhaps the most prominent was Anthony J. Drexel Biddle, the colorful philanthropist who advocated a no-nonsense diet of evangelism and fisticuffs for red-blooded Americans, and whose eccentric ways later were immortalized in the play *The Happiest Millionaire*. But Al Smith, then in his first term as governor, was doubtful that the criminal element in boxing could be controlled; he was also concerned about whether Protestant voters in the state really wanted such legislation. (Catholics for the most part approved the measure, since so many of their number saw prize fighting, not as a moral issue, but as an avenue of escape from the slums.) Though the bill passed the legislature, the dubious Smith refrained from signing it.

When Walker called on the governor one Friday afternoon for an explanation, Smith told him the only way he would act on the bill would be if Walker by Monday morning could get the signatures of 100 clergymen who approved the measure. "And all of them must be *Protestants!*" the governor specified. Back in his office, Walker immediately called Biddle, who he knew had close ties with Protestant religious groups. By Monday morning there were almost a thousand wires on Smith's desk, all from ministers extolling the virtues of prize fighting. "How the devil did you do it?" Walker asked Biddle admiringly. "The devil had nothing to do with it, Jim," said Biddle. "Just the opposite." He pointed out that he had recently given a half-million dollars to his Bible Society. "I merely requested our New York office to notify the state membership about the worthiness of the boxing bill. We are a congenial organization." With this telegraphic spur, Smith signed the prize-fighting bill into law.

Impressed by such maneuvering, Murphy about this time approved Walker as Democratic leader of the senate, his own son-in-law, James A. Foley, having resigned the leadership to accept the post of judge in the New York Surrogate Court. When Walker telephoned from Albany to thank the Tammany leader, he asked, "What about patronage?" "Use your own judgment," said Murphy. "If it's good you'll be an asset to the party. If it isn't—well, the sooner we find it out the better."

Walker's instincts for distributing patronage must have been well grounded; throughout his public life, he kept the Tammany Tiger well fed.

In 1919, when the Senate was debating the ratification of the Prohibition Amendment, Walker again displayed his ingenuity. A Republican senator from Buffalo was emphasizing the case against alcohol by reading a letter from two little girls whose father was in Dannemora Prison for a murder he had committed while drunk. "Help bring papa home," the letter ended, "for he was a good papa."

The Senator put down the note, pointed his finger at Walker and asked sternly, "Would the Senator from New York dare deny that the liquor traffic is murderous? Or that our prisons and madhouses are full of its victims?"

Walker accorded the bombast the treatment it deserved. "I would like to go with the Senator from Erie County to Dannemora Prison 'to bring papa home,'" he said, "if, in return, the Senator will go with me to bring home from Bloomington Asylum the host of religious fanatics and criminals who never have tasted liquor in their lives and have committed the most atrocious crimes."

The 18th Amendment was ratified, of course, but Walker's trenchant debating style nonetheless impressed his colleagues. Perhaps his most famous put-down occurred several years later, when the Senate was debating the Clean Books bill. The Republican lawmakers backing the measure were determined that sexually suggestive books should be censored lest they offend female sensibilities. (The works of D. H. Lawrence were found particularly objectionable.) After much fulminating by Republicans about the need to protect female virtue, Walker rose to offer his comments. "Why all this talk about womanhood?" he said. "I never yet heard of a girl being ruined by a book."

While a senator, Walker maintained a private law practice. One of his cases at this time involved the defense of Stewart N. McMullin, a prohibition agent who had killed a man in the line of duty. McMullin had spent half of his forty years in jail for offenses ranging from manslaughter to forgery to highway robbery; nonetheless, he was employed by the federal government because of his knowledge of the underworld. In early March of 1920, he convinced a taxi driver named Harry Carlton that he wanted to buy a large quantity of whiskey. In short order, McMullin and two other undercover agents were guided by Carlton to one Carlo Carini, an Italian bootlegger on East Seventy-sixth Street, to whom they paid $736 for numerous cases of liquor. Before an arrest could be made, however, Carini gave the cash, which was needed as evidence, to his eighteen-year-old daughter. When the agents drew their guns, the bootlegger ran out of his flat and into another apartment, where McMullin's partners followed him and arrested him. Meanwhile, Carini's daughter ran to the rear of her own flat and attempted to leave via the fire escape. McMullin caught up with the screaming girl and tried to subdue her. Carlton, left more or less to his own devices, then approached the fire escape himself, possibly trying to calm the girl. As McMullin saw him coming, he shot him. Later, McMullin claimed that Carlton had threatened him with a knife.

At the trial, the New York State prosecutors alleged that the prohibition agent had committed murder. Since McMullin was working for the U.S. government, he was defended by the U.S. District Attorney's office, and Walker was named to assist the defense. The nub of the case was this: McMullin, holding the girl out on the fire escape, claimed that he had not shot Carlton until the man, knife in hand, had started to climb through the window after him. The knife was never found, and McMullin concluded that it must have fallen through the fire escape to the street below, where no one thought to look for it. In retort, Carini and his daughter insisted that McMullin had never identified himself as a law officer; they panicked, they said, because they thought they were being held up by robbers. As for the knife, the girl insisted that Carlton had been unarmed and had only been trying to help her as she struggled with a presumed assailant. In view of McMullin's criminal past, it seemed certain that the jury, ironically, would believe the bootleggers.

During the summing up, however, Walker raised a crucial point. "Every time they ask you what became of the knife," he told them, "ask yourselves what became of the cartridge shell fired by McMullin. If McMullin killed Carlton in the room, as the prosecution charges, the cartridge should have been found there." Now the jury saw what Walker was driving at. Just as no knife had been found, neither had a shell. If McMullin had been out on the fire escape, as he claimed, both objects could have fallen through the metal slats. But would Carlton have climbed out on the fire escape unless he *was* attacking McMullin, and unless he *had* been armed? The jury voted for acquittal.

Another Walker case concerned the murder of Nathan Kaplan, known as Kid Dropper, in August of 1923. At the time Kid Dropper was the leader of the most notorious group of Jewish gangsters in New York. Decades earlier, in the mid-1800s, when the whole of the Lower East Side had been populated by Irishmen, the Irish gangs were everywhere, their specialties being cracking skulls, stuffing ballot boxes, and occasional burglary. Yet, said journalist Morris Markey, "These Irishmen did not greatly care about killing each other. The sound of a hearty smash against a flaming thatch was happiness enough. Pistols were expensive and money was scarce, and since politics was the chief reason for fighting at all, the actual death of one's enemy was not considered essential." As 1900 dawned, the Irish learned they could join the police force and be paid for brawling. Moreover, the Lower East Side was seeing a huge influx of Italians; these worthies started up their own gangs, and their weapons were not fists but stilettos. By 1910, still another wave of immigrants—the

Jews—changed the ethnic balance of the East Side once again. The Jews, like the Italians, were not natural fist-fighters, but they were eager to improve their lot; when the area's poverty kept them from realizing their ambitions, many of the Jewish boys, discovering the equalizing effects of the automatic pistol, opted for the gangster's life.

Nathan Kaplan, the Dropper, got his nickname while still in his teens. It was his habit then to jump unwary youngsters while they were shooting craps, cuff them around, and pick up the money lying on the ground. Hence the term "Kid Dropper."

Kaplan's chief gangland rival was Jacob Orgen, called Little Augie by his adherents. In the hot summer of 1923, the feud got so bad —one side being paid to support a strike of laundry workers and the other side being paid to crush it—that even the Irish police abandoned their traditional attitude of let-the-Jews-kill-each-other. Kid Dropper was arrested on the last-resort charge of carrying a concealed weapon (thanks to Big Tim Sullivan and the Sullivan Law) and arraigned in Essex Market Court. There the forces of law and order persuaded the Dropper that, in return for dismissal of the charges, he should visit his brother out West. They even guaranteed him safe passage out of New York and Little Augie's sphere of influence. Surrounded by three dozen police and accompanied by Captain of Detectives Cornelius Willemse in plainclothes, the gangster left the courthouse. Just as he and Captain Willemse seated themselves in a waiting taxi, a trembling little man, so short he could not see into the rear window of the high-backed cab, ran up behind it and blindly fired three bullets, one of which killed the Dropper instantly. The killer's name was Louis Kushner, alias Louis Cohen, and he was possibly the lowest ranking member of Little Augie's gang.

Once more, Walker was the court-appointed attorney for an accused murderer. In his testimony, Cohen explained that fear of the Dropper had driven him to act as he did. He had been told the day before the murder that the Dropper had said he would "get" him as soon as he was released from custody. "I went to a turkish bath that night but couldn't sleep," Cohen lamented. "The next day I went down to the court. . . . The Dropper gave me a look when he reached the sidewalk. I went behind the taxicab and began shooting." Walker decided his only hope of enabling his client to escape a First Degree Murder conviction and the death sentence was to focus on the disappearance of the spent cartridge, as he had done in the McMullin case. Witnesses had testified that Cohen had fired three shots. Three bullets had been found—one in the corpse, one that wounded the cab driver, and one that lodged in the cab. Yet Captain Willemse had a bullet hole in his straw hat. Where was this fourth shell? Walker hammered home at the point: Who had fired the fourth shot? Might not it have killed Kid Dropper?

"We know Cohen attempted to kill the Kid," Walker said. "But to sustain a charge of First Degree Murder you must prove it. . . . Four bullets were fired and only three of them by Cohen. From whose revolver came the fourth shot—the shot that may have killed the Dropper?"

Influenced at least in part by Walker's argument, the jury brought in a verdict of Second Degree Murder, and Cohen was sentenced to twenty years to life. As for the fourth shot, uncharitable people whispered that it had not been fired during the attack, that Captain Willemse himself had later shot a hole though his own hat to show how close he had come to death.

In April of 1924, two events took place that were greatly to affect Walker's future. In that year, the Democrats had control of the Senate by one vote; since there were many crucial bills to be passed, it fell to Walker, as majority leader, to quash Republican opposition by making sure all Democrats attended roll calls. Even one man's absence could upset the party's advantage. Senator John A. Hastings, a flashily dressed twenty-four-year-old with a taste for expensive living was paying the periodic price of overindulgence, laid up in his Brooklyn home with what his doctor described as the grippe. When Walker sent word to Hastings that he was needed in Albany, the senator caught the next train to the capital, where he had himself wheeled into the chamber on a stretcher. As one bill after another came to a vote, Hastings would weakly and dramatically raise his hand to signify "aye." Walker thoroughly appreciated the performance, and he and Hastings became fast friends. In a few years, the younger senator would play a major role in the city scandal in which Walker most personally involved himself.

The death in 1924 of Charles F. Murphy would also leave its mark on Walker. The sixty-five-year-old Tammany leader succumbed to a sudden heart attack that was headlined, ignominiously, as acute indigestion. Mr. Murphy, who had not married until he was in his fifties, left a widow, a stepdaughter, and the aforementioned step-son-in-law, Surrogate James A. Foley. Of the tight-lipped leader's *modus operandi*, the New York *Times* commented: "A caller on Mr. Murphy at Tammany Hall rarely talked to him more than two minutes. With immobile features, Mr. Murphy would listen to him attentively without moving a muscle. A nod of assent or of negation would usually be all that the seeker for favor would receive." So careful had Murphy been with words that, at a Tammany Fourth of July celebration, a reporter once noticed he was not joining in the singing of "The Star-Spangled Banner." Why didn't the boss sing, the reporter afterward asked a Tammany factotum. "Perhaps," replied this gentleman knowingly, "he didn't want to commit himself."

Many people who knew both Walker and Murphy believed that, if the Tammany leader had lived, he would have had the necessary moral and political suasion to discipline Walker during his mayoral years. Certainly Allie Walker, who had learned early in their marriage that her husband was not the most domestic of men, held this viewpoint. "I do think that Mr. Murphy . . . would have controlled Jim to the extent that he never would have become involved the way he did," Allie would say in retrospect, thinking of the shambles of Walker's career and the failure of their marriage. "I think that all of his friends felt that soon he would come to his senses, but they waited too long to try to influence him. . . . Mr. Murphy would have nipped things in the bud."

By 1925, Walker was in his sixteenth year in the legislature and was nearing his forty-fourth birthday; he was reaching an age when he had to think of improving his financial worth—perhaps by leaving politics and concentrating on law, or even by going into business. One of his friends was Arthur Grashoff, an Englishman who had made a fortune marketing ginger ale and soda water. (The coming of Prohibition in 1920 had substantially increased the demand for soft drinks, with speakeasies and saloons were selling ginger ale and soda at inflated prices and then surreptitiously adding liquor to patrons' glasses. More and more mixers were being used in homes as well, as a generation of Americans felt compelled to press highballs on anyone who looked remotely thirsty.) Grashoff knew that Walker's Broadway contacts among theater people, journalists, and sports figures would be of great public-relations value to his business, and throughout the spring the two men talked of Walker's taking an active role in its management.

Then, around Easter, reports began to appear in the non-Hearst press that Walker might be the ideal candidate to replace Mayor Hylan, then ending his second four-year term. While the state senator's support was coming from his Broadway cronies, not from Tammany, it could not help but make an impression on Alfred E. Smith. Murphy's death had freed Smith from any obligation not to scuttle the Tammany patronage scow; the governor needed an attractive candidate to defeat Hylan for the Democratic nomination and thus deliver the political *coup de grâce* to Hylan's master, William Randolph Hearst. Smith knew that Hylan would be difficult to unseat; the machine cares only that its needs be met, and Hylan was seeing to that. Moreover, Hylan was supported by the vituperative Hearst press. "A fellow loses an arm, the good Lord makes the other twice as strong," Smith observed of the mayor. "Hylan has damn little sense. But Lord, what *luck!* . . .

After Surrogate James A. Foley and Supreme Court Justice Robert Wagner turned down his entreaties, the governor considered Walker's candidacy. He was aware of the senator's popularity but repelled by his lack of seriousness. Earlier in 1925, for instance, he had instigated a pointed conversation with Walker that touched on the latter's glibness and then fastened on his fondness for Broadway showgirls.

"The only thing that's worse for a public man than being funny," Smith said, "is for him to chase women if he's married."

"Could you by any chance be thinking of one of the neighbor's children?" Walker asked.

"Jim, I have a genuine, deep-down affection for you," Smith said. "And it's a shame you won't listen to reason."

"It's a great temptation to be like Mayor Hylan," Walker joked. "A solid, substantial man who—"

Smith abruptly terminated the discussion.

A long-time Smith aide and confidant, master builder Robert Moses, has observed that Walker "was no paragon to hold up to youth. He was the product of a crazy age, impish, urbane, polished, sardonic. He was at his best when dependent solely on his wits, when he was unprepared, unrehearsed, and seriousness was purely coincidental."

Moses remembers discussing Walker's mayoral credentials that summer with Smith and other Democratic leaders on a boat trip up the Hudson River to Bear Mountain. Smith was demanding a replacement for Hylan, and the Democratic chieftains and subchieftains were reluctantly discussing substitutes. The governor asked Moses what he thought of James J. Walker. Moses replied that Walker "was incapable of sustained effort."

"What the hell is that?" truculently demanded Boss McCooey.

"That means," said Moses, "that if Walker is given a two-page memo he reads the first page, and then his attention wanders."

On July 2, as we have seen, an enthusiastic Walker delegation, composed mostly of Broadway notables, pressed his candicacy on George W. Olvany, who had succeeded Murphy as Tammany leader, at the Fourteenth Street Wigam. About that time, comedian George Jessel was acting as master of ceremonies at the Café de Paris on

West Fifty-fourth Street. One night he spotted Walker at a corner table. It had been a difficult evening for Jessel. Bea Palmer, the singer who originated the "shimmy" and was the latest craze, had not shown up to perform, and he was stalling by introducing various celebrities from the audience and asking them to entertain. Nora Bayes sang "Shine On, Shine On, Harvest Moon"; Eddie Cantor obliged with a fifteen-minute monologue. Well, figured Jessel, why not introduce Walker and let him say a few words? To get the audience's attention, he later reminisced, he "ordered a fanfare from the trumpet player and a cymbal crash from the drummer," and then announced the presence of "a young man who may be the next Mayor of the great City of New York." Walker got to his feet, addressed the merry revelers, and, much to Jessel's surprise and relief, "held them fascinated for a full half-hour." This was the beginning of a strong friendship; Jessel would make some fifty speeches for Walker during the mayoral campaign that was to follow.

Smith, meanwhile, was still hesitating over his mayoral choice. "Basically, Al Smith had little use for executives of the Walker stripe," Robert Moses has written, "no matter how much he liked them personally. They worried him. He knew that in the end, when hard times came and the mood of the people changed, tragedy was inevitable."

Even the irrepressible Walker eventually realized that he would have to curb his partying and late hours, ostensibly at least, before Smith, family man that he was, would grant him the nomination. Accordingly, a subdued Walker, fortified with ample stores of caviar and champagne and an occasional trustworthy showgirl, holed up in Arthur Grashoff's penthouse apartment on West Fifty-eighth Street. After a few days, his absence from his Broadway haunts began to be talked about; after a couple of weeks, word of Walker's supposed reform reached Governor Smith. In late July, a vacationing Smith summoned Walker to his hotel in Atlantic City.

"How'd you ever do it?" asked Smith.

"Do what?" asked Walker innocently.

"Keep away from the speaks?"

"We all grow up some time, Al."

The governor paused for a moment, still skeptical, and then abruptly decided, for political expediency, to become a true believer.

"Jim, I've decided to approve your candidacy. You're the man to beat Red Mike."

Within days, Tammany Boss Olvany in Manhattan and Boss Edward J. Flynn in the Bronx would, with Smith's backing, announce their support of the state senator; the Walker bandwagon was beginning to roll—straight at the bumbling but hitherto lucky Red Mike Hylan.

A portent of what would happen to Hylan took place on July 4, 1924, when the mayor was seeing his wife off on a vacation trip to Europe aboard the liner *Leviathan.* He was accompanied to the pier by Boss McCooey of Brooklyn, long a strong supporter, and shortly before the ship sailed, the mayor had his picture taken clasping McCooey's hand. Then he remarked to reporters: "Now I am sure of being nominated." Later that day, however, when Smith and George W. Olvany presided at the Tammany Society's annual Independence Day celebration, a fete attended by every city Democrat of any importance, it was learned that Hylan had not been invited. Commented the New York *Times:* "Mayor Hylan was not present, but it was said that the failure of Tammany to send a special invitation to him had no significance, as he was known to have had an engagement to speak elsewhere."

We have already examined the relationship that Charles F. Murphy alternately suffered and enjoyed for two decades with William Randolph Hearst, and how it led in large part to Smith's aversion to Hylan as mayor and his readiness to accept Walker. Now we should look more closely at a reluctant Smith ally, George Olvany, the new Tammany leader, and at a willing one, Edward J. Flynn, the Democratic boss of the Bronx. Nor should we forget Boss McCooey, who still leaned toward his fellow Brooklynite Hylan but also desired to safeguard his patronage arrangement with Tammany.

Olvany, Flynn, and McCooey knew only too well that Tammany could no longer swing elections unilaterally. Throughout the nineteenth century, when most of the immigrants had settled on Manhattan Island, the tiger needed no allies. In the 1880s, just before James J. Walker was born, Manhattan's population was 1,164,000 while that of Brooklyn, its closest rival, was only 550,000. As the years went on, however, improved transportation enabled Brooklyn to become a bedroom adjunct to Manhattan, and its numbers grew; by 1923, its population actually surpassed Manhattan's—2,137,000 to 2,065,000. Yet Tammany's superior organization enabled it throughout the 1920s to continue to call the political tune among the five boroughs. Moreover, Mr. Murphy before his death had supported Ed Flynn for the Bronx leadership, thereby gaining Flynn's personal loyalty. "As Tammany was both the oldest and the most aggressive of the five Democratic organizations," Flynn would reflect, "the leader of Tammany Hall treated the other leaders less like allies than like hand-picked viceroys—which is precisely what they were."

Edward J. Flynn was that rarity among the politicians of the era, the possessor of a formal education, having graduated from Fordham University and Fordham Law School. After two terms in the state assembly, he was elected sheriff of the Bronx; the newly elected Flynn promptly fired the sixty-two job-holders in his office and replaced them with his own people. "It would be nonsense to pretend that devotion and personal ego are all that hold a machine together," he commented, defending the spoils system.

Flynn's elevation to the over-all Bronx leadership came about in this manner. In 1922, when Arthur Murphy, the incumbent boss, died, a slew of candidates vied for the job, but none was strong enough to win the position outright. Acting as a peacemaker, Charles F. Murphy then arranged for a tirumvirate to rule the Bronx and named the thirty-year-old Flynn a member of this body. (Murphy, right after Richard Croker's abdication, had himself been a member of a triumvirate; just as he had emerged from the group to dominate Tammany, he felt sure that Flynn would develop the confidence to rule the Bronx.) "Once a week [in] a funeral hack . . . the three of us would proceed in state to Mr. Murphy's house on East Seventeenth Street," Flynn said of these months of shared leadership. "[Mr. Murphy] would seat himself with his usual dignity and ask, 'How are conditions in the Bronx?' Each of us in turn would reply, 'Excellent.' This would conclude the conference."

Conditions were far from excellent, however, because by the time Flynn and his two colleagues could get together to make decisions, "the patronage in question would be absorbed by some other county, or the question of policy would no longer be important." Party affairs in the Bronx slowed to a standstill. After three months, Flynn became so irate at the pretense that he went down to Murphy's office alone and told him that he intended "to call a meeting of my supporters and have myself elected leader, whether anyone liked it or not." In his anger, Flynn disregarded the fact that he did not have the votes to accomplish this coup. Smiling benignly at Flynn's initiative, Murphy informed him, "There will be a meeting of the committee tomorrow, and you will be elected chairman." And so it came to pass. "His power was so great," said Flynn, "that when he gave what is known in politics as 'the word,' opposition crumbled away."

While serving in the legislature, Flynn had gotten to know Al Smith; in the fall of 1922, one of his first important decisions as boss of the Bronx was to line up with Smith, during the Syracuse State Convention, when Smith refused to run on the same ticket with Hearst. "As time went on, my acquaintanceship with Governor Smith ripened into a genuine friendship. . . . By close observation, I found out how Smith handled things, how he weighed issues, how he adjusted political considerations with broader interests." Smith had no sooner begun his third term as governor in 1924, said Flynn, "than he made known his determination to prevent the renomination of Mayor Hylan." Flynn was an enlightened boss, and he was fully in accord with Smith's programs for social reform. Moreover, he disliked Hylan's connection with Hearst. Just as he had accepted Murphy's authority, therefore, he now accepted Smith's.

Though he allied himself with Tammany, Flynn was not overly impressed with George W. Olvany, a former judge of the Court of General Sessions who was now Tammany's leader. Olvany had been selected after Murphy's death as a compromise among various warring factions; in effect, he had been handed the post. His limitations, Flynn felt, "lay in the fact that he had not fought for the place. . . . A person who has won his leadership by hard battling makes a better leader."

Judge Olvany stood six-foot-two, weighed 210 pounds, and was at his best when the situation called for him to wear a silk hat. With his rise to the bench early in 1924 he developed a pervasive dignity that some of his less successful friends resented. "He don't seem like the same old George," was a remark heard more and more. Judge Olvany thought it unseemly, for instance, to continue taking his lunch perched on a high counter stool at the Record Café in downtown Manhattan. His old cronies interpreted his new sense of fitness as snobbism. George eventually kept both his decorum and his friends by letting it be known that urgent matters of jurisprudence required him to eat lunch in chambers.

Olvany grew up in the Greenwich Village area, played as a boy with Jimmy Walker, went to mass with Al Smith at St. James Church. Possessed of a sense of humor, as witness his oft-repeated remark, "New York is the cleanest and best-governed city in the world," he also believed in periodically mortifying the flesh; in the middle of winter, he and various other hardy souls, members of a club called the Polar Bears, would dash into the surf at Coney Island. Like Flynn, Olvany had a college education, having graduated from New York University. This raised him above the madding Tammany crowd, enabling him to forsake the filling of beer glasses for the practice of law. (In 1905, while serving on the Board of Aldermen, he was reportedly the only one of his peers to remain seated when an excited boy popped his head into the meeting room and shouted, "Alderman, your saloon's on fire!") Olvany rose steadily in the Tammany hierarchy, and when the siren call came that Murphy's mantle might be his, he cupped his ear. No one could find anything wrong with George beyond a great-grandfather back in Ireland who may or may not have been a Presbyterian, so he was offered the leadership. With alacrity, Olvany resigned the judgeship he had held for less than a year and moved his silk hat to Tammany Hall.

In the five years he would be leader(and for two years thereafter), George's law firm would gross over $5 million while practicing before the Board of Standards and Appeals, a municipal agency that decided, among other matters, how substantially buildings and skyscrapers could intrude into the city's air space. Olvany's associates must have been persuasive men, because petitioners who retained the firm to request zoning variances were invariably found to be in the right.

Olvany saw Walker, to use Charles F. Murphy's words about Hylan in 1917, as someone "we can trust and do business with." Flynn's analysis of Walker went deeper: "When he would do something that annoyed me, I felt that his manner was so boyishly disarming that my resentment usually evaporated. This was a beguiling characteristic, but one destined to give him much trouble. Many of the people who surrounded him were superficial and rapacious. He found it hard to believe that any of his friends were bad—or even wrong. In the end, Jimmy Walker became the victim of some of these so-called friends."

Brooklyn's McCooey did not want to dump Hylan; neither did the leaders of Queens and Richmond. Hylan was delivering the patronage, wasn't he? These leaders were far more interested in protecting their local interests than in helping Governor Smith build a political base that would further his presidential ambitions.

By 1925 John H. McCooey had held the Brooklyn leadership for seventeen years. He achieved this suzerainty in America's most populous county through patience, diligence, and hard work; he would hear his constituents' complaints, requests, and demands in his office from 10:30 A.M. to 5:00 P.M. daily; no appointments were needed —just line up outside the door. McCooey always gave his people a straight answer. Yes, so-and-so would do well in that job. No, that eviction notice isn't valid, you can forget about it. But if a journalist asked him a question he wanted to dodge—what his golf score was, how much he weighed, or whom he'd support in an up-coming election—McCooey issued a stock reply: "The situation, as far as I am concerned, is unchanged."

White-haired and mustachioed, jowly, and possessing the kind of unblemished pink skin that, as one reporter put it, "is achieved only by babies and by old men who have lived successful lives," Mc-Cooey considered Hylan his friend. That as much as patronage considerations ensured his support for Hylan against Walker, whom he called "a nice young fellow," in the primary. McCooey was also a friend of Hearst, whom he had pushed for governor at two successive Democratic conventions. When Murphy and the publisher rowed, McCooey would try to patch up their differences; he gave up only when Murphy finally ordered Hearst's "filthy, lying newspapers" banned from Tammany clubhouses. McCooey belonged to nineteen fraternal societies, including the Knights of Columbus and the Protective Order of Elks, and he held the presidencies of the Emerald Club and the Friendly Sons of Saint Patrick. Married, but with his two children grown, McCooey had little home life. Six nights a week, he would attend political dinners; at these affairs, he would wave his inevitable cigar like a scroll of office. Each year he looked forward to his birthday party, when hundreds of his supporters boarded a cruise boat and steamed up the Hudson to Bear Mountain, there to feast on huge quantities of shellfish, chowder, and ice cream. There was little drinking on these outings. McCooey wanted it that way; his constituents were told to bring their women and children, and to stay sober.

At the end of July, Tammany prepared for war. Olvany called a luncheon meeting of the five Democratic borough chiefs at the New York Athletic Club to discuss the mayoralty nomination, but nothing came of it. He and Flynn remained solidly for Walker. McCooey, Maurice Connolly of Queens, and David S. Rendt of Richmond continued to support Hylan.

"Is Mayor Hylan out?" Olvany was asked.

"No one is out," he replied.

Said McCooey: "The situation is unchanged and all we can report is progress."

Said Connolly: "We had a fine luncheon."

Said Rendt: "........."

When Olvany returned from the lunch to the Wigwam on Fourteenth Street, he talked to about twenty of his district leaders, sounding out each man's loyalty.

Mayor Hylan was not so circumspect. He used the occasion to fulminate against a stock-market tip sheet signed by an E. H. Rodney that advised its readers to buy traction stocks. Rodney's reasoning was that Hylan would soon be replaced as mayor and that quite possibly the fare would rise. "Who gave Rodney the information as to what is going on in inner circles?" Hylan asked darkly. "Are not the people entitled to know who on the inside can deliver the people of New York and the Democratic Party to the traction financial ring?"

Finally, on August 6, Olvany told a meeting of the Tammany Executive Committee that the party could not win if Hylan was on the ticket. His advocacy of Walker for mayor received unanimous approval. In the Bronx, Flynn pushed through a similar resolution. Nominated to run with Walker were Charles W. Berry, a long-time friend of Al Smith, for controller, and Joseph V. McKee, a Bronx man suggested by Flynn, for the aldermanic presidency. It was a neat package that contained something for everyone and, theoretically at least, would enable Smith and Flynn, through their personal choices on the ticket, to keep Walker under surveillance. At least that was the plan.

All three Tammany candidates were regarded as progressives. Commented the New York *Times* on Walker: "Among the legislation he has sponsored was a bill to unmask the Ku Klux Klan by compelling publication of its membership roll. . . . He has also been the sponsor of legislation providing for a liberalization of the Prohibition Law. . . . During the administrations of Governor Smith subsequent to 1922, he made a brilliant fight for the governor's legislative program, succeeding in a 100 percent performance while the Senate remained Democratic." Walker played up this appraisal. "I have been trained so long in the Smith school," he said, "that I am used to the idea of a constructive platform containing pledges meant to be fulfilled and capable of fulfillment."

Charles W. Berry, by profession a physician, had been appointed Commanding Officer of the State National Guard by Smith; he was usually addressed, therefore, as General Berry. The post–World War I era was a period of intense patriotism, and the command of the Guard was a signal honor. A Brooklyn resident, Berry had been McCooey's doctor and had long been active in politics, being a past chairman of the Brooklyn Democratic Committee. As the candidate for controller, Berry enjoyed the reputation of someone who knew how to watch his buffalo nickels.

The thirty-six-year-old McKee had served in the state assembly, concentrating on such matters as welfare legislation; despite the well-meaning endorsement of the good-government Citizens Union, he had somehow managed to survive three consecutive terms. McKee had just been named a city court justice for a ten-year term at $17,500 annually—a post he resigned to run for the much lower-salaried job of aldermanic president. This was understandable. Men like John

Purroy Mitchel and Al Smith had in recent years used the aldermanic seat effectively to further their careers.

Hylan, growling that nefarious "orders have been issued by the powers behind the throne," announced that he would run against Walker in the Democratic primaries only five weeks away. Supporting him and a separate slate of candidates were McCooey, Connolly, and Rendt. Yet even Brooklyn did not appear to be safe for Hylan. When Judge Olvany was asked whether Walker could win in that borough, he replied knowingly, "I think he might."

This last bit of presumption irked McCooey exceedingly—all the more because he knew his hold on Brooklyn was in doubt. In 1925 any man Al Smith backed had to be feared. McCooey resorted to bluster. Harking back to the late Patrick H. McCarren, the Brooklyn boss who twenty-one years before had threatened Tammany with the slogan "The Tiger Must Not Cross the Bridge," McCooey revived the exhortation. A cynic was quick to point out that the Brooklyn Bridge was no longer the only easy manner of access between Brooklyn and Manhattan, but McCooey was in no mood for quibbling. Neither, evidently, were Smith nor Walker. Within a week they took up the challenge, speeding over the bridge one evening in a twenty-automobile caravan bathed in the light of red flares and escorted by a fleet of snarling police motorcycles. In Prospect Hall, once the omnipresent bands got "East Side, West Side, All Around the Town" and "Hail, Hail, the Gang's All Here" off their tubas and kettledrums, Governor Smith proceeded to make Hylan look foolish. First he sidestepped the mayor's charge that Arnold Rothstein, a well-known gambler and "fixer" rumored to be the link between Tammany politicians and the underworld, had dictated the machine's choice of Walker. (We shall learn more about Rothstein later.)

Rothstein didn't give the nominating speech at the Wigwam for Walker, said Smith in a marvelous *non sequitur;* it was Daniel E. Finn, who, as all loyal Democrats knew, was "a good, old, upstanding, straightforward character of New York." There was loud applause. "Incidentally," Smith added, "Finn happens to be a member of the Mayor's cabinet." Now there was laughter. "The Mayor either does not know a gambler when he sees one," Smith concluded, "or he does not know who made that nominating speech." In the even louder laughter that resulted, the Rothstein charge was forgotten— at least for the next few years.

Smith then admitted that Hylan was a decent fellow: "As a man that fought his way up the ladder, I have a great admiration for him. I like him. I like his family. I like his good clean life. . . ." Finally came the ostensibly reluctant assessment of Hylan: "But I speak of his ability to be the Mayor of this City. *That* is what we are dwelling on!"

Walker next took the microphone to deliver a long, fact-filled speech in which he pledged that he would keep the five-cent fare and outlined how various new subway and road-building projects would be initiated in Brooklyn—if he were elected. "There is no doubt in my mind . . . of the necessity for the construction of a boulevard from the foot of Atlantic Avenue at the East River to Jamaica . . . Atlantic Avenue is the only street running east and west with a right of way wide enough to be utilized as an artery of traffic. . . ." His remarks were calculated to show his grasp of the transportation situation, and in this he succeeded. The 3,000 people in Prospect Hall and another 3,000 partisans outside the building listening via amplifiers time and again shouted their approval. Everyone went home happy.

At a garden party given for Walker in the Rockaways a few days later, Grover Whalen endorsed the Hylan challenger. This was, in a sense, surprising. Whalen, an executive of Wanamaker's department store, once had been Hylan's private secretary and until the summer before had served as Hylan's Commissioner of Plants and Structures; for six and a half years he had been considered the man closest to the mayor. Who are you for? Whalen was asked.

"This is a Walker party," he answered.

"Will you support Senator Walker?"

"I live at 43 Fifth Avenue, Manhattan, and I'm for the Tammany Hall candidate," Whalen said.

"That's Walker, isn't it?"

"You bet your life," replied the exuberant Whalen, who would eventually play a two-part role in the Walker administration. As the city's official host, he would, with unshakable aplomb and gusto, arrange elaborate ticker-tape greetings for explorers, aviators, and Channel swimmers; as Walker's third police commissioner, he would bring his showmanship to bear, with less success, on crime-in-the-streets, traffic snarls, and speakeasy owners.

Smith continued his stumping for Walker. First he would lay into Hearst and Hylan, then lavishly praise his man's accomplishments in the legislature; Walker had advocated laws calling for improved housing, rent control, penal reform, minimum wages, soldier bonuses, child welfare—all bills Smith had drafted in the governor's mansion. Walker followed up Smith's performances by respectfully outlining how he could help the city grow. Meanwhile, Hylan continued to rail against "traction interests." By early September, it was apparent that most of the Tammany district leaders felt Walker would win—and win big.

In the Fifth Assembly District, the "Hell's Kitchen" that ran roughly from the thirties through the forties and from Seventh Avenue to the Hudson River, Thomas J. ("The") McManus figured Walker had a 10-to-1 margin. McManus was known throughout the city as "The," like a Celtic chieftain. He had supplanted George Washington Plunkitt in the district leadership in the late 1880s and would hold it for forty years, until his death in 1926. ("There is no crime so mean as ingratitude in politics," said Plunkitt, who had made his pile in city construction contracts, "but every great statesman of the world has been up against it. Caesar had his Brutus . . . and I've got my 'The' McManus. . . . Great men have a tender, trusting nature. So have I, outside of the contractin' business.") Thomas M. Farley, leader of the Fourteenth A.D., was guaranteeing 9-to-1 of the total Democratic vote for the machine candidate. (This was the same Farley who was later celebrated in court testimony and song as "Tin Box" Farley. His political clubhouse, on Sixty-second Street near First Avenue, where gambling was said to take place, was fortified with barred windows and massive metal doors, making it almost impervious to police raids; Farley claimed the precautions were necessary to keep the children of the neighborhood from "petty pilfering." He would earn the nickname "Tin Box" in 1931, while he was having his turn at being Sheriff of New York County. Samuel Seabury, investigating the Walker administration for the state, asked Farley how he had managed to bank $396,000 in the previous seven years when his wages totaled only $87,000. Farley replied, "Well, that came from the good box I had." Asked Seabury: "Kind of a magic box?" Farley looked him straight in the eye and said, "It was a wonderful box.") Over in Murphy's old Twelfth A.D., where a gentleman named William P. Kenneally was holding down the city position of Assistant Deputy Controller and simultaneously filling Murphy's brogans by running the district, the vote looked like 4-to-1 for Walker.

Endorsements flooded in. The Interboro Baseball Association, representing more than 200 of the best-known amateur teams in the city, declared that its support was merely a small return for Walker's zeal in legalizing Sunday baseball. Edwin Franko Goldman, who had gained considerable renown for sponsoring free concerts in Central Park, said that thousands of music lovers were tapping out the beat for Jimmy. The Anti-Fanatic League added its endorsement, on the ground that Walker had "shown himself to be . . . a foe of that intolerance which seeks to raise racial prejudice and religious strife among good American citizens." And Broadway's George M. Cohan, already a supporter, loudly proclaimed that every member of the theatrical profession "owed" it to Walker to support him. Cohan, the millionaire showman who had written such songs as "Mary's a Grand Old Name," "I'm a Yankee Doodle Dandy," and "Over There," had been a big name in the theater for over two decades. In the early 1900s he had been instrumental in founding the Friars, the well-known theatrical club in whose revels Walker later was a frequent and enthusiastic participant.

At his headquarters in the Commodore Hotel, Walker relaxed by having mentalist Joseph Dunninger read his mind. Dunninger had already limned the thoughts of Presidents Roosevelt and Harding, Chief Justice Taft, the Prince of Wales, Jack Dempsey, and Babe Ruth. He had even read Mayor Hylan's mind, thereby proving his tenacity. The candidate was asked to write a short statement on a piece of paper and put it in his pocket. Dunninger then astonished those present by correctly stating that Walker's note read: "Democracy means loyalty." "The Senator," the mentalist said afterward, when he had recovered from the strain of his performance, "is not only exceptionally alert and keen, but he is a splendid listener—receptive to reason. His mind is supple and adaptable—not the kind which is always made up in advance." He predicted Walker victories in the primary and the election.

In September of 1925, New York City's population was 5,877,000 —up more than a million since Walker first took his seat in Albany. Grand Central Station, located from Forty-second to Forty-fifth Streets along Vanderbilt Avenue, had been open for a dozen years. The first zoning ordinance had been in force for a decade; it regulated the uses to which buildings might be put, their height in relation to their surroundings, and how fully they could cover their lots (the ordinance also gave Tammany politicians, through their influence with the Board of Standards and Appeals, splendid opportunities to increase their net worth by obtaining variances). The White Plains Road and Jerome Avenue extensions of the transit lines had bound the Bronx tighter to Manhattan. The invention of pyroxylin finishes was enabling the hitherto all-black automobile to burst into greens, reds, and yellows, enlivening the city streets, and Hudson "Super-Six" Coaches were selling for $1,250. Transcontinental telephone service was a reality, and so was a daily airmail route from New York to Washington. In 1920, the first commercial radio stations had begun operating; by 1925, the New York-based radio industry was affecting the life-style of all Americans. Silent movies had been a multi-million-dollar business for over a decade; within a year, the first talking film, *The Jazz Singer*, would appear, expanding the influence of movies still further.

Prohibition was in its fifth year, and more and more men and women were evading its mandate. The life-styles of women were changing in other ways as well. Skirts had risen above the knee, dancing was a "syncopated embrace," even "nice" girls openly drank Bronx cocktails and smoked Sweet Caporals. The flapper era that F. Scott Fitzgerald had described among the rich in *This Side of Paradise* a few years before had filtered down to the middle class. Sociologists explained the metamorphosis of women: Now there were time-saving products and services available in the home, they said, conveniences like canned goods and bakery products, electric washers and irons, ready-made clothes. Now there was woman's suffrage. Now there were Freud's teachings on sex (which finally had come to the attention of nonscientific eyes), the intimacy of the closed-top auto, the sensationalism of the tabloid newspapers. The bobbed-hair woman of the twenties was no longer just a man's better half, his wife, the mother of his children; she was becoming tentatively but determinedly his companion. Most men seemed to approve. This, then, was the milieu in which James J. Walker in 1925 was putting forth his candidacy.

On Primary Day, Smith and Walker were confident. "Jimmy Walker will clean up," said the governor. In Brooklyn, McCooey drew ballot No. 13 when casting his vote. "I have been too long in politics to be superstitious," he said.

The Irish police were vigilant about enforcing the primary laws. Mrs. Arthur Gatti of 76 Charles Street in Manhattan was told by one patrolman that she could not vote because investigation showed she did not live at the address she had given for herself. "I don't care about your investigation," Mrs. Gatti replied spiritedly. "I have lived there all along, as all the neighbors know, and I'm going to vote." She was allowed to cast her ballot after swearing a special residency oath. Isidor Pops of the Bronx was not so fortunate. He was arrested by a Patrolman Kelly immediately after voting, on the ground that he was not a registered Democrat. "Why did they give me the ballot if I didn't have the right to vote?" he lamented. John R. Gadson, a black waiter of 138 West Forty-third Street, came to grief at the hands of Lieutenant Patrick Hickey, who charged that he had not registered in the preceding election. As for Herman Gordon of 102 East One Hundred Second Street, even a rational explanation did not save him from the paddy wagon when it was discovered that the home address he had given was a motion-picture theater. "But I own the theater and have a bed in it and I sleep there," insisted Gordon.

By early evening, it was clear that Walker would win by about 100,000 votes out of 400,000 cast, carrying Manhattan, the Bronx, and Brooklyn. The Tammany chieftains hunkered in Judge Olvany's private office at the Wigwam, savoring the news. Governor Smith, wearing not his usual brown derby but a gray fedora, sat on one side of Olvany's large desk, Surrogate Foley on the other. Various district leaders occupied chairs along the walls. Visitors included Grover Whalen, the one-time Hylan protégé. At about 11:00 A.M., Walker dropped into the Wigwam to give his thanks to the chieftains and party workers. Later, rejoining his wife at his Hotel Commodore headquarters, Walker allowed, "This was as it should have been, a Tammany victory." It remained for the *Herald-Tribune* the next morning to sum up the reasons for Walker's smashing triumph:

Tammany has had in its time many things to answer for, but never have the prosperity and progress of the community received such a serious setback as since the present Democratic Administration was elected to office. New subways . . . have been obstructed for no other reason save that Mr. Hylan neither knew how to build them nor was willing to allow anyone else to build them. The Port Authority program, which would have expedited the handling of merchandise and saved the public millions of dollars, was delayed because Mr. Hylan was incapable of understanding it and fearful that if it were worked out by others his own prestige might suffer.

For eight years this metropolis, so far as governmental development is concerned, has stood still. . . . The Police Department had failed to protect the merchants and citizens against the criminal invasion . . .

Tammany was slow to learn. . . . The campaign conducted by the Governor at last awakened his party to the imperative need of discarding the incompetent whom their organization had twice nominated and elected.

When Hylan arrived at City Hall the morning after his defeat, he was in a belligerent frame of mind. "I am pleased with two things," he told reporters. "First, that I pulled the mask off the big ham-and-egg man from Albany [an overly optimistic reference to his jousts with Smith], and second, that I made the traction and underworld

interests spend an average of $400 an election district to defeat me."
But Hylan soon saw the reality of his situation. McCooey and the
other dissident borough leaders—Connolly of Queens and Rendt of
Richmond—were now closing ranks with Tammany and simply would
not support him if he chose to run as—God forbid—an Independent.
Within hours, Hylan announced his retirement, promising to support his party's choice in the general election. (Walker, ever a charitable man, in 1930 would appoint Hylan to a well-paying city job—
that of a judge in the children's court. "Now the children can be
judged by one of their peers," Walker observed privately.)

Olvany was jubilant, Smith was beaming, all good Democrats were
happy—or relatively so. One of Walker's critics was Socialist Norman
Thomas, himself a candidate for mayor. He said:

> It is quite true that we have not shared any great enthusiasm for [Hylan].
> We have felt that his devotion to the people, while honest enough, has
> been lacking in reason and understanding. . . . But never for one instant
> have we shared the delusion that the people of New York will be better
> off under Jimmy Walker than under Mayor Hylan. The man whom
> Broadway calls "our Jimmy" may be too clever to let the City slide back
> to the naked, roaring vice of the days of Croker, but there isn't anyone
> who does not know that under Walker the underworld of New York
> will flourish as it never flourished under Hylan. There isn't anyone who
> does not know that the transit interests and a lot of others rejoiced . . .
> in Walker's victory.

Walker's Republican opponent in the 1925 election was Frank D.
Waterman, president of the Waterman Fountain Pen Company. A
dry and colorless orator, Waterman nonetheless tried hard to inject
some wit into his speaking style. "I used to think . . . that I was
the only bald-headed man in New York," he told an audience during
the campaign. "Now, as I look out over this gathering, I see that I
was mistaken." A hundred or so sensitive bald heads turned a shade
pinker, and there went another hundred votes. Once such extempo-
raneous boffos were disposed of, Waterman would put on his glasses
and get down to his prepared speech. His voice was quite expres-
sionless. His gestures were few; mostly he let his hands hang at his
sides; sometimes he would cross them on the lectern; in moments
of rare emotional stress, he would extend his forefinger.

In 1923 Waterman had organized the Committee of One Thousand,
which strove to make Mayor Hylan modify his delaying tactics on
subway construction. His efforts earned him the necessary city-wide
fame to be proposed as the Republican mayoral candidate two years
later. Appropriately, his supporters in the race against Walker wore

small brass shovels in their coat lapels and adopted the slogan "Say It with Shovels." Waterman saw little difference between Hylan and Walker in transit matters. "Mr. Walker," he said, "openly stands for municipal operation of subways. There I take issue with him. Municipal operation would mean that every subway employee from general manager to watchman would be selected on grounds of political pull." And, Waterman added, "Tammany control of our subways [would] mean Tammany free to give, without competition, contracts for cars, contracts for steel rails, contracts for equipment, contracts for all kinds of favored Tammany contractors."

As the November election drew nearer, Walker proudly proclaimed his Tammany allegiance. Addressing an appreciative crowd at the Wigwam, he opened his arms wide to indicate the Great Hall and declared, "This was the only place where my immigrant father found welcome, help and assistance when he landed in this country . . . it is the home of an organization which has done more to fight the fight of the City of New York than any political organization that you or I have ever heard of. Nearly all the humane measures that have been written into the statute books of the State in recent years emanated from this building."

In a subsequent radio talk, Walker answered the charge that, if elected, he would permit an "open" city. "I am ready to admit," he said, "that I would rather laugh than cry. I like the company of my fellow human beings. I like the theater and am devoted to healthy outdoor sports. Because I like these things . . . I have reflected my attitude in some of the legislation I have sponsored—2.75 percent beer, Sunday baseball, Sunday movies and legalized boxing. But let me allay any fear there may be that, because I believe in personal liberty, wholesome amusement and healthy professional sport, I will countenance for a moment any indecency or vice in New York."

Though the issues in the campaign were many, the argument boiled down, as political arguments often do, to a simplistic choice: Walker's sixteen years in the Legislature (and lack of administrative experience) versus Waterman's proven skill in running a business (and lack of knowledge about practical politics). The forty-four-year-old Walker also had going for him a carefree personality and a charm of manner that ideally complemented the heady optimism of the Roaring Twenties. Clearly the woman's vote was his. "I believe," Allie Walker said of her husband's appeal, "that many women who have never voted the Democratic ticket wlil vote for my husband."

The gamblers agreed with Mrs. Walker. As Election Day neared, offers of 15-to-1 on Walker were going begging. Waterman money was nowhere to be found. One betting firm stated that in New York election wagering no candidate ever had been quoted at such odds; even the immensely popular Harding and Coolidge had only been 12-to-1 favorites.

On election eve, Walker paid a symbolic visit to a rain-soaked rally at Charles Francis Murphy's old Anawanda Club, at Twentieth Street and Second Avenue. A torchlight parade of about fifty automobiles and several hundred club members had been scheduled, and the candidate was expected to watch it from a reviewing stand. As the first line of marchers neared him, however, Walker ran out into the muddy street, shook hands with District Leader William P. Kenneally, accepted a small American flag, and strode with Kenneally at the head of the parade. Bathed in a red glare from the torches, the procession wound through the streets of the district for an hour before it ended back where it began. As Walker took the speaker's platform, he looked up at tenement windows jammed with blurred Irish faces and at grimy tenement walls and fire escapes temporarily made festive with red-white-and-blue campaign banners. "When you vote tomorrow you will be voting for Murphy," he acknowledged, "but I will get the benefit of it." The crowd cheered his words lustily. Afterward, Walker explained that his physician had advised against his making any more speeches (his weight had dropped below 115 pounds as a result of his campaign exertions), but that he had wanted to end his campaign in Mr. Murphy's district.

Election Day was among the quietest New York had seen. There was little talk within the 100-foot zone around the polling places, nor were any arguments or fights reported. The weather was mild and bracing, what one newspaper referred to as "good Republican weather," meaning that such weather encouraged the casual anti-Tammany voter to go to the polls. (Tammany leaders made sure that their people turned out in any weather; neither rain nor snow nor sleet could substantially lessen the machine vote.) Before casting his ballot, Senator Walker was asked to comment on his chances for victory. Ever the actor, he pretended to give the matter much thought. He took off his hat, ruffled his hair, and narrowed his eyes before saying, "I don't care to make any predictions." Then Walker and his wife placed their ballots very slowly in the box so that motion-picture cameras could record the historic moment for concerned movie audiences everywhere. Frank D. Waterman also declined to predict victory, which suggests that he was a prudent businessman after all. But he and his wife did agree to pose for the cameras.

"Smile at each other," said one picture taker. The Watermans complied.

"Now kiss each other," demanded another.

"Nothing doing," said the candidate emphatically.

"Why not?"

"You know," said Waterman, "no businessman would do that."

"Don't businessmen kiss their wives?"

"Not in public," said Waterman, offering his wife his arm and beating a righteous retreat.

When the votes were totaled late that night, it was learned that Walker had carried all five boroughs, compiling a plurality of 400,-000. The Democratic candidate's running mates, General Charles W. Berry and Judge Joseph V. McKee, were swept with him into the controllership and the aldermanic presidency. Yet the victory was clearly Tammany's. Just four years before, the machine had re-elected the already forgotten John F. Hylan to the mayoralty by an even greater margin.

Walker and his party arrived at Tammany Hall at 10:15 P.M. amid the applause of the crowd around the Wigwam. With police clearing a path, Walker made his way into Tammany's executive committee room. Olvany and Smith rushed to greet him, and the governor slapped him on the back. The three men later posed for photographs with clasped hands. "The chain of unity is now formed," an ebullient Smith remarked. (Over in Brooklyn, Boss McCooey, who must have been feeling cold patronage winds despite having delivered his borough by more than 100,000 votes, wistfully opined that "All's well that ends well.") The three Tammany leaders trooped upstairs to the Wigwam's ballroom, packed tight with campaign workers, and delivered brief addresses. There were three cheers for Walker, another round of cheers for Smith, and still another round for Olvany. Capping off the hurrahs, Joseph Humphreys, a boyhood friend of the governor's who was now a prize-fight announcer, called in stentorian tones for "Three cheers for the mothers and fathers who made them all." Smith, ever ready to pay homage to his Irish mother, waved his hand to Humphreys to show how he appreciated the thought. Soon afterward, Walker went off into the night to celebrate his victory, first at other rallies and then with Broadway friends, male and female. Back in their apartment at the Hotel Commodore, Mrs. Walker was asked where he might be. "Was ever a wife with her husband on Election Night?" she answered with a forced smile. "If I see him by about five o'clock in the morning, I will consider I am doing well."

A few days after his victory, Mayor-elect Walker—without Allie—headed South on a four-week vacation, the first of many such sojourns that would mark his administration. His first stop was Atlanta,

Georgia, where, with an eye toward helping Governor Smith get the 1928 presidential nomination, he sought to dispel his hosts' distaste for Tammany. "I am sorry if I disappoint the cartoonists," Walker told a dinner gathering of Southern Democrats. "I haven't the realization of avoirdupois falling over my neck, nor can I smoke a cigar at an angle of 45 degrees, and I haven't the Bowery twang that I am sure was expected. I am sorry if I disappoint, but I am just a normal human being, the symbol of Tammany Hall, that organization that during the last six years in New York City appropriated $198 million for the construction of free public schools." Walker then asked his audience to look further at Tammany's (meaning Smith's) progressive record. "Witness laws providing for workmen's compensation, widows' pensions, child welfare, shorter hours for women and children in industry. . . . I respectfully direct your attention to our stand on woman suffrage, the direct primary, consolidation of our State departments. . . . Again, this month, following the leadership of New York's great Democratic Governor, the people of the State approved his plan for a bond issue of $100 million for the maintenance of that great army of unfortunate wards of the state." The reaction of the Southern politicians to Walker was loud and enthusiastic, but more for the man than for what he had to say about Tammany and Smith. Prejudices die hard and, despite Roman Catholic Smith's credible record, his voice did have a Bowery twang.

After the Atlanta speech, Walker went on to Miami, where he was greeted by a beaming trio of Sunshine State mayors. There he announced plans for a bear-hunting expedition (it never took place), assured Southern women that they and their children could safely walk the streets of New York (although the city was then having one of its periodic crime waves), and went deep-sea fishing but caught nothing. He broke up his Florida stay by visiting Cuba as a guest of its president, who sent a warship to bring Walker and his party to Havana. For several days, he was whirled from celebrating masses in private chapels to speech-filled lunches to gala theater performances. Just before he left Cuba, Walker spent an afternoon at Oriental Park, where a special race was run in his honor; for the occasion, the horses were named "City Hall," "White Way," "Bowery," "East-Side, West-Side," "Fifth Avenue," and "So Long, Jimmy." In the vacationing Walker's entourage throughout the festivities, incidentally, was his crony Arthur Grashoff, the soda-water entrepreneur in whose penthouse apartment he had hidden from Al Smith's scrutiny that summer.

Walker had no sooner returned to New York, on December 8, than he made it clear he would follow Judge Olvany's lead regarding patronage. "So far as politics is concerned," Walker said, "I shall recognize Judge Olvany as the City leader." Olvany was not immediately overjoyed by Walker's decision. At the Wigwam, he was already besieged by office seekers. There was scarcely a district leader who had not asked for a commissionership for himself or a member of his family. "It looks as if Senator Walker was trying to find more work for me," Olvany commented, "and it's bad enough as it is." He permitted himself a mirthless laugh, then added, "I suppose I ought to be much obliged for the compliment."

Walker was indeed giving Tammany the green light on patronage. For one thing, he felt it was the machine's due. But, more importantly, he was letting the Tiger know he did not wish to burden himself with the granting and withholding of favors. Such uses of power had no place in Walker's easygoing life. And though Olvany might temporarily complain, he and the other sharp-eyed Tammany leaders realized that the mayor-elect had presented them with the keys to the city. Yet Walker's attitude was predictable. In the exuberant year of 1925, he mirrored perfectly the mood of the men and women who had elected him to the mayoralty. Listen again to the words of Bainbridge Colby, the man who had first formally advanced Walker's candidacy to Judge Olvany: "He knows the City in all its moods. He knows its big and good heart and the fervor with which it lives. He is a New Yorker of New York." All this was true. For Walker, his first term of office was a time in which to live, love, laugh, and be happy. He would not be cheated of his destiny by the responsibilities of public service. During the next four years, no New Yorker would work so hard at having fun as Gentleman Jimmy.

1926

"O grandson of Conn, O Cormac," his own son asked one of the storied Kings of Ireland, "what is good for the welfare of a country?

"This is plain," answered Cormac. "Frequent assemblies of wise and good men, to investigate its affairs, to abolish every evil and retain every wholesome institution."

"O grandson of Conn, O Cormac," again asked his son, "what are the duties of a prince in the banqueting hall?"

"A prince shall light his lamps and welcome his guests with clapping of hands, offering them comfortable seats. The cup-bearers shall be active in distributing meat and drink."

〜〜〜

In the first days of his administration, Walker appointed Abraham Rosenbluth of the Bronx a city magistrate. At the reception that followed, State Senator Benjamin Antin shook hands with Walker and said, "The new magistrate is my brother-in-law."

"I didn't know that," said the mayor, surprised but smiling.

"I know you didn't," said Antin's friend, James F. Geraghty, Democratic leader of the Ist Bronx A.D., "we put one over on you."

Walker's attitude toward patronage was, as we have seen, quite relaxed. When he took office in 1926, he nonetheless appointed two superior men to head two critical city departments—police and health.

As a candidate, Walker had made the charge that gambling and prostitution were commonplace in the city. He felt this was due in large part to the inadequacy of incumbent Police Commissioner Richard E. Enright, who, while holding the rank of lieutenant, had been jumped to the post in 1917 by his fellow Brooklynite, Hylan, over the heads of 122 higher-ranking officers. Enright was the first commissioner to be promoted from the ranks; tradition called for a civilian in the job. He had used his presidency of the Lieutenants' Benevolent Association, ostensibly an organization to help widows and orphans, to indulge in considerable departmental intrigue. Enright had cultivated politicians as well; he knew how to do favors and how to elicit them in return.

To replace Enright, Walker needed a commissioner with genuine organizational ability and a stern sense of rectitude. The new mayor's choice was George V. McLaughlin, a bluff, no-nonsense type who had been State Superintendent of Banking. McLaughlin dealt with problems with speed and decisiveness, was known for skipping his lunch if a good game of handball offered itself, and was under obligation to no politician. Civic and business leaders hailed the appointment. "Mr. McLaughlin is capable of giving New York a splendid police administration," said Harry H. Schlact, president of the Downtown Chamber of Commerce. "It was my pleasure to be associated with him in the investigation that led to the elimination of many abuses by State bankers dealing in foreign exchange. He is a splendid investigator."

Before McLaughlin was in office a month, his men knew he was running a clean department. Perhaps the most significant of his acts during this period was to restore Lewis J. Valentine and three other promising lieutenants to the eligible list for captain. Enright had denied advancement to all three men three times without explanation, thus effectively shelving them. Presumably, they had not been cooperative with Tammany politicians and their allies in the other boroughs. McLaughlin soon named Valentine a captain and then appointed him head of the newly reactivated Confidential Squad, which had been created by Reform Mayor John Purroy Mitchel more than a dozen years earlier, and was charged with investigating reports of graft among policemen. Walker's first police commissioner would be in office fifteen months. Working through honest policemen like Valentine, he would greatly irritate Tammany.

The other department that badly needed a shake-up in 1926 was the Department of Health, which New Yorkers were shortly to learn was permitting the sale of impure and adulterated milk. This chicanery had been outlined to Mayor Hylan the year before, when the Hebrew Retail Grocers' Association of Brownsville and East New York (the two largest Jewish ghettoes in Brooklyn) pointed out that inspectors were being bribed to approve bad milk. A man called Harry Danziger, the association claimed, was arranging the sale of such milk under the protection of Tammany politicians. But Hylan had taken no action. Possibly prodded by Governor Smith, to whom even the suggestion of impure milk was cause for colic, Walker tapped Louis I. Harris as his health commissioner. Harris had been with the department for eighteen years, knew its workings intimately, and was widely respected as an expert on public health. On the surface, Harris was not a forceful personality. But in reality he possessed a fierce determination to root out corruption. Within three months after his appointment, Harris would see to it that the public learned the extent of the extortion and bribery involving the city's health department. In so doing, he too would encounter the wrath of concerned politicians.

In early January, however, New York was far more concerned about song writer Irving Berlin's marriage than about incipient corruption in the police and health departments. Berlin, a widower, had proposed on the telephone to twenty-two-year-old socialite Ellin Mackay, daughter of multimillionaire Clarence H. Mackay, on the morning of January 4, and a city clerk performed the ceremony in the Municipal Building that afternoon. "Don't think the marriage was sudden," Ellin explained to the press. "We have known each other for years. His songs won me, of course." Mr. Mackay, a prominent Roman Catholic, professed himself "stunned" at the news that his daughter had married Berlin, who was fifteen years Ellin's senior and a Jew.

No greater example of the ghetto success story exists than the life of Irving Berlin. Born Israel Baline, he began his career as a singing waiter in a Bowery beer hall called Nigger Mike's. When he was required to provide some entertainment for his initiation into the Friar's Club in 1911, young Berlin casually wrote the now classic "Alexander's Ragtime Band." More than a thousand popular songs followed, including "When the Midnight Choo-Choo Leaves for Alabam'," "Play a Simple Melody," "When I Leave the World Behind," "Oh, How I Hate to Get Up in the Morning," "A Pretty Girl Is Like a Melody," and "Always" (written for Ellin just before their elopement). Berlin went into business for himself in 1919, deriving millions of dollars over the years from sheet-music and record sales. A devoted friend of Walker, he had written him a 1925 campaign song:

It's a 'walk-in' with Walker
It's a 'walk-in' with Jim
He's a corker—and one of the mob
A real New Yorker—who's fit for the job.

Berlin and Ellin, had, of course, been seeing each other for some time. A year before their marriage, in an effort to end what he regarded as an infatuation, Mackay had sent his daughter abroad. Ellin used her exile to good advantage, particularly in Rome, where she had an audience with Pope Pius XI and eventually obtained a dispensation to marry outside her faith. Mackay would have had more insight into his daughter's independent nature if he had read an article she had recently written for *The New Yorker*, in which she attacked what she considered the idiocy of the Social Register set. So keen a journalist was Ellin that, just before leaving on her Atlantic City honeymoon, she remembered to phone Harold Ross, her editor at *The New Yorker*, about a second article she was writing. "Hello, Miss Mackay," Ross said, taking her call. "It's Mrs. Berlin," she replied. "I shan't be able to get my piece in on time. I'm leaving town in 20 minutes."

The Berlins were delighted that their clandestine courtship was over and that their married life (which would last five decades) had begun. No longer would a lovesick Irving have to compose songs like "All Alone (by the Telephone)." No sentimentalist, Mr. Mackay remained unappeased. Ignoring the fact that his own Irish immigrant father had been penniless until he discovered gold in Nevada during the 1870s, Mr. Mackay, who had increased the family fortune to some $30 million, continued to feel Ellin had married beneath her. In the days following the union, he hinted that he would disinherit his daughter. Berlin countered by saying he was giving Ellin $2 million as an indication that her husband was no fly-by-nighter. Even when the couple returned from their honeymoon, Mr. Mackay kept himself aloof. "I'm sorry to say I have not received any word from him," Ellin said. "I'm supremely happy but . . . I have a very heavy heart." (Mr. Mackay eventually was reconciled with his daughter and son-in-law, and, after the crash of 1929, Irving was permitted to loan him money to straighten out his financial affairs.)

About this time, Walker visited the legislature at Albany, where he conferred with Democratic and Republican leaders alike. His purpose was to get state approval of a request for $275 million in additional borrowing power for the city, so that subways could be built. He found his former colleagues predisposed to help, particularly when he assured the Republicans that none of the money would be spent to "recapture" existing subway lines. (The specter of city government taking over anything from private enterprise was anathema, then as now, to Republicans; the Interboro Rapid Transit line and the Brooklyn-Manhattan Transit line—the IRT and BMT—were to remain privately owned, and a source of great dissatisfaction to city officials, until 1940, when they were purchased for $1,650,000,000.) Throughout Walker's administration, charges of graft, favoritism, and ineptitude about transit matters would be commonplace. But at least on January 11, the day Walker first journeyed to Albany to ask for transit cooperation, good will was omnipresent. Declaimed John Knight, the Republican majority leader of the Senate: "What are the characteristics of Senator Walker that have brought him success? Near the front I would place his geniality, his ability to approach and be approached . . . his wonderful ability to grasp problems." Replied Walker: "Kindly handclasps, such as I have had here, mean more than all the front-page glory."

As January wore on, Commissioner McLaughlin impressed his stamp deeply upon the police department. On one occasion, he appeared unexpectedly at a day of police trials in Brooklyn. The first case involved Patrolman John Fagan, who had entered a restaurant on Coney Island Avenue in civilian clothes and, after hanging his coat and pistol on the wall, joined some men at a table. One of them, Matthew Gompert, then took the gun and used it to wound a third man. The prosecution alleged that Fagan later tried to help Gompert escape and that the off-duty patrolman had been drunk. McLaughlin sat forward on his chair and demanded of Fagan, "Well, what is your defense?"

"I had a cold that night, Commissioner," said Fagan, "and I couldn't sleep. I took some whiskey on the advice of my doctor."

Looking steadily at Fagan, McLaughlin delivered his verdict. "You fellows don't know my attitude in these matters," he said. "I don't believe your story and I believe you were drunk. . . . I have made up my mind to dismiss you from the force."

"Commissioner," Fagan said tremulously, breaking under the strain, "won't you please give me another chance?"

"No, I won't," replied McLaughlin.

The new commissioner's usual day began at 9:00 A.M., when, clad in a black alpaca coat, he would take his seat behind a desk in his spacious office. His first caller might well be a policeman whom he wanted to commend for some particularly good bit of work. "I am proud of you, Ryan," the commissioner would say, addressing a uni-

formed patrolman. "I like the way you tackled those fellows. . . .
But I am pleased because you used your head as well. You are a
third-grade detective from today."

Later in the morning, the commissioner visited the line-up. A
couple of dozen unkempt men stood against the wall of a large chamber in the dingy, downtown Centre Street headquarters, while detectives, each wearing a mask to conceal his identity, walked slowly
past the suspects, scrutinizing their faces for signs of last night's offense or next week's outrage. Interest focused on a trio of toughs
who had earlier exchanged shots with policemen. The first man was
young, barely twenty; white-faced and reed-thin, he was a consump-
tive—a product of the dank, sunless tenements. The second culprit,
equally young, had the slack mouth of a drug addict; already in the
1920s morphine and heroin had made inroads into the city, at least
among criminals and thrill-seekers. Only the third man looked the
part of a hardened criminal—heavy-jawed and bellicose. "They are
bad fellows," said McLaughlin. "Just the kind who buy pistols by
mail. What makes them criminals? I suppose we can blame social
conditions in a measure. Perhaps their homes were bad. . . . It is
certain that when the home fails, everything fails with it." Although
sensitive to the conditions that cause crime, McLaughlin was unwav-
ering in his approach to the criminals themselves. "Needless sentiment can be wasted upon the lawbreaker," he observed at the line-
up. "Frequently he regards those who would favor him as simple-
minded people."

McLaughlin was greatly concerned about the availability of hand-
guns, a situation he believed increased the likelihood of violence.
"We caught a boy the other day with a pistol still new and shining
from the mail, bought for $14 with ammunition complete," he said.
"How can we expect to make the Sullivan Law in this state effective
. . . when other states sell pistols here by mail?" Even in 1926, the
police commissioner named drugs as the next most serious cause of
violence. "Seemingly it is . . . comparatively easy to obtain drugs in
quantities," McLaughlin said. "A large number of criminals are con-
firmed addicts and habitually dangerous in the way of any irrespon-
sible man. I scarcely know what to suggest about the control of drugs."

In the afternoon, the commissioner usually received a steady stream
of reports from subordinates. The phone in McLaughlin's office
seemed only to bring news of murders, burglaries, thefts. A gem
robbery had taken place uptown. Within an hour, the patrolman who
spotted the thieves entering their getaway car had come to headquarters and identified two photographs from the rogues' gallery.
A few minutes more, and a description of the thieves had been

wired to every precinct house. Toward evening, McLaughlin was told that the getaway car had been found; there was still no trace of the men. "Well, keep after them," he said. The commissioner reached for his hat. Before going home, he would pay a call on the detectives investigating the robbery. He would see for himself how they were progressing.

What kind of policemen were working for McLaughlin in 1926? Let us look at one of the most important members of the force, Police Inspector John D. Coughlin, who headed the 1,200 detectives assigned to Manhattan.

"Irish and austere," was the way a contemporary journalist described Coughlin; black, sooty eyebrows and frosty eyes looking out from behind a pince-nez earned him the characterization. His attire was somewhat dapper—John D. affected silk shirts and a pearl solitaire—and he was known for a wry wit. After an apprenticeship in the plastering and building trades, Coughlin had joined the department in 1895, when Theodore Roosevelt, then police commissioner, made a plea for honest, strong-bodied men. Never a believer in "clues," Coughlin from the beginning of his career put his trust in information gleaned from stoolies or extracted from suspects. His conversation was studded with the addresses where burglars had hidden out, where robberies had occurred, where young women had been killed; the work of the department was his life. Nor did the scandals that periodically swept the department ever involve him. John D. lived quietly and frugally with his sister in the Bronx, his idea of excess being a day at the racetrack. As chief of detectives in Brooklyn during the Hylan administration, he had apprehended a particularly offensive strangler named Pluto and as a reward had been transferred to his present job in Manhattan. McLaughlin did not care for many of the officers he inherited from Commissioner Enright, but he respected John D., and regularly asked him for advice.

The force that McLaughlin ran was, of course, composed largely of men less motivated than Coughlin. To the average patrolman, who was probably Irish and Catholic, his job represented security. The chances are that he came from a tenement district and that most of his boyhood friends were driving taxis, digging ditches, or serving time in jail. A first-grade patrolman earned $2,810 a year. He expected his hours to be gruelling, and they were. After six eight-hour days starting at 8:00 A.M., he had thirty-two hours off; his next two six-day stints, with thirty-two hours off after each, began at midnight and at 4:00 P.M. respectively; then the round-the-clock cycle started all over again. Almost all this tour was on foot patrol, no matter how freezing the cold or sizzling the heat.

Every good cop knew who the top hoods were, and every good cop worried about the traffic in weapons and drugs that made law enforcement more difficult. Hold-up men opted for Smith and Wesson pistols, bootleggers preferred foreign firearms because of their greater accuracy at long range, killers used sawed-off shotguns. Patrolmen did not really expect the flow of guns to lessen. Until recently, even the police property office had been guilty of recirculating weapons. Confiscated firearms had been sold by the department to pawnbrokers until the guns began to reappear too frequently in the property office. Now they were taken out on a city tug and dumped into the Narrows. As for drugs, some three-quarters of the apprehended criminals were addicts. Patrolmen knew that most of the buying and selling was carried on between Fifty-ninth and Seventy-second Streets on Manhattan's West Side. They felt there was little they could do about it. Morphine was averaging twenty-five dollars an ounce, and heroin, recognized as more powerful but not yet fully in vogue, sold for the same price.

About speakeasies the patrolmen worried not at all. Prohibition was unenforceable and everybody knew it, although few politicians admitted it.

Walker's first six weeks in office were a continual round of luncheons, dinners, and entertainments. On February 9, while in Albany to pursue the lifting of the city's debt limit so as to build the needed subways, Walker paid the price for his excesses. Suffering from what his physician called "nervous exhaustion and an attack of bronchitis," he was confined to his suite at the Hotel Ten Eyck. Governor Smith was much disturbed by Walker's collapse but kept his comments within the bounds of political protocol. "The friends of Mayor Walker," he said, "ought to be more considerate of him, and have a livelier appreciation of the strenuous daytime duties of their chief executive and therefore not expect him to attend so many affairs in the nighttime." Walker, who had earlier bewailed the wear, tear, and laundry expense on his dress shirt, had gamboled at more than one hundred functions in the forty days he had been in office.

Walker returned to New York the next day. "It was getting on my nerves staying in Albany," he said. He and Allie were temporarily living at the Hotel Commodore, because the family home at St. Luke's Place was undergoing considerable renovation—at least by the standards of the times. The cost of the improvements would amount to some $25,000; the bill would be picked up by Jules Mastbaum, multimillionaire president of a chain of motion-picture theaters, who had known Walker since his earliest days in the legislature. There is little doubt that Mastbaum was genuinely fond of Walker; there is no doubt at all that State Senator Walker had fought hard for a law that greatly benefited Mastbaum's theater chain—permitting movies to be shown on Sunday.

Within a few days, Walker went to Atlantic City, in Mastbaum's private railroad car, for a brief rest. Before leaving, he acknowledged that he had attended too many social affairs, but added that his purpose was "to come into direct contact with the people who have honored me with the greatest gift within their power." For the next month. Walker canceled his public engagements, spending several long weekends at Atlantic City and on the Jersey Shore. During this period the St. Luke's Place remodeling was completed and the Walkers moved back in.

On March 13, Walker returned to the banquet scene. Along with Governor Smith and Judge Olvany, he was present, both on the dais and on the stage, at the annual dinner of the Inner Circle, an organization of City Hall reporters. The Inner Circle affair always spoofed the city administration, in song and dance, and the journalists' jibes were never sharper than in this latest production, "The Duke of Jazzland." First a reporter dressed as a court jester appeared in front of the stage curtain and sang of Hylan:

> The King isn't King any more,
> He's lost all his powers of yore.
> He thought that he'd be Mayor for life,
> But he forgot that Tammany could give
>   him the knife.
>
> The primary made him feel sore,
> He let out a horrible roar,
> But since Al pried him loose,
> He's not even a deuce.
> Oh, the King isn't King any more.

When the curtain parted, it revealed the "Day Duke" (whose hours were 6:00 A.M. to 6:00 P.M.—and who was played by Charles F. Kerrigan, Walker's private secretary) addressing a group of "Jazzlanders":

Under King Mike the slogan was razz; we have made it jazz. The axe has been supplanted by the sax. . . . Under the old regime the symbol of power was the blackjack; we have made it the night club. We have made it a clean city; there is a bathtub on every stage.

The Day Duke then began to complain that, though it was 6:00 P.M., the Night Duke had not yet shown up for work. This worthy, played by Walker himself, then was rolled on stage in a bed. Arising to the tune of "Oh, How I Hate to Get up in the Morning," Walker sang this show-stopper:

> Let Charlie K be Duke by day,
> And I'll be Duke by nights.
> By every test, I'm at my best,
> Beneath electric lights.

The machinations of Governor Smith and Judge Olvany were similarly satirized, but they did not participate in the skits. Why, they must have wondered, had Walker ever agreed to go on stage, in a spoof that hit so close to home? The reason, of course, was what the assembled reporters loved about the Mayor: His utter lack of pretense, his refusal to deny that his private hours, and many of his public ones, were devoted to anything but good friends and good times.

When Walker did officiate at City Hall, he brought a personal touch to his duties. He could meet a delegation of civic leaders from Munich, Germany, and reduce what might have been a boring, hour-long ceremony to a convivial two-minute round of laughs. "Mr. Mayor," the delegation chairman would begin, ready to launch into the usual superlatives, "we bring you the greetings of Munich, the first City of Bavaria . . ."

"That's fine," Walker would interrupt, "I accept your greetings in the spirit they are offered." Here he would pause, ". . . and I wish we had some of the things you get in Munich." Then he would wink —in distaste for prohibition and appreciation for Munich's beer. People would begin to laugh, and the ceremony would be over.

It was impossible to keep Walker at the day-to-day discipline of administrative detail. Shortly after the Inner Circle dinner, the Mayor set off on a week-long southern trip. His first stop was Cincinnati, where he was guest of honor, on March 17, at an affair sponsored by the local branch of the Friendly Sons of St. Patrick. In his after-dinner speech, he again pushed Smith as a possible presidential candidate in 1928, just as he had done in Florida the previous December; Walker continued to sound this refrain on every stopover. His train took him through Atlanta, where he was cheered heartily, and deposited him in St. Petersburg, Florida, where he watched the New York Yankees with Babe Ruth win a spring training game from the Philadelphia Phillies. The principal excitement of the next few days occurred when the yacht on which the mayor was a guest temporarily went aground in Sarasota Harbor.

En route back to New York, Walker almost came to grief at the jaws of a frisky alligator, a gift—presumably from a well-wisher—he discovered only when the train was underway. The reptile fastened its teeth onto his trouser leg and required considerable coaxing before letting go.

At the end of March, New Yorkers began to learn what had been happening to their milk supply. Harry Danziger, who had been passing himself off as a power in the Health Department, was arrested, on Commissioner Harris' initiative, as an extortionist. The blustering Danziger had been forcing legitimate dealers to pay him money by threatening to sour or steal their milk through strong-arm tactics. He came to grief at Ebling's Casino, at Third Avenue and One Hundrel Fifty-sixth Street in the Bronx, when Harris arranged for a detective to be present while Danziger extracted tribute from a group of dealers. Once he accepted the money, he was taken into custody.

At first the public thought this was the end of the affair. But then it developed that Danziger, during Hylan's reign, had indeed had connections within the department—principally with Thomas J. Clougher, who had been personal secretary to the previous health commissioner and whom Harris, with instinctive good judgment, had fired. Besides extorting money from honest men, Danziger had been taking bribes from unscrupulous dealers and seeing to it that departmental approval was given to impure milk. Commissioner Harris estimated that approximately 1,200,000 of the city's daily supply of 3,000,000 quarts of milk had been adulterated in the previous two years. The graft amounted to about $1 million. The impure milk not only was a serious danger to infants but probably had caused a number of typhoid deaths. "We have evidence," Harris said, "that some of the milk was adulterated with water that flowed from a dirty stable hose. Even if the water were clean, it would lead to grave conditions, especially in the treatment of the sick."

Danziger was no stoic. In his confession, he told the Bronx district attorney that ninety cents out of every dollar he had extorted or accepted as a bribe had gone to health department employees and mysterious "others." This meant that Danziger had passed on about $900,000 of the graft. Who had gotten this money? Even before the case came to trial, it was clear that most of it went to Clougher, who had made it his business, while working for Hylan's health commissioner, to impress the dealers with Danziger's importance. Now it was rumored that Clougher, after taking his cut, had in turn funneled much of the money to a powerful Tammany district leader. Harris, who had already suspended a half-dozen or so men among the pitifully small group of seventy-odd milk inspectors in his department, promised further revelations in court. Clougher would not be arrested for another month, and he would not come to trial on bribery charges until early June.

While the case was pending, Walker saw Allie off for Europe aboard the liner *France;* she was accompanied by her mother, Mrs. Ella Traver Allen. The two women were guests of an American Hotel Association delegation that was taking a nine-week tour of the Continent. Their schedule sounded like a Baedeker's dream: meetings with King Albert of Belgium and King Victor Immanuel of Italy, a reception with the president and assorted members of the German Reichstag in a convivial Berlin beer hall, other receptions hosted by the presidents of France and Switzerland and the Lord Mayor of London, an audience with the Pope. "I am doing more for Europe and the people of Europe today than I could do in the next four years," said Walker with a straight face at the pier, "by giving them the opportunity of seeing Mrs. Walker. I also have a deep-seated regret that I am losing my mother-in-law."

Shortly after his wife's sailing, Walker inspected the facilities of Bellevue Hospital; with him was Joseph V. McKee, president of the board of aldermen. Conditions at the city-run hospital were, according to the New York *Times,* "overcrowded, insanitary, poorly ventilated, lacking sufficient light and air, dark and depressing, all of which is proving a tremendous handicap to the hospital's highly efficient staff." The mayor's party focused its attention on Bellevue's psychopathic and out-patient facilities. Erected 108 years before as a combined penitentiary and hospital, the four-story women's psychopathic building was a firetrap, with wooden stairways that would burn rapidly; bars on the building's windows would prevent escape and pose a further hazard. "All the women who are sent to Bellevue for observation," read a report the mayor issued later, "are thrown together . . . moral and immoral, sane and insane. In the very next cot to a woman with a homicidal or suicidal mania may be one who is absolutely sane, but is there because of a temporary nervous disorder." The men's psychopathic building, Walker found, was almost as bad. Patients with all sorts of mental problems were herded together, and it was difficult for the layman to tell them apart. A young man who looked perfectly normal approached Walker and protested that he was being kept in Bellevue against his will.

The mayor patted the boy's hand and expressed his sympathy, half believing him.

"What's your name?" he asked.

"Jupiter is my name," was the reply.

The out-patient building was an ancient red-brick structure, far too small for the 1,200 adults and children who called there for treatment every day except Sunday. They were kept waiting for hours on end, and many were forced to stand because there were not enough benches. The crowding was so great that patients with infectious diseases like measles and diphtheria waited among those with minor ills. Dr. John J. McGrath, head of Bellevue's board of trustees, told Walker it would cost $6 million to erect new psychopathic and out-patient facilities. The mayor answered he would ask for special appropriations, not only for Bellevue, but for "all other city hospitals" as needed. "If the newspapers will tell the story to the people," Walker said, "it should convince them that action should be taken." Added Aldermanic President McKee: "I think we should use every cent possible to correct the physical disabilities we have here."

For his sensible appointments and humane attitudes, Walker was ringingly praised in mid-April by the Citizens Union, a group usually diametrically opposed to Tammany. Among the CU's comments:

° Hylanism is dead . . . The meetings so far of the Board of Estimate have been marked by a return to decorum . . . The Mayor has presided with dignity.

° Mayor Walker has effected a complete reversal of Hylan's policy with respect to transit. For the first time in many years matters have been discussed frankly . . . with a view to getting at the facts.

° Police Commissioner . . . McLaughlin entered upon his duties with energy and sincerity . . . A new spirit of honest effort among the rank-and-file has developed.

° Dr. Harris . . . is another Walker appointee who promises better things in his Department.

On the negative side, the CU regretted Walker's frail health. "He appears to have been . . . anxious to gratify the wishes of his numerous friends to exhibit him at all sorts of evening social gatherings. These festivities have frequently been prolonged far into the night. A temporary halt was called . . . but to all appearances the lesson has not as yet been learned."

With Allie in Europe, Walker appeared alone at two important social functions. The first was the thirty-first annual New York Spring Horse Show, where his saddle mount, Cedar King, competed but failed to win a prize. In fact, when the mayor took the bridle from the hands of a groom, the big chestnut gelding backed and plunged so strongly that Walker was pulled across the ring some twenty feet; the groom had to come to his assistance. The mayor, who later was presented with a bridle and full saddle equipment, retired to a box. Walker's attendance at Mr. and Mrs. William Randolph Hearst's annual costume ball caused more of a stir. The mayor, who was not in costume but in evening clothes, arrived at the ball at about eleven o'clock, in time for supper in the ornate Gothic Room of the Hearst residence. His presence was taken to mean that he felt no personal animosity toward Hearst for his support of Hylan and that he desired the publisher's good will. As Franklin Delano Roosevelt, while governor of New York in 1932, would say of Walker, "Hell, he's friends with everybody. . . . He's friends with the Pope, he's friends with Anti-Christ."

The Broadway that Walker so enjoyed was rocked in late May by controversy involving showman Earl Carroll, who found himself being tried for perjury. This entrepreneur, almost in a class with Florenz Ziegfeld and his Follies and certainly the equal of George White and his Scandals, chose to call his productions Vanities. Previously he had drawn criticism from the mothers of America by issuing radio calls twice daily for girls, the younger and more inexperienced the better, who wished to pursue theatrical careers. "I am looking for fresh ones," he said. "They get old in a few weeks."

In 1926 Carroll's avid thirst for headlines caused him to host a late-night theater party for about two hundred persons, including the cast of the current Vanities and many newspapermen. To liven up the proceedings, Carroll about 4:00 A.M. had a bathtub brought on stage. Joyce Hawley, a seventeen-year-old chorus girl, then walked out clad only in a chemise and shoes. While Carroll held up a cloak in front of her, she stripped nude and got into the tub, which he had filled with what passed for champagne. Scooping out a glassful, he declared, "Gentlemen, the line forms on the left." With that, fifteen or twenty wine-snobs lined up for tastings, and the girl in the tub, clearly no trooper, collapsed in tears.

After the first stories on the party appeared, Carroll began to feel the disapproval of the more conservative elements of the community. He decided to opt for respectability. The gathering, he said, "was a party which any man, even a minister, might have attended with his wife." Carroll continued to be assailed for his hospitality, however, and the caterwauling eventually caused him to be summoned before a federal grand jury. Since this was the middle of the Prohibition era, the jury was far more interested in whether the liquid in the tub was champagne than if Joyce was nude. At this point, Carroll blundered: he decided to claim (1) that the liquid was ginger ale and (2) that no girl had ever bathed in anything at the party. He was indicted on two counts of perjury.

In the trial that followed, New Yorkers learned that Carroll's party had led off with a Charleston contest and then progressed to a pretty-girl competition; afterward, various cuties from the Vanities, in negligees and bathing suits, chatted with the guests. This was pretty tame stuff even then, and at least one of the celebrants, Philip A. Payne, managing editor of Hearst's morning tabloid, *The Mirror,* was planning to leave when, he testified, he was stopped by Carroll.

"Don't go yet," said the showman. "I'm going to have a girl take a bath in a tub of wine."

Whether the tub contained champagne or merely ginger ale, Joyce Hawley's testimony temporarily removed Carroll from his Broadway haunts and sent him to the Big House. The supple youngster swore she had been offered $1,000 to bathe on stage. While she was waiting for her cue, she said, an aide of Carroll's had poured her several drinks and then had given her some of the liquid from the tub.

"What effect did the liquid have on you?" she was asked.

"It got me drunk," Miss Hawley replied. "I stood behind a curtain until Mr. Carroll said, 'Baby, all right,' and came up to me with a cloak and led me to the tub. . . . I took off what I had on . . . and then I sat in the tub about five minutes. Then Mr. Carroll . . . invited the men to take some of 'this beautiful drink.' . . ." After the oenophiles formed a line, "I started to cry and he had the tub moved off stage and bawled me out."

"What did you do then?"

"I put on my clothes and came back to the stage crying. Mr. Carroll came up to me and said, 'Damn it, keep your head up or get off the stage.' "

Joyce never did get her money from Carroll, which may or may not have motivated her testimony. She subsequently put her fame to use, however, by appearing in the *Greenwich Village Follies,* where she was paid several hundred dollars weekly for re-creating her bathtub specialty.

Though the court found that he was telling the truth in saying the liquid in the tub was nonintoxicating, Carroll was judged guilty of perjury in saying that no bath had taken place. He was fined $2,000 and sentenced to imprisonment for a year and a day. After various futile appeals and a ten-day delay of commitment in order to put flowers on his mother's grave, he was sent to the federal penitentiary in Atlanta, Georgia. En route, Carroll was taken from the train to a South Carolina hospital in a supposed coma, and there he remained for two months. When he finally did enter prison, doctors there diagnosed his illness as imaginary. After five months he was paroled. Penitent though not humbled, he still defended his special vision of the Broadway girl: "We show her in her most lovely mood . . . sans costume, sans silk manufacturer, sans shoemaker. All we rely on is the hairdresser, the pearl manufacturer and the heaven-sent smile." The New York *World* felt his crusade was less idealistic: "Mr. Carroll is convicted of perjury. His real crime is obnoxious vulgarity."

Soon after the Carroll trial, an urbane con man named Jules (Nicky) Arnstein was picked up by the New York police on an old charge of grand larceny involving stolen securities. Arnstein was then married to Ziegfeld funny-girl Fanny Brice, whom Walker knew well. He spent only a few hours in the Tombs, as the foreboding city lockup was called, before he was released on bail, and the charge was soon dropped. "The D.A. knows I have no bonds," he protested. "They are just trying to make a sucker out of me."

Arnstein's arrest in 1926 nonetheless brought back to the public's mind the events of 1921, when he allegedly had been the mastermind behind a series of messenger-boy "robberies" that cost Wall Street firms some $5 million in negotiable securities. No one denied the mustachioed Nick's charm and attractiveness to women, but heretofore he had not been known for his intellect. "Mastermind!" commented a loving Fanny Brice when she heard of the charge, "Nicky couldn't mastermind an electric bulb into a socket!"

Actually, there was great doubt that Arnstein had engineered the securities scheme. It was true that he had been pointed out to the messenger boys in restaurants and other public places where he held court as "Mr. Arnold"—the Big Boss. The members of the ring needed the cooperation of the Wall Street runners in order to set up the phony "robberies"; they evidently felt that Nicky's aristocratic mien would bolster the boys' confidence in the undertaking. But many knowledgeable citizens felt that Arnold Rothstein, the notorious gambler (whose murder in 1928 would greatly embarrass the Walker administration), was the "Mr. Arnold" in question. Nicky, the rumors went, had merely allowed himself, for a fee, to be used as front man. Even the police, meaning no disrespect to Arnstein, doubted that he possessed the requisite organizational ability for the enterprise. Moreover, while none of the $5 million in bonds was ever recovered, Rothstein paid Nick's bail money and all his legal costs.

While her husband's case was dragging through the courts, Fanny opened in the 1921 Ziegfeld Follies. With consummate showmanship, Florenz Ziegfeld had decided, in view of Nicky's perilous situation, that Fanny would be just the girl to sing the plaintive "My Man." (Flo had previously asked Channing Pollack to adapt the number from the famous French song "Mon Homme.")

> It costs me a lot
> But there's one thing that I've got
> It's my man. . . .

"Do you think you can make them cry?" asked Ziegfeld. Fanny thought she could, and she was right; her performance was a highspot in one of the Follies' most successful runs.

Though Arnstein's first trial ended in a hung jury, he eventually was convicted of conspiracy and sentenced to a two-year term. He entered prison in May of 1924 and was paroled and temporarily reunited with Fanny in December of 1925. Two years later the long-suffering Miss Brice decided that her man posed an even greater psychological problem out of jail than in jail. She divorced Nicky for infidelity.

Now Walker found himself under pressure to lend the weight of the mayoralty to the milk inquiry. After Thomas J. Clougher's arrest, Dr. Harris ascertained that the city prosecutors, with the exception of the Queens district attorney's office, were foot-dragging on the investigation. Additionally, even though the milk conspiracy involved all five boroughs, a grand jury in Queens, say, could not bring indictments for wrongdoings committed in Brooklyn or Manhattan. The Citizens Union asked Governor Smith for a special state attorney general to coordinate the case. Smith's unofficial reply was that such a request would have to come from Walker. In turn, Walker explained that he would not take such an action unless importuned by Dr. Harris.

On May 26, at about five o'clock, the health commissioner called on the mayor; he remained in Walker's office for almost two hours. There is no record of what the mayor said to Harris, but the outcome to their private conversation was that the health commissioner did not ask for a state attorney general.

Clougher eventually was indicted in Manhattan, the Bronx, and Queens. (There was no indictment, not so strangely enough, in Mc-Cooey's Brooklyn.) On June 15, a guilty finding was returned against Clougher on two counts in the Bronx, and there were hopes that, in order to escape the maximum sentence of twenty years, he would name the higher-up "others"—the political leaders with whom he had shared the $900,000 in milk extortion and bribe money. But Clougher had his code, and like any mortally wounded Irish hero, stayed mum. He even announced through his counsel that he would not ask for the mercy of the court. His defiance was well founded, for he received a comparatively mild sentence—from five to ten years. As for the indictments in the other boroughs, for which he could have received another thirty years, the trials were postponed indefinitely.

At the time of the Bronx sentencing, Dr. Harris declared: "Clougher . . . has much to tell and has told nothing. With sentences from accumulated convictions staring him in the face, Clougher would . . . throw light on the whole corrupt situation." Yet the milk scandal middle-man was never brought to trial on any of the other indictments. Moreover, he would leave Sing Sing on a conditional pardon, rich and content, after serving a little over two years of his sentence. The milk investigation would continue in 1926, but only against Clougher's aides and henchmen; his superiors were never revealed.

At his board of estimate meetings, Walker was often tardy, but he brooked no lateness from others. After one morning session, the board was scheduled to reconvene at 3:00 P.M.; most of the members were still waiting in the chamber or in the corridors outside when the mayor arrived shortly after four o'clock and took the chair. Conspicuous by his absence was Controller Charles W. Berry, whose own seat was at the left of the mayor's. Much business was hurriedly disposed of. Then the board turned its attention to the plea of financier J. P. Morgan and other interested individuals, who were opposing a zoning change in the Murray Hill district, at Madison Avenue between Thirty-sixth and Thirty-seventh Streets, that would allow commercial enterprises in that staid and monied residential area. As Morgan's attorney prepared to address the chair, one of Walker's assistants whispered to him that action on the zoning measure required the full membership of the board.

Frowning and gesturing, the mayor conferred with Aldermanic President McKee and then angrily told those assembled in the chamber: "It is a great pity that the Controller cannot take the trouble to walk across the street to attend to the city's pressing business."

Walker's anger was widely reported in the papers, and the next day Berry sent him a public letter. "Assuming that you are quoted correctly," it read, "I am very sorry to have annoyed one whose lifelong record of punctuality is so widely known." The controller maintained that he had been in the chamber at 3:00 P.M., the hour for which the session had been called by the mayor, and had waited forty-five minutes. "When you did not appear," Berry's letter to Walker concluded, "and as the controller's office is a busy one, I went off to attend to other city business. You arrived at 4 P.M."

At the first meeting of the board after this dispute, both men were obviously embarrassed. As Walker and Berry took their seats, each looked straight ahead, concerning himself with his own affairs: the mayor became absorbed in one of the documents that littered his desk while the controller conversed with some aides. Finally Walker nodded to Berry with his most engaging smile and got a broad grin in return. The board celebrated the reconciliation of its principals by approving $1 million for a memorial to John Purroy Mitchel, to $be erected at the Central Park gateway at Fifth Avenue and Nine-tieth Street.

A few days later, the city gave a tumultuous greeting to Lieutenant Commander Richard E. Byrd, Jr., the naval officer who had been the first explorer to fly over the North Pole, and to Floyd Bennett, his pilot. Chairman of the reception committee was Grover Whalen, the Wanamakers' executive who would be a prominent figure in many lavish city welcomes yet to come. For Commander Byrd, there were shrill harbor whistles to signal his arrival by boat, a blizzard of paper snow, and hundreds of miles of ticker-tape as he and Bennett walked from the Battery to City Hall. Planes buzzed overhead, crowds filled the sidewalks from curb to curb, and the police had all they could do to keep the streets clear for the heroes, who were fol-lowed on foot by 300 distinguished citizens of New York. At City Hall, a white-haired admiral forgot himself momentarily, interrupt-ing the proceedings to lead the crowd in three cheers for Byrd. A Southern congressman, who represented Byrd's own district in Vir-ginia, set up a portable organ and then sang "Carry Me Back to Ole Virginney." "Now, everybody, join me in the chorus," he shouted. And everybody did—guests, politicians, the explorers crew—although New York accents clashed amusingly with the song's sentiments.

"I believe aviation has pulled the teeth of the Arctic," Byrd said in his formal address to his hosts. "There is no place on the face of the earth a plane cannot fly." Mayor Walker handed out medals to Byrd and four members of his party, including Joe de Ganahl, a coal passer. "This boy worked sixteen hours a day shoveling coal all through the expedition," Byrd said aloud to the mayor before whispering some-thing else in his ear. Walker grinned, led de Ganahl to a conspicu-ous place on the platform and said to the crowd, "And if anything else is necessary to prove the courage of this young man, let me tell you he is just getting ready to be married."

Perhaps the most uninhibited member of the Byrd party was Dick Konter, known as "Ukulele Dick" and author of *Dick's Ukulele Guide*. Konter had shipped on as an able-bodied seaman for the combined sea-and-air assault that made the North Pole conquest possible. He was met in New York by twenty young women who were formerly his pupils, all playing violently on ukuleles in honor of the maestro's return. Throughout the festivities, Konter flourished a ukulele that had made the trip to the Pole aboard Byrd's plane and was covered with the signatures, not only of Byrd and Bennett, but of other Polar explorers—Amundsen, Ellsworth, and Nobile. Behind his exuberance, however, Ukulele Dick hid a sad heart. His purpose in making the trip had been to introduce his instrument to the Eskimos; it was not until he reached Spitzbergen, the jumping-off point for the flight, that he learned there was not an Eskimo on the island. Walker found him irresistible.

Police Commissioner McLaughlin began a drive against nightclubs in early June of 1926, its object being to force them into a 2 A.M. closing. Prohibition, which had been the law of the land ever since the Eighteenth Amendment superseded the Volstead Act on January 17, 1920, had killed or was bleeding to death the great Broadway hotels and restaurants. The Hotel Knickerbocker and its bar, which had served the city's best free lunch and boasted Maxfield Parrish's celebrated painting of Old King Cole, was long since gone. So was the Manhattan Hotel, where the cocktail of the same name had been conceived. And the once elegant Hotel Claridge, though it still survived, was definitely second rate. Delmonico's, where dozens of superb dishes, such as Lobster à la Newburgh, had originated, was forced to close, as was Reisenweber's, which once employed 1,000 persons and offered a dozen dining rooms seating as many as 5,000 customers. Jack's, with its Irish whiskey, Irish bacon, and flying wedge of waiters to eject the unruly, Churchill's with its fabled clientele, Monquin's with its superb French cuisine—all were gone. Broadway was already losing its charm. Though the theater was never better, the ban against liquor and wine had drastically reduced the profit margin that enabled the first-class hotels and restaurants to operate. They were replaced by garish speakeasies, blaring arcades, fruit-juice holes-in-the walls.

The nightclubs that sprang up on the vacated premises of such storied establishments as Rector's, where a late supper had been a must for socially prominent theatergoers, were—as Commissioner Mc-Laughlin knew—forced to evade the Prohibition Law as best they could. On the one hand, they were legitimate businesses, not speakeasies; the clubs booked entertainers, served food, and paid license fees. On the other hand, they had to serve liquor, surreptitiously but diligently, to make a profit. The hypocrisy lent itself to a good deal of police bribery. Since it was obviously impractical to close the nightclubs altogether, McLaughlin thought he would curb them by an early curfew. The time he selected, with no advance warning, was 2:00 A.M. The city's twenty-two licensed establishments, places like the Lido, Ciro's, the Silver Slipper—representing an investment of some $5 million, and already hard pressed by tens of thousands of speakeasies—set up a cry that reached City Hall.

Walker, knowing he had to back up his police commissioner, decided to compromise. Effective in the fall, the mayor suggested in a bill he offered to the Municipal Assembly, all establishments with musical entertainment would have a 3:00 A.M. closing. Violators would commit a misdemeanor, he said, explaining why he was for the later hour, and when a law "may send offenders to jail it would not do to leave it without flexibility."

Even a 3:00 A.M. curfew did not please some nightclub owners, and they subsequently expressed their grievances at a public hearing before Walker and other city officials. Nathaniel Lieberman, a lawyer representing some of the owners, complained that the proposed bill would not regulate the speakeasies.

"Are you seeking to stay open because the dives you mention are open all night?" Walker asked. (The speakeasy problem was insurmountable, as we shall see later.)

Switching his tactics, Lieberman stressed the expense of operating a nightclub, with its musicians and entertainers, and suggested the closing be extended to at least 3:30 A.M.

"I know these places—at least I did until recently," said Walker, maintaining that most of the clubs already closed by 3:00 A.M. "How many keep open after 3?"

"A good many."

"The Lido is not open after 3," the mayor said, "nor is the Montmarte or the Mirador. Nor a lot of others. I know the class of people who stay out after 2:30, and I know where they stay and where they go after they leave the nightclubs."

"These clubs entertain people from all over the world," said Lieberman. "You've been entertaining people [too]. . . . You have been doing practically nothing else for months."

"I want you to understand I have been doing plenty of other things," said Walker heatedly.

"Every time I am down in the federal building," Lieberman said, "I hear the band playing in front of City Hall."

"Are the cabarets getting jealous of the bands?"

"No, your Honor, we don't use brass."

"Well, *you* seem to have plenty of it," said Walker. "Tell me, in what other city do people stay out after 3 in the morning? People come here and make a cesspool of New York."

Taking up the mayor's charge that out-of-towners were giving New York a bad name, David Stone of Maxim's Supper Club on West Thirty-second Street declared: "If a man is out at night why shouldn't he go home when he *wants* to? This is a free country. All he has to do is ask for his check."

"And sometimes when he gets it, he can't go home," interrupted Walker. "It's too long a walk."

"He never asks for the check," said Aldermanic President McKee jokingly, pointing at Walker.

"I get it without asking for it," replied the mayor.

"Why must you pass an ordinance to make people go home?" Stone wailed, while the chamber rocked with laughter. "Why doesn't the bill affect the Masons or the Elks?"

"Do you put the average nightclub in the same category with the Elks or Masons?" Walker asked. "One is a detriment to the town and the other is an ornament."

In a related move, Commissioner McLaughlin continued his shake-up of the police department, shuffling Irish names like the toast-master at a Holy Name breakfast. On one July day alone, he reduced a deputy chief inspector, an inspector, and three deputy inspectors to the rank of captain, replacing them with men he felt would better enforce the law; since all ranks above captain serve at the pleasure of the commissioner, the shifts could be arbitrary and unexplained. John W. O'Connor, who was demoted from deputy chief inspector, was replaced by an officer named Lyons, who was in turn replaced by an officer named Murphy. At the same time, McLaughlin promoted Lewis J. Valentine, whom he had made head of the Confidential Squad, to deputy inspector. It was a move that boded ill for Tammany—and perhaps for straight-arrow police commissioners.

Despite the criticism of City Hall welcomes that was voiced at the nightclub hearing, Walker was not deterred. On successive days shortly thereafter, amid the usual brouhaha, he gave city keys and scrolls to Bobby Jones, the first golfer to win both the National and the British Open Tournaments, and to Ronald Amundsen and Lincoln Ellsworth, who had crossed the North Pole and the Arctic Ocean in the dirigible *Norge*. Ten days later, handicapped by a knee injury sustained, we are told, in a bathtub accident, Walker limped forward before an appreciative crowd to greet Umberto Nobile, the Italian aeronautical engineer who had piloted the *Norge*.

By July 20, Walker felt obliged to attempt a settlement of the IRT subway strike, which had been inconveniencing New Yorkers for two weeks; he suggested a conference of strikers, city officials, and IRT management at which the issues could be arbitrated, only to have his plea rejected by IRT President and General Manager Frank Hedley. This contrariness was to be expected from Hedley, who thought the subway's problems could be resolved only by raising the five-cent fare and who was openly contemptuous of the politician's practice of calling a conference or appointing a commission to get at the facts. "*I* will study the situation," the general manager was fond of saying, "and then do as I please." Besides their demands for better hours and better pay, the hard core of strikers, only about 300 in number, wanted the IRT to dissolve its tame company union and recognize a genuine union in its place. This sharing of power was anathema to Hedley, who declared that any meeting with the strikers would be a "betrayal of about 13,000 loyal employees who are members of the Brotherhood of Interborough Employees."

The sixty-five-year-old Hedley had been in charge of the IRT system for twenty-three years; he was perhaps the foremost expert on rapid transit in the United States. "Any fool could be president of a railroad company," he once said, "but the general manager has to know something." His great-granduncle had helped build the first steam locomotive near Newcastle-on-Tyne in 1813; his father was a master mechanic for the London & Southwestern Railway during Queen Victoria's time. Hedley himself had arrived in New York with his machinist's tools in 1882 and worked his way up through the Erie Railroad, the New York Central, the Manhattan Elevated, and the Chicago El; in 1913, the year before the IRT began its operations, he was enticed back to New York to head the company. During his general-managership, he off-handedly developed such devices as a "recorder-coaster" (which encouraged motormen to coast when possible to cut costs), multiple doors on subway cars to alleviate crowding, coupling mechanisms to reduce the danger of telescoping in a collision, and the nickel-in-the-slot turnstile to hold pilferage down to respectable levels.

As a descendant of British workingmen, Hedley enjoyed making New York's Irish pols jump to his railroad whistle as much as he enjoyed his $75,000 annual salary. Only the Transit Commission, which was controlled by the state, had jurisdiction over him. (Another agency, the Transportation Board, was run by the city, but its powers were limited to transit construction.) "This isn't an alibi,"

Walker told the strikers after Hedley's rejection of his arbitration proposal. "It's the law. You know that controversies have been started in the hope that the five-cent fare would be raised. You know I am against that. I feel that the companies can pay a living wage and still run on a five-cent fare. . . . Before I would alter that opinion I would have to be shown that it can't be done."

By this last admission, Walker was acknowledging that he was as much in the dark about the IRT's finances as the strikers; the IRT (like the BMT) was a private corporation and did not have to show its books to the city. Yet Hedley was forever crying poverty. Once, when he was assailed by city officials because his cars were so dirty, the general manager insisted that he could not afford to clean them as long as the fare held at five cents. "I saw a car with clean windows today," he said, "and when I got back to the office I raised hell to find out who spent all that money." A couple of days after Walker's attempt at intervention, the 300 strikers capitulated. They marched in a body to the IRT yards at Lenox Avenue and One Hundred Forty-seventh Street and asked to be taken back on the job; Hedley munificently agreed. It was not until 1934 that an effective Transport Workers Union was formed, and not until 1937 that it succeeded in getting closed-shop contracts from the lines.

Besides Thomas J. Clougher, only two other men of importance were convicted in connection with the $1 million milk scandal; both were Clougher's underlings, and both received minor sentences. One was Fred W. Kehoe, formerly a Deputy Assistant Corporation Counsel attached to the department, the other was William H. Kautzman, superintendent of milk inspectors. The cases against them were clearcut. Kehoe, for instance, could not explain to the court how, on the basis of his declared income, he had been able to bank $122,000 in the years 1924–25. How had the corruption been organized? Light was cast on the tangled web on August 9, when former Supreme Court Justice Charles H. Kelby, who had finally been assigned by Governor Smith to investigate the scandal, made his report to the mayor. There was no real organization to the milk bribery, Kelby found, until October of 1923, when "the Special Service Squad was organized by the then Health Commissioner [Frank Monaghan] and his personal secretary [Clougher]." The squad, drawn from the ranks of the department's inspectors, "was responsible directly to him and his secretary. . . . [Its] activities became so notorious that they were a matter of common talk in the Department." Dishonest inspectors annually took in some $2,500 apiece in bribes, as much as their median salary, yet the real cream rose to the top.

Though Kelby's report contained no such charge, the rumor that

Clougher's superior—who absorbed the cream—was a prominent Tammany district leader grew so insistent that Judge Olvany felt obliged to issue a blanket disclaimer. (The name most often mentioned was Charles L. Kohler, leader of the 10th A.D. and a one-time health department official.) "I made inquiries of my own when it was charged that some Tammany 'higher-up' was being protected in the milk investigation," Olvany said, "and I know this is not true." The denial did little to convince skeptics. "Dr. Harris long ago wanted a state investigation," said William J. Schieffelin, chairman of the Citizens Union. "Mr. Olvany does not want a state investigation . . . because it might involve a powerful member of the organization."

The health department, reported Kelby, had also been guilty of betraying the public trust in a more traditional way—misusing funds to pad the payroll. Between 1921 and 1925, the board of estimate, in response to repeated emergency requests, appropriated $1 million to the department to combat the ravages of various communicable diseases that loitered just offshore, ready to overwhelm the city. A favorite such threat was bubonic plague. The diseases were nonexistent, of course; the money was used to pay the salaries of non–Civil Service (and politically well-connected) employees.

When Judge Kelby issued his report, Walker was on a ten-day vacation in the White Mountains of New Hampshire; he no sooner returned to New York than he learned of three murders of policemen within the week. The first officer had been killed when he tried to arrest two hold-up men at Eighth Avenue and Forty-ninth Street; the second victim, a motorcycle patrolman, had been shot by hoodlums driving a stolen automobile in the Brownsville section of Brooklyn. Now Walker was informed of the killing of a detective at police headquarters—the first such crime to be committed there. The mayor was outraged by the attacks. He called for quick trials and severe punishments to be given to killers in such cases. "I have never known in my experience as a practicing lawyer," Walker said, "that the defendant's case in a criminal action suffered through delay in trial. . . . Oftimes material witnesses absent themselves and the state's case loses much of its strength."

John Singer, the detective who was shot in police headquarters, had arrested a Negro named Eugene Pierce for auto theft. Together with the car's owner, Louis Kuku, they drove downtown to the Tombs in the early hours of the morning. "I drove the car and Detective Singer and the Negro sat in the rear seat," said Kuku afterward. "The Negro laughed and chatted all the way . . . When we were halfway here, Pierce told the detective he was hungry and said that he had no money. 'Well, if you're hungry, I'll buy you a meal,' Singer said, and we stopped at the next restaurant . . . There was not the slightest indication that any harm would befall the detective."

Singer was in the process of booking the suspect at about 2:00 A.M., asking questions of him and of Kuku, when Pierce asked if he could go to the water cooler. Singer, seated at the detective's desk and bending over the card on which he was writing, didn't even look up. "Sure, help yourself," he said. As Pierce passed by the detective, he grabbed the latter's gun. Singer got to his feet and smilingly held out his hand for the pistol, saying, "Don't do that, Pierce." Three shots followed in rapid succession, Kuku bolted from the room shouting for help, and the detective lay dead on the floor. He left a wife and two children.

Because of the early morning hours, only a skeleton staff was on duty at headquarters, and Pierce simply ran out the entrance into the surrounding streets. Within minutes, however, a bulletin describing him went out over signal-box telephone to officers on the beat. Look out for a Negro, the alarm went, six feet tall, about twenty years old, and (this last bit of information was volunteered by Kuku, the witness) wearing a watch fob made of dimes on his coat.

About 5:30 A.M., Patrolman John White of the Clinton Street Station saw a Negro walking toward him along Delancey Street. White stepped back in the doorway of a store, took out his pistol, and waited; when the man was opposite his hiding place, the officer saw the fob of dimes. Night stick in one hand, pistol in the other, White brought the butt of the gun down with all his strength on Pierce's head and soon subdued him. Within six hours a grand jury returned a First Degree Murder indictment—which called for a mandatory death penalty.

A few days thereafter, doubtless thinking of the families of men like Detective Singer, Walker asked the board of estimate to approve a statute that would grant full-pay pensions to the widows of policeman killed in the line of duty.

In mid-August, screen lover Rudolph Valentino was in New York, promoting his latest film, *Son of the Sheik,* when he complained of severe stomach pains and was rushed to Polyclinic Hospital. There the surgeons removed an inflamed appendix and tried to repair two perforated gastric ulcers. Valentino received more than a thousand get-well messages, including a concerned phone call from Mayor Walker, and he appeared to be mending satisfactorily. Then, a few days later, he developed peritonitis. On August 23, he came out of a coma, looked up at Joseph Schenck, head of United Artists Corporation, and said, "Don't worry, chief, I'll be all right." With that, he died. The news set off a torrent of grief among women around the world. Some of Valentino's admirers did more than cry. In a Manhattan tenement on Cherry Street, Mrs. Angelina Celestina, the twenty-year-old mother of two children, drank iodine, shot herself twice, and collapsed in a heap on her Valentino picture collection. Happy to report, she later recovered.

The day after Valentino's death, the hysteria began in earnest. Clad in full evening dress, the body had first been laid out on a gold-draped catafalque in mortician Frank E. Campbell's finest room, which contained a number of *objets d'art*. When Campbell saw the 30,000 mourners waiting outside his funeral home he ordered his staff to remove all valuables. As the first visitors filed past the catafalque, they tried to rip buttons from the body's clothing or rub the cosmetics from its face. Campbell's solution was to encase Valentino's remains in a protective silver-bronze coffin and demand police reinforcements. Commissioner McLaughlin himself showed up to supervise the crowds, which had pressed forward and broken Campbell's huge plate-glass windows. Mounted policemen repeatedly charged the mob, and after one such cavalry sweep, twenty-eight pairs of women's shoes were gathered up. To combat these police tactics, mourners rubbed soap on the sidewalks and streets so the horses would slip and fall. Men, women, and children were in the mob, and they were of all social stations. Mrs. Alfred E. Smith, wife of the governor, filed past Valentino's bier, and so did Mrs. Richard P. Whittemore, widow of a recently executed murderer.

Who was this Valentino whose slick black hair, luminous eyes and expressive face made female hearts pitterpat to the beat of the tango he performed so well? (And not only women were impressed with the actor; when it came time for heavyweight champion Jack Dempsey to have his nose repaired, he asked his doctor to make the nostrils flare with passion just like Rudy's.) The eighteen-year-old Valentino came to this country in 1913 from his native Italy, where he was known as Rodolpho Guglielmi di Valentina. Within a couple of years, he found there was a steady demand for his dancing skills in New York supper clubs; he also convinced a young woman named Bianca DeSaulles that she should divorce her wealthy husband and marry him. Before Bianca and Rudy could wed, however, two unfortunate events took place. First, Valentino got caught blackmailing some well-heeled New Yorkers whom he had provided with girls, and then Bianca fatally shot her ex-husband when he tried to take their daughter away from her. Everybody's attorneys agreed the best thing for all concerned was that Valentino leave town.

Like many another ambitious entertainer, he headed for Hollywood, where he played the nondescript, dark-visaged bad guy in a dozen films. Only when he made *Four Horsemen of the Apocalypse* did he tango his way to stardom. Then, in 1921, Valentino made *The Sheik*—racing on a white steed over desert sands—and his fame became international; movies like *The Young Rajah, Blood and Sand,* and *Cobra* followed; in 1925 he demanded and got $200,000 a film, plus 50 percent of the profits—unheard of largesse for the time.

In his private life, Rudy was less successful. The imperious male on screen, he was in reality a soft target for domineering women. His first wife, whom he married at the beginning of his Hollywood career, much preferred a female roommate; Valentino won a divorce when she testified on the witness stand that she had never allowed the marriage to be consummated. In 1922, just after his triumph in *The Sheik,* Valentino cleaved unto one Natacha Rambova, born Winifred Hudnut, who was the stepdaughter of cosmetics tycoon Richard Hudnut. Natacha's first gift to her husband was a slave bracelet. She insisted she have the final word on his scripts, publicly berated him for stupidity, and—worst of all—compared him unfavorably to Douglas Fairbanks. This second marriage also appears to have been unconsummated. "A man may admire a woman without desiring her," Rudy philosophized. He and Natacha divorced shortly before his death.

When the police finally got the mob under control at Campbell's Funeral Home, 150 persons a minute, hustled along by arm-grabbing bouncers, filed by Valentino's bier. Despite his travails, Mr. Campbell appreciated the publicity. Each of the reporters covering the wake received a personal coffin plate, inscribed with the recipient's name and birth date and with room for a death date; each was guaranteed a fancy funeral, when needed, "on the house." Valentino's own funeral took place at St. Malachy's Roman Catholic Church on West Fifty-first Street, with 500 mourners inside and 100,000 sightseers outside. Women as disparate as demure Mary Pickford, the golden-haired actress, and raucous Texas Guinan, the saloon hostess, sobbed in the pews. Valentino's death called for hyperbole, and the New York newspapers met the challenge. "The Sheik rode silently and alone into the desert of death," one story read; "a desert where the sandstorms of censure can never penetrate."

Just after Rudy's funeral, New York gave a lavish ticker-tape welcome to Gertrude Ederle, daughter of an Amsterdam Avenue butcher and the first woman to swim the English Channel, in the process besting the time of the five men who had previously accomplished the feat. Miss Ederle debarked from the Cunard liner *Berengaria,* which had brought her back to America, amid blaring band music, harbor whistles, and the cheers of the assembled crowd. From the Battery she was taken by limousine to City Hall, escorted by the ubiquitous Grover Whalen, chairman of the mayor's Welcoming Committee. Her face deeply bronzed from exposure to sun and salt water, Trudy was escorted past 10,000 persons gathered in City Hall Park and brought up to Walker in the Aldermanic Chamber. "When history records. the great crossings," Walker told her, "of course they will speak of Moses crossing the Red Sea, Caesar crossing the Rubicon and Washington crossing the Delaware. But very frankly, your crossing of the English Channel must take its place alongside of them."

Miss Ederle next rode with Whalen through tens. of thousands of cheering New Yorkers to Amsterdam Avenue between Sixty-fourth and Sixty-fifth Streets, where her father's butcher store and, next door, the five-story tenement he owned were situated. The front of the Ederle shop was festooned with red-white-and-blue bunting, and in the window was a cardboard model of the English Channel, with bright green waves moving up and down, powered by a small electric motor. Amid them, using the crawl, was a cardboard Gertrude hitting the water at sixty strokes to the minute. Beneath the scene, a verse read:

> Pop Ederle by cutting meat made for
>   himself a name
> His daughter Trudy by cutting waves
>   won victory and fame
> You see here how she fights the sea
>   and how she puts it over
> Hurrah for her, first of her sex to
>   swim from France to Dover.

Forty-two relatives and countless friends visited the Ederle home to pay Trudy homage, while her father and mother served sausage, cold cuts, and near-beer.

That night, Walker and Whalen took the young celebrity, dressed in a satin evening gown, to see a special Ziegfeld revue (there were no Follies as such in 1926). "It would be hard to say," Whalen reflected later, "who laughed the louder—Jimmy or Trudy—during the last number of the show, which happened to be a parody on 'Hard-to-Get Gertie,' glorifying Miss Ederle's conquest of the Channel." Afterward the mayor's party went to the Club Lido, where Walker —3:00 A.M. closing or no—danced with Trudy into the early morning hours.

A visitor from England about this time was Captain A. J. Murdocke, an arbiter of men's tailoring, who had come to America to attend the National Association of Clothiers' convention. His first act after debarking was to rush to City Hall to pay his respects to Walker.

"Mr. Mayor," he said unabashedly, "you have a simply marvelous figure."

"Wait until you see the 1927 city budget figure," Walker replied, referring to a budget increase of almost ten percent that would mean the highest taxes ever for property owners.

"Well, I certainly think you are the best-dressed mayor I have ever had the pleasure of meeting," said Murdocke.

"I wear New York-made clothes," Walker protested.

"But I really envy your figure," said Murdocke. "You will always have a good waistline."

"The nervous strain of my job keeps me slender," allowed Walker.

Despite his light-hearted manner, Captain Murdocke was dead serious about clothes. On that first day in New York, his costume consisted of an Oxford gray double-breasted morning suit, a pale blue shirt, a tie of darker blue dotted with red figures, a red boutonniere, brown hat, and brown kid shoes. "It really isn't done, you know," he said, apologizing for calling on the mayor in such informal attire, "but I couldn't get my luggage ashore in time to change to a pearl gray topper, morning coat, and gray striped trousers." So far as predictions went, Murdocke thought the coming season would see the "athletic silhouette" prevail; the shoulders of men's coats would be well padded and the waist cut close. "Women love cave men," he explained.

It is no wonder Murdocke warmed to Walker, who cared so much about his clothes that he designed them himself. The style of the mayor's business suits always remained the same; only his sports attire responded to the moods of fashion. The suits were quite form-fitting, moving social observer Lucius Beebe to say that Walker might be called "a snappy, keen or sharp dresser, and in the Broadway mode at all times." The back of the coat had to hang absolutely straight, the sleeves quite narrow; the breast pocket was not on the conventional slant but straight across; the vest had seven buttons instead of the usual six. So slim were Walker's hips that he had to devise a system whereby the vest buttoned to (and held up) his tapering trousers. And while he sometimes liked cuffs on his sleeves, he wanted none on the trousers, lest they become dust-collectors.

The mayor usually wore three shades of the same color: perhaps a blue suit, a lighter blue shirt, and a blue tie, tightly knotted, of still another shade. He favored light gray hats with broad brims that flopped down on the right side, French cuffs on his shirts, and dark shoes.

Walker wore contrasting colors only in sports and at-home clothes. Yet he took a sensuous delight in gaudy fabrics that were, by the standards of the day, almost feminine; indeed, he enjoyed talking with women about color combinations and materials, and often did so. For his dressing gowns and pajamas, he chose exotic fabrics that were Oriental in appearance; the gowns fit tightly around the torso and flared below the waistline.

For over two decades, beginning in 1914, Jeann Friedman was the tailor who cut and sewed these designs for Walker. Friedman thought so highly of his patron that he named his son after him. In most ways, Walker was a perfect client. He never returned a coat or suit to Friedman; if any displeased him, he gave it away.

On the afternoon of September 23, Walker was among 75,000 fight fans jamming Pennsylvania Station, waiting to leave by train for Philadelphia, where that night Gene Tunney would challenge Jack Dempsey for the Heavyweight Championship of the World. The mayor traveled in a private car chartered by publisher Paul Block, the unctuous owner of a string of small-city newspapers, who never managed to gain more of a publishing toehold in New York than the *Brooklyn Standard-Union* but meanwhile gratefully paid Walker's hotel, haberdashery, and traveling expenses. ("What a man! What a man!" he would say admiringly of the mayor.) With them were Broadway producer George White, James P. Sinnott, a former reporter for *The Morning Telegraph,* the turf newspaper, and now press secretary of the New York Police Department, and the Marquis de la Falaise de la Coudray, husband of Gloria Swanson. It was a convivial group.

Dempsey, although he was as much as a 5-to-1 favorite over Tunney, had not fought in three years. Born in Manassa, Colorado, he ran away from home at the age of sixteen and wandered through the towns of the West, working as a laborer and miner. A natural brawler, he supplemented his income by taking on tough saloon patrons. His short left hooks traveled no more than eight or ten inches, but they invariably floored his opponents. Acting as the promoter, the bartender would then pass the hat, giving the young man 50 percent of the take. Dempsey soon began to fight professionally; in 1916, he even boxed in New York, suffering three broken ribs in a match that netted him thirty-five dollars. It was not until he came under the tutelage of a manager named Jack Kearns that the fortunes of the Manassa mauler-to-be began to rise. Though Kearns was a small man, his ego was immense. Impressed by Kearns' patter and his wardrobe (the manager would change his clothes three times a day), the naive Dempsey agreed with a handshake to share his future earnings with him on a fifty-fifty basis. Thereafter, the fighter referred all queries regarding his career to Kearns with the comment, "He's the doctor," earning the manager the nickname "Doc."

Spurred on by his mentor, Dempsey proceeded to demolish such luminaries as Gunboat Smith, Fireman Jim Flynn, and Bull Sadee before beating Jess Willard for the heavyweight championship in 1919. Later, he survived the charge that he had been a draft dodger during World War I, then rolled over France's Georges Carpentier, the Midwest's Tommy Gibbons, and Argentina's Luis Firpo. Jack began to hobnob with such celebrities as Walker, newspaperman Damon Runyon, band leader Paul Whiteman, and dancer Fred Astaire, and married a Hollywood actress.

Tunney's father, an immigrant from Ireland, had worked as a stevedore on the Greenwich Village docks; young Gene grew up in the Village and attended Catholic grade and high schools, just as Jimmy Walker had done a generation before. When World War I came, Tunney joined the Marine Corps, where he spent more time boxing than soldiering. During one unlucky match in France, which was witnessed by General John J. Pershing and Crown Prince Leopold of Belgium, he broke the knuckles of his right hand against an opponent's skull, thereby supposedly ending the possibility of becoming a devastating puncher. "If you want to know what a breakable mechanism the human hand is," he said later, "just be a boxer with cracked knuckles." Tunney persisted in his chosen trade, however, and gradually developed skills at ducking and slipping punches that marked him as a superb ring strategist. Meanwhile, he strengthened his hands by doing fingertip pushups. Turning professional after the war, Gene won the light-heavyweight title from Battling Levinsky, then fought a bloody series of encounters with one-eyed Harry Greb (who thrashed Tunney in the first of five meetings and then, predictably, was beaten more and more badly by the analytical Tunney in the remaining bouts). After besting those ubiquitous stalking-horses, Carpentier and Gibbons, Gene earned his chance at Dempsey.

A complicating factor of the match, and the reason it was held in Philadelphia rather than New York, was that James A. Farley, Chairman of the New York State Athletic Commission, had revoked Dempsey's boxing license, presumably because he had not honored an agree-

ment to fight Harry Wills, the Brown Tiger of Harlem. This un-
friendly act was most unlike Farley, who had used his office to give
out thousands of free tickets to countless bouts, thus earning for
himself the proverbial host of friends a state-wide Democratic leader
needs. "The gratitude of the average man for a prize-fight is un-
bounded," journalist Alva Johnston explained at the time. "It is not the
money saved that is important, but the pass is a sort of decoration,
like the Star and Garter, which shows that the bearer amounts to
something." Two years later, when Franklin Delano Roosevelt was
elected New York's governor, Farley would become the state's Democratic boss. The reason for Farley's harshness toward Dempsey in
1926, however, was not personal but political. In an effort to keep
placated Harlem's votes, he wanted the champion to meet the Negro
Harry Wills—and possibly lose his title to him. Dempsey, believing
that a fight with Tunney would draw more spectators (and make
more money), had declined.

The ringsiders present in the crowd of 135,000 at Philadelphia ran
the gamut from politics to finance, from philanthrophy to outright
thievery, from sports to movies. Governors Pinchot of Pennyslvania,
Moore of New Jersey, Small of Illinois, Ritchie of Maryland, Robinson of Delaware, Byrd of Virginia, and Groesbeck of Michigan were
there, and Mayors Kendrick of the host town and Hague of Jersey
City, as were Charles Schwab of Bethlehem Steel, Edward Stotes-
bury of J. P. Morgan, Vincent Astor, Percy Rockefeller, Walter Chrysler, and Tommy Hitchcock. Gambler Arnold Rothstein, one of the
few people to pick Tunney, was perhaps the best-known member of
the underworld in attendance. Baseball's John McGraw, Jacob Rup-
pert, and Wilbert Robinson settled into their seats, as did Charlie
Chaplin, Norma Talmadge, and Tom Mix. Walker, one of the last
celebrities to come down the aisle, received the most applause.
    Though the crowd did not realize it, the fight was all but settled
in the first round, when Tunney unloaded a straight right to the
champion's cheek that staggered him to his toes. Through all the
rounds that followed, Dempsey's legs never recovered from this jarring punch, and he could not leap at his opponent with the flurry
of punches that was his style. "I hit him hard enough to knock
down a horse! I know I've got the title!" Tunney told his seconds.
The fight went the scheduled ten rounds, but the outcome was
rarely in doubt, and Tunney was awarded the decision. "What happened?" his actress wife asked Dempsey afterward. "Honey," said
Dempsey, $850,000 richer but with eyes swollen shut, nose flattened,
and lips puffed, "I just forgot to duck."

A couple of days later, Tunney took his place in the cavalcade of heroes passing through New York, posing on the steps of City Hall with all the pols and campaign contributors Tammany could fit into the picture. Father Patrick H. Drain, pastor of St. Veronica's Church in the Village, where Tunney was christened and reared, was also present; he praised the boxer as "the type of man the Church and State depend on—an athlete of Christ." Walker told the crowd that "Gene Tunney . . . will compare as favorably in any endeavor as he does in the ring." The mayor was prescient. Tunney's keen intelligence, zest for reading, and zeal for self-improvement would soon make him the biggest success story the ring has ever known; in addition to the fortune he would make boxing, he would lecture on Shakespeare at Yale, make a movie (*The Fighting Marine*), marry a society heiress, become friendly with George Bernard Shaw, and spar with Ernest Hemingway. That day in New York, however, Gene was a young man who wanted to tell the world what willpower could accomplish. "I first got my inspiration to win the heavyweight title on a day seven years ago while quartered in my barracks in Paris," he said. "I was belittled, ridiculed . . . But I went on, I had confidence in myself."

These were the sentiments that Jimmy Walker's New Yorkers, the Irish, Jews, Germans, and Italians, wanted to hear; how splendid it was, in the golden years of the 1920s, that someone who wanted to make something of himself could succeed on so grand a scale.

Walker was in Syracuse in late September, calling the Democratic State Convention to order at its first meeting, but exercising no major role thereafter. It was clear that Smith would once again be the gubernatorial standard-bearer, and most of the delegates simply used the occasion for partying. Walker amused himself as best he could, yearning for Broadway but savoring an exchange he had with an upstate man who offered him the keys to some of the wine cellars in Steuben County.

"When we elect a man to high office we know we can trust him with a couple of bottles of wine," the delegate said.

"A couple of bottles won't go far in this convention," replied Walker.

With Calvin Coolidge in the White House, Smith ran for governor in 1926 against Republican Ogden L. Mills, a member of the House of Representatives who later would be appointed Secretary of the Treasury. Searching for an issue that would cut down the traditional Democratic plurality in the city, Mills seized on the recent milk scandals and tried to connect the governor to them. All through October,

New Yorkers were to hear that Smith had hushed up Tammany's part in the graft-taking (indeed, he *had* stepped gingerly) and that the city's milk supply was still impure. Smith characterized as preposterous the charge that he was protecting Tammany. "If Congressman Mills has any milk-graft evidence he is suppressing for campaign purposes," he said, "then he isn't fit to be Governor." Meanwhile Dr. Harris, while he refrained from discussing Tammany's past role in the milk graft, insisted that the health department now had cleansed itself. "The impression must not be allowed to go out," he said, "that the milk supply of the city is no better off than it was 18 months ago."

As the campaign continued, Mills remained all but silent on how he felt about such relevant issues as public power, wage and hour reforms for women workers, road building, grade-crossing elimination, aid to public hospitals and orphanages, and workmen's compensation; instead he insisted that the city's milk supply was still impure. Smith, learning that a long-time Hearst newspaper editor named Victor A. Watson was lending advice to Mills, happily dragged his old adversary into the controversy. In a speech at Hornell, New York, the governor charged that "the presence of Hearst's man Watson in the Mills headquarters at a salary greater than that paid to the Governor for a whole year's work" was responsible for the milk strategy. "It seems that in every political contest in which I take part," Smith said, "I am called upon to wage the real fight against the sinister figure of Hearst and all that he stands for."

After sending his wife, Allie, off to Europe again in early October (she would not return until November 1), the mayor made ready to play host to royalty. Queen Marie of Rumania was coming to town, and Tammany sachems were breaking out their silk hats, morning coats, and gold-headed canes. The usual foolscap scroll, replete with gold leaf and hand lettering, was feverishly prepared by Hector Fuller, Walker's factotum, whose dignified mien and resonant tones could be admired in Bleeck's Artists and Writers Restaurant on West Fortieth Street, where, with perfect diction, he would recite Tennyson, Swinburne, and the other English Romantics from memory as long as listeners refilled his glass.

Finally the day of Marie's arrival came. Amid streams of water shot hundreds of feet in the air by circling fireboats, she was escorted from the liner *Leviathan* onto the city's tugboat, the *Macom*. A handsome woman with a full figure, Marie had her worries. Back home her eldest son, Crown Prince Carol, had been forced to renounce his right of succession to the throne because of his liaison with a beauteous commoner, Mme. Magda Lupescu. To tabloid readers of the day, the name "Lupescu" conjured up dark, smoldering passions; they were hopeful that Queen Marie would elaborate on the infatuation.

Alas, Marie waved aside all such personal questions from vulgar reporters with regal disdain. Escorted by Grover Whalen, she then slowly proceeded by car up Lower Broadway to City Hall. Chill rains that had fallen earlier in the morning held down the crowds, but the granddaughter of Queen Victoria still received several rousing ovations. Gracious and charming, she seemed to be able always to keep her face in profile. After an exchange of compliments with the mayor and the presentation of Fuller's scroll, she and Walker immediately began their ride to Pennsylvania Station, where a special train was waiting to take Marie on her American tour. En route to the station behind a phalanx of motorcycles, the mayor bundled a lap robe over his guest in the open touring car; at that moment, a construction man perched overhead in a half-completed skyscraper called out in a foghorn voice, "Hey, Jimmy! Have you made her yet?"

Marie never lost her smile. "You Americans are quite droll," she told Walker.

The queen would travel the breadth of America, from Washington, D.C., to California, and sometimes it seemed that she would never go home. Her reasons for coming were many: lucrative contracts from a newspaper syndicate for interviews, fees from an automobile company and a vanishing-cream manufacturer for endorsements, the need to press Washington for a $100 million loan for her country. Marie enthralled Americans with her regal manner and her at-arm's-length charm—qualities they admired so much for having seen so little. When she stopped off again in New York before returning to Rumania, the motorcycle policemen who had escorted her at breakneck speeds, often at risk to themselves, learned firsthand the real meaning of *noblesse oblige*. Instead of the expected fifty-dollar tip, each man was gifted by Marie with her autographed photograph.

On the other side of the Atlantic, Allie was likewise enjoying herself. In Berlin, she had been received by Field Marshal von Hindenburg, Germany's president. "When I was introduced," she said, "he kissed my hand, which one wouldn't expect Mr. Coolidge to do. But I think it's a charming European custom." Allie had been invited to Europe by the Hamburg-American Line to dedicate a new ship, the *New York*—the idea being that the presence of an American mayor's wife at the launching would help heal whatever animosities remained from World War I. The Berlin papers devoted much attention to her visit. Allie gave the German newsmen their first inkling of how to dance the Black Bottom, and she took them aback when she described the Charleston, which had just been introduced to Germany, as "old-fashioned." The stories praised her dancing skill and the "diminutive shapeliness" of her feet.

On the eve of the gubernatorial election, Smith and Olvany led a motorcade of supporters through the streets of the East Side. One hundred and fifty cars left the Biltmore Hotel at about eight o'clock and wound their way to Martin McCue's clubhouse on Forty-sixth Street near Second Avenue; the crowds there were so dense the autos could not make any headway, and McCue had each of his club members holding not one but two Roman candles, so that the whole neighborhood blazed with light. Next on the tour was the late Charles Murphy's Anawanda Club, down on Twentieth Street; here the governor left his limousine and shook hands with everyone he could reach. On the parade went, past Essex and Hester streets, through Seward Park, where Smith had the inevitable baby thrust upon him for the obligatory kiss, until the raucous motorcade reached the Downtown Tammany Club, on Madison Street. There, amid cheering and fireworks, the governor spoke of his early days on the Lower East Side. "There was one thing Tom Foley always said," he told the crowd, and at the name of Smith's old political mentor men in the audience solemnly removed their hats, "and that was always to go home early on the night before election. And so I'm going to give you all the same advice."

No one took this sentiment more to heart than Brooklyn's John H. McCooey, who showed up at his polling place at 6:00 A.M. the next day to follow his custom of casting the first ballot in his district. When he found the place, which was located in a tailor shop, locked, he summoned a policeman and ordered him to break open the door; after a few minutes the tailor arrived, breathless and apologetic, explaining that his alarm clock had not gone off. No matter, the boss voted on time. Walker and his wife did not cast their ballots in Greenwich Village until a few minutes after 3:00 P.M.; the mayor explained that he had let Allie go to Europe only after she had promised to return in time to vote. After greeting Mrs. Margaret Fay, a campaign worker, with a kiss, Walker called Smith's re-election "a foregone conclusion."

The mayor was right. Smith beat Mills in the city by a plurality of some 483,000—greater than Walker's own 1925 plurality of 402,213. Though Mills carried upstate New York, his margin there was not substantial enough to offset this advantage, and the governor handily won a fourth term. Judge Robert F. Wagner, another protégé of Charles Murphy, was also swept into office, winning his first term in what would be a distinguished senatorial career. New York State simultaneously made its feelings evident about Prohibition. In a special referendum, the vote was 4-to-1 in favor of modifying the Volstead Act so that each state could choose for itself whether to be wet or dry; in the city the count was 7-to-1. Voting machines, which had been tested in only one assembly district the previous year, were now used city-wide, considerably speeding returns. John R. Voorhis, the politician who four decades before had led William H. Walker into the Tammany camp, tried out the new-fangled machine but declared he did not like it. The ninety-seven-year-old Voorhis, now a Grand Sachem of the Society, admitted he had been very courteously received by the election inspectors. "They had me sign my name twice, and I thought possibly they were going to give me two votes. . . ."

On November 8, a Gershwin musical called *Oh, Kay!* opened successfully in New York, with Walker in the audience. The show marked the American debut of Gertrude Lawrence, who played the "Kay" of the title and sang two of Gershwin's most memorable tunes: the classic "Someone to Watch Over Me" and the lively "Do, Do, Do." (The latter song might have become more popular at the time had it not been boycotted by radio—principally because some female vocalists were delivering the lyrics with sexual innuendo.) *Oh, Kay!*'s book was pure froth. Kay was the sister of an impoverished English duke who had turned to rum-running, aided by a hapless bootlegger-butler (wonderfully played by Victor Moore); they were using the Long Island estate of an out-of-town playboy to unload their booze, and all was going well until he returned; then Kay found herself romantically involved with him, and he found himself torn between her and several other women, and all the while the girls in the chorus piped out their lines and showed off their knees. Walker enjoyed himself immensely, and after the show he went backstage to meet Miss Lawrence. There he also met the English-born Betty Compton, one of four ingenues who, wrote a critic, led "the snappy chorus in some brilliant displays of agility." If there was such a thing as a typical flapper, Betty might well have been she, with her jet-black, tightly bobbed hair, eyes that could be enticing and a mouth that could pout, and a dancer's sensuous figure. She attracted Walker immediately. He was forty-five at the time, Betty twenty-two. As much as anything else, the age difference explains the relationship that was to ripen between them.

Walker's next trip to Philadelphia after the Dempsey-Tunney fight was an unhappy one. Jules Mastbaum of that city, one of his earliest benefactors (the man who had paid for the remodeling of 6 St. Luke's Place), had died of complications following an abdominal operation at the relatively early age of fifty-four. Mastbaum, head of the Stanley Corporation of America, had built up a chain of movie theaters that extended from upper New York to Virginia, and as far west as Ohio. He was a philanthropist as well, and his latest instance of generosity was a $1 million Rodin Museum that was being built in Philadelphia even as he died. Rushing to console Mastbaum's family after hearing the news, Walker declared, "No man was closer to me than Jules Mastbaum. I can't realize that he is dead." Despite the less than ten-year difference in their ages, the millionaire had always treated Walker like a son; after his death, his widow would keep up the friendship between the families, even occasionally going on trips with Allie.

When he returned to New York, Walker, nearing the end of his first year in office, found little time to mourn Mastbaum. The mayor's favoritism toward a mysterious group called the Equitable Coach Company, which sought bus franchises in Manhattan, Brooklyn, and Queens, was now coming under scrutiny. It was important, he had explained to the Board of Estimate, that "new management, new money and new blood" be brought into the transit situation. The Equitable was certainly new; it existed only on paper, and no one was quite sure who its real backers were. Walker could not, of course, grant the franchises unilaterally. Twelve of the board's sixteen votes were needed for such multimillion-dollar decisions, with the mayor, controller, and aldermanic president having three votes apiece, the Manhattan and Brooklyn Borough presidents two each, and the remaining Borough presidents one each. Controller Berry, in questioning the Equitable Coach proposal, wondered why the mayor was not giving more consideration to competing bids made by companies with more transit experience; why, for instance, was a BMT offer to establish a Brooklyn bus line not receiving more consideration?

This line of thinking from the controller, a friend of Boss McCooey, was supported by Brooklyn Borough President James J. Byrne, McCooey's brother-in-law. Together they had five votes on the board of estimate, enough to stymie Walker's efforts. The Equitable debate would drag on for the next eighteen months; even then the full facts would not be known until the Seabury investigation of the city government in 1932. Suffice it to say now that the mayor was once again being hospitable to his friends. State Senator John A. Hastings, who two years before had been carried into the legislature on a stretcher when Walker, then majority leader, needed his vote, now was asking a favor; he stood to make, and perhaps to share, millions of dollars through stock options in the Equitable—if only the company got its franchises.

1927

It was to a gathering of Ulstermen that Bricriu Poison-tongue came, and he seated himself by the shoulder of Conchobar. Then Bricriu got to his feet and said to all present, "Come with me, to partake of food and drink at a banquet with me."

Fergus, speaking for the nobles of Ulster, made answer, "No, for if we go our dead will outnumber our living, because your Poison-tongue will make us fight with one another."

"If you do not come, you shall fare worse," said Bricriu.

"What will you do?" said Conchobar.

"I will stir up such enmity among the Kings, the leaders and the heroes, that the blood will run for days, if you do not join me in my feast."

"We will not be threatened," said Conchobar.

"I will make father and son fight," said Bricriu. "Or I will make a quarrel with mother and daughter. If all else fails, I will make the Ulster women beset each other with blows, so that their breasts become flaccid and loathsome."

"Sure, it is better that we come," said Fergus.

〰〰〰

During the first week of the New Year, Walker officially opened phone service between New York and London. His hook-up with the Lord Mayor of London was to have gone through at 1:30 P.M.,

New York time, but static was so bad that the connection was three hours late. After the initial exchange of pleasantries, the conversation went like this:

Lord Mayor: "Can you hear me?"

Walker: "I can hear your Lordship very well."

Lord Mayor: (Sentence not clear.)

Walker: "I didn't quite get that."

Lord Mayor: "Yes."

Walker: "I find it a great delight to talk to you."

Lord Mayor: (Sentence not clear.)

Walker: "Hello, there."

New York's mayor some days thereafter found himself in a more meaningful dialogue, trying to get Equitable Coach's bid for bus franchises through the board of estimate. By now the company's ownership had been revealed, although there was still no mention of Hastings' part in advocating its petition. Equitable's principal shareholders, it turned out, were three Ohio men: Frank R. Fageol, president of the Fageol Motor Company (owned by American Car & Foundry), Charles B. Rose, his vice-president, and William O'Neil, head of General Tire and Rubber. These entrepreneurs hoped to profit by supplying the city with buses and tires, and to profit again by operating the lines. They believed Hastings had Walker's ear; as a result, they agreed to award the Brooklyn senator and his "associates" one-third of the Equitable's common stock, which would have returned $6 million in dividends alone during the company's first ten years of operation. As for raising the huge sums of money needed to put buses on the streets, the Equitable's representative explained, rather vaguely, that the "company has been assured of adequate financing provided the franchise as now proposed is granted."

Toward the end of January, Walker in executive session with the board of estimate pushed through the preparation of bus franchise contracts. His argument was that, in his view, the Equitable would provide the best service throughout Manhattan, Brooklyn, and Queens. (He did, however, favor a second company to service the Bronx, thereby pleasing Aldermanic President McKee, who was from the Bronx, and Henry Bruckner, the borough president.) The mayor threatened to stump the city if the procrastination continued. "I am quite capable of going into the Academy of Music in Brooklyn," he told reporters afterward, "comparing the record of the Equitable Coach Company and its offer with the previous history of the BMT, and I am quite capable of going into Carnegie Hall in Manhattan and doing the same thing."

Subsequent events proved, of course, that opposition on the board to the Equitable bid was justified. Controller Charles W. Berry, as we have seen, smelled a sellout and tried to block it, as did Manhattan Borough President Julius Miller. But at the time, partly because it was difficult to work for Tammany and simultaneously to criticize its machinations, Walker's adversaries gave the impression of simply indulging themselves in foot-dragging, at the expense of the public. Controller Berry, wary of dealing with an unknown transit company, could not point with pride to the records of the existing companies in the field; as for the borough presidents, the best that could be said of them was that they appeared to be confused. At the most recent executive sessions, Julius Miller had opined that the streets were already crowded and buses would add to the congestion.

"As I understand it," said Walker, quickly squelching him, "what you really want is to deprive the poor people of buses, so that the streets may be given over to limousines."

No one else made a motion, and the board adjourned. The decision to prepare the contracts, though it did not ensure that the Equitable would get the franchise, all but disposed of its rivals, most of whom were not prepared to bid on virtual citywide operation. One company, Service Bus, which was backed by International Harvester's guarantee to supply it with $12 million in equipment, did try to submit an offer, but it was ignored. The snub was all the more painful because Service Bus had pledged a five-cent fare (as opposed to the Equitable's sliding fare), posted a $100,000 bond (the Equitable offered no bond), and promised more frequent passenger service than its rival.

Drained by his transit exertions, Walker promptly left on a three-week trip to Cuba as a guest of publisher Paul Block. "I have seen the bus situation through to a stage where definite developments are pending," the mayor commented.

Whenever Walker was out of town, Aldermanic President McKee automatically became acting mayor; on this particular occasion, McKee decided to conduct a campaign against what he regarded as vice on the Broadway stage. The targets were three shows called *The Captive*, *The Virgin Man*, and *Sex*, and the police were ordered to close them forthwith. At the last moment, however, McKee wondered if he was acting wisely. The closing of the last two shows would not jeopardize the health of the American theater, but *The Captive* had received much critical applause. In need of encouragement, McKee called Havana and asked Walker to endorse the closings. "I'd advise you to wait," said Walker, expressing particular misgivings about raiding *The Captive*. "That show has been running for quite a while. If we pull it now we admit either that we didn't know about it or that we tolerated it."

On the other end of the long-distance line, McKee hesitated before answering. "I can't," he said finally. "The police are already out with the warrants."

Critical praise goes only so far; *The Captive* decided not to fight the police raid and closed before coming to trial. So did *The Virgin Man*. It remained for Mae West, author and star of *Sex* (which featured the ample but imperious Mae doing the shimmy in a skin-tight gold dress) to defend the freedom of the American stage. In an effort to put the subject of decency in perspective, she elected to stand trial. "People want dirt in plays, so I give 'em dirt," she explained. "Know what I mean?"

Her hair still a brassy gold and not the platinum it would be in later years, the twenty-seven-year-old Miss West had been bankrolled in her theater venture by a racketeer—a not uncommon arrangement in New York of the period. Mae's patron was Owen ("Owney") Madden, recently paroled from Sing Sing, where he had been imprisoned on a manslaughter conviction, and now one of the city's biggest bootleggers. He considered Miss West a sensitive artist. Yet the curvaceous Mae, with the candor only a true genius dares to express, would open her violet eyes wide and describe her work habits thusly: "When all my notes are typed and put together, I have a play. See? I put in the real stuff at rehearsal. Know what I mean?"

Miss West, who had been reared in Brooklyn's Greenpoint section —"Greenpurnt," as she would say—made her way up in the world through stock-company rolls (Little Eva in *Uncle Tom*), burlesque, (off-color songs), and vaudeville. (When not singing, she indulged in weight-lifting, once supporting four men on her shoulders.) As she matured, Mae decided that her favorite colors were flesh, white, silver, and gold—not necessarily in that order—had a pier glass placed at the foot of her canopied bed, and delighted in paraphrasing one of Walker's favorite remarks by saying, "I'll match my private life with any woman's." Yet Miss West could take violent exception to the sexual innuendoes that were already circulating about her. "Because my plays have dealt with sex and the dregs of humanity," she once earnestly wrote to the New York *Times,* "some persons see fit to assume that I write vividly about such subjects because I know them by experience. . . . Nobody ever sees me in nightclubs or cabarets. . . . I am, in fact, retiring by nature. . . . I do not drink, I do not smoke. . . . I have my books."

For her defiance of Aldermanic President McKee and the police, in 1927, the author-actress got twelve days on Welfare Island and immense amounts of publicity. (Before *Sex* voluntarily closed, it drew 300,000 paid admissions.) Mae stood up well under the prison discipline, her complaints centering on the quality of the underwear issued to the inmates; it itched, she said, and "nearly drove me wild." The warden, congratulating her upon her release with a handshake and a broad smile, declared that she was "just a wholesome woman trying to serve twelve days."

The very next year, Miss West would author another hit play, *Diamond Lil,* which Mayor Walker, knowing when a superior show-woman had him upstaged, would studiously leave alone.

Shortly after his return from Cuba, Walker was faced with what was, for a Tammany mayor, a horrific situation. For months now, Police Commissioner George McLaughlin had been ordering raids against various clandestine gambling establishments. Using Lewis J. Valentine's Confidential Squad, the commissioner had even invaded political clubhouses, looking for evidence of bookmaking and gaming. At first, the results were not gratifying. On one occasion, for instance, a police investigation showed that two men had been mortally wounded when gambling in the Harry C. Perry Club on the Bowery; yet neither Perry, who was chief clerk of the City Court, nor anyone else would give testimony in the matter. Although bloodstains and the revolver used in the shootings were found on the premises, the killings were never solved. Another time, Valentine's men un-successfully raided the Upper East Side clubhouse of Thomas M. Farley, an early Walker supporter in the 1925 primary. There was much scurrying about within the club, which was fortified by thick "ice-box" doors and barred windows; when the police entered in force, they discovered hastily concealed gambling paraphernalia. Far-ley had a glib explanation for the crowd in his clubhouse at 2:00 A.M., however, and the charges were soon dropped. "The members that was there was busy packing baseball bats, skipping ropes and rubber balls, because our May Day party took place [the next day]," he would say.

Though they were not bloodied, the Tammany district leaders and their counterparts in the other boroughs were increasingly dis-turbed by McLaughlin's and Valentine's attentions. Their voices rose like the wails of suppliant choir boys, but the commissioner remained unmoved. Nettled, the leaders turned to Walker, who was caught in a curious conflict of loyalties. Though it was true that Smith had urged McLaughlin's appointment on him, Walker felt he owed the commissioner the same support he owed the machine.

Matters came to a head on March 12, when McLaughlin authorized

Valentine to raid three Brooklyn political clubhouses. Caught amid various evidences of gambling in one of them, the People's Regular Democratic Club, was Alderman Peter J. McGuinness, who was also the district leader. He was arrested on a charge of bookmaking. Eight other men were arrested on the same charge, and 150 others for disorderly conduct, but it was the "Fighting Greenpoint Alderman" who made the headlines. In New York, embarrassing a district leader in this fashion was just not done. McLaughlin obviously lacked a sense of fair play.

The raids on the three clubs had been carefully planned. First, wiretaps had established that bets on horseraces were being accepted. Next, fearing that police in the local precincts might tip off the pols, the members of Valentine's Confidential Squad, without revealing their targets, "borrowed" patrol vans and uniformed policemen from other station houses. McGuinness and his colleagues were taken entirely by surprise. The alderman, a six-footer who weighed 230 pounds and had the massive physique to be expected of the stevedore he once was, "expressed himself· indignantly" to his tormentors.

McGuinness had not been entirely unwary. Two weeks before the raid, according to testimony given by a detective who had infiltrated the clubhouse, the district leader had walked hurriedly into the room where the betting was going on and shouted to the bookmakers, "Boys, the cops are around. Get these. fellows out of here quick." While the room was being cleared of bettors, McGuinness sought sanctuary in his private office.

Though the gambling charge against him was soon dismissed, McGuinness behaved impetuously. He assailed McLaughlin in a vitriolic speech at a board of aldermen meeting. This lack of humility provoked McLaughlin into revealing what had been found in the McGuinness clubhouse: receipts indicating that $600,000 yearly was being bet on the races in the establishment, with a profit of over $60,000. "The records on which the [estimate] is based were taken from a safe labeled 'Peter J. McGuinness,' which safe was in a room on the door of which appeared 'Peter J. McGuinness, Private,' " McLaughlin announced. "The only persons who had access to this room were . . . McGuinness and the professional gamblers." Madder than ever, the district leader denied the safe was his. "The safe in question," he retorted, "is the property of the club. . . . The only man who has the combination is Frank Miller, treasurer of the organization. He was not present at the time the raid was made. . . . I have not the combination and never did have it." Asked what Miller's business was, McGuinness replied he understood he was a salesman, but of what he did not know.

When Miller finally was located, he too pleaded ignorance of the combination. "When I was elected treasurer," he said, "they tried to give me the combination of that safe, but I have forgotten what it was. . . . I never saw that safe open in my life."

Greenpoint, the district Alderman McGuinness represented, had once been a sylvan place, surrounded on three sides by the East River and Newtown Creek; in the early 1900s, however its waterfront grew grimy under the proliferation of factories, its air was made foul by the belchings of smokestacks. Property values fell, and many of the Irish residents, appalled at the non–English-speaking immigrants who had been brought in by manufacturers to provide cheap labor, began to move. A concerned citizen versified in a local paper:

> Oh those on high who watch mere mortals act
> Send us a fighter strong, clean and intact,
> That we may save our fair town from decay
> And from the chains of unrest break away.

The hoped-for fighter was not long in coming. Stevedore McGuinness, already the most popular man on the Greenpoint waterfront, decided in 1913 that he would go into politics. Ruling the district at the time was James A. McQuade, who would later explain, during the Seabury investigations, that he had amassed a half-million dollars in bank depostis by "borrowing" the money to feed the "thirty-three starving McQuades." A frequenter of saloons and racetracks, McQuade had his admirers, but he was ultimately to prove no match for the abstemious, glad-handing McGuinness, who over the next few years repeatedly accused the entrenched leader of being responsible for Greenpoint's inferior schools, broken sidewalks, and bands of thieving gypsies. The tactics were effective. In 1919, McGuinness, then thirty-one, won a handy victory over McQuade's man in the aldermanic race. (The real power in the city lay in the Board of Estimate, which could grant franchises, issue bonds, and set the municipal budget. About all the board of aldermen could do, besides wheedle favors for their districts, was reduce but not enlarge the budget; it was made up of some sixty-five politicians, most of whom were amiable hacks; nonetheless, the board of aldermen handled the mundane problems that the average voter was concerned with.) "What's the matter with Park Avenue Jim McQuade?" McGuinness asked the electorate during his campaign. "Don't he think his own people are good enough to have showers? Why shouldn't Greenpoint be right up there with Flatbush and places like that?"

In another election four years later, McGuinness won the district leadership. But McQuade still retained the backing of Boss McCooey, and for the next half-dozen years he not only hung on in city government but kept challenging McGuinness, fruitlessly as it turned out, for the Greenpoint leadership. It was this continuing strife, in fact, that was responsible for the gambling in Peter's club. McGuinness was that rarity in machine politics, a personally honest man, but he was forced to offer gambling facilities for his supporters lest they move away to McQuade's club, which had long been supplying such services. It was Peter's bad luck, the night of Commissioner McLaughlin's raids, that he was in his clubhouse but McQuade was not in his.

Like so many lower-echelon Irish pols of his day, McGuinness wore black high-top shoes and white cotton socks. He loved nothing better of an evening than to say good-bye to the wife ("the old champeen"), stride down to his clubhouse, and receive petitioners while seated behind his decrepit desk. There he would accept his "contracts." "I get one hell of a kick out of that," he would say. "Sometimes I even do favors for people in Jersey." To honor his friends, McGuinness had founded an organization he called the Grand Benevolent Order of Pork Chops. "What the hell, I had to have something to call me ole pals," he explained. "I call them pork chops because all the old Aldermen loved eating pork chops." In Greenpoint, Peter's friends were beyond number; he was easily the district's most-in-demand honorary pallbearer. (Among the Irish pols, his loyalty was unimpeachable: years later, when Walker was in disgrace, McGuinness would throw his arms around him, while reporters looked on, and say, "Jimmy darling me old pal, stay in Brooklyn if they won't give you a job over there. I'm sheriff here, and you can be me first deputy, me dear old pork chop.")

By the end of March, the protests by district leaders over gambling raids had reached such a pitch that McLaughlin, as prudent as he was uncorruptible, decided that he would quit. After fifteen months in office, he resigned his $10,000 police commissionership to accept an executive vice-presidency of the Mackay Companies, the telegraph and cable enterprises headed by Clarence H. Mackay, at a yearly salary of $75,000. (Mr. Mackay, who had not yet gotten over his pique at his daughter's marriage to Irving Berlin, had been casting about for a successor to run the family-owned business for the past year.) There were broad smiles among the leaders at the Wigwam when they heard the news; Judge Olvany said of the hard-driving commissioner, "He should not be criticized for leaving the Police Department at this time in view of the extraordinary offer that has been made him. He is a young man with a growing family."

Perhaps the happiest of all district leaders on this occasion was Alderman McGuinness. "The City of New York has lost a good official," he announced with a straight face at a City Hall press conference. "I am very glad to see him elevated, and I trust that peace and prosperity may be his to the fullest extent and that no misfortune will mar the new career he is entering upon."

Named by the mayor to succeed McLaughlin was Joseph A. Warren, a close friend and former law associate of Walker who had been serving in his administration as Commissioner of Accounts. In this post, Warren acted as a special investigator for the city. Most recently he had looked into an outbreak of violence in the Tombs, in which the warden and a keeper were killed and three prisoners committed suicide; his report held the head of the Department of Correction responsible for the oppressive prison conditions that led to the rebellion, and called for his resignation. Yet Warren was a Tammany man (the first member of the Wigwam to be named police commissioner since the administration of Mayor Van Wyck in 1898), and Walker felt he could depend on him to accommodate the machine.

"I can go to bed and rest with Joe Warren as Police Commissioner," the mayor said, in a good example of double entendre.

Walker did not know his man. "I appreciate the honor the Mayor has shown me," Warren declared. "With whatever brains and energy I possess, I shall endeavor to continue the policies of Commissioner McLaughlin."

It was not that Walker was not explicit. Warren was to demote Valentine, by now an Inspector, and disband the Confidential Squad; he was also to transfer Valentine to a precinct so remote that the only gambling game was catching public transportation to get there. Unfortunately for the mayor, behind Warren's nervous manner and unimposing physique was a total integrity that completely paralleled McLaughlin's. The new police commissioner went back to his office and summoned Valentine, who fully expected to be fired and had written out his letter of resignation.

"Inspector Valentine," he said, "you will carry on as usual. . . . You will continue your gambling raids whenever you think advisable, and you will raid any premises in New York City where you think gambling is going on. . . . That is all."

It was no accident that commissioners like McLaughlin and Warren relied so heavily on Lewis J. Valentine—a dedicated policeman contemptuous of graft or political pressure, who always went by the

book. Valentine, who had joined the force in 1902, spent his early
years walking a beat in the Williamsburg section of Brooklyn, where
he quickly proved himself tougher than any of the hoodlums who
questioned his authority. After ten years, he was promoted to sergeant. A widower, he had married his late wife's sister; they lived
quietly in Bensonhurst with the children of both marriages, and all
of Valentine's spare time was spent studying for the Civil Service
exams that might raise him to lieutenant and captain. He fixed up
an office for himself in a corner of his cellar; there he would read
aloud from textbooks in an authoritative voice until he had committed
the material to memory. In 1917, during the administration of John
Purroy Mitchel, Valentine was tapped for the newly formed Confidential Squad and soon afterward made lieutenant. Hard-eyed and
suspicious, he was the perfect man to investigate corruption among
his peers. When Mayor Hylan came to office in 1918, however, Valentine was consigned to eight years of purgatory. As we have seen,
Commissioner Enright bounced him from one unpleasant assignment
to another and three times passed him over for promotion to captain.

Early in 1926, Lieutenant Valentine received a phone call in, yes,
Greenpoint, where he was currently in exile; the voice on the other
end of the line, summoning him to headquarters, was that of Commissioner McLaughlin.

"Why weren't you promoted?" McLaughlin asked when the lieutenant stood before him.

"I don't know, sir," said Valentine stiffly.

The commissioner laughed and waved him out. Days later, Valentine was named acting captain (at the princely salary of $4,000) and
assigned to head the Clinton Street Station on the Lower East Side.
There he threw himself into the running of the precinct, prowling
through its streets at all hours to make sure his men were doing their
job. Just as Valentine was checking up on his subordinates, so the
commissioner was watching him. McLaughlin wanted to re-create
Mitchel's Confidential Squad, and he needed a tough, uncorruptible
officer to run it; after three months, he decided he had his man.
Valentine accepted the assignment, was named a deputy inspector and
later a full inspector. "Those were the glittering days of Prohibition,"
he would explain later. "Vice was rampant. Broadway harbored every
known criminal. Gangsters had loose trigger fingers. It was the era
of beer-running, bathtub gin, peeephole speakeasies, and killings and
more killings." Valentine made gamblers the special target of the
Confidential Squad. "The gamblers were a menace," he said. "They
mingled with Wall Street tycoons, society bluebloods, and city officials. Tammany leaders were their secret partners. . . . These mighty

gamblers could throw ten years' salary at a prying police inspector to hold him off until the right string was pulled by Tammany to get him off the trail."

After McLaughlin's resignation, Valentine kept up his antigambling drive under Commissioner Warren, making more than a thousand raids. Even the lack of convictions did not discourage him. "Only one politician was convicted, only to have his sentence suspended," he admitted. "The utter disregard of these gamblers for our courts continued to amaze me."

Walker was never more popular than in the spring of 1927, and New Yorkers heard still another song written in his honor by Irving Berlin:

> Who told Broadway not to be gay?
> Who gets his picture taken three times a day?
> Jimmie!
> We're glad to show,
> That we all know,
> That Jimmie's doing fine.
> Can't you hear those old New Yorkers hollering:
> Gimmie—gimmie—gimmie Jimmie for mine!

One of the New Yorkers who thought so highly of Walker was publisher Paul Block, who had opened a joint brokerage account with the mayor; it was a curious account because Walker put no money into it but between March 9 and June 15 drew $102,000 out of it. (By the time the account was closed in August of 1929, he had withdrawn a total of $246,000.) Block was later to explain to Judge Seabury that the concern of his ten-year-old son Billy had motivated him to help Walker make ends meet.

"The youngster said, 'How much salary does the mayor get?' and I told him $25,000, which was his salary at the time," Block would testify. " 'Well,' the youngster said, 'can he live on what he gets?' And I said, 'Well, I suppose he can, but it probably is a problem.' "

After Block opened the joint account, it happened that he, his son Billy, Walker, and John H. Delaney, chairman of the board of transportation, journeyed to Brooklyn to watch a chemist, Dr. Robert S. Beyer, change copper into gold. Acting as their guide was the ubiquitous Senator Hastings. He and Block, together with the chemist, were the chief stockholders in the Beyer Company.

"Dr. Beyer had promised us," Hastings would say, "that he would effect some rather unique processes that heretofore had been attempted but were not successful. He was going to, I think, temper copper in an electric vacuum furnace that he had . . . and he was working on a process for the changing of metals."

"What metals? Gold?" Hastings was asked.

"Probably, this fellow is good."

Though the actual transmutation of copper into gold was held up by a few technical problems, Hastings and Block took up the slack by pointing out that Dr. Beyer had developed a synthetic tile that might be of use in the city's subways. Beyer could make the tile, Hastings would say, "at considerably reduced cost, and would be able to underbid any competitor for any particular job."

Everyone present, particularly Billy Block, was impressed; Walker suggested that Chairman Delaney look into the tiles posthaste; obviously, it was important that the city practice economies. Unfortunately, the board of transportation's humorless engineers vetoed the tile purchase (but not until Hastings had sold his stock for a $50,000 profit). The Beyer tile, said the engineers, was "almost identical in quality and kind with our standard station finish tile." Still, Hastings and Block cannot be faulted for having tried to save the city some money.

On April 11, Walker and Allie celebrated their fifteenth wedding anniversary aboard the liner *New York* as guests of the Hamburg-American Steamship Company. Most of the important people in the city government were present, as were admirers of the mayor ranging from art dealer Sir Joseph Duveen to philanthropist Sophie Irene Loeb. Allie, wearing a gown of rouge chiffon and a gray felt turban, was smiling and cordial; in moments of repose, however, her face would take on a pensive, hesitant expression, for she worried about Walker's philandering. He had not yet taken up in earnest with Betty Compton, the young actress he had met the previous November at the opening of *Oh, Kay!*, but he continued to pursue various showgirls casually. Allie, with her thickening waist and double chin, did not protest; Jim would eventually settle down, she hoped, and meanwhile appearances had to be kept up.

Walker could joke, in defense of his numerous vacations, that "a politician does his full duty only when he leaves town," and he was an equally lighthearted host. On and on came the visiting heroes and heroines to New York, while citizens cheered and sanitation men grumbled. The president of Cuba was followed by an Italian aviator who was followed by most of the U.S. fleet, moored resplendently in the Hudson. In early May, however, the mayor angrily asserted his political authority. Parks Commissioner Francis D. Gallatin, a Hylan appointee eight years before, had aroused Walker's ire by ordering the removal of some newsstands in City Hall Park, on the ground that the vendors were not exercising their God-given (and Tammany-given) right to vote. "If trucks are backed up here to take away those stands," Walker declared, "Gallatin will go on the first truck." He went on to say that he was concerned not with whether or how the vendors voted but with the fact that the news-dealers, many of whom were widows, had been in the park for years and had no other livelihood. Perhaps, Walker said at a board of estimate meeting, Gallatin should spend less time worrying about vendors and more time preparing the plan, long overdue, that would tell the board how he was going to spend a $1 million appropriation to restore Central Park. Either the parks commissioner "ought to resign or the board of estimate members ought to walk out," the mayor snapped.

Taking the hint, Gallatin, who had long been a Tammany sachem, bowed out huffily, saying, "When I am criticized by the Mayor, no matter how unjustly, I feel I can do nothing but resign." He was replaced by Walter R. Herrick, who had known Walker since they had been state senators together. "It's a funny thing," the new commissioner said, "but Mrs. Herrick, when she came in on Monday night [the day before Walker offered him the job], had been through the park and she said to me, 'I'm afraid Jimmie is going to have that park come back on him. It's in horrible shape.'"

Soon afterward, Walker publicly rebuked Welfare Commissioner Bird S. Coler, who, like Gallatin, was a Hylan appointee. It seemed that the mayor and the board of estimate had alloted more than one-third of a $15-million hospital appropriation to Kings County Hospital alone, because new surgical and maternity facilities were needed. Walker's grievance grew out of the fact that Coler had allowed the funds to be shifted to the construction at the hospital of a medical laboratory, to be used by students at Long Island College.

"While the more necessary buildings have been held up," he told the apprehensive Coler at a board meeting, "you are pushing this laboratory to completion for the benefit of a private institution. . . . This is a course to which this Board never gave its consent. . . . And yet you have continued upon this laboratory enterprise until the Medical Board of Kings County Hospital came to City Hall and protested."

Admitting that the laboratory was 70 percent completed, Coler murmured something to the effect that there must have been a misunderstanding between himself and Dr. Walter H. Conley, his medical superintendent. "Dr. Conley?" exploded Walker. "Why, you know Dr. Conley has gone to Europe to make a survey of hospital methods. . . . We can't get his evidence now."

At Kings County, conditions were such that 600 surgical cases were often crowded into an area unsuitable for half that number, while the wards, some of them seventy years old, were without sufficient daylight and air. "You don't mean to say, Commissioner," an irate Walker demanded of Coler, "that a laboratory conducted by students is more needed than hospital beds?" "What made Bellevue is its laboratory," retorted Coler, indicating the dreams of medical prestige that motivated the misuse of funds. For the mayor, who was as concerned about the lives and feelings of people as he was careless about money, this was an infuriating answer. Walker ordered that the laboratory building be converted immediately into the anticipated medical pavilion. Only the fact that Coler, a one-time unsuccessful gubernatorial candidate, was entrenched more firmly in the Democratic machine than the unfortunate Gallatin kept him his job.

June saw the greatest welcome yet that Walker and the city could give: Charles A. Lindbergh was back in town. Early on the morning of May 20, the young airmail pilot from Missouri had taken off from a Long Island runway in his monoplane, *The Spirit of St. Louis;* thirty-three and a half hours later, he landed outside of Paris, the first solo flier to cross the Atlantic nonstop. It is difficult now to appreciate the courage Lindbergh's feat required. Grover Whalen was present when the daring aviator took off for Paris. "The only moment of hesitation I noted," he would write of Lindbergh's behavior that historic morning, "was when he asked the Wright engineer (who had just finished tuning the engine), 'Shall I go?' The engineer replied, 'Go on, kid,' and turned away. I could see that he had tears in his eyes."

Lindbergh had gambled and won, and now Whalen was readying the city to pay him homage. The aviator flew up from Washington, where he had been received by President Coolidge upon his return from France, escorted by an honor guard of twenty-three planes. After he landed his seaplane in the Narrows, he boarded the municipal tugboat *Macom,* while 30,000 well-wishers aboard 400 nearby ships cheered themselves hoarse, and 200,000 more shouted and waved from the Bay Ridge, South Brooklyn, and Staten Island shorelines. The head of the French War Veterans in the United States, embracing Lindbergh on board the *Macom,* impulsively took the Legion of Honor from his own coat and placed it on the aviator's, saying, "Comrade, what is mine is yours."

At the Battery 80,000 people waited for Lindbergh. Standing in his open touring car, waving to the crowd, he nearly somersaulted backward to the pavement when the car suddenly lurched forward; Whalen grabbed his legs as he fell and hauled him back into the rear seat. Walker and some 100,000 other citizens greeted Lindbergh at City Hall. Referring to the modest aviator's habit of referring to himself and his plane as "we," the mayor declared, "That well-known inclusive word 'we' was quite right, because you were not alone in the solitude of the sky and the sea, because every American heart . . . was beating for you. Every American . . . was riding with you in spirit." Lindbergh accepted his scroll from Hector Fuller, Walker's man-of-all work, with the abrupt bow and quick-flashing smile that had become his trademark. Then he and the mayor rode off through the city, in ideal, sunny weather, surrounded by mounted police. They turned north on Park Row past the Pulitzer Building, gay with the flags of all nations; up past police headquarters and along Lafayette Street; through Astor Place; past the Hotel Lafayette at Ninth Street and University Place, where Raymond Oteig, owner of the Lafayette and the donor of the $25,000 prize for the New York-to-Paris flight, smiled down from a balcony; then up the splendid vista of Fifth Avenue, while millions of onlookers threw themselves completely into the emotions of the moment.

Everywhere the ticker-tape, confetti, and torn telephone-book pages were ankle-deep. "I guess when I leave here," Lindbergh told Walker, "they'll have to print another edition of the telephone book."

At the Fourteenth Street intersection, long lines of trolley cars waited, filled with people craning their necks for a glimpse of the aviator. At Twenty-third Street, the procession, which now included 10,000 marching troops and scores of bands, stopped at the Eternal Light monument, where Lindbergh placed a wreath in memory of New York's soldiers and sailors who had died in the First World War. At Thirty-fourth Street the Waldorf Astoria's windows were crowded with spectators, and at Thirty-ninth Street the Union League Club had put up a special grandstand for members and guests. Finally, at Central Park, Walker formally introduced the aviator to Governor Smith, who presented him with the state Medal of Valor.

That night, escorted by Walker and Whalen and their wives, Lindbergh was dragooned into attending a dinner in his honor given by Postal Telegraph's Clarence Mackay at his $6 million Long Island estate. As Lindbergh's cavalcade passed the Mackay gate, located a full mile from the main house, Japanese lanterns of red, white, and blue flickered in the trees, and the floodlit gardens, modeled after those at Versailles, beckoned invitingly. Mackay had invited eighty prominent citizens to dinner and 500 to the reception that would follow. But Lindbergh, terribly tired and, if the truth be known, incredibly bored, lasted only through the dinner. Afterward, he quietly slipped away, ordering a chauffeur to drive him back to New York. By this time Mackay was happily organizing the reception line that would show off his prized guest amid his precious paintings and tapestries. It fell to Grover Whalen to tell him that Lindbergh had left.

"He was so shocked by the news he could hardly speak," said Whalen of Mackay. "When he did regain his composure, he told me he felt ill and was going to his room."

In his attempt to save the five-cent fare, Walker found a champion in sixty-nine-year-old Samuel Untermyer, an attorney whose forensic skills were so appreciated by his clients that he was worth $1 million before he was thirty. Thereafter he often turned his attention, for little or no money, to city and state service. It was wise to have physicians in attendance when Untermyer conducted a cross-examination. Once he reduced to tears the bull-doggish Grover Whalen, a one-time private ash-hauler, while forcing him to admit that his trucks had illegally dumped their loads on city property. Now, as special counsel for the transit commission, he obtained from James L. Quackenbush, general counsel of the IRT, the admission that the company's subway lines had earned in 1926 a profit of $6,569,573, or 22 percent of the original cash investment.

"The five-cent fare appears to be ample, does it not?" Untermyer said to Quackenbush.

"I do not believe it will be ample to pay—"

"How much more than 22 percent would you like to earn?"

"Just enough more—"

"As much as you can get, is that it?"

Quackenbush defended himself by saying that a respectable profit margin was necessary if the IRT were to sell its bonds at reasonable rates of interest—in order to finance further capital outlays.

"That brings us back to the question again," said Untermyer, "that the Interborough itself, at a five-cent fare, earns a very handsome profit."

"Treating the subway alone," admitted the beleaguered Quackenbush, "I think nobody can deny that."

Untermyer next interrogated Thomas L. Chadbourne, who owned 10 percent of the BMT stock.

"Now that BMT isn't starving at this fare, is it?" Untermyer said.

"No, not starving, but not getting what it ought to get," replied the wealthy Chadbourne.

"It is earning $6.50 a share on the common stock, is it not?"

"I think a little more than that, but that will do."

"How much more would you like to get?" asked Untermyer.

"Well, I should think—"

"Fifteen percent or 50 percent?"

"It ought to be able to make $8 a share."

"You are going right up with your earnings every year, aren't you?" Untermyer persisted.

"Yes, they are advancing very handsomely."

"Don't you think they will get to $8 without advancing the fare?"

"I sincerely hope so," said Chadbourne.

In essence, Untermyer wanted the formation of a unified city transit system (which would involve recapturing the IRT and BMT). If the city were to take over existing lines and join them to new ones, he felt, fiscal policies could be established that would forestall a fare increase. Walker was properly grateful that the attorney was fighting his battles. "The Transit Commission, with the aid of Mr. Untermyer," he said, "has a duty under the statute to prepare a readjustment plan, and they must do the negotiating. I have every confidence in . . . Mr. Untermyer."

By the time he was twenty-one, Samuel Untermyer's fees from his New York law practice amounted to $75,000 a year. He got into the millionaire's club, however, by going to London; there he dropped unannounced into the board of directors' meeting of a large investment firm, shouting: "Five minutes of your time, gentlemen!" Within twenty-four hours he sold the English bankers a consortium of American breweries and pocketed a million-dollar fee. As the years went on, his courtroom foes included J. P. Morgan, United States Steel, John D. Rockefeller, and the New York Stock Exchange, all of whom, at one time or another, conducted raids on the public exchequer. When Henry Ford distributed millions of anti-Semitic pamphlets in dozens of languages, Untermyer filed a libel suit that forced Ford not only to recant but to put out pro-Semitic literature.

Perhaps the attorney's greatest triumph, at least in terms ordinary citizens can appreciate, was not paying his electricity bill from 1903 to 1911. It was, he said, too high. The bill eventually totaled $7,-200, and ninety-three attempts were made to collect it. New York Edison did not dare to black out Untermyer as it would have done to ordinary mortals, fearing to offend him. "Ye Gods!" the utility company's executives must have said to themselves; "what if he gets us into court!" The specters of rate reductions, public ownership, even outright confiscation haunted their dreams. Once the bill was cut in half, Untermyer paid it.

A lifelong asthma condition got the attorney up at four each morn-ting; he often worked sixteen hours a day. His memory was prodigious, and his courtroom powers of persuasion were also impressive. On one occasion, assigned to defend a woman who had fatally stabbed her husband and was pleading self-defense, he encountered a troubling detail. The deceased had been stabbed in the back, which indicated that he had not been so aggressive after all. Playing down this ap-parent incongruity, Untermyer extolled the virtues of the accused as wife and mother. The red-eyed jury not only brought in a verdict for acquittal but donated $500 for his client's support.

When World War I came, Untermyer, who was of German descent, did all he could to keep the United States out of the conflict; in one instance, he may have been overenthusiastic when he recom-mended to Berlin that the Kaiser buy the New York *Sun* for use as a propaganda organ. Yet, as the second biggest stockholder of Beth-lehem Steel, which sold more than $1 billion in munitions to the Allies, he managed to keep his emotions in perspective.

If the attorney had a weakness, it was for orchids; he seldom ap-peared anywhere without a fresh one in his lapel. Sixty gardeners were employed on his 171-acre Greystone, New York, estate to humor the idiosyncracy; in addition, they also raised out-of-season grapes, nectarines, and peaches in hothouses. Any legal associate of Unter-myer could be easily identified in court: he would be wearing an orchid. Untermyer's health had broken temporarily with the death of his wife a few years before his involvement with the city's transit affairs; but now he was fully recovered—ready for a fare dispute that would not be settled in the courts until 1929.

Certainly the most rambunctious witness at the transit hearings, which continued through July, was ex-Mayor Hylan, who showed that his knowledge of transit problems was extremely limited but that his antipathy for Untermyer knew no bounds. (In part, this was because the attorney had persuaded him, back in 1918, to appoint Frederick H. Bugher as his first police commissioner. Bugher would click his heels in Prussian military fashion when entering the mayor's office, but his sense of obedience ended with the mannerism; he totally ignored Hylan's recommendations on police matters. Hylan fired him after three months and replaced him with the more politically minded Enright.) At this point in the hearings, Untermyer was trying to make it clear that the existing IRT and BMT lines had to be re-claimed by the city and merged with the about-to-be-built subway lines if there was to be a chance of keeping the five-cent fare. To prove his point, he cited the report of the board of transportation, whose members were appointed by Hylan and whose findings he had approved, that it would require a first-year fare of ten cents to make new lines self-supporting.

"Oh, they may have thought that," Hylan pooh-pooed, "just as you thought that you were going to get a half-million-dollar fee in the Stokes case (Stokes being a big spender eager to divest himself of his wife) and only got $200,000."

Untermyer remained unruffled. "As I understand it, then," he said to Hylan, "you cannot shed any light on how the city should deal with the question of deficits arising from the construction of new subways."

"When we get to that we will answer your question," the ex-mayor royally rejoined, referring to himself in the plural.

"In the meantime, you know, do you not, that the city is putting out this money?"

"The people of the city will take care of that. What they want is service."

At various stages in the hearing, Hylan waved photostatic copies of pages from the *Congressional Record,* which he said contained incriminating charges against Untermyer. It turned out that the charges, which had been made thirty-seven years before, had long since been dropped. At other times Hylan would not hear Untermyer out ("I am not going to answer your tricky questions your way"). Hylan even brought along his own stenographer.

"Several months ago . . . we concluded that we ought to reorganize the Five-Cent Fare League and watch you," he said to the attorney.

"I ask to strike out that answer," said Untermyer to Transit Commission Chairman John F. Gilchrist.

"I want my stenographer to take it down," said Hylan. "That is what we are doing, watching you."

"Don't you know it's mandatory upon the commission to prepare a readjustment plan?" Untermyer asked.

"It isn't mandatory to put you in it," shot back Hylan. "Do you know what I think, Mr. Untermyer? I think you are trying to get your son nominated for Supreme Court Judge." (In fact, Untermyer's son, Irwin, was several years later elected to the state supreme court, largely as a result of the assistance he provided in the transit hearings.)

The next day, Hylan was back. He forced his way into the hearings shouting, "May I make a statement!"

Chairman Gilchrist began calling for the sergeant-at-arms. "You've had your opportunity," he said, banging his gavel.

"I have here the record showing the payment of fees by the IRT to this man!' yelled Hylan, pointing at Untermyer.

Unfortunately, there was no sergeant-at-arms. The attendant, one J. W. James, a much smaller man than the bulky ex-mayor, took one look at him and went in search of a policeman. For the next few minutes, Hylan continued shouting, claiming that Untermyer was in the pay of the traction interests. Finally, before any policeman appeared, he strode defiantly from the hearing room.

Tammany Grand Sachem John R. Voorhis, the old friend of Walker's father, celebrated his ninety-eighth birthday on July 27. He could remember New York as it had been in the 1840s, so simple and rustic that it seemed impossible it could have changed so radically in so short a time: then its residents felt they were in the country when they watered their horses at Corporal Thompson's Inn—near what is now Fifth Avenue and Thirtieth Street; Washington Square was Potter's Field; garbage disposal was handled by the pigs; the first six-story building was arousing controversy; and the gentry still walked to the other side of the street if they saw an actor coming. Voorhis' family had been New Yorkers since the 1660s; his relatively well-to-do parents gave him a private-school education, but young Voorhis enjoyed working with his hands. He went into carpentry and stair-building, and then into Tammany politics. As leader of the Ninth Ward, he left Tammany in 1871, after the scandals of the Tweed Ring, and formed what he called the "Voorhis Democracy"; his organization helped decide many a city election. In 1889, Richard Croker lured him back to the Tammany fold. Over more than half a century, under Mayors Havemeyer, Wickham, Cooper, Grace, Edson, Hewitt, Grant, Gilroy, Van Wyck, Low, McClellan, Hylan, and now Walker, Voorhis held the offices of excise commissioner, police commissioner, dock commissioner, police commissioner again, police justice, elections commissioner, superintendent of public buildings (replacing William H. Walker), and, since 1918, president of the board of elections. He avoided exercise, regarded Daylight Saving Time as a cruel deceit, ate but twice a day, and bemoaned the growing adulteration of decent whiskey. On his birthday, Voorhis arose at 5:20 A.M., had his usual substantial breakfast, leisurely read the newspapers, and arrived at the Municipal Building at about eleven. A steady stream of callers had already left messages of congratulations, and there was a heap of telegrams as well, from Governor Smith and others who could not drop by in person. Voorhis posed for photographers, cut a huge birthday cake, and was informed by Chief White Horse Eagle (the Osage warrior whose face was profiled on the buffalo nickel) that he had just been named an honorary Indian chief; he would be getting his war bonnet and full regalia within the week.

Asked who he considered the greatest living American, the Grand Sachem replied, "I am."

While Voorhis engaged in public tomfoolery, Walker pursued his private weaknesses, notably his romance with Betty Compton. Leaving a banquet at the Hotel Commodore in honor of Mrs. Hearst's Free Milk Fund for Babies, at which he had been the toastmaster, Walker offered the actress, who was one of the 3,000 guests, a crosstown ride in his official car. To get through the Times Square traffic, he had his driver use the limousine's siren. "I'm impressed," said Betty. A few days later, Walker arranged another meeting, at a quiet dinner party in Paul Block's suite at the Ritz-Carlton. All that early summer, Jim spent most of his free time with Betty. It was his first real infatuation since his relationship with showgirl Yvonne Shelton years before. But the romance was to be interrupted by the European trip that he and Allie, together with some friends, would shortly be taking.

The day after Voorhis' birthday, Walker finally persuaded the board of estimate to award bus contracts in Manhattan, Brooklyn, and Queens to the Equitable Coach Company. As we have seen, twelve of the sixteen votes were necessary to pass the resolution. Comtroller Berry was unalterably opposed to the award; thus far he had been backed by Brooklyn Borough President James J. Byrne, whose two votes added to Berry's three precluded passage. Walker, one vote short of his objective, went to work on Byrne. Just before a board meeting, the mayor delivered an ultimatum: he would take the stump in Brooklyn, he promised, and oust Byrne and McCooey from their jobs if they persisted in supporting the bid of a BMT subsidiary for a franchise in that borough. As a sweetener, Walker would see to it that Brooklyn was voted twenty-five miles of new subways, at a cost of some $150 million. (Bronx Boss Flynn had already been won over to Walker's side by being permitted a separate bus franchise; Aldermanic President McKee, a Bronx man, and Borough President Henry Bruckner were guided by Flynn's wishes.) Walker was most persuasive with Byrne.

When the board of estimate opened its afternoon session, the mayor jumped several times on the calendar and declared, "The Chair moves the adoption of No. 14. The Clerk will call the role."

Controller Berry not voting, thirteen votes for passage were quickly obtained. Walker then moved "the adoption of No. 39, so far as it refers to the Surface Transportation Company." A similar vote followed.

Few people in the audience at the hearing knew what was happening. Item No.14 contained a resolution awarding bus franchises in Manhattan (crosstown lines only), Brooklyn, and Queens to the Equitable. (As the price for his votes, Manhattan's Julius Miller had insisted that only crosstown lines, which would not be in competition with the subways, be established in his borough.) Item No. 39 awarded the Bronx franchise to Surface Transportation; later the Staten Island franchise was given to another favored applicant. It was a case of a little something for everybody.

"We object to this procedure—" one dazed bus competitor started to say, before he was gaveled down by the mayor.

"We have respectfully listened to you . . ." Walker intoned. "We refuse any longer to permit you to use this Board to get publicity for yourself."

When the bus man tried to speak again, the mayor ordered a policeman to silence him.

Twenty-four hours later, the Equitable group threw a party. The hosts included Frank R. Fageol of the Faegol Motor Company, Charles B. Rose, his vice-president, J. Allan Smith, his New York representative, and William O'Neil of General Tire & Rubber. Among the guests were the mayor and Senator Hastings. The following night, Walker saw O'Neil off for Europe, visiting him in his stateroom.

On August 9, the day before Walker officially signed the bus contract, Equitable's J. Allan Smith paid to the Equitable Trust Company $10,000 in cash for a letter of credit to be made out in the mayor's name. The next day, with the signing out of the way, a bank officer, escorted by Senator Hastings, delivered the letter personally to Walker at City Hall. That night the Walkers and their friends themselves sailed to Europe.

Testifying before Judge Seabury, Hastings would explain the apparent bribery thusly: he and Smith were close friends; they lunched together quite often at the Recess Club, where they had gotten to know Arthur Loasby, president of Equitable Trust. Smith knew that the Walkers and their friends were going to Europe and that they would be bringing a large sum of money with them to meet expenses. He told Hastings it would give him great prestige with Loasby if he could march into the bank and buy the mayor a letter of credit. Hastings, always willing to do a favor, arranged for Senator Bernard Downing, a member of Walker's party who was arranging the details of the trip, to temporarily turn over the group's funds to him.

"I got the $10,000 from Senator Downing," Hastings would testify.

"I gave it to Smith and Smith opened [the account] at the Equitable Trust and his prestige was advanced, he told me, as a result of it."

The mayor and his friends, while in Paris, spent $3,000 over the letter of credit. When the overdraft came in, Hastings said, Smith asked him to straighten out the matter with Senator Downing. Hastings evidently had some difficulty getting in touch with Downing, so he asked Smith to "pay the sum, and I would have it reimbursed when I got the money."

That was how it came to pass that J. Allan Smith, the representative of the Equitable Coach Company favored so fiercely by Walker for the past year and a half, paid for the Mayor's letter of credit and overdraft. It was, Hastings would testify in 1932, only an innocent transaction. By that time, Senator Downing, the only man who could have corroborated this account, had died.

Just before Walker left for Europe, two bomb explosions about 11:15 one night wrecked the Twenty-eighth Street subway stations. The greatest damage was done in the BMT stop on Broadway, where the men's washroom was demolished and the change booth hurled twelve feet, down onto the tracks. In the IRT station on Fourth Avenue, the force of the explosion buckled the sidewalk overhead. Scores of people were injured but, amazingly enough, only one man was killed.

The terrorism was caused by the furor over the imminent execution of Nicola Sacco and Bartolomeo Vanzetti, the two anarchists who had been convicted and sentenced to death in 1921 for the murder of a paymaster and a guard during a robbery in Braintree, Massachusetts. Great doubt existed even then as to the guilt of Sacco and Vanzetti. Many people thought they were being used as scapegoats, at a time when anyone who criticized the workings of the capitalistic system was thought to be evil incarnate. Various appeals held up the carrying out of the sentence for years, and the governor of Massachusetts even appointed a special committee to advise him on the matter. On August 3, 1927, a committee found that the original verdict had been correct, and a date was set for the execution. The decision set off a wave of violent protests throughout the northeast.

In New York, the motorman of an incoming train in the BMT stop managed to bring it to a halt before hitting the change booth on the tracks; the woman inside the booth suffered only minor lacerations. On the East Side, Thomas Buckley, the change agent there, had his booth blown to bits. "Suddenly everything went black," he said. "I did not hear the explosion and I did not see any flare-up. . . . I was on the floor when I came to my senses." Because it was late at night, few people were waiting on the platforms; otherwise the toll would have been dreadful.

Police Commissioner Warren, fearing more explosions, canceled all vacation leaves and put his men on stand-by alert. "All subway and elevated stations are to be guarded," he said. "Public buildings will also be guarded where it seems wise to do so."

Luckily, further violence in the city did not materialize. On August 22, while Walker was aboard, Sacco and Vanzetti were put to death.

~~~

If Walker's tour of Europe, in the late summer of 1927, did not establish him as an international celebrity, it at least stamped him as a spiffy dresser: he took along four dozen suits, a dozen ensembles of sports coats and striped white trousers, 100 ties, a half-dozen topcoats, morning coats, top hats—the list could go on and on. Lasting about nine weeks, the tour was crowded with as many lunches, receptions, and dinners as the human mentality could devise and the human stomach could endure. Besides Walker and Allie, the party consisted of Senator Bernard Downing, Tammany politicians Walter Herrick and William McCormack, and scroll-reader Hector Fuller; Miss Evelyn Wagner, the mayor's secretary and niece of Senator Robert F. Wagner, would join them in London. The group sailed on the Cunard Line's *Berengaria,* probably the most prestigious steamer of the 1920s. Originally a German ship called *Imperator,* it had been turned over to Cunard as part of the spoils after the war; the *Berengaria*'s first-class accommodations were so lavish that the bathrooms boasted marble walls. *Bon voyage* champagne parties lasted through the evening as dozens of prominent New Yorkers saw Walker off, with the ship not scheduled to leave its moorings until the fashionable hour of midnight. On the pier, the Police Glee Club, accompanied by the Firemen's Band, sang Irving Berlin's "Jimmie":

> Can't you hear those old New Yorkers hollering:
> Gimmie—gimmie—gimmie Jimmie for mine!

The next morning, Walker—wearing a blue blazer and white trousers, the wide brim of his hat tilted at a rakish angle—took the customary constitutional around the promenade deck. So many passengers came up to shake hands with him, however, that he was forced to discontinue the walks. Such popularity made it all but inevitable that Walker would be chosen auctioneer for the ship's pool; this was a post that required a man with great presence, a steady line of patter, and considerable wit. The auction pool, which at the time enjoyed a great vogue, was simply a field of consecutive numbers grouped around the ship's average daily run—about 600 miles in good weather. Passengers would pay a nominal fee for the numbers, assigned by lot, and later the numbers could be disposed of— and bid up—at auction, with half the proceeds going back in the pool. A persuasive auctioneer could increase the value of the pool many times over by encouraging bettors to trade numbers back and forth, as the excitement reached a peak just before the mileage was announced. With Walker officiating, the first day's pool of $1,500 was won by Robert C. Scripps of the Scripps-Howard newspaper chain, who later, as a gesture of appreciation, sent two cases of champagne to the mayor's suite. (One of the marvelous advantages of being at sea on a foreign liner, Americans discovered, was that they were freed from the restraints of Prohibition.)

During the voyage, Walker, the sponsor years before of legalized prize fighting, put on the gloves with George Mason, an English lightweight who was now the *Berengaria*'s gym instructor. (In 1924, Mason once had the honor of going a few rounds with the Prince of Wales, who was aboard the ship incognito; that evening Mason solemnly mounted the royal gloves, crossed at the proper angle, on the gym wall.) Walker's boxing experience was less dignified. When he sent out a straight left to Mason's nose that brought tears to his eyes, the instructor instinctively retaliated with a hard left to the stomach that brought Walker to his knees and the bout to a halt.

One evening the mayor hosted a party in a private dining room in honor of Senator Downing's birthday. There was much sentimentalizing and speechifying, and not much attention was paid to the hour. "I am crossing the ocean tonight in the Imperial suite of this wonderful ship," Walker declared, "but I can't help but remember that there was a man, my father, who crossed this ocean with a coil of rope for his pillow, and how he would rejoice tonight were he alive to do honor to you, Senator Downing." Finally, the group moved on to the *Berengaria*'s smoking room, where they found most of the first-class passengers impatiently awaiting their arrival. The mayor and Hector Fuller, it seemed, were sharing the auctioneering duties that night, and while they had forgotten the event, the other passengers had not; they wanted the betting to begin. As Walker entered the room, an upper-class English voice enunciated distinctly:

"I don't quite see why we should all be kept waiting here until nearly eleven o'clock. I, for one, am not in the habit of waiting on the pleasures of Lord Mayors." Taking the floor, Walker defended his tardiness by saying, "I had no idea that this auction was conducted on stock-exchange principles. I thought it was merely a recreation among gentlemen."

On deck the next day, Walker and the Englishman he had offended, a wealthy importer named C. Peto Bennett, made their peace. Such was the mayor's charm that Bennett insisted that Walker and his party visit his home ("the finest roses in England") on their way from Southampton to London. As the *Berengaria* pulled into Southampton, a fleet of huge Daimlers summoned by the importer waited at the dock. After a brief stop at the Englishman's manor house, where Allie was laden down with hundreds of long-stemmed roses, the Daimlers sped Walker's party on to its destination.

In London, Walker and his friends stayed at the Mayfair; he and Allie saw a musical called *Lady Luck,* then went on to a late supper at the Café de Paris off Leicester Square, where the mayor provided the piano accompaniment as Miss Aileen Stanley, an American entertainer, sang, "Will You Love Me in December as You Do in May?" At a press conference the next day, Walker outlined his difficulties in getting buses on the streets of New York; while he was in London, he said straight-facedly, he hoped "to see a good deal more of London buses," with an eye toward learning more about successful bus operations in general. A tour of the city's public buildings and monuments followed—with Walker, chatting amiably all the while, visiting the Lord Mayor's residence, the Guild Hall, and Trafalgar Square. The British newsmen were impressed. "He is a mayor of the type not often seen in this country," one wrote. "He shows it is possible to sleep until midday and still retain a reputation for hustling."

Dublin was next on the Walker itinerary, and there he was greeted at a formal dinner by President of the Irish Free State, William T. Cosgrove. Afterward a ball was held in the mayor's honor at the Gresham. The high spot of his trip to Ireland, however, was his visit to Castlecomer, the village in County Kilkenny his father had left when emigrating to America in 1857. Several of Walker's cousins still lived in Castlecomer, and together with all the country people from miles around they were there to welcome him when he stepped from his limousine. "Three cheers for William Henry Walker's boy!" someone yelled, and the crowd responded lustily. Walker, standing on a kitchen chair produced for the occasion, declaimed "Mine own people! To have looked into the eyes of villagers who knew my dear father, to stand in their hearts as a symbol of that great opportunity that America offers!"

Back briefly in London, Walker acted like an ordinary tourist. While Allie and Evelyn Wagner went shopping, he went to see the Tower of London. "I'd like to see this working," he said to the Beef-Eater, indicating the beheading block frequented by Henry VIII's wives. "I wonder if you can arrange it." The Beef-Eater was not amused. "I don't think it will be possible today, sir," he said. The Cheshire Cheese for lunch, the Royal Box at the greyhound races—the hours passed quickly. All too soon, Walker and his party crossed the Channel on their way to Germany.

In Berlin, the American ambassador warned Walker that he might expect communist demonstrations, as a result of discontent with American handling of the Sacco-Vanzetti case. The mayor, assigned a German policeman for protection, made light of the matter. "I'm so thin nobody could hit me anyway," he joked, patting his guardian on the shoulder.

By train the mayor proceeded to Baden-Baden, the celebrated spa whose mineral waters had rejuvenated the livers or at least the psyches of countless true believers. There Walker drank, but not deeply, at the Trinkhalle, while pretty girls served up the bitter waters. He spend most of his time dining and dancing at the resort hotels, and at the race track, where he helped King Gustav of Sweden handicap a few races. At one formal dinner, his American host remarked that Walker had been so well received abroad he should turn his thoughts to the presidency. "Don't you think I have enough trouble as it is?" the mayor rejoined. After a few days, Walker and his party drove on to Munich, where they were guests of the Burgomeister at Hofbrau Haus, the famous beer hall. He also inspected the wine cellars under the Rathaus, or City Hall; many of the casks bore wooden carvings depicting past burgomeisters, each holding a well-filled cup. "There are some things about civic government we might well learn from Bavaria," Walker said. After strolling through the city, he turned serious. "I am amazed at the cleanliness of Munich's streets," he said. "I understand that there are stringent laws against littering [them] with trash. We have such laws in New York, but what we seem to lack, and that is probably due to the various nationalities that make up our citizenship, is civic pride."

The combination of Walker's absence and the humid summer weather made for little news from City Hall, most of whose functionaries had fled for relief to Breezy Point or the Rockaways. Perhaps the best story involved the police department. Commissioner

Warren, noting that three patrolmen (two of them Irish) were brought up on charges stemming from drunkenness during one forty-eight-hour period in August, huffed that he was personally cracking down on police boozing.

Dewey Hock of the East One Hundred Tenth Street Station, one of a group of policemen busily celebrating the promotion of their captain, Vincent J. Sweeney, to the rank of deputy inspector, had been the first culprit. Hock's joyous mood allegedly took the form of firing five shots in the air near the precinct house. One of the bullets entered a living room window, where it nicked a chandelier, broke some plaster, and sent the elderly female occupant down to Warren's office to render her complaint in person. In the second instance, Patrolman Leonard C. Tobin, in civilian clothes and admittedly drunk, was accused of trying to rob a man and wife at pistol-point while they were sitting in their car at Twelfth Avenue and Fifty-ninth Street. A fellow policeman overpowered Tobin after a struggle and locked him in his own precinct house. The last officer to be arraigned was a bleary-eyed John Condon. Out of uniform, Condon had been observed by a foot patrolman carrying a bulky object from a store on Horatio Street to a waiting automobile. Before the officer could investigate, the car sped away; when he reached the store, he found it had been burglarized. A few hours later, he noticed the same car, with a cash register in the back seat, parked in front of a bar on Ninth Avenue. Deductions were swiftly made. Condon, who had stopped off for a few nightcaps, was arrested when he returned to the auto.

None of the suspended policemen had a clean record. Hock, the fast gun, had previously been reprimanded for failing to report another officer's suicide. Tobin, the would-be Jesse James, and Condon, the cash-register specialist, had already earned twenty complaints between them.

Now the mayor and his party were in Italy, where they stopped first in Venice, planning to sun and swim at the Lido, on the shores of the Adriatic. Here Walker temporarily lost track of his luggage. Meeting a fellow New Yorker who was a habitué of the Lido and was wearing, in early afternoon, bright silk pajamas, the mayor was told not to worry. "Everybody here does it, Mr. Mayor," said his informant, referring to the pajama-wearing. "No one dresses until evening, many of them not even then."

"How do you know whether people are just going to bed or just getting up?" said Walker.

"This is one place nobody cares."

Oddly enough, the "Night Mayor" of New York thought the pajamas undignified and would not wear them in public. Not so the other members of his party, who bought several pajama suits in startling blues and golds and reds and, even after their baggage arrived, continued to wear them. Hector Fuller, for instance, wore his pajamas to the beach, over his bathing suit. But Walker remained true to his blazers and white trousers; he did not put on a bathing suit either. "I hate to swim," he said. The truth is, he was self-conscious about his spindly legs.

St. Mark's, with its Byzantine architecture, the gondolas on the Grand Canal, the Palace of the Doges—the mayor enjoyed all the sights. At a farewell luncheon in his honor, a Venetian host gave him the supreme accolade, if we remember that Mussolini had just come to power in Italy. "I am quite sure that you, Mr. Mayor," he said, "are all that a typical Fascist should be."

In Rome, the mayor's party met with Monsignor Joseph Breslin, vice rector of the American College in the Vatican, who had formerly been a curate of St. Joseph's, the church where Jim grew up and where he and Allie had been married. Monsignor Breslin was arranging a private audience for them with Pope Pius XI. When the day arrived, all went smoothly. Preceded by helmeted, pantalooned, pike-bearing Swiss Guards, scarlet-clad "Sedari" (the bearers of the Papal Sedan Chair), and Noble Guards in full-dress uniform with bearskin busbys, Walker and his party passed through one ornate anteroom after another. Pius XI, clad entirely in white and wearing a bejeweled cross on a gold chain, received them in his chambers. At the end of the audience, Pius presented the mayor with a gold medal bearing the Papal likeness, Allie with a gold rosary.

From their suite at the Excelsior, the group ventured forth to see Rome—the ancient aqueducts, the Colosseum, the Fontani di Trevi, St. Peter's Basilica. Nights found them in cabarets, where the sophisticated patrons took a worldly view of what Americans in the 1920s considered shocking behavior. In one cabaret, for instance, Walker and his friends noticed two white women dancing with black men; the mayor's party quickly took its leave.

Before departing from Rome, Walker had a second audience with a world-famous leader; this time it was Mussolini. "Come, let us talk together!" Il Duce said to Walker in English, leading him into his private office. For the next forty-six minutes, the two men conversed alone. Walker was impressed with Mussolini's knowledge of New York and its large Italian population. "My own home in Greenwich Village," he told Il Duce, "is almost surrounded by Italians, who through hard work have risen high in the social scale." Motion-picture taking followed. Mussolini himself directed the setting up of the cameras and lights, telling everybody where to stand. "It is evident that even in little things he is determined to be the boss," said Hector Fuller admiringly.

The fascist leader liked Walker, whom he found "young, not only in appearance, but also in spirit . . . a man of great talent, an idealist yet practical. . . . He is highly fit to govern the great metropolis where millions of Italians live." Walker voiced his feelings about Mussolini more casually. "It's from the chin up that he has got it," he said. "You don't notice the rest of him.

Walker left Rome in an overnight sleeper, bound by express train for Paris. "Did you enjoy crossing the Alps?" he was asked when he arrived at the Gare de Lyon. "To tell the truth, I never really noticed them," he said, alluding to the comfort of the train. The Parisians were appreciative of the mayor's clothes. "His blue shirt might have inspired a poet to an ode," one reporter rhapsodized. Said another journalist: "One of the important reasons for liking him is that he is such a sworn foe of the dry regime. Could such a lovable man refuse the cheer of good wine?" After checking in at the Crillon, Walker tried to sort out his speaking engagements. In view of the lavish meals he was encountering on the trip, he worried aloud about putting on weight: "I'll have to be careful about my diet, you know, or when I get back I'll be better fitted for an aldermanic job." That evening the mayor, together with many New York cronies who happened to be in Paris, explored the uninhibited cafés of Montmarte.

The next day—in top hat, morning coat, wing collar, gray tie, spats, and black shoes—Walker laid a bronze wreath at the Tomb of the Unknown Soldier. A half-hour late for the ceremony, he remained blasé. "Paris is a wonderful place," he said; "no one seems to mind when you come, so long as you come." Afterward he was the luncheon guest of the Anglo-American Press Association at fashionable Drouant, where he was introduced by the reporters' bearded president, who jokingly chided him for his habitual tardiness. "I've heard," Walker replied gracefully, "that all human sins may be condoned, even that of being late. But as for whiskers, that's a man's own fault." In his talk, the mayor mentioned that 30,000 members of the American Legion would within a few hours be holding their annual convention in Paris. He used their coming to decry those Americans who lived abroad and apologized for their country's supposed materialism. "My country wants nothing but to be of service," he said. "I hope that the 30,000 American boys who are making a pilgrimage to France will instill a new pride of country in the hearts of these lukewarm Americans. . . . We want no apologies for our country. New York will not tolerate it. For ours is a city that has been the gateway to America—giving everyone opportunity, asking in return only character, integrity, industry, willingness to work." The luncheon lasted the whole afternoon, with the mayor ending up at the piano, playing his favorite tunes. That night he went to a boxing match, where he watched Spider Pladner, a French flyweight, take a disputed decision from Frankie Ash, an Englishman; and once again, he journeyed to Montmartre.

On succeeding days, the hectic socializing continued. He visited the mother of Charles Nungesser, the aviator who had recently disappeared while attempting to fly the Atlantic, presenting her with a check for one million francs, the proceeds of a New York benefit performance at the Roxy Theater. He was received at Hotel de Ville, the Parisian City Hall, an honor previously bestowed on Woodrow Wilson, General John J. Pershing, and Charles Lindbergh. At the Invalides, the sight of the many crippled veterans affected Walker greatly. "As I stand here in your presence and see your patience and your superb bravery," he said, "I am more convinced than ever that there is a God." Meeting Marshal Ferdinand Foch, who in World War I had commanded the combined armies of France, England, and America, he impetuously urged, "Marshal, fight like hell for universal peace!" On Sunday, along with thousands of French and American veterans, the mayor went to Notre Dame, where the Archbishop of Paris celebrated a special mass to welcome the Legionnaires back to France. Twenty-four hours later, Walker stood on the reviewing stand as the American Legion staged its dramatic parade, around the Place de l'Etoile, under the Arc de Triomphe, down the Champs Elysée to the Place de la Concorde. He was repeatedly cheered by the marching men, who recognized him immediately. When the New York delegation passed, it burst into "East Side, West Side, All Around the Town." Confessed Walker afterward: "I got forty-eight thrills in less than an hour as the forty-eight banners of the States marched by."

The mayor and his party returned to New York on the newly launched *Ile de France;* with its ultra-modern interiors, all stark and sleek and hopelessly rectangular, it would soon become the most popular liner of the late 1920s. Once again, he was chosen the auctioneer for the ship's pool. He also presided on Concert Night, another traditional passenger entertainment; on this voyage of the *Ile* it featured the performances of such travelers as the Metropolitan Opera's Anna Case, accompanied by the New York Symphony Orchestra's Walter Damrosch. Walker was relaxed and happy. To make his mood complete, he learned by ship's radio that his fellow Greenwich Villager, heavyweight champion Gene Tunney, had beaten Dempsey in their rematch: a knockout in the tenth round. The mayor's trip had, of course, been a comic opera of sorts. But it was not so very different from the Grand Tour taken by countless well-to-do Americans during the brash, optimistic decade we call the Roaring Twenties. Walker radiated this optimism. "I feel myself enormously benefited by the insight into foreign municipal processes," he reflected about the trip. "London with its fine old traditions and courtesy; Dublin with its progressive spirit; Berlin with its spick-and-span cleanliness; Rome with its modern vitality and ancient loveliness; Paris with its cultural eminence—to visit these cities has been a privilege and a pleasure." Allowing for the hyperbole, we must admit the man enjoyed himself.

≈≈≈

On Walker's return to New York, and all during October, the transit wars flared anew. He continued to hear objections to the Equitable Coach award, and it required all his glibness to silence his critics. At a board of estimate meeting, the mayor quickly cut off the counsel for a bus competitor, who said he had not been given the opportunity to speak at the July board session.

"The time of this Board cannot be taken up with such facetious objections," Walker said. "It is too bad that such nonsense can delay several of the boys here who want to go to the game this afternoon." (He was referring to a World Series game scheduled between the New York Yankees and the Pittsburgh Pirates.)

Stewart Browne of the Real Estate Owners' Association then tried to speak; Browne, slightly deaf, was usually permitted to stand at the railing enclosing the board, quite close to its members. Walker resolved this problem of proximity by having two policemen escort him away from the rail and back to a seat.

A second bus competitor then shouted that he, too, had been ignored at the July session.

"Ignored you, did I?" said the mayor. "I've worn out eight tonsils on you. Go on up and root for the Yanks." And with that he took his own advice, going up to the Stadium to see the game.

So far as the subways were concerned, Charles E. Smith, Controller Berry's transit advisor, came out for a seven-cent fare. And while Berry disclaimed responsibility for Smith's report and for its publication, he declined to state whether he thought the fare should be held at a nickel. Both Samuel Untermyer, the transit commission's counsel, and James H. Delaney, chairman of the board of transportation, declared that Smith's conclusions were based on false premises and were, according to Delaney, "a rehash of the arguments presented by the opponents of Mayor Walker, whom the people elected by something like a 500,000 plurality."

While making a subway inspection in Brooklyn, Walker was asked whether he would change his mind about raising the fare. "Even if there were an eight-cent, ten-cent, or fifty-cent fare there could be no better service as long as no more trains can be operated on the existing lines during rush hours," he replied. "I am still standing where I have always stood. Five cents is enough."

A week later, when the board tentatively approved an unprecedented $524,922,000 budget for 1928, some $50 million more than the current year's, there were acrimonious exchanges between the mayor, Controller Berry, and Aldermanic President McKee. The first budget "proposed for adoption" by Walker was for $517,922,000, and McKee supported the measure, with the proviso that the budget be rescrutinized before final adoption, with an eye toward avoiding a real estate tax boost.

"The Chair concurs," said Walker, "We have eleven days in which such action may be taken."

"I shall have to vote no on that motion," said Berry.

"I can't see why the burden should be passed on to us," complained McKee, objecting to the controller's holier-than-thou attitude.

"Suppose you specify, then," said Walker to Berry, "just what items you prefer to have omitted."

"I would leave out of it, first of all, the $20,210,000 allotted to the transportation board for subway construction," said Berry.

"Is this the only objection you find to the budget?" Walker asked.

"No, I think there are some things that should be put into the budget as well as taken out," said Berry.

"What items would you like to have added?"

"I should add $4 million for snow removal during the coming winter, $2,200,000 to anticipate judgments and claims that will be entered against the city, and $800,000 to meet the expenses of the transit commission."

"All right," Walker said, "let's make it a 100 percent honest budget. To that end I now ask the unanimous consent of the board to substitute the motion that the budget as proposed for adoption be fixed not at $517,922,000 but at $524,922,000, and that there be included in it [the items] suggested by the Controller."

"This budget," said Berry, "is more or less an imposition on the taxpayer."

"I feel no fear in spending the taxpayer's money," retorted Walker, "as long as they get 100 per cent service for every dollar spent."

"I certainly will never vote for a $525 million budget," said Berry somewhat illogically, in view of his previous complaints.

"But I have included the very items which you have enumerated. . . ." protested Walker. "Besides, we have eleven days in which we may take out some items or replace them."

"After all, this is our budget," interjected McKee. "It represents the legitimate cost of government."

"I'm casting my three votes for this motion," said Walker.

After Berry voted "no," McKee voted "yes," re-emphasizing that the final budget should be cut in some way so that it did not radically affect the tax rate.

"With that understood," McKee said to the mayor, "I vote with you. . . . I do not think that any one member of the board should say to the rest of us, 'Not for me!'"

All the borough presidents went along with Walker, too; the motion passed easily, only nine votes being needed.

Because of his European trip, Walker had missed the New York opening of the 1927 Ziegfeld Follies. Now he visited the revue to see himself impersonated by the bug-eyed Eddie Cantor, handing out keys to the city to Gertrude Ederle, Lindbergh, and anyone else who showed the remotest interest in acquiring one. Finally the on-stage "Jimmy" stopped, not because he was exhausted, but because he had run out of keys. Walker was delighted with the burlesque, and he had even had a hand in it. "Before the show opened," Cantor recalled, "Jimmy took me to his tailor, a little fellow on Fifth Avenue, who made me a morning suit exactly like Jimmy's, and I dropped in at the Knox Hat Store for a high silk hat." The mayor liked the show so much, Cantor added, that he came back often. "One night I introduced him to the audience," the comedian said, "and gave *him* a key—to my dressing room. He made a speech from his seat in the first row. He ad libbed and we started to kid around . . ." To Cantor, Walker "was a combination of George M. Cohan, James Cagney, and John Barrymore. He was the best off-the-cuff speaker I'd ever heard. . . ."

The current Follies was the finest in years. It was the first one whose songs were written by a single man—Irving Berlin, and the first one with a single star—Cantor. The comedian stayed on-stage —strutting, singing, and doing his inimitable double-takes—for two hours of the show's two-and-a-half-hour duration. When not impersonating Walker, he appeared as a brassy petshop owner selling a spavined dog to an unwary customer, a timid beau being violated in a taxi by his girl friend and, of course, in the blackface and white gloves he had helped to popularize. Among the Berlin songs delivered by Cantor were "You Gotta Have It," "Learn to Sing a Love Song," and "It All Belongs to Me." The strain of being on-stage so long was debilitating, and the comedian had agreed to it only because he wanted to free himself from a long-term Ziegfeld contract. "I lost a year from the contract and five years from my life," Cantor quipped. (Indeed, before the show's run was finished, he came down with pleurisy.) Besides Cantor, the Follies, which cost almost $300,000 to produce, boasted some interesting special effects. In one spectacle, "It's Up to the Band," ninety girls in white dresses played white pianos and white kazoos. In another scene, "Jungle Jingle," an actress rode across the stage on a live ostrich.

Florenz Ziegfeld had become internationally famous for his glorification of the American showgirl. He got the idea of putting phalanxes of regal-looking, gloriously unclad women on stage from his first wife, Anna Held, a French chanteuse ("Won't you Come and Play wiz Me?") so popular in the United States during the first decade of the 1900s that a cigar was named in her honor. Before Ziegfeld's first Follies in 1907, showgirls earned no more than thirty dollars a week; when Flo burst into full producing bloom, he paid even the least of his creatures hundreds of dollars weekly, and threw in the services of personal maids as well. (Delores, his highest-salaried creation, earned $650 a week.) There was method in this showmanship: Ziegfeld well knew that his shapely, well-publicized hirelings all but guaranteed the enthusiastic patronage of every New York man-about-town. Stage-door Johnnies may have waited in the wings, but they also bought plenty of tickets for themselves and their friends. "The Follies' opening night became a national event," Eddie Cantor later explained. "Girls from every part of the country stood backstage. The dressing rooms were filled with so many stars the skies looked deserted. Forty-second Street was a bobbing black sea of high-powered imported cars. The lobby of the New Amsterdam Theater glittered with aristocracy—the Stotesburys and Huttons, Replogles and Cosdens, Whitneys and Astors rubbing silk hats and ermine wraps in a dignified but eager scramble to see and be seen."

Walker enjoyed everything about Broadway, but he particularly reveled in the Follies; along with everyone else, he wondered who Ziegfeld's new girls would be. And the producer seldom disappointed. "With his telegram pad in one hand and his telephone in the other, he kept the wires sizzling to make the world safe for beauty," Cantor said, describing Ziegfeld's work habits. "He would get up at six in the morning, take the telephone into his bed and start calling up his press agents, managers, actors and authors—who had probably gone to sleep an hour before. . . . He wanted an Indian scene rewritten so he could bring out his girls in crowns of feathers four yards long. . . . He had seen a picture of a girl's legs in the papers and wanted her traced. . . . He had just learned that Earl Carroll was made a judge in the beauty contest at Atlantic City and took it as a personal affront." In all his Follies and in such musicals as *Whoopee, Show Boat,* and *Rio Rita,* the producer with manic determination mixed pink skin with white satin, pampering his girls and trumpeting their pulchritude.

By now Walker had resumed his affair with Betty Compton, who with her innocent eyes and splendid legs might have been a Follies girl herself. The brown-eyed dancer, twenty-three years his junior, was spontaneous and uninhibited, and she ideally complemented Jim's personality; both of them lived for the moment, and the moment had to be gay. But Betty could turn moody—suddenly and, to Walker's way of thinking, without provocation. Already she was balking at the various subterfuges that he used to conceal their intimacy. With his days largely taken up by the commonplaces of life at St. Luke's Place and his mayoral duties, the evenings were almost the only time they could meet. And though Walker stayed up often and late, he usually first officiated at semipublic fetes and banquets, only afterward going to private parties. What this meant was that Betty and he were rarely together for more than a few hours at a time, at various trysting places. It was an awkward situation, and it annoyed the actress. She told Jim she wanted him to leave Allie and his St. Luke's Place home so she could see more of him. Walker procrastinated. He was not yet ready for this step.

In her professional life, Betty was more successful at having her way. George Gershwin, who had written the music for *Oh, Kay!,* was about to open a new show, *Funny Face,* at the Alvin on West Fifty-second Street, and she would be cast in a featured role. The show, almost without plot, was noteworthy for its songs. Its star was Fred Astaire, who played the thirty-two-year-old guardian of four young girls—all avid for romance. His sister Adele would be one of the girls and Betty would be another, singing and dancing to "Birthday Party," "What Am I Going to Do?" and "Blue Hullabaloo." The show would be a hit, and she would stay in it for almost a year. Said one critic about Betty's spirited performance: "It is a tribute to her that the part does not pale—it is not due to her lines."

In the state-wide elections that November, the mayor won another transit victory; the voters passed the constitutional amendment, strongly supported by Governor Smith, that would permit the city to borrow $300 million outside its debt limit for new subway construction. A 400,000 majority in the city for the amendment overcame resistance upstate by a 2-to-1 margin. "Now we can keep our pledge to complete the new subway routes," Walker commented.

Almost all Tammany and organization candidates were swept into office handily. One of the few Republicans who ran successfully for office in the city was Ruth T. Pratt, who was re-elected to the Board of Aldermen; indeed, Mrs. Pratt, whose Madison Avenue clubhouse put her in the heart of the Republican "silk-stocking" district, had been New York's first, and was now its only, woman alderman. The mother of five children, she was an outspoken critic of Tammany chicanery who never lost her dignity—not even in the Breughel-like atmosphere of the aldermanic chamber. Shortly after her re-election, however, she became outraged upon learning that Peter J. McGuinness, chairman of the Aldermanic Seating Committee, was planning to scatter the Republican minority (seven members out of some sixty-five) in widely separated seats about the chamber, so as to hinder what little effectiveness it enjoyed. President McKee, who had not been in the city when the plot was devised by McGuinness, smilingly assured Mrs. Pratt that Republican solidarity would be preserved. As for McGuinness, he was merely having a bit of fun. Over the years he had come to value the Republican lady highly. When Mrs. Pratt later left the board (to go to Congress), he eulogized her in the chamber thusly: "Ruth, when you go down to Washington you want to take along that beautiful fur coat that your dear husband gave you. . . . The people there are cold as ice. Why you know yourself, Ruth, that here in the Board of Aldermen . . . there isn't a single man who if you were cold and unhappy wouldn't put his arms around you and hug you and make you feel good. But you'll never in your life find such loving hearts in Washington. So you'll sure need that coat, Ruthie me darling."

Elected to the board of aldermen in 1927, too, was Republican George U. Harvey of Queens, who even then was launching what would become known as the Great Sewer Scandal.

Maurice E. Connolly had been borough president of Queens since 1911; on a $15,000 annual salary, he maintained an $80,000 home, rode in chauffeured limousines, and thought nothing of putting down $146,000 in cash to make a real estate purchase. He had often been investigated on graft charges during his sixteen years in office, but nothing illegal had ever been proved. Now Connolly was becoming enmeshed in a scandal involving the heavy-handed assessment of $16 million from the borough's taxpayers for forty miles of new sewers.

It was not that Queens had no experience with corrupt political figures. Connolly's predecessor as borough president, Lawrence Gresser, had been indicted for allowing false claims by contractors against the city; subsequently he was removed from office by the governor. Gresser, in turn, had succeeded Joseph Bermel, who in 1907 had sold the city eighty-seven acres of swampland for a quarter of a million dollars ("I will make Queens blossom like a rose") and shortly thereafter resigned and sailed to Europe ("to take the baths at Carlsbad because of my health"). Bermel's predecessor, Joe Cassidy, who managed to amass a half-million-dollar fortune in two years on a $5,000 annual salary, went to Sing Sing for selling a judgeship for a paltry $10,000. And even before Queens was incorporated as part of New York, there had been Patrick ("Battle-Axe") Gleason, the last mayor of Long Island City. Gleason, who acquired his nickname as a result of his politeness in requesting plunder, fell from a ferry boat into the East River one dark night. Since the whereabouts of his loot, stashed in cash in nooks, crannies, and holes in the ground, could have been found only by reading an indecipherable code in the deceased's papers, the money presumably is still moldering.

In 1927 Queens was the city's fastest-growing borough; its population of 800,000 had increased tenfold over the last three decades. Most of its residents were of modest means. They earned an average yearly wage of $1,275—the lowest in the five boroughs—and lived in small homes, worth no more than $7,500, in unimproved neighborhoods. All through the 1920s they had suffered unusual tax assessments. Now the bills for new sewers became staggering. Mrs. Mary Brennan, a widow, was confronted with a $5,000 demand; Carmine Scocca, a laborer who earned thirty-two dollars weekly, was assessed $700; Jacob Gescheidt, a new homeowner, received a sewer bill for $1,645. Queens had long endured corruption, but these levies were too much for even its most patient residents. A group of taxpayers hired Harry H. Klein, an aggressive attorney, to represent them at public hearings at the board of assessors, and their protests encouraged some contractors (who were *not* building the sewers) to declare they could do the work for a third of the price. It was Alderman-Elect Harvey, however, who took up the cause politically, asking Governor Smith to investigate conditions in Queens. Harvey himself had been assessed $550 on his home and fifty-foot lot, and the experience brought on some analytical thinking. "The man across the road," he pondered, "must pay as much for the same piece of sewer . . . and people behind us for a mile back must pay [as much]. . . . At the rate charged against me, that one stretch would alone yield a lucrative amount of graft."

At various hearings, attorney Klein brought out the fact that James Rice, the sixty-seven-year-old, $7,250-a-year "chief engineer" for the sewer project was "utterly unfit and incompetent. . . . He has been carried along for twelve years as a dummy and rubber stamp." Rice himself admitted that he was looking for "anything I could get in an engineering way" when he met Connolly in 1915; he was so eager for work that he blindly followed all the borough president's directives regarding the sewer network. The most important of these suggestions was that Rice specify that only a special lockjoint pipe be used in Queens sewers. Though this type of pipe was not much different from others that could do the job, it had been patented and therefore could be bought only from the company owning the patent. The man representing this concern was John M. Phillips, who shared his profits with Connolly. "Contractors can do the work only if they get the pipe from Phillips," said Klein. "They must pay him whatever he asks. Then they pass this little saving on to the people of Queens."

Jack Phillips lived on an even grander scale than Connolly. The "Pipe King," as he was called, kept up a $150,000 home in Freeport, Long Island, maintained a racing stable and several Pierce-Arrows, and dined off a $200,000 gold dinner service presented him by dutiful contractors. His neighbors considered him a splendid fellow.

If Connolly was experienced at municipal theft, Phillips was a master; his skills had been honed to a fine edge by years of relentless skulduggery. In 1911, as a simple ward-heeler, he had been involved in the scandal that cost Lawrence Gresser, Connolly's predecessor, his job. For years, Phillips had been sending in bills to the city for repairing perfectly good pipe; then he charged some $400 for work another plumber had been paid $115 for, and had actually done; at a loss to explain the misunderstanding, he was indicted for grand larceny, but the charge was later dropped. In 1915, as a city purchasing agent, Phillips plied an insane asylum with so much rotten beef that he was fired. His ascent into the headier regions of embezzlement began in 1918, when he obtained the Queens franchise to sell the lockjoint pipe. Shortly thereafter, he convinced Connolly of the wisdom of working wrench-in-glove.

Though the borough president had not yet been formally named in the sewer charges, he was beginning to feel beleaguered. "No contractor need buy sewer pipe from Phillips nor from anyone else if he does not care to do so," Connolly protested. "He can even make the pipe himself in conformity with our specifications if he wants to. . . ." Then the borough president went on the attack, questioning the motives of attorney Klein in representing the taxpayers. "Often, in order to secure retainers," he said, "lawyers misrepresent the facts to prospective clients." Klein immediately hit back. He said he would prove that of the $93-per-linear-foot cost of the Jamaica sewer, thirteen dollars was labor, leaving eighty dollars for material—and that five dollars was the actual cost of the material used. This left unexplained the seventy-five dollar excess. Declared Alderman-Elect Harvey: "Phillips is the most feared man in Queens. We must be on the right track or he would not be lying low, afraid to come forward and defend himself." At first nobody knew Phillips' whereabouts; in Freeport, his Japanese houseboy announced to callers the master was not at home; later it developed the Pipe King had gone to Atlantic City; there, outside of New York's jurisdiction, he was immune to subpoena.

On a personal level, Walker's attitude amid this travail was almost gleeful. He was no friend of Connolly's, who had been a Hylan supporter and had carried his fiefdom for Red Mike in the 1925 primary. Tammany had long been resentful of Connolly's domination of his borough; the man who succeeded him, the leaders felt, might be more amenable to working with his colleagues in Manhattan. And so, temporarily, matters rested. With Connolly seeking to delay the sewer investigation, Phillips in seclusion, and Walker enjoying the show.

In late December, Samuel Untermyer continued his jousting with the subway interests. Seeking to force the IRT to buy 432 new cars, the transit commission counsel insisted at public hearings that subway crowding was approaching the danger point.

An engineer testifying for the IRT placed the "upper limit of comfort" for passengers at 162 persons a car, with 44 sitting and 118 standing. Untermyer asked if this situation did not present a difficulty for older people, women, and children, and for those in ill health and of fragile physique.

"Fragile people have no business riding during the rush hours," the engineer sternly replied.

"What are you going to do with the estimated increase of 141,-000,000 passengers a year by June, 1930?" said Untermyer.

"They'll find places somehow," said the IRT man. He went on to state the average number of passengers per car during the day now was only twenty-two on local trains and forty-four on express trains.

"Don't you know that's perfectly absurd?" said Untermyer.

"You don't ride on the Brooklyn cars," said Charles C. Lockwood, a member of the transit commission, to the witness. "I do."

"Why don't you run more cars?" asked Untermyer.

"Except during rush hours, passengers get a fair chance for seats," the engineer retorted.

"A fair fighting chance," said Untermyer with heavy irony.

"Some passengers generally prefer to stand," said the witness.

At the same hearings, Health Commissioner Louis I. Harris came out for new cars, saying that respiratory infections spread and worsened in subway crowding.

"Personal experiences that I have gone through," testified Harris, "make me feel that [the subways] have become intolerable. One does not have to be fragile . . . to realize that such travel is an ordeal that requires unusual powers of resistance." Explained the commissioner, who was below average in height: "A short person suffers particularly. It is impossible to breathe with a solid mass of humanity packed around you. I speak rather feelingly."

So the year came to a close, at the great feast that was New York in the 1920s, with municipal thieves and civic leaders sitting side by side at the banquet table—each striving for the self-improvement he most desired.

After much eating and drinking, the heroes of Ulster sprang up from Bricrui's table to exhibit their strength. Loegaire and Conall each pushed away a wall, and Cu Chulainn lifted an entire corner of the palace—so he and his wife could see the stars from their bed. All present murmured wonderingly at this, and there was general agreement that Cu Chulainn should have the champion's portion. But Loegaire and Conall disagreed.

Later, Loegaire was traveling in his chariot when a dark, heavy mist overtook him. As soon as he stopped, he was challenged by a giant—carrying a club as big as the wheel-shaft of a mill—who thrashed him so soundly that he fled, leaving behind his horses and chariot. In like manner, Conall met up with the giant, received a similar beating, and fled as Loegaire had done.

When Cu Chulainn encountered the giant, the outcome was far different. It was he who set upon the tormentor of the heroes of Ulster, and he who pummelled the giant with his own huge club, until there was no fight left in the evil fellow, who ran from the field in his tattered brogues, crying all the while for mercy.

"Thine is the champion's portion," said Bricriu to Cu Chulainn when he heard of these feats.

"Not true, Bricriu," said Loegaire and Conall. "We know his friends from the fairy world are helping Cu Chulainn in these heroics. We shall not forfeit our claim to the champion's portion."

*So the men of Ulster were not yet able to effect a settlement
and choose a leader. . . .*

January was a time of doldrums. Walker's municipal activities, while
the sewer scandal developed, were for the most part humdrum, the
sole exception being his appointment of a new press secretary,
Charles S. Hand, the newspaperman who had reported Smith's rout
of Hearst at the 1922 Democratic State Convention for the New York
World. To relieve the tedium, the mayor arranged a boxing match
with band leader Paul Whiteman,who outweighed him by more than
a hundred pounds, at the Hotel Belvedere. Whiteman, who had just
performed Gershwin's *Rhapsody in Blue,* specially written for the
occasion, at Carnegie Hall, was then at the height of his fame, earning $300,000 a year. To jazz he had brought the orchestration and
finesse that previously were limited to classical pieces. His musicians
were the finest in the country. Grossly overweight (there was a Broadway joke that a long-distance air flight could be held around Whiteman), he possessed the sleekness of a well-fed otter—the resemblance
accentuated by his moon face, his thinning, slicked-back hair, narrow
eyes, and tiny, waxed mustache. In the 1920s, all New York danced
to his tune, yet he did not dance himself.

Whiteman's boxing match with Walker lasted only two rounds,
with the portly musician wheezing and puffing and the diminutive
mayor darting around him, throwing flurries of lefts and rights. The
bandleader was at a particular disadvantage, the newspapers reported,
"since the mayor was hitting both his chins with regularity, while
he had the mayor's single chin to aim at." Later, Whiteman explained that the bout was part of his plan to lose weight; he would
be taking his orchestra to Europe shortly and feared his personal
excess-baggage charges would make the trip unprofitable.

The mayor, also in the interests of physical fitness, had not been
drinking since his return from Europe—one of his periodic flights
of abstinence. The Rev. Dr. Christian F. Reisner of the Chelsea
Methodist Episcopal Church told his congregation: "Mayor Walker,
in his generous way, gave me permission to tell you 'I no longer drink
champagne nor alcohol in any form, nor have I since last September. . . . While I enjoyed the exhilarating high spots from alcoholic
stimulants, the low spots of the next morning collected a heavy toll.' "

If Walker and the Methodists were not drinking, few other New
Yorkers were following their example. Bootleggers were peddling

their product and in many cases making it themselves as never before. "Jean," a typical entrepreneur, had been a waiter at Sherry's
who encountered tipping problems once Prohibition forced that elegant restaurant to discard its wine and liquor cards. But Jean, who
had a few acquaintances in the underworld, knew that Sherry's regulars continued to thirst. Accordingly, he lined up a source of supply
(the booze being brought down from Canada or up from Cuba, or
even landed on the Jersey shore), quit his job, and called on his old
patrons at their homes. He sold them good liquor at top prices, getting $150 for a case of Scotch, and keeping fifty of it for himself.

As Prohibition's span lengthened, Jean, who by this time was netting nearly $100,000 a year, would buy his liquor in bulk and bottle
it himself. He would buy suitable Scotch bottles, for instance, from a
firm in the Midwest in lots of 10,000—all perfect imitations. His
labels were printed in England, on English paper, and they likewise
could not be told from the real thing. Jean had his output bottled
by hand. "Two good men can turn out 50 cases a day." Using Scotch
malt smuggled down from Canada as a flavor base, he added alcohol
and water and—presto—instant booze. A perfectionist, Jean even wet
down the ersatz Scotch bottles and their paper wrappings in a salt
solution, to make it appear that the cases had undergone a stormy
trans-Atlantic crossing.

Even full-time breweries flourished in New York during Prohibition. Perhaps the largest of these was the Phoenix, which ostensibly
produced breakfast cereal, and was located on Tenth Avenue between Twenty-fifth and Twenty-sixth Streets. Time and again the
federal authorities tried to stage surprise raids that would close the
Phoenix; on each occasion they were thwarted by the city police.
It was not uncommon, for instance, for New York's finest to arrest
federal agents as they stood on the streets or sat in parked cars in
the brewery's vicinity, waiting to make a raid, on the ground that
they were suspicious-looking characters. Thus warned, the Phoenix's
operators would slam shut their fortress-like steel doors.

Each of the 800,000 half-barrels the Phoenix produced yearly cost
the brewery's owners no more than $2.75 but was sold to distributors
for twelve dollars. This amounted to a net profit of $7,400,000.
The distributors, incidentally, marked up the half-barrels to eighteen
dollars before selling them to speakeasies. These middlemen were
usually good citizens without police records; many were Tammany
and organization politicians supplementing their incomes. Certainly
the brewery could not have operated without Tammany approval.

A major owner of the Phoenix in 1928 was Owen ("Owney")

Madden, the Liverpool-born hoodlum who, as we have seen, was one
of the financial backers of Mae West's *Sex,* and one of the biggest
bootleggers in New York. Madden's parents had brought him to
this country at the age of nine, the family settling in the squalid
West Side tenements of Hell's Kitchen. By the time he was sixteen,
Owney was a leader of the Gophers, a gang of young toughs who in
the early 1900s robbed freight trains, rolled drunks, and turned a
dishonest half-dollar any way they could. The Gophers, the *Morning
Sun* declared, "contain about the only gangsters of Irish descent left
in the city"; this basically was true—the Irish having made the discovery that a position with the police department, while it still permitted them to consort with criminals, nonetheless offered a pension
plan. In Feburary 1912, the twenty-year-old Madden allegedly shot
and killed one William Henshaw, who had been dancing with one
of Owney's girls at a district shindig and was about to get into a cab
at Ninth Avenue and Sixteenth Street to escort her home. Though
the dying man told police Madden was his slayer, the cabdriver and
other witnesses disappeared, and no action was taken. A few months
later, Madden himself was shot—presumably in revenge. It happened
on the night of November 5, 1912, right after the voters of the nation
had elected Woodrow Wilson, the Democratic governor of New
Jersey, to the presidency (a victory regarded with horror by Tammany, which rightly saw in Wilson's incorruptibility a threat to its
federal patronage). Owney, standing in the Arbor Dance Hall at
Seventh Avenue and Fifty-second Street, was moodily watching his
wife, Loretta, with whom he had been spatting, cavorting on the floor.
She had dared him to come to the hall by threatening to dance with
members of the Hudson Dusters, the Gophers' hated rivals. Owney
had taken up the challenge, feeling that Loretta's egalitarianism
would ipugn his manhood. Nobody knows precisely what happened next. Perhaps it was a friend of the dead Henshaw, perhaps
it was some Hudson Duster, but in the crush one or more assailants
came up to Madden, shot him in the stomach, and then disappeared
into the crowd.

"Who done it, Owney?" asked a waiter.

"I done it myself," Owney replied, tight-lipped, while sprawled
on the floor.

Making a remarkable recovery, Madden resumed his journey along
crime's byway. In 1914, when he was out on bail on a burglary
charge (his forty-third arrest), he took offense at Patsy Doyle, who
had been stabbed by one of Owney's gang and had thoughtlessly
complained to the police. "I have it planned to croak Doyle because
he is a squealer," Madden told two of his associates. He sent them
to a saloon on West Forty-first Street, where the offender was en-

joying a glass of beer, and there they killed Doyle by firing six
bullets into his body. Unfortunately, there was a witness to the shooting, and the two killers were tried and convicted of Second Degree
Murder. To escape the death penalty, they implicated Owney, who
was convicted of manslaughter and given twenty years.

In 1923, Madden was paroled, having served less than half his sentence. Physically, he was still the same: his hair black and combed
straight back, his nose big and beaked, his chin virtually nonexistent.
And his speech was still studded with the expected "deses," "dems,"
and "doses." But a character change had taken place in Owney in
prison; where before he was rash, now he was shrewd. It did not
pay, he realized, to knock heads openly with other hoods and with
the law—not when bootlegging was regarded by so many citizens
as a legitimate enterprise, and when so many cops, feeling the same
way, regarded the graft as their due. Ten months after he was out
of jail, Owney bankrolled himself for his new career by a few judicious
armed robberies; though he was arrested for each transgression, the
charges in each case were dropped. Once he was firmly established
in bootlegging, Madden went into nightclubs—becoming associated
with the Silver Slipper, the Cotton Club, and some people claimed,
any and all of Texas ("Hello, Sucker") Guinan's *boîtes*. His enterprises became more and more respectable. Said social arbiter Lucius
Beebe: "Millionaires and their ladies drank the Madden booze in
many a joint. . . . [He] became the elder statesman of the rackets
of New York. His word, except among madmen and low competitors
who had designs upon his life or his money, was always good."

Now there was no reason for Madden to maim or kill; there was
plenty of money for everyone, and gangsters moved easily among
the well-to-do and the respectable. Prohibition had seen to that.

During the early years of his mayoralty, Walker was sounded out
on various job offers. The firmest of these may have been from the
Stanley Corporation of America, the motion-picture-theater chain that
had been headed by the late Jules Mastbaum. Following the wishes
of Mastbaum's widow, Stanley's board of directors in February 1928
offered Walker the presidency at a $150,000 annual salary. He de-
clined, saying that he intended to serve out his full term as mayor,
and left the city for a week-long tour of the South as the representative of the new (and presumably clean) Tammany. Stopovers included Baltimore, Washington, New Orleans, Mobile, Atlanta, and
Winston-Salem, where Walker sought to evaluate presidential sentiment for Governor Smith in areas where the anti-Catholic Ku Klux
Klan was strong.

On the way to New Orleans, Walker's train paused briefly at Mont-

gomery, where several hundred Alabamians serenaded him from the
station platform with a song written in his honor:

> You may go from pole to pole
> Meet the fellows young and old
> And you'll find that they like you . . .
> If we had our way today
> We would nominate you, too . . .
> Al Smith's first and Jimmy's next
> Is what we would like to do . . .
> Get this right. . . . There is one guy
> Who has captured every eye . . .
> Jimmy Walker, we like you!

The mayor's longest stay on the junket was in New Orleans itself,
which he providentially visited during Mardi Gras. Arriving at night,
he went directly to the official reviewing stand, where he watched
the passage of colorful floats representing various historical events.

When Columbus went by in a replica of the *Nina*, Walker doffed
his hat.

"There is the greatest man who ever lived," he said. "Except for
him, I'd be in Ireland now instead of New Orleans."

Before his visit was over, Walker reviewed two more parades,
toured the city by car and foot, attended two official balls, and went
to the local racetrack. It was a full schedule.

Back in New York briefly, the mayor tried vainly to bring a sem-
blance of order to the chaotic subway situation. From Upper Manhattan and the Bronx, down the West Side to Fulton Street and
across to Queens and Brooklyn, lay long, ragged trenches covered by
timbers—excavations designed to link four of the five boroughs by
rail. Hylan's blustering during his eight years in office had put the city
in terrible shape; he had initiated the construction of subways but
had not made it clear whether private or public interests should operate them, what would happen to the existing IRT and BMT, and
how the fare could be held. The New York *Times* commented that
the situation had three sides (the companies running the existing
lines, the government agencies regulating them, the public using
them), as well as three angles (the fare rate, ownership of the new
lines, and reorganization of the system). "The whole cannot be understood without a knowledge of all," said the paper.

In mid-March, Walker, tiring of the transit mathematics, left town
on a Florida vacation. What he wanted to do, said the mayor, "was
put on a pair of overalls and just fish. No speeches, no receptions,

no politicians, no dress clothes this time." He went directly to Miami Beach, attended some exhibition baseball games played by the Newark Bears, a minor league team then owned by Paul Block, and did go fishing—aboard the yacht of Brooklyn shipbuilder William H. Todd.

Meanwhile, the expected financing that would have enabled the Equitable Coach Company to convert paper promises into public conveyances was still not forthcoming. The mayor had originally counted on the promise of Anson W. Burchard, head of General Electric, to put his company behind the deal. Unfortunately, Burchard died just before the bus franchises were granted. At roughly the same time, the mayor also contacted such potential backers as William H. Woodin, chairman of American Car & Foundry, and Charles E. Mitchell, chairman of National City Bank—but received negative responses. In an effort to have General Electric fulfill Burchard's moral commitment, Walker had clandestinely approached two of its representatives, Charles W. Appleton and Owen D. Young, asking them to honor Equitable's claim.

On March 17, the day after Walker left for Florida, J. Allan Smith, Equitable's New York agent, wired a cryptic message to Frank R. Fageol in Ohio that underlines the influence that all concerned felt Senator Hastings had on the mayor, who was referred to as the "boy friend":

NO ANSWER YET YOUR SUGGESTED FINANCING STOP HE [Hastings] NOTIFIED BOY FRIEND [Walker] TIME LIMIT [for beginning operations under the franchise] WAS APRIL 15 STOP HAVE MADE PROGRESS UPSTAIRS [GE] AND ARRANGED MEETING YESTERDAY AFTERNOON BETWEEN JUDGE [Appleton] AND BOY FRIEND [Walker] BEFORE HE [Walker] LEFT FOR FLORIDA STOP JUDGE [Appleton] REPORTED FAVORABLE PROGRESS AND EXPECTED SEE HIS BOSS [Young] TODAY AND ADVISE ME MONDAY

GE eventually retreated from the financing with a firm refusal, however, and Walker and his associates were forced to strike out in another direction. In their desperation, they conducted lengthy discussions with the Brooklyn-Manhattan Transit Corporation, one of the companies that had vainly tried to bid against the Equitable. Representing the mayor in the negotiations was Parks Commissioner Walter Herrick. It was suggested to Brooklyn-Manhattan that, in exchange for financing, the company might be awarded the Brooklyn bus franchise. These conferences dragged on, without any commitment from either side, for the rest of the year.

Now the Queens sewer scandal was entering another important phase. Supreme Court Justice Townsend Scudder had been appointed by Governor Smith to investigate charges of collusion against Borough President Connolly; the judge and his special counsel, Emory R. Buckner, had chosen to conduct the preliminary inquiry in secret, lest advance knowledge of the evidence mounting against him should enable Connolly to take preventive counter measures. The borough president temporarily blocked this approach by getting a court ruling that Scudder, as an impartial jurist, could not conduct a secret investigation. In turn, Governor Smith topped his strategem by having the legislature pass a bill specifically authorizing Supreme Court Judge Clarence Shearn to act in an investigatory capacity. For some weeks, of course, Connolly and his colleagues had been doing all they could to destroy possible evidence. Contractors working on the Queens sewers one after another reported their offices had been burglarized; strangely enough, only their records had been stolen. Nor had the authorities been able to subpoena Jack Phillips, the "Pipe King," who stayed in Atlantic City, visiting his Long Island home only on Sundays, when he could not be served. When reporters did manage to corner Phillips, who was hiding his normally bald head under a toupee, the dialogue went like this:

"Why does sewer pipe cost four to eight times more in Queens than anywhere else?"

"I can't say that it does. I ain't never had a contract with the city in my life."

"When did you last see Connolly?"

"I ain't seen that ——— ——— in seven or eight months."

"Then you had a falling out?"

"I ain't sore at him."

"Then you're still good friends?"

"We ain't never been good friends."

"What did you do with the $8 million Harry Klein says you stole from the city?"

"I'll give you 99 percent of everything you find."

The Scudder-Shearn inquiries nonetheless turned up considerable evidence, and Connolly indicated he was feeling the heat. He demanded that the city appropriate $100,000 for a special legal fund he could use to defend himself. Walker, who had a genuinely soft heart for miscreants, now felt obliged to say some kind words for the borough president. "The fact that a man is accused of something isn't going to drive me away from the support any man is entitled to," said the mayor. So great was the immediate public outcry that Walker had to reverse himself. "I mean that the city should bear the cost only if the accused is acquitted," he said. On April 2, Connolly resigned, thinking the gesture would ensure dropping of the charges against him.

Such was not to be the case, for public indignation now was fanned by two happenings. Jack Phillips had been located by the federal government down in Florida, where he was recovering from a kidney attack caused by his heavy drinking, and arrested for failing to file income-tax reports; he had earned $4,575,000 in 1925, 1926, and 1927, the tax men said, and owed them nearly $747,000. In a related event, the New York legislature passed a law threatening witnesses who fled the state to evade subpoena with a $100,000 fine; figures in the sewer scandal thereupon returned to Queens with amazing alacrity. What resulted was a grand jury indictment of Connolly and Phillips, along with two sewer engineers, on three counts of conspiracy. The former borough president said of his coming trial: "As I have been above reproach, I do not fear it."

As for Phillips, he never would stand trial. Back again in Atlantic City, his drinking would increase and his kidney condition worsen. He would die, in midsummer, of acute alcoholism. There would be a splendid funeral mass at the Church of the Holy Redeemer in Freeport, attended by Jack's wife and son, his fellow Spanish-American War Veterans, 500 Elks, and all the local cabdrivers who had enjoyed his customary twenty dollar tips. There the priest would eulogize: "Judge not that you be not judged."

Connolly was too tough to take the bottle as a way out. He would twist and turn, and there would be many more developments in the sewer scandal, as we shall see, before he was brought to bay.

On April 9, Walker culminated his courtship of the South for Governor Smith by going to Atlanta, where he helped dedicate a huge equestrian figure of Robert E. Lee, carved in granite on a nearby mountainside. There, among a covey of Dixie governors, senators, and congressmen, he was introduced at the unveiling—sixty-three years after Lee's surrender to Ulysses S. Grant at Appomattox—as the representative of the city that had raised more funds for the memorial than any other in the country. Delivering the principal address, Walker said in part that in Lee "God joined the warrior and the saint. . . . I am proud that I am an American because he was one." Referring to the Civil War, the mayor got in a boost for Smith by declaring pointedly, "The time has come, my friends, when we should all disregard geographical lines." The reception afterward was notable chiefly for a brief moment of embarrassment. Passing a man with a camera, Walker thought him a newspaper photographer. He struck as statesmanlike a pose as one can while carrying a plate of barbecue. Minutes later, the man rushed up with a finished photo —and a polite request for "two-bits, please."

When he returned to New York, the mayor received still another surprise. The four Democratic aldermen from Queens informed him they planned to elect Bernard M. Patten to the borough presidency as Connolly's successor. The decision enraged Walker. Though Patten was his Commissioner of Markets, the mayor had given him the post only as a peacemaking gesture toward Connolly after the 1925 primary. To Walker's way of thinking, a fresh face was needed if Queens voters were to be kept in the Democratic fold. A stormy meeting at City Hall between Walker and the aldermen followed. Scores of Queens officeholders loitered outside, seeking to stiffen their colleagues' resolve; by opting to preserve the status quo, they were protecting their own jobs. Indeed, so certain were the ward-heelers of Patten's success that they had already placed the traditional floral horseshoes, bearing the legend "Good luck, Bernie," in the office of the Queens borough president. Inside his chambers, the mayor berated the aldermen, saying that the Queens taxpayers were entitled to "a new deck." Walker's threats were unavailing. The next day Patten was elected.

Republican Alderman George U. Harvey of Queens, outvoted 4-to-1 by his Democratic colleagues, was cheerful about their refusal to clean house. "The people of Queens," he told them, "will have something to say about this next November. [They'll] simply throw you out of office, the whole gang."

Sitting in the crowded City Hall room where the special election was held, Walker said nothing, but his frown showed he knew Harvey was right. Within hours, the Central Queens Allied Civic Councils, representing 110 organizations and some 400,000 individuals, announced plans for a series of meetings to demand "that civic welfare be placed above politics." In November, Republican Harvey would be voted into the borough president's office.

In the less than two and a half years Walker had been mayor, the city had welcomed more than 200 dignitaries and celebrities from thirty-five countries, including a king, two queens, nine princes and princesses, and countless prelates, statesmen, politicians, industrialists, artists, inventors, educators, Channel swimmers, airmen, explorers, and golfers. Each greeting generally began amid foghorns and fireboats in New York harbor, with the distinguished visitor being transferred from his incoming ocean liner to the municipal tugboat, *Macom*. Once the guest reached dry land at the Battery, the inevitable motorcade and City Hall reception followed. These were trying days for Grover Whalen, who supervised the welcomes. Though some 40,-000 important New Yorkers usually wished to attend the functions, he had room, in the grandstand and at the lunch or dinner for only 2,500. Nonetheless, Whalen remained cheerful about the hurly-burly, saying that it had "succeeded in convincing the people of the rest of the country, and even of the world as a whole, that this city is not too engrossed in night life, finance and other material activities to acclaim those whose achievements are of signal distinction."

Whatever one may think of this philosophizing, the greetings themselves were comparatively inexpensive. Only $200,000 had been spent by the city in all, the largest share in behalf of Lindbergh's reception ($71,850), with Commander Byrd's a far-behind runner-up ($26,-490). (It should be pointed out that many of the welcomes, as in the case of Queen Marie, had been wholly or partially paid for by private contributions.) The Japanese fleet ($667), some French aviators ($459), and a delegation from Hungary ($299) were, all fair-minded citizens would agree, real bargains. Dollar for dollar, however, the city easily got top value from the fete given the Italian ambassador ($125). In contrast, $12,000 was spent for the reception tendered President William Cosgrove of the Irish Free State, including $7,208 for a dinner at the Biltmore—which says something about which ethnic group then ran New York.

With all the furor about the transit situation, Walker was fortunate to have in Whalen a man who knew how to distract the masses. On May 2, a federal court granted the IRT's petition for a seven-cent fare, creating consternation among vote-conscious Tammany politicans. The city, represented by Samuel Untermyer, immediately appealed the decision, sending the case to the U.S. Supreme Court. Since the two-cent increase amounted to some $75,000 a day, and since the court was unlikely to hear the case for at least seven months, the city was faced with the need to put up a $15 million bond against the event it lost. Walker vowed he would run again for the mayoralty in 1929, to prove his "determination to uphold the five-cent fare."

In fact, the case would not be decided by the Supreme Court for another year; meanwhile, the fare remained at five cents. But Red Mike Hylan nonetheless burst into full rhetoric, using the occasion to excoriate Walker and Untermyer. "They only pretended to make a fight in opposition in order to hoodwink and fool the people," he said. "This is in accordance with [their] deal with the traction interests, who supplied the funds to drive me out of power."

About this time, too, the first reports began to appear about growing friction between Walker and Police Commissioner Warren. Tammany and machine pressure over Warren's attempts to close politically sponsored gambling dens was becoming more and more difficult for the mayor to withstand. The raids made by Valentine's Confidential Squad had resulted in few convictions, but they were nettlesome. "Joe, when in hell are you going to do something about Valentine?" Walker had complained. Warren's answer was to promote Valentine from inspector to deputy chief inspector.

Walker was forced to the realization that, to stop the raids, he would have to fire his old friend; it was perhaps the only inconsiderate act he ever performed in his public life. The mayor found some justification for himself in a police report for the first quarter of the year showing a sharp increase in crime over the same period the year before. While he was steadfast in his honesty, Warren did dissipate his energies on petty administrative details. Perhaps his poor health made him shrink from confronting his deputies personally, as McLaughlin had done, and demanding results. At any rate, most policemen felt that Warren would not last the year as commissioner, and in this they were right.

No clearer indication exists of the differences in character between Walker and Governor Smith than the nature of the men surrounding them. Walker's casual ways with people and with money attracted those who hoped to bask in his reflected publicity, like publisher Paul Block, or to profit from the relationship, like Senator Hastings. But Smith was a moralist. His friends, who respected him for his administrative abilities, admired him all the more for his righteous ways. On May 16, William F. Kenny, a construction executive who was unknown to the general public, testified before the Senate Campaign Fund Investigating Committee in Washington that he had just contributed $70,000 to help Smith's drive for the presidential nomination.

"Do you expect to make further contributions?" a senator asked.

"I hope so," said Kenny.

"How much?"

"Within the limit only of my ability."

Since Kenny had a fortune estimated at $30 million, this was no idle promise. Shipbuilder William H. Todd (who had been good for $5,000—although nominally a Republican), banker Herbert H. Lehman ($10,000), and banker James J. Riordan (who contributed $5,000—and who as head of the U.S. Trucking Corporation had once made Smith, temporarily out of office, the chairman of his board of directors), subsequently made similar declarations of loyalty to the governor.

Bill Kenny epitomized these men, who wanted nothing from Smith by way of publicity or favors. Almost all his construction firm's business came, not from the city or state, but from the private sector—particularly gas and electric companies. The only city business he ever accepted was with the fire department; over a period of years it brought his company, he admitted, "not enough profit to pay the salary of one good man"; the work was taken on for sentimental reasons—Kenny's father had been a Battalion Chief. When the department, in gratitude, made him an Honorary Deputy Chief, he responded by donating an ambulance, coffee truck, and searchlight engine.

"Do you expect anything from the Governor in the event he is nominated for and elected President?" a senator asked the jowly, mustachioed Kenny.

"I do not," he replied. "All that I have done for the Governor is because of my love and affection for him."

As boys, hanging around Engine Company No. 9 on East Broadway, Kenny and Smith shined the brass, groomed the horses, and ran errands. Sometimes they were allowed to ride on the wagons to a fire. In his teens, the newly married Kenny took a job with the Edison Company at $13.50 a week. He dug trenches, next bossed some workmen, and progressed to ownership of his own dump carts. Kenny possessed a genius at getting construction projects underway and finding the right men to complete them. His first million was not long in coming.

Kenny's political contributions to Smith began in 1904, when Al was running for the assembly, with a $1,000 gift; by 1926, Al's last gubernatorial campaign, the ante was up to $10,000. What the contractor gave Smith as much as money, however, was companionship. On the top floor of the Kenny Building at 44 East Twenty-third Street, was an opulent meeting place for Bill's cronies that he called the Tiger Room.

"Is it painted in black and yellow stripes?" asked a senator at the time of the hearing concerning the $70,000.

"That's just newspaper bull," said Kenny. "I call [the place] that because I'm a good Tammany Tiger."

What the room did offer, however, was a tiger rug on the floor, a tiger painting over the mantel, and a tiger bas-relief on the fire screen. It was not uncommon for the entire cast of the Ziegfeld Follies to entertain on the room's stage, although the girls had to wear more clothes than usual—in deference to Al Smith's wishes. There was twenty-four-hour food and drink service, and guests could comfortably be put up overnight. Here Kenny and three of his brothers (who likewise became wealthy in his business) would gather for poker parties with Smith and New York's mostly Irish political leaders, as well as Irish entrepreneurs like banker James J. Riordan and bookmaker Timothy Mara (who later became the owner of the New York Football Giants). Though the betting had a five-dollar limit, Al usually stayed out of the game—his poker being abysmal.

Shortly after the Senate hearings Kenny would be off for Houston, Texas, taking an entourage of Smith supporters in three private railroad cars to the Democratic National Convention, where he hoped to see his friend nominated for the presidency.

"Let Al worry about politics," he said. "I'll stick to building."

While Walker and Smith, two Irish-American politicians with widely divergent views on morality, were mingling with the lace-curtain classes, thousands of their shanty-Irish counterparts continued to scratch out a criminal living. It was true that the organized gangs of New York (and particularly Manhattan) were now largely populated by Italians and Jews. But in that section of Brooklyn called Irishtown, the waterfront area between the Navy Yard and the Fulton Ferry and around the approaches to the Brooklyn and Manhattan Bridges, the boyos were still conducting the internecine feuds that were known to a generation of tabloid readers as the dock wars. The motives of the combatants, like their wants, were simple. Any man tough enough to bully the hard-working, hard-drinking stevedores could extort about two hundred dollars a week for himself; a stevedore who didn't hand over a percentage of his pay didn't work, and if he tried to he would be beaten or even killed.

On the night of May 16, the day Kenny was questioned in Washington about his relationship with Smith, a waterfront gangster named Edward McGuire was shot to death on a dock under the Brooklyn Bridge. According to the police, he was the tenth man to lose his life "in the struggle for the leadership of the old Bill Lovett gang"—Lovett having been killed in 1923. McGuire, evidently an idealist, had shot craps with four rivals for the leadership and had won—whereupon the losers shot him. The woman who identified his body was Anna Lonergan, who had been Lovett's widow, but who in 1928 was married to Matty Martin, one of the men suspected of killing McGuire.

Anna Lonergan had made a career of identifying the bodies of her loved ones and their enemies. As a child, she attended St. James' parochial school on the Lower East Side—Al Smith's old parish. Later the family moved to Brooklyn. In her formative years, Anna felt the heavy hand of her father, an odd-jobs man who ran a bicycle shop, if she was not in her bed each night by nine. During World War I, however, the eighteen-year-old girl used her nubile good looks to gain employment in Broadway supper clubs, and the bedtime rule had to be relaxed. Anna danced at Rector's and Churchill's, and the experience, at the very least, taught her how to attract the male eye.

The first body Anna identified was that of her father. In 1923, still in show business though living at home in Brooklyn, she noticed her father and brother "Peg-Leg" (he had lost a leg under the wheels of a trolley car as a boy) talking with two Irishtown "tramps." She told her mother, who rushed over to the bicycle shop and, after an exchange of cordialities, fatally shot Mr. Lonergan. Arriving at the scene, a now contrite Anna immediately sent for a priest. "Mama," she said, "what have you done to Papa?" Wild Bill Lovett, then terrorizing the docks, had been courting Anna for some time. As a dutiful future son-in-law, he hired Mama a good lawyer, who persuaded the jury that Mr. Lonergan had pulled the gun and his wife had simply wrested it away from him in the struggle. An acquittal resulted.

Lovett had long been calling on Anna, sitting mutely in the Lonergan parlor, staring at the sister while pretending he was there to see Peg-Leg. Heretofore she had not encouraged his suit. "I don't talk to people who go around shooting people," she said. And Lovett did enjoy the sound of gunfire. He had taken over the Irishtown dock leadership in 1920 by shooting to death Dinny Meehan, then the boss, as Meehan lay sleeping in his bed. A year after that, Lovett killed a man for pulling a cat's tail. Anna, an animal lover herself, found it easier to overlook that particular peccadillo. All in all, Wild Bill probably killed about 20 men during his lifetime. "The papers only gave Bill credit for seven," Anna argued. "He killed nearer twenty-seven in Brooklyn." Lovett also did fun things with guns at social gatherings. Once he shot the pork chops out of the fry pan at an Irishtown dinner party; another time, disapproving of a friend's imitation of Charlie Chaplin, he shot off his derby hat (the friend suffered a simple flesh wound).

So grateful was Anna for Lovett's coming to the aid of Mrs. Lonergan, however, that she put aside her scruples and, a month after Mama's acquittal, married him. They settled in a small cottage in Ridgefield Park, New Jersey, where they sought to leave behind the evil influences of the city, making only occasional sojourns into Brooklyn. One mishap marred the three months of their idyll. That occurred when Lovett came home late one night, declared, "I want to see if you can take it," and shot off Anna's big toe. In October of 1923, Wild Bill met with disaster while visiting Irishtown to collect tribute; when the police found him, his body was riddled with bullets, his head crushed with a stevedore's bale hook. Naturally, Anna identified the body.

The dock wars continued. Convictions were impossible, because no witnesses could be found to testify against the transgressors; the police consoled themselves with the thought that "they" were only killing each other. Anna, who had moved back to Brooklyn, again found herself in the thick of the fighting. Her brother Peg-Leg had achieved a bit of a reputation as a hoodlum and had thrown in his lot with Matty Martin, one of the men attempting to succeed Wild Bill. Matty accompanied Peg-Leg to his sister's home for a relaxing drink after a hard day of head-cracking, and very soon another romance blossomed. In February of 1924, after three months of widowhood, Anna married the new dock boss.

Matty's big problem was that he was a sleep-walker; it was not unusual for him to get up in the middle of the night, go down to the kitchen and eat everything in the icebox, and then, still comatose, unfold and read the evening paper. Sometimes he would be found like this when the rest of the family came down for breakfast. Anna's Mama, who lived with them, was intolerant of this eccentricity. "Take him away," she told her daughter; "he gives me the horrors." Anna and Matty moved to Bushwick, quite a few miles from the docks. More of a homebody than Wild Bill, Matty seemed content; he liked tinkering with his five new-fangled radio sets—although he never was able to eliminate the static. He was more compassionate than Bill, too, and probably had no more than eight or ten notches in his gun.

Back in Irishtown on Christmas Eve, 1924, a lonesome Peg-Leg wondered how to celebrate the holidays; with a couple of friends, he decided to venture into Gowanus and have some sport with the Italian patrons of the Adonis Social Club. Drinking heavily, Peg-Leg and his pals spread good will by calling the Italians "ginzoes" and chasing Irish girls out of the club, telling them to "come back with white men." The climax of the evening came when party or parties unknown fatally shot Peg-Leg and his companions. Al Capone, who would later achieve the distinction of being named Public Enemy No. 1 by the FBI but was then little known outside Chicago, happened to be in the club that night; the police arrested him for the murders, but the charges eventually were dismissed. Anna always attributed the killings to Capone. "You can bet it was no Irish-Americans like ourselves who would stage a mean murder like this on Christmas Day," she said. A dutiful sister, she journeyed to the morgue for the identifications.

Now, in 1928, Anna and Matty appeared to have settled down. Each day Matty would come home from the docks, play his radios, and pour himself a couple of hard belts. Nobody was killed unless, as in the case of the dice-rolling Edward McGuire, he tried to muscle in on the extortion money. Always a devoted churchgoer, Anna frequently importuned St. Theresa, the Little Flower, to protect Matty from all danger and harm. "I always pray that [he'll] have good company and not go bad," she said.

Anna had cause for pessimism. In December of 1930, Matty Martin would himself be fatally shot in a De Kalb Avenue speakeasy. His widow, still a handsome woman, would live on, remembering past bloodshed and past glories.

Throughout May and June, one of Walker's favorite pursuits was to tour the subways. His descent into the ditches was always an event. At Sixth Avenue and Fifty-third Street, for instance, where the crosstown line to Queens was being constructed, Walker and the members of his party were lowered eighty feet to the floor of the tunnel in a large, flat-bottomed scoop. The bar from which the scoop was suspended was equipped with loops of rope for the passengers to grab. Taking hold of one, Walker remarked, "I'm the first straphanger in the new subways." Down in the murky tunnel, where water dripping from the rock ceiling created five-inch-deep puddles, the mayor was treated to a litany of construction difficulties. Reaching Eighth Avenue and Fifty-seventh Street, at the bottom of five levels of transit, Walker got into a truck for the underground ride to Washington Heights; all along the Upper West Side, he noted, the excavation was nearly complete.

The mayor had been the guest of Sam Rosoff, the most colorful of the subway builders. In 1925, Rosoff, then the owner of a sand and gravel pit and a small contracting company in Newburgh, New York, put in a bid for his first subway section, under St. Nicholas Avenue between One Hundred Twenty-second and One Hundred Thirty-third Streets. (Contracts were let, through competitive bidding, in ten-block sections.) His price for the work, $4,600,000, was so low that he almost didn't get the job; after all, who had ever heard of his company? Rosoff was informed he'd have to put up a $250,000 bond. A friend of his, Edward Luther, whose business it was to finance such ventures, offered $150,000 of the sum.

"Where the hell am I going to get $100,000?" asked Sam.

"How about the Rosie National Bank?" said Luther.

"She'd never let me have it," sighed Sam.

Rosie was Rosoff's wife, and for years, while he had gone broke in one contracting job after another, and while huge gambling losses had taken away most of the money he did manage to make, she had managed to take her housewife's percentage. Mrs. Rosoff was at her most relentless when Sam came home after an occasional winning night at rolling dice. If he won $10,000, say, he would find only $5,000 in his pocket when he woke the next morning; Rosie had appropriated the rest.

Though at first skeptical, Mrs. Rosoff eventually agreed to finance her husband. With his mind freed from mundane financial concerns, the rotund Rosoff threw himself into the ditchdigging—bawling out orders, slogging through the dirt and muck, perspiring through the hatband of his beat-up fedora. His knowledge of engineering was entirely self-taught. Yet he was the first subway builder to put steam shovels in the trenches, to use underground conveyor belts to bring the dirt to central loading points, to haul it out quickly via trucks and ramps. The faster the work went, Rosoff realized, the greater the profit. Even while he was finishing that first section under St. Nicholas Avenue (which was completed a year ahead of time), he started digging on two other sections. All together, the three jobs represented $27 million in contracts.

A Russian Jew, Rosoff had immigrated to this country at the age of eleven. He sold newspapers, slept on subway grates, and finally got a job as a laborer on a construction gang. Unlike Bill Kenny, whose trek toward making millions in construction was straight upward, Rosoff was a late-bloomer. For twenty-five years he drifted from one enterprise to another, buying up rusty railroad tracks and selling them as scrap, wrecking buildings, laying roadbeds. By 1928, of course, the subway work had made him a rich man.

Rosoff's greatest pleasure, despite his success, was to go into the ditches himself. He delighted in dining with friends, all in evening clothes, and then insisting that they visit his latest excavation. For Sam, nothing was so real as earth, nothing so important as its moving and shaking.

Late in May, Walker kept thirty-seven of his department heads waiting in his City Hall anteroom for some ninety minutes before warning them that they would be held personally responsible for the wrongdoing of their subordinates. "No man, no matter how well I know him, no matter what his party or influence or power, can hold a place in this administration unless he shows himself to be capable and continually on the job," he admonished. "Some people think the mayor is largely responsible for any laxity that there may have been because he is generally known to be good-natured."

In truth, it was Walker who, by his example, was responsible for the municipal laxity, and only a happy-go-lucky city, such as New York in the 1920s, could have tolerated him. A good indication of the prevailing mood was the craze for marathon dancing. At Madison Square Garden in mid-June, even while Walker was making plans to attend the Democratic National Convention in Houston, a marathon derby was entering its fifth day; thirty-four couples were left, vying for the $5,000 prize and gliding glassy-eyed to "Ain't She Sweet?" "Lucky in Love," and "Me and My Shadow." Patricia Salmon of Shelby, Montana, "danced" for four and a half hours while unconscious, supported by the arms of her partner, Guy H. Shields of Los Angeles. (The rules required that the contestants keep in some semblance of motion but did not require them to be awake.) "Once or twice I felt like stopping," said Shields. "But then I said to myself, 'Oh well, she may come to.'"

When Vera Campbell of 45 East Fifty-fifth Street slumped at one point into a stand-up faint, her trainer ran onto the floor, slipped a thermometer between her lips, and took a reading.

"Lovely," he said. "Only two degrees above normal. A cold compress will bring that down during the next rest period."

Pluckiest of the competitors undoubtedly was sixteen-year-old Gloria Petrick, the youngest entry in the marathon. Her feet, tightly taped around the ankles, had swollen so badly that she had graduated from wearing dance pumps to bedroom slippers to small-size men's shoes to large-size men's shoes. When her feet grew too big for the latter, Gloria had to be carried to her tent.

Gloria wanted to continue wearing galoshes, but the medical staff decided she was a poor risk. Still the band played on, that June day in Madison Square Garden . . . "Let a smile be your um-brel-la . . . on a rai-ny after-noon . . ."

※※※

Walker, who originally had been named Smith's floor leader, arrived in Houston for the Democratic National Convention on June 25. But an attack of the grippe, helped on by his fondness for partying, had weakened him, and Smith had second thoughts. The governor decided to rely on Franklin Delano Roosevelt, the upstate Democratic politician who, in 1910, had defied Charley Murphy in his bid to send "Blue-eyed Billy" Sheehan, a convivial hack, to the U.S. Senate.

Roosevelt had not only survived his initial clash with Tammny but prospered. He backed Woodrow Wilson for the Democratic presidential nomination in 1912 and, after Wilson's election, went to Washington as his assistant secretary of the navy. In 1920, he ran for vice-president on the national ticket headed by James M. Cox of Ohio, who was defeated by Warren G. Harding. Despite the attack of polio that made him a cripple, able to walk only haltingly with the aid of canes and leg braces, Roosevelt had nominated Al Smith for the Presidency at the bitter 1924 convention, extolling him as the "Happy Warrior." (The Roman Catholic Smith's bid had been thwarted by William G. McAdoo of Tennessee; the convention, rent by religious bigotry and deep-seated feelings about Prohibition, eventually compromised on John W. Davis of West Virginia, who was soundly beaten by Coolidge.) Now in 1928, almost certain of the presidential nomination. (In the fall, FDR would win the governorship while Smith would lose the Presidential race in a Republican landslide for Herbert Hoover.)

Smith's decision about changing the floor leadership appeared to bother Walker not at all. Accompanied by Charles F. Kerrigan, his assistant, Charles S. Hand, his press secretary, Grover Whalen, chairman of his Welcoming Committee, and William E. Walsh, chairman of the board of standards and appeals, Walker radiated ease and cordiality as he greeted the cheering crowds at his convention hotel. Spatless for once, he lifted an immaculate white panama hat and waved it in appreciation for his reception. At Smith headquarters, a large group of well-wishers, mostly women, awaited him.

"How long will it take to nominate Al Smith?" said one young Texas lady.

"What's the shortest time on record?" countered Walker.

Though Smith won the nomination on the first ballot, there was much foot-dragging on the part of the South and of delegations from rural areas generally; the prejudice was both religious—against upstart Irish Catholics—and geographical—against New York "wets" who wanted to repeal Prohibition. Moreover, the country was still enjoying Coolidge (and Republican) prosperity. The stock market, entering its most spectacular phase before the crash that was sixteen months away, was making paper fortunes for everyone; skyscraper-building was reaching its peak in New York's Grand Central area, with towers going up forty to fifty stories and more; and few people noticed that the bubble was only a bubble, let alone that it might burst. Even Roosevelt in a letter to a friend at the time complained, quite rightly, that Smith's chances for the presidency that November were none too good. As for Walker, he steered his own course, leaving directly from the convention for a six-week tour of the West, the Pacific Coast, and Canada. It was his seventh extended vacation since taking office in January of 1926—a total of 149 vacation days in two and a half years, not including long weekends. His need for relaxation had taken him to Atlantic City, Cincinnati, Florida, Cuba, the White Mountains of New Hampshire, Palm Beach, Cuba again, Europe, and the South.

While Walker was traveling on the Pacific Coast, Police Commissioner Warren came under criticism again when the New York *Telegram* published a survey it had made of killings in the city through the first six months of the year. Out of 121 homicides, the report asserted, the killers had been brought to justice in only twenty-two cases, and only two persons were convicted of murder in the first degree. The *Telegram* thereupon concluded that in New York the odds were 11-to-2 that a killer would never be sent to prison and 11-to-4 that nobody would be indicted for the crime.

The killing that received the most publicity that summer was that of Francesco Yale, better known as Frankie Yale, a Brooklyn-based gang leader who had made the mistake of trying to doublecross Chicago's Al Capone. Since being accused of the Peg-Leg Lonergan murder, Capone had, through a system of alliances, built up his Midwest bootlegging operation on a national scale. His representative in Brooklyn was Frankie Yale, a one-time murder-for-pay specialist ("I'm an undertaker," he would say of his profession), who had risen to the presidency of the *Unione Sicilione,* the predecessor of the Mafia. It was Yale's responsibility to oversee liquor landings on Long Island and then arrange for the cargo's transportation to Chicago by truck. Sometime in 1927, however, many of the trucks were highjacked and Capone suspected that Yale was doublecrossing him. He sent an aide, James de Amato, to Brooklyn, ostensibly to ingratiate himself with Frankie, but really to spy upon him. De Amato was shortly thereafter shot down dead in the street.

For a while, Capone brooded but did nothing. As a young man in Brooklyn, he had been given his start by Yale, who had hired him as a bouncer in the Harvard Inn, Frankie's headquarters on the Coney Island waterfront. It was at the Harvard Inn, in fact, that Capone's unwelcome compliment to a hoodlum's sister had earned him the three prominent knife cuts that resulted in his "Scarface" sobriquet. Al's mind was finally made up when a disgruntled Yale henchman proved to him who had ordered the highjackings and the De Amato killing.

Now Capone moved swiftly, dispatching assassins to New York from the Midwest. On the sunny afternoon of July 1, 1928, Frankie Yale was driving along the streets of Brooklyn in his sporty coupé when the traditional black sedan pulled up alongside and forced him to the curb. A fusillade of pistol shots rang out, noisily sending the gangster to his death. The police later found a sawed-off shotgun and a machinegun in the abandoned sedan; the killers had not needed to use them since Yale had not been protected by bodyguards. Frankie was given a splendiferous funeral—a nickel-silver $15,000 casket, innumerable garlands of flowers, and files of swarthy mourners wearing wide-brimmed hats and dark suits. His send-off may have been the most lavish mobster's funeral New York ever witnessed, though it could not compare to the ones given fallen warriors in Chicago.

Frankie's murderers were never found. Searching for the colleague who had fingered Yale, Warren's police first picked up Giuseppe Periani, otherwise known as "The Clutching Hand"; next they interrogated Giuseppe Speranza, whose record of eleven arrests included two for murder; both men eventually were released for lack of evidence.

Walker's Health Commissioner, Dr. Harris, who had done so much to clean up the milk scandals, handed in his resignation about this time. Ostensibly, he was leaving the administration to accept a post as consultant to the National Dairy Products Corporation that would pay him several times his $10,000 municipal salary. "Yes, I suppose everything I did wasn't satisfactory to some politicians," Dr. Harris said. "But so far as the Mayor is concerned, I have never had any indication from him that he was dissatisfied. I am leaving office absolutely of my own volition." Walker had remained loyal to his health commissioner, but he must have felt relief about his resignation. Only the lower-echelon milk grafters like Thomas J. Clougher had gone to jail; the higher-up pols had not even been named. The machine was eager to get back into the milk racket and had been exerting the usual pressures on City Hall to replace Dr. Harris. Walker had not been willing to do this, but he had struck a compromise—refusing to push through the necessary appropriations to hire additional inspectors and sufficient laboratory staff.

That July found Tammany Grand Sachem John R. Voorhis celebrating his ninety-ninth birthday. After the obligatory party and cake-cutting in his board of elections office, he was interviewed in his Greenwich Village home, which he had helped build with his own hands in 1865. A three-story-and-basement brick house at the corner of Greenwich and Bethune Streets, it was so close to the tracks of the Ninth Avenue El that one could almost touch the trains by leaning out the second-story windows. Voorhis allowed that the noise of the trains thundering by bothered his visitors, but said it did not trouble him. Nonetheless, he would not permit a radio in his home, feeling the sound would be an invasion of his privacy.

Walker returned to New York in early August, bringing back tales of unexpected Smith strength in the Far West. Wearing a light-gray suit and a panama hat and carrying a walking stick, the mayor looked jaunty. Despite the heat, he wore a vest. Reporters asked Walker what he thought of a renewed federal effort that summer to close speakeasies and enforce Prohibition in the city. "If the law is being violated, it ought to be stopped," he parried. "I'll say this, though. After traveling 10,000 miles I wasn't in one place where there was any difficulty to see and get liquor." And with that he pleaded fatigue and went on to his home.

The mayor's residence, however, was no longer St. Luke's Place. He had left Allie earlier that summer (although she would continue until the fall to hope for a reconciliation) and moved into a suite at the Ritz-Carlton, at Madison Avenue and 48th Street, where Paul Block also lived. The reason, of course, was his infatuation with Betty Compton. Now Walker made no secret of his feelings for the young actress. When his brother George visited him at the Ritz, the insurance man was taken aback by the framed photographs of Betty throughout the suite.

"He had pictures of that woman all over the place," George told their sister, Nan.

"Don't try to interfere," she answered. "What's done is done. And Jim is Jim."

Walker's decision not to conceal the affair any longer appalled his newspaper friends. But they were determined that his career would not suffer. Not one word about his relationship with Betty ever appeared in print while he was mayor, and even at the time of the Seabury investigation in 1932, she would be mentioned only once and then as the "unnamed person."

For Walker, the time for subterfuge was over. He still remembered, with humor but also with distaste, how one of his and Betty's "love nests," a house in Queens, had been moved out from under them—the result of highway construction. Robert Moses, who then was not only Smith's secretary of state but in charge of New York State parks and public improvements, described the predicament vividly. "Jimmy and a friend with their girls shared a love nest on what is now the Grand Central Parkway. We took it in acquiring rights-of-way. Jimmy, who had approved the plans without looking at them, was in a state." On the other side of the proposed parkway was the Creedmoor State Hospital, and eating into the institution's grounds was a small truck farm cultivated by one of the Creedmoor custodians. "The worst thing would have been to cancel or reroute the project," said Moses, who always liked Walker despite recognizing his weaknesses, "and have the Republicans in Albany find out why. We convinced the custodian he needed a bigger farm. . . . The Mayor and his chums promptly bought the old one [and] moved the nest over. That's how parkways are built."

Betty and Jim had celebrated the house-moving with a small, exclusive party. Everyone had a little too much to drink and, amid the hilarity, the heavy eye make-up Betty used became quite smudged—much to her chagrin. "Betty always wore too much make-up," reflected the other woman in the "love nest" years later.

New York that August suffered the worst subway crash Manhattan had seen to date. Sixteen people were killed and more than a hundred injured when an IRT express, leaving the Times Square station at the 5:00 P.M. rush hour, ran over a defective switch. Eight of the ten cars had passed over the switch, with the train rapidly gaining speed, when the ninth car was suddenly shifted onto a spur track. The jarring wrench split the car in two, hurling it against the retaining walls and crumpling it like a tin can.

As soon as Walker heard of the accident, he rushed to the scene, going down into the subway fifteen minutes after the wreck. Even in this brief time, speedy police work had resulted in most of the victims being taken to hospitals by ambulance and taxi. After talking to some of the injured in nearby French Hospital, the mayor went to the West Thirtieth Street Precinct House. There the police told him the switch that had caused the accident had been known to be faulty; indeed, IRT maintenance men had labored to repair it only minutes before the tragedy. Walker then asked the police if they had questioned the switchman; detectives answered they feared the company was keeping him under cover, so its attorneys could coach him on how to respond. The mayor lost his temper. "Notify [IRT] President Hedley," he said, pounding his fist into his palm, "that unless the man responsible is turned over to the police for questioning forthwith I will order [Hedley's] arrest."

Within a half-hour, Hedley appeared at the precinct house, bringing with him W. S. Baldwin, the switchman the police had been seeking, plus a battery of lawyers.

The IRT president explained that the train, a ten-car express from Van Cortlandt Park, was one that habitually was turned at Times Square and put onto the northbound-tracks.

"Switchman Baldwin, the day maintainer, could not get the switch over," Hedley said. "He notified the trainmaster, who told him to send the train down the main line. Baldwin handles the switch from the tracks. He told the motorman to proceed downtown. The forward trucks on the ninth car passed, but the rear truck passed over to the spur track."

What caused the switch to open with a train on the tracks? Said Hedley candidly: "I don't know."

Nobody ever did pin down the reason for the malfunction. An investigation showed the equipment was in good working order; the switchman obviously had guided the train onto the main line. Perhaps the cars had been overloaded, forcing the switch to slip under the weight; perhaps the motorman had accelerated the train too quickly, thus adding to the strain. Whatever the cause, sixteen persons died.

Walker and his administration were coming under increasing attack for their dubious enforcing of Prohibition in New York from Assistant U.S. Attorney Mabel Walker Willebrandt. Mrs. Willebrandt, who complained of the small force of Prohibition agents she was forced to make do with, declared that the mayor, with a police force of 17,000 men, should be better able to control the illegal drinking. Since New York's nightclubs, which were "nothing more than saloons for rich men," all have to be licensed by the city, she added, Walker was in a position to make a "splendid showing" if he really wanted to cooperate with the federal authorities. Meanwhile, Mrs. Willebrandt was plunging ahead for God and the Volstead Act, going over the head of the local U.S. attorney and leading her gallant band of agents in a series of raids against the city's clubs and speakeasies.

Before Mrs. Willebrandt launched her crusade, Prohibition agents tended to be brusque. They would drop into a place suspected of selling liquor (or smash their way in if necessary), arrest the owner, waiters, or bartenders, and padlock the establishment. As fast as they closed one place, two more bistros sprang up nearby. The most famous of the federal liquor men by far were Izzy Einstein and Moe W. Smith, who from 1920 until their retirement in 1925 arrested some 4,600 people, knocking off fifteen to twenty establishments a week. It was a rigorous schedule that did not allow for the niceties. Izzy and Moe, each of whom weighed in at about 250 pounds, wore a variety of disguises in carrying out their duties. To gain entry to a country club. they wore knickers and carried golf clubs; to get into a dive, they dressed like stevedores; to raid a nightclub, they wore evening clothes, The job paid only $3,600 a year, but it provided an extensive wardrobe. Unlike their colleagues, who often used axes and strong-arm methods, Izzy and Moe rarely indulged in violence. Their most physical encounter came when they tried to arrest two Polish brothers who operated a Third Avenue saloon. The brothers started swinging, and their wives proceeded to assault the agents with brooms. Moe, who had been a featherweight boxer in his youth, fighting at half his Prohibition weight, laid out the men but could not bring himself to belt their wives. Izzy ran out of the saloon and got the police. After their enforced retirement, made necessary because they had become so well known, Izzy and Moe became successful salesmen with the New York Life Insurance Company. They were active, too, in the Grand Street Boys Association on West Fifty-fifth Street, where Walker also was a long-time member.

The raids instigated by Mrs. Willebrandt in 1928 were more refined. She insisted that the agents be big spenders and good conversationalists, able to make friends with club owners and patrons alike before blowing their whistles; the agents could even bring along their girlfriends. (One of her diligent hirelings visited Texas Guinan's place twenty-three times, buying booze on each occasion.) By September, some thirty-six Broadway restaurants and nightclubs had been padlocked. Moreover, Mrs. Willebrandt had initiated criminal prosecution against café owners, which was thought not sporting by purists; the two most prominent saloon hostesses, Helen Morgan and Miss Guinan, were speaking of early retirement. But such raids were costly. The agents, who were known to buy orchids for their girls, spent $40 for champagne, $10 for a pint of Scotch, as much as $2.25 for a cocktail. In all, the Willebrandt drive ran up some $75,000 in bar tabs. Ultimately, the government got back only $8,400 in cash and fines, and no convictions resulted, not even of the Misses Morgan and Guinan. Yet Mrs. Willebrandt, speaking about her efforts, could say, "No one knows what Prohibition is, because up to the present it has not had a fair chance."

Walker had a more realistic view, in this instance at least, of human nature. Referring to the statement of Herbert Hoover (who had just received the Republican presidential nomination to run against Smith) that the eight-year-old national Prohibition was a "noble experiment," the mayor commented, "I am willing to admit that it is noble, but I am compelled to ask when it is going to start." Nonetheless, he ordered Commissioner Warren to compile a report of premises that had been raided by the police. Mrs. Willebrandt was not impressed. In early September, she announced with heavy irony that Walker himself would make a "first-class inspector of nightclubs." Retorted the mayor: "If I were to qualify as an inspector I don't think I should need to become a reckless purchaser of orchids or of Staten Island champagne to learn facts which are known to virtually everyone."

William L. D'Olier, a prominent contractor who had done $1,600,-000 worth of work on the Queens sewers, was found dead in Mount

Zion Cemetery in Maspeth, Long Island, on September 2, a bullet hole in his right temple. The death occurred a couple of weeks before he was scheduled to testify in the trial of ex-Borough President Connolly. D'Olier appeared to have been beaten, and though *rigor mortis* had set in, the gun was not in his hand but on the ground beside his body; moreover, his fingerprints were not on the gun. The police insisted it was suicide. "My husband was murdered to silence him," said D'Olier's widow. A Queens grand jury agreed, castigating the police and calling the death a murder, but the case was dismissed for lack of evidence. A taxi driver originally swore that he had seen D'Olier and Connolly together twice within the last two weeks, but later he changed his testimony, saying it must have been someone who looked like the politician.

The conspiracy charges against Connolly meanwhile had been considerately reduced from three to one, and that a misdemeanor; he figured to get off lightly. On September 25, with some $8 million stolen from the taxpayers of Queens, Jack Phillips dead almost three months of cirrhosis, and most witnesses cowed, the ex-borough president's trial finally began. That Connolly was convicted at all was due to the energy and intelligence of the special prosecutor, Emory Buckner.

Born in Wheeler's Grove, Iowa, Buckner was the son of a Methodist minister, and as such destined to be a thorn in the side of fiscally careless New York politicians. After graduation from Harvard Law School in 1907 he proceeded to New York, where he became an assistant district attorney in Manhattan and later a special prosecutor. Buckner's initial success came in 1911, when he convicted a prominent lawyer of having received stolen goods by painstakingly going back over the testimony and itemizing a total of 105 times that the defendant had contradicted twenty-one witnesses. A few years thereafter, he sent to Sing Sing on a bribery charge one David Maier, later to become an intimate friend of Walker and a member of the mayor's Welcoming Committee, but then the owner of a string of whorehouses. Success followed success, and in 1925 Buckner was appointed U.S. district attorney. As such, he shipped Earl Carroll off to Atlanta for lying about plunging Joyce Hawley into a tub of champagne and treated William V. Dwyer, perhaps the biggest bootlegger of them all and a partner of Owney Madden, just as disrespectfully. (After Buckner had convicted him of trafficking in $40 million worth of booze over a two-and-a-half-year period, Dwyer told him, "While you were speaking, I thought to myself, 'I really *should* be convicted.'")

By 1928, Buckner had resigned from federal service and was acting as a special prosecutor in the trial of Connolly. As the proceedings went on, Buckner showed that from 1917 to 1927 some 90 percent of all sewer pipe laid in Queens had been bought through Phillips—at enormous profits to the Pipe King. In one instance, Phillips charged the city forty dollars a foot for pipe he had purchased at twenty-one dollars, making a profit of $76,000 on an $876,000 job. Buckner then hit hard at the connection between Phillips and Connolly. The prosecutor revealed, among other financial facts, that Connolly, between October 1925 and November 1927, had spent $145,454 in cash (on a salary of $15,000 a year).

Realizing that he had to make a clear and continuing impression on the jury of the connection between Phillips and Connolly, Buckner drew up a chart that may have been the largest ever used in a criminal case. Thirty feet by seven feet, it showed in a series of graphs how the burgeoning rates for Queens sewers oddly paralleled the increasing opulence of Connolly's life-style. While one graph indicated that the residents of Queens paid four times as much for sewers as anyone else, another pointed out that the ex-borough president spent at least four times as much as anyone with a comparable income. Amid the droning of witnesses and the objections of defense attorneys, such a chart becomes to jurymen, in the words of a journalist of the period, "as attractive as a Fragonard panel." Long before the end of the trial, the chart's 210 square feet were indelibly impressed on the jury's memory.

In mid-October, Connolly and a minor coconspirator were found guilty; they received the maximum sentences that could be given them—a year's imprisonment and a $500 fine. Two and a half years later, after the failure of two appeals, they journeyed to Welfare Island to serve their terms; Connolly's coconspirator made an inconspicuous arrival, but the ex-borough president drew up before the prison in a chauffeured limousine. Despite effusive greetings from prison guards and the warden and the frantic popping of photographers' flashbulbs, Connolly was moody. "Why make a Mardi Gras out of it?" he shouted. Ten weeks later, in March of 1931, he walked out of jail a free man, able to enjoy his considerable wealth for some years before his death.

At the state convention that October, Walker endorsed Smith's decision and put Roosevelt's name in nomination for governor. "I would be the last one to come upon this platform and suggest a man for your consideration," he declared, "unless I knew that man was a genuine American, and by that I mean a man who had studied and who knows the Declaration of Independence and [refuses] to forget what has been written in that immortal document." This scarcely veiled reference to religious intolerance brought the Democratic convention to its feet, cheering Roosevelt while condemning anti-Catholic attacks on Smith. Roosevelt's ebullient personality, unaffected by his semiparalysis, began to have its effect on the delegates, too. What had been a dull and lifeless convention, dispirited about finding any gubernatorial nominee to replace Smith, changed into an enthusiastic political gathering. Roosevelt was swiftly nominated, and Herbert H. Lehman was selected to run as lieutenant governor.

That fall found Betty Compton with her best Broadway part to date, opening in *Hold Everything*, a Ray Henderson musical. For a girl of only twenty-four, Betty had considerable theatrical experience. When she was seven, she had emigrated to Canada with her mother from her birthplace on the Isle of Wight; at age seventeen, she made her stage debut with a Toronto stock company. Married at eighteen to a Canadian attorney, she was divorced within a year. Betty then gravitated to New York, where she put her dancing talents to work in a series of musical revues; in 1926, she had attracted attention in *Oh, Kay!*, where she met Walker, and the next year had been similarly successful in *Funny Face*.

Hold Everything was a spoof of the prize-fight game. It concerned a young boxer whose romance with his girl friend is temporarily broken up by Betty, in the part of a vampish society flapper. Yearning for his true love, the boxer loses all interest in his upcoming championship match. At the last moment, fighter and girl friend are reunited, and he becomes a battler again. Curtain. *Hold Everything* made a star of Bert Lahr, whose portrayal of Gink Schiner, an older, punchdrunk fighter, was replete with shadowboxing, shouting, and double takes. In her role, Betty sang and danced her way through three numbers: "An Outdoor Man for My Indoor Sports," "For Sweet Charity's Sake," and "It's All Over But the Shoutin'." She was one of three girls in the show whom the reviewer for *The New Yorker* called "the prettiest principals I remember having seen collected." Added Percy Hammond of the *Herald:* "Miss Betty Compton peeps her carols prettily though inaudibly, and as a man-hungry flapper from Old Westbury, she is smart and good to look upon."

Sidney Solomon, a friend of Walker whose various occupations ranged from hotel-keeping to dress manufacturing, had made it known to the mayor in 1926 that he wanted to take over the management of the Casino in Central Park. A dilapidated, sixty-year-old building, the Casino stood in the Seventies, just inside the Fifth Avenue border of Central Park; it served pedestrian food and was unimaginatively run. Walker ascertained that the ten-year-lease of the operator, Carl F. Zittel, a small-time theatrical publisher, would expire in mid-1928, and arranged for Parks Commissioner Herrick to transfer the lease to Solomon. The one-time dress manufacturer had grandiose plans for the Casino. He intended to spend some $400,000 remodeling and redecorating the building; there would be a stone terrace and a rooftop fountain, the dining room would be silver, maroon, and green, and black glass would mirror the dancers in the ballroom. Gourmet chefs would be hired, and, anticipating that patrons would bring their own liquors and wines, stiff fees would be charged for set-ups and glasses. Finally, the Casino would have, not just one, but two of the best-known orchestras in the country—Leo Reisman's and Emil Coleman's.

Solomon's plans would become reality in 1929, and Jim and Betty, together with the rest of fashionable New York, would make the Casino their rendezvous. "The Casino will be our place, Monk," said Jim, calling Betty by the pet name he had given her.

In October of 1928, however, Zittel's friends were suing the city, saying that Walker and Herrick, by authorizing such an elaborate transformation of the Casino, were violating the park's recreational purpose. Nathan Straus, Jr., president of the Park Association of New York, demurred, insisting that "the public interest would not be injured." Embarrassed by the implied (and justified) accusations of favoritism, Walker got testy. Whatever the outcome of the suit, he said, "There is one thing certain. Zittel will not get the new lease." Added Herrick defensively: "The city certainly needs such a place. When we were abroad with the mayor we were entertained in just such a restaurant."

On the night of November 4, gambler Arnold Rothstein was found critically wounded by a gunshot in the service area of the Park Central Hotel at Seventh Avenue and Fifty-sixth Street. He had made his way down the back stairway, his hand clutching the wound in his stomach, and had told an elevator operator, "Get me a taxi." When the police were summoned, the forty-six-year-old Rothstein refused to tell them who had shot him. He was taken to Poly-clinic Hospital, where two days later, as some forty million Americans were casting the ballots that overwhelmingly repudiated Smith and swept Herbert Hoover into the White House, he died, still not naming his assailant. The Rothstein killing brought Walker the most insistent public criticism he had thus far encountered, for it underscored the ineffectiveness of the police in dealing with organized crime. Yet the police and District Attorney Jaob Banton, knowing Rothstein's ties with many Tammany politicians, were understandably reluctant to dig too deeply into his affairs. Already a lawyer for the gambler's family had asked D. A. Banton to investigate his business records. "If those papers are ever made public," the lawyer said, "there are going to be a lot of suicides in high places."

The official foot-dragging was all the more obvious because the murder suspect could so easily be identified. Rothstein had gone to the hotel in response to a telephone call, which he received in his customary "office"—a table in Lindy's Restaurant on Seventh Avenue. "McManus wants to see me at the Park Central," he told a friend. Rothstein entered Room 349, from which the call to Lindy's had been placed, and there he was shot. His assailant then threw the revolver out the window onto the street; there it was found by a cab driver who turned it over to the police, but smudged the fingerprints. Although Room 349 had been registered in the name of "George Richards," an expensive Chesterfield overcoat was found in the room's closet with the name "George McManus" embroidered inside. And a hotel maid named Bridget Farry, shown a photo of McManus, himself a gambler, was certain he was the man who earlier in the evening had occupied the room and done a good deal of drinking there: "Sure, he's the one. I'd know him anywhere." Moreover, McManus had a motive. Ten months earlier, Rothstein uncharacteristically had dropped some $250,000 in a poker game run by McManus, but characteristically had paid off only in IOUs. As the weeks dragged on and he did not ante up, the other participants, not daring to pressure someone of his underworld stature, began to badger George. They felt he had an ethical responsibility, so to speak, to see all debts were settled. But Rothstein, who needed ready cash for the narcotics empire he was building (drugs being strictly a cash-and-carry trade), and with hundreds of thousands of dollars tied up in bets on Hoover for president and Roosevelt for governor, had been in no hurry to make good. "They'll get their money," he had said, "but when I want to give it to them."

Days went by after Rothstein's killing, and the police were still not able—if indeed they were trying—to locate McManus. Finally on November 27, three weeks after the shooting, the gambler decided to give himself up. His lawyer called a detective they knew and arranged for the surrender to take place in classic fashion, in a barber shop at Broadway and Two Hundred Forty-second Street. When the detective, John Cordes, arrived, the tall, well-built McManus, minus his collar and polka-dot tie, was in the barber's chair; he had just gotten a haircut and was about to be shaved.

"Hello, George," said Cordes.

"Hello, Jack," was the reply.

Sitting down in a nearby chair, Cordes then leafed through a magazine, waiting until McManus was finished.

This companionability was too much for Walker. While he did not want Rothstein's ties with Tammany politicians to be revealed (and a careful perusal of the gambler's papers might well have done that), he felt the police should appear more assiduous in their efforts to bring in his murderer. He gave Commissioner Warren "four days to solve the case or retire." After all, most of Rothstein's business records had by now disappeared, the steel filing cabinets housing them mysteriously having been removed from the dead gambler's home at 912 Fifth Avenue by unknown parties.

Arnold Rothstein developed his bookmaking and gambling skills in the early 1900s under the protection of "Big Tim" Sullivan, who ruled the Bowery and the Tenderloin. (Though Mr. Murphy bossed Tammany Hall, Sullivan's districts were fiefdoms within the organization and were run independently.) Arnold's greatest coup during this period was the taking of $250,000 one night from Percival H. Hill of the American Tobacco Company, whom he had lured to his gambling house with the assistance of Peggy Hopkins, a stage beauty of the period. Though many people had to be given their percentages, Rothstein still cleared half the money. It was not until the summer of 1912, however, that the gambler, then thirty, began to emerge as a power in his shadowy world. One reason was the murder of Herman Rosenthal, a gambler acquaintance of Rothstein; the killing, which was played up by the *World*'s Herbert Bayard Swope, exposed Tammany and police protection of gambling operations. Another factor was Big Tim's failing mental health, which prevented him from smoothing over the situation as he once might have done. Casting about for a shrewd, quiet fellow who could be its link with the underworld, Tammany's eye fell on Rothstein.

Over the next few years, Rothstein provided all manner of services for the Tiger—hiring hoodlums to stuff ballot boxes, posting bail bonds for the unlucky, serving as a bag man for the gathering of tribute. Similarly, Arnold handled the fixing of nightclub violations, the granting of boxing licenses, the evasion of laws and ordinances great and small. In each instance, he took his cut. While he was still in his thirties, his fortune had grown to a half million dollars.

Rothstein used the money to expand his bookmaking operations. He became a discount man for bookmakers—giving them insurance, for a fee, when bettors wagered too heavily on various favorites. In 1919, when members of the Chicago White Sox conspired to lose the World Series to Cincinnati, he was charged with having put up the money to persuade them. Said Ban Johnson, then president of the American League: "The man behind the fixing was Arnold Rothstein." In a prepared statement, Rothstein denied the accusation, saying that some "cheap gamblers [had] decided to frame the Series and make a killing . . . [and] used my name to put it over." The grand jury believed him, and he was not indicted. Amazingly enough, the jury did return indictments, not just against two other gamblers and eight ballplayers, but against Rachel Brown, Arnold's chief bookkeeper, who had been in Chicago keeping a painstaking record of all the bets. It gives one pause.

In the early 1920s, Rothstein branched out once more, financing and protecting "bucket-shops." These were high-pressure stock-dumping operations on the fringe of the law; the idea was to sell as much stock in as short a time as possible and then clear out—before anyone complained to the authorities. Profits were enormous, and Rothstein's worth was now several million dollars. Nat J. Ferber, a reporter for the New York *American* who completed a detailed investigation of the shops, pointed out that almost all the bucketeers had close ties with the Tammany middleman: "He had helped one get a ticker wire; he had lined up a high-price lawyer for another; he had gotten a third an interview with a Tammany leader. Rothstein, more than anyone, was in on the birth and death of [the] bucket-shops."

By the late 1920s, with the permissive Judge Olvany ruling Tammany, Rothstein had spread his financial tentacles still further. He had always bankrolled bootleggers in their endeavors (Jack "Legs" Diamond, who was once his bodyguard, had been one of his earliest beneficiaries). Now Arnold, always able to anticipate trends, was buying and selling cocaine and heroin. Here the profits were potentially even greater than in bucket-shops. After Rothstein's death, U.S. District Attorney Charles H. Tuttle got his hands on the gambler's few records that had not been spirited away. The information Tuttle gleaned from them enabled him to stage simultaneous raids in three locations, which netted almost a million dollars in drugs. "Drug traffic in the United States [has been] directed from one source. . . . Arnold Rothstein was that source," Tuttle declared.

It was ironic that Rothstein should have been killed, probably by the boozy McManus, a minor cardsharp feeling pressure from his confreres, over a mere $250,000 in poker debts. The shooting kept him from collecting his bets on Hoover and Roosevelt in the elections, which would have brought him some $570,000. As matters stood, he left an estate of $3 million.

The four-day ultimatum Walker had given Warren to solve the Rothstein case came and went. In early December, the mayor went to Wanamaker's department store and spoke to Grover Whalen, its general manager.

"Grover, I've got to make a change of police commissioners," he said. "This Rothstein murder has raised hell. . . . Police morale is shot to pieces. . . . I'm here to ask you to be the top cop."

His health now shattered, Warren was embittered by Walker's treatment of him; he knew he was being sacrificed to hide a corrupt political situation. His first letter of resignation said as much, and the mayor refused to accept or make it public. Walker's former law associate then submitted a second letter, coldly formal but correct. Eight months later he was dead.

Whalen set up a great appearance of police activity. He hit "police laxity," merged some squads and established others, and demoted numerous officers. Inspector John D. Coughlin, the head of detectives who had been highly thought of by both McLaughlin and Warren, was retired. "I don't think the Detective Division has been sufficiently active," said Whalen. "I know of no arrest by detectives in the [Rothstein] case and the usual routine of bringing in witnesses for questioning seems to have been ignored." (In fact, McManus was in jail on a murder indictment, and Bridget Farry, the maid who had identified him, was being held as a material witness.)

In a related move, the new commissioner demoted Deputy Chief Inspector Lewis J. Valentine to captain and disbanded his Confidential Squad. "Oh, yes," said Whalen in reply to a reporter's question, "Captain Valentine is being sent out to command the Fifty-ninth Precinct over in Long Island City." The idea of a "personal investigation bureau" was, Whalen said, repugnant to him; it demoralized the force.

Whalen's insistence that justice would be done in the Rothstein case pacified those who wondered when McManus would come to trial. As matters turned out, he was not tried until almost a year later—after the November 1929 mayoral election. During most of that time, he would be free on $50,000 bail, while an increasingly nervous Bridget Farry would be kept in jail. When the case did come before a jury, she understandably decided that McManus was not the man she had seen in the hotel room after all, and District Attorney Banton put up such a weak prosecution that the judge directed a verdict of not guilty. Smiling and relaxed, McManus left the courtroom wearing the Chesterfield coat that only minutes before had been part of the evidence against him. He died of natural causes, in Sea Girt, New Jersey, twelve years after Rothstein.

Of Grover A. Whalen, a journalist of the 1920s said, his is "the square-jawed, black-mustached face that swarms over the scenes of the period like the cupids in the old religious paintings." And indeed, it was for his work as head of the mayor's Welcoming Committee that Grover was best known. But Walker's third police commissioner was more than a mere glad-hander. He was an energetic businessman who projected an image of utter efficiency. Whether this reputation was deserved is another matter.

Born in a tenement on East Broadway, the son of a local Tammany leader who made a good living in real estate, Whalen was educated at DeWitt Clinton High School, Packard Business College, and New York Law School. By 1917, at the age of thirty-one, he had developed a friendship with Rodman Wanamaker, heir to the then-thriving department store; together the two young men helped persuade the Business Men's League, of which they were forceful members, to endorse Hylan for the mayoralty. Once he was elected, Red Mike rewarded Grover with a job as his personal secretary.

Since Whalen, his chin at a belligerent tilt and his bearing imposingly military, had a habit of preceding Hylan at public gatherings, the mayor within a year decided to move him into a less noticeable job, commissioner of plants and structures. No sooner was the new commissioner installed, however, than he was informed that one of the main cables of the Brooklyn Bridge had slipped three inches in its tower saddle on the New York side. Grover personally inspected the slippage, walking up the cable hundreds of feet to the tower, before ordering the bridge closed. It was weeks before it was fully restored to traffic; all the while, much to Hylan's chagrin, Grover stayed in the headlines. There was never any further slippage, and Whalen afterward admitted, "What caused the movement I have never been able to determine."

After the fortuitous episode with the bridge, over the next few years the commissioner threw himself into a multiplicity of projects —not all of which really concerned his office. He revitalized a Staten Island trolley line, reorganized the ferries, made laboratory tests of bootleg whiskey for the police, took over the city's purchasing board, and commandeered the municipal radio station. Occasionally, Grover did remember that Hylan was the boss. In 1923, to celebrate Red Mike's recovery from an illness, he staged a party. As Hylan arrived in the plants and structures' offices, trumpets sounded, ferryboat captains in dress uniforms saluted, and an ode was read that proclaimed in part:

> We have been like a ship without a rudder;
> We have missed the captain's skill;
> Though we've worked for our Mistress the City,
> The while he lay grievously ill.

Whalen's stroke of genius, however, was his leadership of the Welcoming Committee, which was initiated during the Hylan administration but achieved full splendor under Walker. In that post, he invariably upstaged Red Mike. All eyes instinctively were drawn to a man who knew that the Prince of Wales must be greeted in top hat and tails, while a transatlantic flier who had merely made the Azores necessitated only a fedora and a blue-serge suit. Tammany pols yearned to be instructed in the niceties.

Hylan must have wondered what welcoming had wrought. When Grover began suggesting that he run for senator or governor, Red Mike, who knew his limitations, realized that his protégé had mayoral ambitions of his own. He thereupon called Rodman Wanamaker, sometime in 1924, and advised him that Grover was just what his department store needed.

"But I wouldn't want to take him away from you," said Wanamaker.

"Never mind me," said Hylan.

As a gardenia-wearing Wanamaker's executive, Whalen devoted his energies to Chippendale bedroom suites, the latest in Limoges, and the prevention of shoplifting. In the summer of 1925, when he came out for Walker in the primary fight, Red Mike promptly labeled him a "traitor." After Walker's election, Grover got even with Hylan by not inviting him to the City Hall reception for Lindbergh.

In planning the welcomes for distinguished visitors, Whalen's greatest accomplishment was making sure that all motorcades began promptly at 12 noon. While it was not difficult to get New Yorkers to turn out for Byrd, Gertrude Ederle, or Lindbergh, there was understandably less excitement over General Horatio Vásquez of San Domingo, Hassan Tagi Lader of Persia, or George Kojac, the Ukrainian-American 100-meter backstroke champion. Yet at noon, Lower Broadway was always packed with people taking their lunch break. The more obscure the guest, the more he was touched by the warmth of his reception.

With Smith discredited by a presidential loss so overwhelming that he had not even carried New York, Governor-elect Roosevelt

State Assemblyman James J. Walker, age thirty-two, in 1913. *(Culver Pictures)*

Allie Walker in 1918, six years after her marriage to the young legislator. *(Culver Pictures)*

Walker's Greenwich Village birthplace and home, 6 St. Luke's Place.
(Wide World Photos)

Walker being sworn in for his first term as Mayor by State Supreme Court Justice Robert F. Wagner.
(Wide World Photos)

Former marine Gene Tunney, flanked by Mayor Walker and Grover Whalen, the city's official greeter, gets a military welcome after winning the heavyweight boxing championship from Jack Dempsey in 1926.
(Culver Pictures)

Charles A. Lindbergh stands at attention with Walker during a tumultuous New York reception celebrating his nonstop solo flight across the Atlantic in 1927. *(Culver Pictures)*

Gertrude Ederle, the first woman to swim the English Channel, is feted by the Mayor's Welcoming Committee. *(Culver Pictures)*

Walker, Allie, and their party before their audience with Pope Pius X during a trip to Europe in 1927. Standing behind the Mayor's right shoulder is Hector Fuller; behind Mrs. Walker is her secretary, Evelyn Wagner; State Senator Bernard Downing is at the far right. *(Wide World Photos)*

Twenty-three-year-old Betty Compton (far left), as she appeared with Fred Astaire in the 1927 musical *Funny Face*. Adele Astaire is on her left. *(New York Public Library)*

Walker in a pair of cuffed trousers, such as he rarely wore, and an even rarer pensive mood, on the boardwalk at Atlantic City. *(Museum of the City of New York)*

Fighting the good fight for the five-cent fare at the Transit hearings in 1931, Walker is assisted by Comptroller Charles Berry (behind his left shoulder) and Attorney Samuel Untermyer (far right). *(Wide World Photos)*

To help Tammany celebrate the move of its headquarters from East Fourteenth Street to Union Square at Seventeenth Street in early 1929, Walker, Sachem John R. Voorhis, and Alfred E. Smith watch the laying of the building's cornerstone. *(Museum of the City of New York)*

Although Walker, then forty-eight years old, had been estranged from Allie for a year, he shows up at the polls with his wife to cast his ballot in the 1929 mayoral contest against Fiorello LaGuardia. *(Wide World Photos)*

On a visit to Europe in 1931, Walker dedicates a memorial in Paris to American doughboys who fought in the World War. *(Wide World Photos)*

Plagued by the Seabury investigations, Walker (wearing the peaked beret he adopted in France) returns to New York in late September, 1931, and is greeted by his assistant, Charles Kerrigan, and his fourth and last police commissioner, Edward P. Mulrooney. *(Wide World Photos)*

Still sprightly, Walker in 1932 leads thousands of New Yorkers down Fifth Avenue in a "Beer for Taxation" parade that sought repeal of Prohibition. *(Wide World Photos)*

In May of 1932, a beleaguered Walker was finally called before his accuser, Samuel S. Seabury, at the end of the state investigation into the affairs of the city government. *(United Press International)*

Walker and his last "benefactor," realtor and theatrical magnate A. C. Blumenthal. *(Wide World Photos)*

With Brooklyn leader John H. McCooey (left) and Tammany leader John F. Curry (center), Walker talks strategy at the 1932 Democratic National Convention, at which New York's governor, Franklin D. Roosevelt, was nominated for the Presidency. *(Wide World Photos)*

Betty Compton, Walker's second
wife, and the former Mayor, then
fifty-five years old, attend a dog
show in 1936.
(United Press International)

In November of 1946,
James J. Walker's spirit is consigned
to his God in a Solemn High Mass
of Requiem at St. Patrick's
Cathedral. *(Wide World Photos)*

indicated at year's end that he was taking the reins of government firmly in hand. Now all state patronage, he told Walker during a brief conference at his East Sixty-fifth Street townhouse, would be funneled not through Tammany but through Bronx Democratic leader Edward J. Flynn. Twenty-four hours later, he made the decision public, naming Flynn his secretary of state and chief advisor on city affairs. Though the Bronx man's alliance with Tammany had helped put Walker in office, his reservations about Judge Olvany and the mayor were well known. In choosing him, Roosevelt was quickly asserting his independence.

Franklin Delano Roosevelt was by birth and breeding the antithesis of Tammany's pushy newcomers. His family, having emigrated from Holland in the 1600s, had become charter members of the Hudson River aristocracy. Young Roosevelt was reared on a 500-acre estate in Hyde Park, New York, where future oil magnates and bank presidents were his boyhood chums. He went to Groton and then to Harvard, where he belonged to Hasty Pudding and served as editor of the *Crimson.* He attended Columbia Law School and, though he flunked his finals and did not graduate, he later passed his bar examinations.

Despite FDR's privileged background, he was genuinely concerned with progressive social measures. Unlike their wealthy neighbors, the Hyde Park Roosevelts had always been Democrats; even in the years before the Civil War, though they were abolitionists themselves, they refused to change their party affiliations. (Republican Theodore Roosevelt, a fifth cousin of Franklin, represented the Long Island branch of the family.)

Still in his twenties, FDR won election to the state senate from conservative Duchess County, a decided accomplishment for a Democrat. When Theodore Roosevelt ran against Republican William H. Taft as a Progressive in 1912, splitting his party and permitting Woodrow Wilson to win the presidency, cousin Franklin was an indirect beneficiary. A strong Wilson supporter, he was named assistant secretary of the navy under landlubber Josephus Daniels. If Roosevelt was a "white flannel yachtsman," at least he was an experienced one; naval officers were soon bringing him their problems directly. He was particularly effective during World War I—breaking up cliques, supporting competitive bidding for contracts, creating submarine-chaser squadrons.

In 1920, Roosevelt's stature was such that he was nominated for the vice-presidency at the Democratic convention in San Francisco. Initially, both he and presidential nominee James M. Cox had planned to play down Wilson's fight for the League of Nations, correctly feeling that the country was moving away from internationalism. But after a meeting with the ailing president, whose health had broken down almost completely during his second term, they could not bring themselves to disclaim his stand, even for political expediency. It was foreordained that the Cox-Roosevelt ticket would lose to Harding-Coolidge—and badly. "While I waited for the returns," said FDR, "I felt that if one could be beaten on such an issue, there was something rotten about the world."

The next year Roosevelt, his own health impaired by the strain of campaigning, was stricken with infantile paralysis following a swim in the icy Maine waters off Campobello Island. For a while, he was completely immobile; then therapy and willpower brought about a partial recovery; only his legs remained paralyzed. At the 1924 New York Democratic Convention, waves of cheering had rolled through Madison Square Garden when FDR, a lone figure on crutches, appeared at the rear of the speaking platform. As he swung his slow, determined way toward the microphones to put Smith's name in nomination, the delegates roared their approval. Smiling and triumphant, he had ringingly delivered his "Happy Warrior" speech. And when he concluded with the lines from Wordsworth, "This is the Happy Warrior . . . this is he . . . Whom every man in arms should wish to be," the delegates knew that in FDR the party had a second "Happy Warrior."

The friendship between Smith and Roosevelt ripened over these years; each respected the other as a skillful, dedicated politican. Up until the 1928 elections, however, it was always Smith who spoke for the democracy of New York. Now Roosevelt was the leader. Whatever restraint Smith had been able to exert on Tammany and Walker, through Celtic blood and allegiances, had disappeared as though it had never been.

1929

"My plan," said Queen Medb to Ailill, "is to keep these three heroes with us tonight, and to test them further."

Next day the heroes attempted the wheel feat. Leogaire seized a chariot wheel and hurled it halfway up the castle wall; Conall followed this splendid effort with an even better toss, sending the wheel as far as the top of the wall. Then Cu Chulainn put his back into an awesome throw that sent the wheel over the wall and into the outside courtyard, where it sank to the depth of a tall man's stature in the hard and rocky ground.

These feats elicited many cheers—each of the heroes having his own staunch adherents.

〰〰〰

In mid-January, Allie Walker sailed with a woman friend aboard the liner *President Roosevelt* for a six-week vacation in Cuba. When Mrs. Walker, escorted by Charles Hand, the mayor's secretary, got to the Hoboken ferry, which was to take them across the Hudson to the ship's New Jersey pier, she discovered that she had left her ticket and the keys to her luggage back at St. Luke's Place. The chauffeur was sent to retrieve them, and the party continued on its way. Unfortunately, the chauffeur had not reappeared when the *Roosevelt's* last whistle warned all visitors ashore, so the liner was held at the pier. Finally, after a fifteen-minute delay, the man arrived—with the ticket but with the wrong keys. Allie was forced to have her trunks opened en route by the ship's locksmith.

It would be unwise to make too much of this anecdote, but it does illustrate the kind of woman Mrs. Walker had become—ineffectual, a trifle sad, no more able to cope with the gay, sophisticated games of Walker and his show-business friends than the mayor himself, living for the moment, could control the shrewd, patient avarice of his Tammany associates. The newspapers explained that "a bad cold" had kept Walker from being on hand for his wife's sailing.

The next day, the mayor recovered sufficiently to attend funeral services for Sophie Irene Loeb, a distinguished New Yorker whose welfare work had made her widely known both in the United States and in Europe. Brought to this country from Russia at the age of six, she was raised in Pennsylvania. As a young woman she came to New York, where in the early 1900s she became interested in the problems of widows and children trying to eke out a livelihood in the slums. Largely through her efforts, a state board of child welfare was appointed in 1915 (on which she served), with powers to pay living allowances to widows in their homes so as to keep families together and avoid institutionalizing the children. In the years thereafter, Mrs. Loeb saw to it that annual appropriations to aid the indigent mothers were increased from $100,000 to more than $5 million. At the same time, she served as a staff writer for the *Evening World* and authored a dozen books of an inspirational and sociological nature. Among her activities, Mrs. Loeb helped to bring about free maternity care for needy women, penny lunches in the public schools, off-hours use of the schools as community centers, play streets for slum children, and housing relief for slum dwellers. For her social work, she never accepted any pay.

Mrs. Loeb's funeral at the Free Synagogue House on West Sixty-eighth Street was attended, not only by Walker, but by such dignitaries as newly-sworn Lieutenant Governor Herbert H. Lehman and Rabbi Stephen Wise, then perhaps the leading spokesman for the city's Jewish community. "Few persons in the United States have done as much for mothers and children," Walker said of the fifty-two-year-old humanitarian, his voice breaking with emotion. "The blessings of everyone with whom she ever worked, and above all the blessings of the children whom she aided, will go with her to her eternal resting place." Added Lehman: "She made her presence felt in so many circles that her loss is almost irreparable."

Bird Coler, the commissioner of public welfare who had been

assailed by Walker in mid-1927 over his use of city hospital appropriations to build a laboratory and other facilities for Long Island College, turned in his resignation the last day of January 1929, and promptly launched an attack of his own. Coler, whose thirty-year political career and eleven years as commissioner had been curtailed by the mayor's consolidation of the city's hospitals into a separate municipal department (thus effectively reducing his importance), contrasted the regimes of Murphy and Hylan to that of Olvany and Walker; he declared that the present incumbents, besides having been sold "a gold brick" on the matter of the hospital merger, were permitting too much indiscriminate patronage. "You can't make a hospital part of a political machine," he said, "and make it work." Would-be appointees to posts in public welfare now appeared in his office, Coler stated, merely bearing slips of paper signed by Tammany officials. "In the old days, the leaders would come down themselves and recommend a certain man," he said, "and if that man manifestly was not fitted for the job you could talk to that leader and he would suggest someone else. . . . Nowadays [it's impossible to] turn down the men. . . . Judge Olvany may not know it but the [Tammany] secretary, James F. Eagan, is doing it. Under the administration of Mayor Hylan, I was never interfered with at all. Under the leadership of Mr. Murphy, I was never interfered with on the appointment of physicians." Commented Judge Olvany: "They're the ravings of a man who has lost his job."

Yet Coler's charges of indiscriminate patronage in city medical departments were not without merit. Dr. William Schroeder, the newly appointed commissioner of hospitals, soon proved this when he named his two top deputies, James H. Fay of Manhattan and Edward P. Cadley of Brooklyn. Fay was vice-president of the Anawanda Club, Mr. Murphy's old organization; Cadley, a close friend of McCooey, had been chief clerk in the borough president's office. "They were my personal choice," insisted Schroeder with bland insouciance.

The Equitable bus-franchise scheme meanwhile was coming to an abortive end. Certificates of convenience and necessity, which required the company to establish bus routes in Manhattan, Brooklyn, and Queens by early 1929, had been issued by the transit commission, but no rolling stock had been produced. Financing could not be found. To hush the funny-money whispers, Walker publicly announced that the board of estimate, when it originally approved the Equitable franchise, had thought that the late Anson W. Burchard, then head of General Electric's finance committee, was guaranteeing the Equitable's credit. "The Board believed that all the resources of General Electric were behind the petition for a franchise," the mayor claimed.

"At that time, the board did not know [the promise] was limited to a moral commitment [but] thought it was a legal commitment."

Walker's confreres on the board, who with him had approved the Equitable award, now were loath to give it further favorable treatment; the publicity was posing too many difficulties. By the spring, the transit commission declared the Equitable franchise nonoperative, thus ending Senator Hasting's dream of becoming a millionaire. Nonetheless, Hastings managed to meet expenses. During the three and a half years he championed the Equitable cause at City Hall, he was paid some $60,000 for services rendered.

In the same casual way that he had run Tammany for the previous five years, George W. Olvany in mid-March suddenly resigned its leadership. Just before opening a routine meeting of Tammany's executive committee, he handed a letter announcing his intentions to James F. Eagan, the society's secretary. Then he proceeded to deal with the assembled district leaders, who know nothing of the letter, on mundane political matters, while Eagan sat and fretted. When the business was concluded, Olvany sat stony-faced through a long pause. Eagan looked at him expectantly but received no direction. Finally the Tammany secretary rose and announced he had a statement from Judge Olvany he should read aloud.

"Because of ill health and on the advice of my physicians, I resign as leader of Tammany Hall," was the brief message of resignation.

Complete silence followed. After a stir, a voice cried, "What does that mean?"

"Possibly you did not understand me," said Eagan, who then read the letter a second time. With that, the meeting broke up.

Subsequently it was learned that Dr. Harlow Brooks of 47 West Ninth Street and Dr. Walter Timme, a neurologist of 1 West Sixty-fourth Street, had informed Olvany that he was "overdoing it" and that his condition was such that he should take a long rest from his arduous duties. "Mr. Olvany was reluctant to give up his work," Dr. Brooks said, "but we insisted that he must take a long vacation. He said that he could not take such a vacation and still occupy his place in public life."

At a gathering of Democratic moguls in a private home a few days later, Al Smith put a different interpretation on Olvany's decision. "Did you lose your nerve?" he asked him.

"The condition of my health made it imperative that I resign," Olvany replied, his doleful countenance showing no emotion.

At the same affair, Walker remarked, "I would have appreciated it, George, if you had given me twenty minutes' notice."

"The condition of my health," intoned Olvany, "made it imperative that I resign."

Smith's and Walker's doubts about George's true motivations were justified. During Olvany's brief stint as Tammany's leader (and for two years thereafter), his law firm earned some $5 million in legal fees for its powers of persuasion before the board of standards and appeals. The board's five members were appointed by the mayor, but only with George's approval; indeed, William E. Walsh, the chairman, had been a close friend of Olvany's for the previous fifteen years. A word of explanation is in order here to explain the board's powers. During the reform administration of John Purroy Mitchel in 1917, an attempt was made to curb skyscraper construction and thereby preserve light and air for the citizenry. Obviously, the value of a residential property would greatly increase if high-rise apartment houses could be erected, or if the area could be rezoned for business. It was the board of standards and appeals that granted such variances. Builders were willing to pay large sums to law firms with political connections, believing, in their naivete, that the smile, the wink, and the nod were more likely to capture air space than all the costs per-square-foot devised by man. Whether any of the legal fees were passed on to other interested parties was not the concern of the petitioners.

Olvany's law firm specialized in a second interesting area—condemnation proceedings. In these instances, speculators with clairvoyant powers would buy land at nominal prices, only to find that the city was convinced it must have the property—for a school, park, or garbage dump—whatever the cost. Good businessmen that they were, the speculators did not rely completely on the occult, but retained attorneys with a certain knowledge of municipal affairs. One visionary represented by Olvany optioned a piece of land for $25,000, then found that the city would pay him $449,000 for the tract. No piker, he thought that the $87,000 legal fee (a fifth of the profit) was money well spent.

At the Seabury hearings in 1931, Olvany would maintain that his influence on zoning and condemnation proceedings had been minimal. Though it was true that Board Chairman Walsh would stop off for advice at Tammany Hall "on the way home," their discussions always remained on a high ethical plane.

"Have we got it this way?" George's interrogator asked. "That the only occasions in which you ventured to interject your personality into the situation . . . [were] where you acted . . . to help someone that needed help?"

Olvany nodded calmly. "As a good Samaritan," he replied.

George kept so much in the background regarding standards and appeals matters, in fact, that quite often the firm of Olvany, Eisner and Donnelly used an intermediary to represent its clients' interests before the board. When realtor Fred F. French needed zoning help to erect the $100 million towers of Tudor City on Forty-second Street and the East River, for instance, he immediately called on George's firm. There one of the partners, John F. Donnelly, explained that "for convenience" he was assigning the case to a third party—a lawyer named Frederick J. Flynn, who had no visible connection with the firm. French, who was interested only in results, made no demurrer and a fee of $75,000 ultimately passed hands. When the first payment of $20,000 came due, French made out a check to Flynn, who deposited it in his bank account and then cashed a check of his own for a smiliar amount. Flynn thereupon delivered the money to Donnelly in person; he saw nothing unusual in carrying this much cash through the streets, explaining that his bank was only three blocks from the law firm's offices. A second $20,000 check was converted to cash in like manner. A third payment of $10,000 from French brought about a variation: Flynn endorsed the check and delivered it to Olvany, Eisner and Donnelly; then Donnelly took the check to the firm's bank and exchanged it for a cashier's check, which he deposited to the firm's account; the canceled check that went back to French, of course, had only Flynn's endorsement.

Forty-five years old in 1929, Fred Fillmore French conducted his business at 551 Fifth Avenue. His working day began promptly at 9:00 A.M., when he strode to the lectern in the building's private auditorium and exhorted his sales force to make the world safe for real estate. (Any salesman who arrived late was forced to listen at the keyhole; French ordered the doors locked before he began speaking.) One of his recurring themes at these get-togethers was that his men should master the art of smiling: "Stand before your bathroom mirror and practice smiling for ten minutes in the morning and at night. . . . Get smiling into your system." Yet French had a spiritual side. "The best example for a sales talk is the life of Jesus Christ," he would say. "He is the best salesman of all time. He said, 'Knock, and it shall be opened unto you.' What he meant was 'Keep knocking until the door is open, and if it isn't opened pretty soon, knock down the door!' " At the end of the talks, with his hirelings so keyed up they could barely be restrained from crashing out of the still-locked auditorium (to call on clients, naturally), French gifted them with reprints of various inspirational essays—works such as Elbert Hubbard's "Message to Garcia." Meanwhile, everybody kept smiling.

French was at the peak of his career when planning Tudor City.

He prided himself on working late and sleeping little, keeping a clean desk, and not employing women ("they can't hew to the line"). He chose not to speculate about why the firm of Olvany, Eisner and Donnelly would use intermediaries such as Flynn (to whom it paid commissions ranging from 15 to 20 percent) or why it chose to receive its fees in cash.

Throughout March and most of April, Tammany tried fruitlessly to agree on a replacement for Olvany. With some seventy leaders (men and women in equal numbers) each voting a fraction of the twenty-three votes representing the twenty-three assembly districts, the early caucuses were tentative, bumbling affairs. At one such meeting, the male leaders showed up, only to discover they had forgotten to invite their female counterparts. (The women were mere window dressing in the politics of the time—in brief moments of candor, they were referred to as "water buffaloes"—but a legal caucus could not be held without them.) On one point, however, the district leaders were firm; the new Tammany chieftain must come from their ranks; no "statesmen" need apply. Gradually, three strong candidates emerged: Edward J. Ahearn of the Fourth A.D., who was disliked by Walker but favored, at least to a degree, by the supporters of former Governor Smith; Martin G. McCue of the Twelfth A.D., a former prize fighter who had served with Walker in the legislature; and John Francis Curry of the Fifth A.D., whose thirty-five years of political experience made him second in length of service among the male subchieftains. Of these men, the one least acceptable to Smith was Curry, who saw Tammany strictly as a city-oriented machine and had long decried the "New Tammany" that Smith had molded to attain national prominence.

As the days lengthened into weeks, however, it became apparent, from the various delaying tactics used by Curry's rivals, that he was the favored candidate. Behind the scenes, Walker was heard to remark in praise of John Francis that "The successful leaders of the Organization have been district leaders, such as Murphy, Kelly and Croker." Smith, Senator Wagner, and Surrogate Foley all resisted Curry's bid, but their influence was waning. "It is fiction, this 'New Tammany,' " Curry trumpeted. "I will carry out the politics in which I grew up." The leaders rightly understood that he was promising them, the middlemen, more generous slices of the municipal pie; they reacted with growing enthusiasm. Yet it would be wrong to think that Curry did not have standards. In his Fifth A.D., just north of Hell's Kitchen, he had built up a powerful vote-producing constituency. "Curry was always on the job in the musty cellars of the clubhouse on West 57th Street, or was rapidly climbing a tenement stairway to comfort the widow of a departed henchman," wrote one admirer. "In brief, he got things done. He [also] obtained his share, and a little more, from the cornucopia horn of plenty fed by the political patronage of a vast city."

Clear-skinned and blue-eyed, Curry at fifty-five radiated good health. A one-time shortstop for the Palisades Baseball Club and track star for the West Side Athletic Club, he had retained a trim physique, smoking but three cigars a day and drinking not at all. Often he would walk the six miles or so from his midtown headquarters to City Hall. His dress was conservative, his white hair and mustache close-clipped. His manner was never boisterous but always cordial. He possessed that God-given quality of the true boss, the ability to show anger when necessary but to reveal irritation not at all.

Curry had been brought to America in 1872 by his Irish parents, with his seven brothers and sisters, as a six-month-old infant. He left school at thirteen, went to work for the Western Union Company, learned telegraph operation and shorthand, eventually mastered accounting. When John Francis was twenty-one, his local athletic reputation was such that Daniel McMahon, then the leader of the Fifth A.D., made him an assistant district captain. Curry rose steadily in the political ranks and in 1902 was elected to the state assembly. Two years later, noting that McMahon was spending as much time in Florida and southern California as in his West Side clubhouse, he successfully challenged him for the leadership. Marrying in 1906, Curry moved into a tenement at 131 West Sixty-first Street, only a block from the house where he himself had been reared, and there he and his wife brought up their five children. Virtually his only departure from the neighborhood was when he visited the offices of his insurance company (made prosperous by his city connections) on downtown Lafayette Street.

As a member of Tammany's executive committee, Curry championed all causes dictated by local needs and ignored the larger issues. With Charley Murphy among the dear-departed, Smith defeated, and Olvany nursing his health, Curry was a man whose time had come. It would be Walker, who had long wanted a Tammany leader more answerable to him than to Smith, who would do the necessary arm-twisting among the district leaders. The mayor was given the political clout to effect his wishes on April 8, when the U. S. Supreme Court denied the IRT's bid for a seven-cent fare, which had been approved by a lower court eleven months before; the decision made Walker's renomination certain.

On the morning of April 23, in what the New York *Times* called "a return to the old idea of centering the effects of the Organization on the City and abandoning thought of further excursions into national politics," Curry was elected leader of Tammany Hall. The final result of the balloting, which was held in Tammany's new colonial-style headquarters at Seventeenth Street and Union Square, was Curry 12 1/6–Ahearn 10 1/3.

Socialist Norman Thomas was one of the few New Yorkers who received the news of Curry's victory with indignation. "The mask is off Tammany," he said. "A district leader of the old school sits in the seat of Tweed and Croker. Jimmy Walker is Mayor and Grover Whalen is Police Commissioner. The old gang is on the job. Who cares about the punishment of the Rothstein murder, the Equitable bus-franchise fiasco, the gross waste of an ever-increasing budget?"

The U.S. Supreme Court's denial of the seven-cent fare lent still more luster to a mayoral image that only thinking citizens and blue-noses questioned; Smith's comment years before about Hylan—"What luck the man has!"—thus far summed up Walker's career as well. At a luncheon held on the day of the court's decision, McCooey told him, "You can safely count on a 100,000 plurality in Brooklyn." Public officials generally were gleeful about the ruling, which they felt would force the private owners of the IRT and BMT to look with favor on the city's unification plans. (IRT stock, which earlier that morning had risen to 55 in anticipation of a favorable decision, fell to 33 1/2.)

Lost in the celebratory mood was the news that the IRT, whose legal and incidental expenses regarding the seven-cent-fare gambit amounted to about $1 million, was charging the cost to "operating expenses." Since these expenses had to be deducted before the city received any payment for its own considerable investment in the IRT, the New York taxpayer had in effect paid for the IRTs suit. Samuel Untermyer could only marvel, not at the inequities of the law, but at the mysteries of bookkeeping.

As popular with the citizenry as the retention of the five-cent fare was the acquittal in mid-April of Mary Louise Cecilia Guinan, better known as Texas Guinan, of the charge of "maintaining a nuisance" at the Salon Royale on West Fifty-eighth Street. The federal prosecutor had claimed that liquor had been sold there, and that the fortyish Miss Guinan, who received half of the club's net profits, had encouraged its sale; the hostess had countered that she was merely "a singer, dancer, welcomer and wisecracker" who sought to bring "sunshine into the lives of tired businessmen."

Invited to describe some of the divertissements she encouraged at the nightclub, Miss Guinan said one of her favorite stunts was "to have a guest walk five times around a walking cane while holding it in one hand," then try to walk "straight" to some designated person. Because he had probably lost his sense of balance, the victim would "fall all over." Her guests, she added, also enjoyed rope-jumping, tugs-of-war, and leapfrog. The prosecutor then asked Miss Guinan how she would characterize the reputations of the young girls who assisted her in her hostessing responsibilities.

"These children are above reproach," she declared.

"Are you trying to keep them so?" the prosecutor asked.

"I am and I do. People adore these children, and you have never heard a single word against any one of them."

"You use the word 'sucker' often, don't you?" the prosecutor continued.

"Yes, there are plenty of suckers. I am one of the biggest suckers in the world."

"Would you define the word 'sucker' as used in the nightclubs?"

"Oh, it is used as you would say, 'Don't be a sucker and go home so early.' It is as if you said 'pal.' It is always used in a spirit of fun and good fellowship."

Though the prosecutor strongly assailed Miss Guinan in his summing up, it was to no avail. "She was a partner in crime with the Salon Royale," he said. "Wisecracks similar to that about throwing out the drunken man from Chicago because 'that's what he gets for bringing his own' were her stock in trade. It was her business to make a poor bird like that feel cheap. Why, with their spotlights and their wisecracks they would make you feel so cheap you'd pay a waiter $5 for a piece of bread.

"In four months, Miss Guinan made $28,600 or thereabouts. Do you think she could have made that *not* aiding and abetting?"

After deliberating for barely an hour, the jury brought in a verdict of not guilty. "Give the little girl a great big hand," someone cried, echoing one of the hostess's favorite remarks.

Born in Waco, Texas, Miss Guinan originally pursued a career in films, where her range-land background earned her the accolade "the female Bill Hart." With the advent of Prohibition, however, she found her true calling, becoming the best-known figure in New York's night life and opening up new clubs as fast as federal agents closed down the old ones. "That was in the days," pointed out Stanley Walker, a celebrated newspaperman of the period, "when a club could get as much for a quart of White Rock as a quart of bourbon was worth. Of course liquor was sold—but Texas, cagy with the law, let the headwaiter attend to the booze-selling on his own responsibility." Along the way, Miss Guinan fell into partnership with Larry Fay, a swarthy, horse-faced racketeer, and they jointly operated several cabarets. Fay, who came from Hell's Kitchen and specialized in selling "protection," brought to the café business the same brash talk and heavy fists that had enabled him to take illegal percentages off taxi-cab and milk-vending operations. He would open a nightspot like his El Fay Club on West Forty-fifth Street without putting a cent down for rent, supplies, or services. Creditors would be stalled off with a list of the celebrities attracted by Miss Guinan who had promised to attend opening night; anyone who persisted in demanding cash was roughly dealt with.

Though Fay was in the process of being eased out of the rackets in 1929 by harder-knuckled entrepreneurs (several years later, he would be fatally shot by a nightclub employee in an argument over wages), Texas Guinan was never more popular. Her monied patrons, with the stock-market crash six months away, basked in her unabashed contempt.

In mid-May, the news that the Casino in Central Park was planning a twenty-five dollar cover charge for its opening night aroused so much controversy that New Yorkers stopped blaming Police Commissioner Whalen for the eighty unsolved murders during the last three months. The remodeled Casino, of course, was a project Walker had been pushing; he saw the restaurant as an exclusive hideaway where he might bring Betty Compton. To justify the charge, the Casino's management promised that the café would be a "dining place for the fashionable and the fastidious." The opening-night guest list would be consistent with "the patronage of a group of prominent New York businessmen and social leaders headed by Anthony J. Drexel Biddle, Jr., who are backing the project."

"Didn't I tell you so?" said Carl F. Zittel, the lessee of the old Casino who had been forced out by Walker's machinations. "That's why they wouldn't renew the lease I had there for ten years. I didn't have a chance to bid on this millionaire's proposition." Before the black-glass ballroom of the Casino opened, Zittel promised, he would once again seek an injunction, on the ground that the remodeling was a structural change in a Central Park building and thus an illegal act. "My attorney is preparing to reopen the original case," he said. "The Dieppe Corporation [headed by Walker pal Sidney Solomon] falsified its affidavits when it said its changes were only interior alterations. They've rebuilt the whole Casino."

Within the week, Sidney Solomon, who was particularly displeased by a report that he was asking $12,000 for the hat-check concession, more than the annual $8,500 he was paying the city for the rental of the whole premises, hit back at the criticism. "Why do we have to defer to Bolshevists all the time?" he asked. "There are five other restaurants in the park now that make 5-, 25-, and 50-cent sales. And when you speak about our rental to the city, don't forget that we are investing almost $400,000 in reconstructing this building. In ten years' time, this all becomes city property."

By early June the Casino remodeling was almost complete. While gardeners were raking the terraces around the green-and-white-trimmed exterior, women sat on the floor of the west pavilion—a domed building with walls painted in a tulip design of green and cream—sewing together specially woven carpets. At the center of the structure was the black-glass ballroom, trimmed in gold and silver. On the east side of the ballroom was the conservatory, a companion room to the pavilion, but with a darker color scheme. All that remained was for Solomon to decide which of the 2,400 applicants for opening night would fill the 600 seats available. Already the guest list included such New York socialities as Charles M. Amory, James P. Donahue, John Randolph Hearst, William K. Vanderbilt, Jr., William Rhinelander Stewart, Jr., and Adolph Zukor, not to mention Florenz Ziegfeld. A lesser-known but equally avid partygoer, dropping in on the Casino while the work was going on, told Sidney that when the design was conceived "genius rolled the ball." He got his reservation.

Just before the Casino's unveiling, Tony Biddle, chairman of its board of governors, democratically announced that the opening-night cover charge had been reduced to ten dollars. Referring to the fruitless lawsuits of Carl Zittel, Biddle said, a trifle defensively, "All we wanted to do is something for the public. It's absolutely the truth." He brightened a bit while announcing some luminaries of the restaurant staff. René Black, out of France by way of some of California's best clubs, would be *maître d'hôtel*. The chefs, Frederick Beaumont and Edouard Gabriel, had been lured from the Plaza; previously they had served Louis Rothschild. Gabriel was regarded as the greater artist, Biddle explained, but "has no English, and therefore cannot deal with American supplymen."

So great was the demand for reservations by the distinguished and the wealthy that there were not one but two opening nights. Walker, still estranged from Allie and living at the Ritz-Carlton, attended the second night with Betty Compton. Guests, met at the door by liveried footmen, ordered from a menu that included Caviar des Grands Ducs, Frivolités Escoffier, Cardinale de mer à l'Américaine, and Poussin désosse Armenonville; they digested their meal to the rhythm of "Sweet Sue—Just You," "You're the Cream in My Coffee," and "Ain't Misbehavin'."

The mayor's preoccupation with the Casino was such that, while the work was going on, he actually pored over the plans and made suggestions for improvements. In one instance, he insisted on relocating the entrance so that the headwaiter could see incoming patrons sooner and thus have more time to decide whether they deserved red-carpet treatment. (Walker's attentions to the Casino and to Betty that spring were a source of annoyance to Governor Roosevelt, who could not understand why the mayor could not find time to confer with him when he came down from Albany.) Walker even helped decorate Solomon's private office, which eventually featured green *moire* walls, a gold-leaf ceiling, and a blue tile bath. In the months to come, he would hold informal political conferences in this den while Betty waited in the ballroom. The mayor drank champagne, but she preferred beer. In deference to Prohibition, the well-chilled drinks would be brought into the Casino for them one bottle at a time from a car parked outside the restaurant just for that purpose. Other well-to-do patrons made similar arrangements or asked waiters to be their suppliers. On his first evening at the Casino, Walker was so ebullient that he tipped bandleader Leo Reisman $100 after the bandleader had played "Will You Love Me in December." Solomon protested, saying he was paying Reisman $2,800 a week to play without being tipped. Walker reacted by giving the hat-check girl $200.

During the first week in June, the Casino was opened to the general public. Breakfast, lunch, and dinner were served; there were tea-dancing in the late afternoon and supper-dancing until 3:00 A.M. Evening dress was required in the ballroom and the connecting dining room, but more casually attired patrons could be accommodated in the pavilion. The cover charge, now down to three dollars, was not levied until the supper-dancing began.

Republican Ruth Pratt, the former board of aldermen member who had gone on to Congress, chose to attack Walker that June, saying that his city administration was the worst in history. "I want to tell you a little about what my three years in the Board of Aldermen taught me. . . . Never has there been such mismanagement of public affairs, such waste and graft. . . . [The mayor] relies on his popularity. . . . Who was so powerful in the Equitable bus group as to hold up bus franchises in three boroughs? Who were the men so powerful they received protection after the murder of a noted gambler?"

The Citizens Union, by now thoroughly disenchanted with Walker, was equally caustic in its election-year appraisal of his administration:

Mr. Walker gained most of his practical education in the legislative halls at Albany. He was an agile debater and a resourceful leader. Even when personal knowledge of the subject at hand failed him, he was invariably able to parry the thrusts of his opponents and beat a graceful, if not glorious, retreat. . . . Mr. Walker must have become conscious early of the great differences between the responsibilities of the role he had been playing at Albany and those of the great office to which he had succeeded. The readjustment was a slow process and, in fact, has never been actually effected. . . . His difficulties in this connection may be explained by recalling that a legislative program has a life of three or four months and then dies with the session, while the program of a City administration continues through four long years.

The City Trust Company, which consisted of two New York neighborhood banks catering to depositors with modest amount of capital, had failed for some $5 million in February of 1929, soon after the death of its founder, an Italian immigrant named Francesco M. Ferrari. Now, in early July, Robert Moses, who had been conducting a state investigation, issued a devastating critique. It castigated Frank H. Warder, a Tammany hack who had become state superintendent of banking, for allowing Ferrari to manipulate bank funds to deceive and defraud. Warder, Moses declared, was "a faithless public official who accepted gifts and gratuities . . . knew of the dishonest management in the Ferrari banks and deliberately prevented exposure." Similarly, the report condemned Francis X. Mancuso, a general sessions judge who had been the City Trust Company's board chairman, saying that his escape from prosecution was only "due to the weakness of the law." Mancuso, who was also a machine politician, had claimed his naïveté hal made him a mere rubber-stamp, but, Moses wrote, he "must have known that he was lending not only his own name to the Ferrari enterprises, but also the dignity and weight of his position on the bench."

Francesco Ferrari, who immigrated to the United States while in his early twenties, went to work for a private bank at One Hundred Eighth Street and First Avenue. Although he was "shrewd, vain, pompous and boastful," his personal magnetism soon made him a power in the Italian community. He joined social and fraternal clubs, contributed heavily to charities, cultivated important people. By 1921, he was able to obtain a license to open his own bank, at One Hundred Ninth Street and Second Avenue; this enterprise later became the Harlem Bank of Commerce. Within a few years, its capitalization grew enormously, ostensibly at least, and Ferrari opened a second bank. "It will suffice to say," Moses commented afterward, "that these funds were never actually paid in, and the transactions were bold and complicated frauds." By 1928, Ferrari's two banks were merged into what became known as the City Trust Company, and his diverse activities had expanded into involved real estate transactions. "One of Ferrari's usual practices," said Moses, "was to hire a number of people to work independently on different phases of the same project. . . . As one witness remarked, 'Ferrari had as many lawyers as he had hairs on his head.'" After Ferrari died, the house of banking that he had so delicately set up simply collapsed. Moses' investigation followed.

What had enabled Ferrari to get away with his bogus dealings so handily, of course, was his influence with Superintendent of Banks Warder. An ineffectual man, Warder was so timid that when he accepted appointments, first to the New York county clerk's office and then to the state department of banking, he still kept his name on the Civil Service rolls. Tammany's power was such, Moses said, that "he was recorded as on leave of absence from 1915 to 1929, being regularly restored to some vacant post as each successive leave was exhausted. When he became Superintendent of Banking, he still held as an anchor to windward a $2,500 job."

Ferrari had given Warder and his family such gifts as oriental rugs and a Chrysler car, not to mention chickens, eggs, and liquor. From a red memo book kept by a Ferrari lieutenant, Moses discovered that $30,000 had been paid to Warder "for approval of the [City Trust] merger without examination"; additional evidence showed that a second $30,000 bribe had also been accepted by Warder. (The extent of the bribery was impossible to gauge. Just as nobody could figure out how much money Ferrari had embezzled as opposed to losing through mismanagement, the amount of his "gifts" could only be estimated.) "Had the fundamental requirement of a proper audit been made in an examination," Moses wrote, "gross fraud and overstatement of [assets] would have been disclosed to the extent of hundreds of thousands of dollars."

In his report, Moses went on to condemn the help that Judge Mancuso had given Ferrari. "It is not too much to expect," said Moses, "that Judge Mancuso should have familiarized himself with the provisions of the State Banking Law. . . . I find it impossible to conclude that [he] did not know that Ferrari and other officers were daily violating the law. . . . I believe that Judge Mancuso deserves censure for his lack of frankness."

Warder subsequently was convicted of accepting a bribe of $10,-000 and sentenced to five to ten years in Sing Sing. Though Mancuso was indicted for improperly accepting twelve $1,000 checks from Ferrari, the charges were soon dropped; in September of 1929, he would resign from the bench.

On July 31, a rumor circulated through the city that Walker had been shot, or at least shot at, in a midtown apartment hotel, and New Yorkers who knew Betty Compton's temper were not entirely surprised. The couple's romance was often tempestuous and unpredictable; slaps and punches thrown in alcoholic partying, by Betty far more than Jim, were not uncommon; a sharp remark by the slim, nonathletic mayor could bring on a formidable attack by Betty. All the evidence indicates, however, that the shooting rumor was bogus, gaining credibility only because Walker's whereabouts could not immediately be pinpointed. "The reason my office was unable to reach me," the mayor later announced at a press conference, "was because I was walking unescorted through the streets from one place to another to keep several appointments." He had, of course, been with Betty Compton, and while she may not have shot at him, she had kept him incommunicado for several hours.

Two weeks before, a real shooting had taken place that marked the beginning of the end for Jack ("Legs") Diamond, one of Prohibition's cruelest gangsters. At the time, Diamond was part-owner of the Hotsy-Totsy Club at Fifty-fourth and Broadway. Previously he had been the $1,000-a-week bodyguard for Arnold Rothstein, whose sudden demise had left the thirty-three-year-old killer in a superb position—with money, prestige, and access to many of the gambler's contacts. Now Legs would indulge in a senseless shoot-out at the Hotsy-Totsy, thereby throwing away his new-found eminence. At the club late that July night, Diamond, who often lost all restraint when drinking, was chatting with some patrons about the merits of a contemporary prize fighter. Most of the debaters had at one time or another been enrolled at Sing Sing. Logic became lost in passion, gunfire burst out, and two of the patrons were killed. In all, twenty-four bullets were fired, and eighteen of them were found in the bodies. Nobody disputed Commissioner Whalen when he called the fracas "a drunken brawl."

Long before the police arrived at the Hotsy-Totsy, of course, Diamond and an associate, one Charles Greene, had fled the scene. For the next six months, while the authorities sought them in vain, witnesses to the shooting were eliminated. Thomas Ribler, the cashier at the club, simply disappeared. "He said he was going to Far Rockaway for a swim," his mother told the police. William Wolgast, the bartender, was found riddled with bullets in New Jersey. Herman Henry, a patron, was shot to death in Philadelphia. Even Hymie Cohen, the Hotsy-Totsy's manager and a pal of Diamond, was silenced. "Legs made it as easy for Hymie as he could when he had him turned off," explained a fellow gangster.

Picked up in Chicago in early 1930, Greene would stand trial for the murders and, with no witnesses to testify against him, be acquitted in February of that year. A month later, Diamond would surrender to the law by walking into the West Forty-seventh Street police station; he too would be acquitted. Yet the Hotsy-Totsy murders, as we shall see, finished Diamond on Broadway. "Such a cheap killing in a man's own joint," wrote a contemporary journalist, "was looked on as horribly sloppy work, fit only for the provinces or the Brooklyn waterfront, and the boys marked him for lousy." Somebody —perhaps it was Owney Madden, the admirer of Mae West who was a leader of New York's bootleggers passed the word that Diamond was to be regarded as a pariah. He would survive for only two years after the shootings.

Born in Philadelphia, Diamond, whose real name was Nolan, had the usual upbringing in an Irish tenement neighborhood. In 1913, as an eighteen-year-old, he came to New York with his younger brother, Eddie, joining a junior auxiliary to the Gopher gang in the Chelsea district. There Legs gained his nickname for the fleetness of foot he displayed as a package thief. Standing five-feet-ten, he weighed less than 150 pounds. Darkly handsome, with "a little arrow of care between his brows, even when he is laughing," Diamond could be mannerly and charming when he wished to be. In 1914, he pleaded guilty to burglary and served time in the penitentiary. After his release, he moved to East One Hundredth Street and fell in with the Car-Barn Gang. By 1918 he was in the army, but he went AWOL and eventually was picked up by the MPs on charges of desertion, carrying a concealed weapon, and theft. Diamond was shipped overseas anyway, with the Twenty-second Infantry Regiment, but made so much trouble that he had to be returned to America. Court-martialed for nonperformance of duty (and for hitting "Sergeant Mahon in the leg with an iron bar"), he was sentenced to five years of hard labor at Leavenworth—but was released after one year by Presidential clemency. From this time on, during an underworld career that lasted a dozen more years until his death in 1931, he never again received a prison sentence, although he was arrested on seventeen occasions—five of them for homicide.

After the war, Diamond settled in the Lower East Side, gaining a reputation as the best truck and warehouse-thief in the area. In October of 1924, while driving his automobile, he was wounded in the head and the foot by shots from rival gangsters. Legs continued on his way, driving himself to Mount Sinai Hospital for the necessary repairs, then motoring home. Three years later, while serving as a bodyguard for Mobster Jacob (Little Augie) Orgen, he and his boss were caught, while standing on the corner of Norfolk and Delancey streets, in a more deadly burst of gunfire. Little Augie was killed, and Legs took two bullets through the chest—a mishap that eventually resulted in a tubercular condition. Diamond's next employer, Arnold Rothstein, frequently assigned him to escort winning gamblers home from his dice and card games; this gave rise to a grim joke at police headquarters; whenever a gambler was found robbed and murdered, the investigating officer was likely to ask, "Did Legs take him home?"

For a brief time after Rothstein's death, Diamond, with his fierce temper, was the most feared of New York's gunmen. The Hotsy-Totsy murders, however, marked him as something less than human —even with the underworld. After a short trip to Europe, Legs settled with his wife, Alice, in a small house in the Catskills, where he tried to take over the liquor traffic. Legs gave the organizing effort his all. At least one recalcitrant buyer was strung up by the neck, the better to apply lighted matches to the soles of his feet. But the hard-drinking Diamond ultimately failed in his ambitions. Not only was his liquor inferior and his methods extreme, but—most important—his victims, realizing death was waiting to pay him a call, refused to knuckle under.

In October of 1930, when Diamond was trying to forget his business worries in the company of his girl friend, Marion ("Kiki") Roberts of the Follies, at the Hotel Monticello in the Catskills, some strangers came to his room and shot him five times. (Miss Roberts reported that she was in the bath at the time, and the running water had drowned out the noise of the shooting.) Legs recovered but did not take the hint. Six months later, at the Saratoga Inn near Cairo, New York, a shotgun blast peppered his body with some eighty pellets. Again he recovered. In December of 1931, Leg's enemies struck a third time, this time with finality. He and Miss Roberts had been celebrating his acquittal on kidnaping and torture charges with a festive evening in Albany, New York. Later, as he lay in a drunken sleep, he was shot sequentially, first in the head, then in the back of the neck, then in the face. It was a thorough job. (Miss Roberts, quite properly, went into hiding.)

"So they got him at last," a ranking New York police officer commented at the time, thinking of the gangland antagonisms Diamond had stirred up. "I expected to see him taken long before this."

On August 1, the city's Republican party, more in desperation than in hope, gave its approval to Fiorello H. LaGuardia's mayoral candidacy. For one thing, the Republican leaders had not been able to convince any of their more genteel stalking horses to challenge the popular Walker. For another, the disputatious LaGuardia, a well-known congressman, was threatening a primary fight if denied the nomination. So the nabobs of strict probity, careful breeding, and good manners met in the Mecca Temple on West Fifty-fifth Street to endorse the short, stocky, noisy Italian-American for mayor. With forced smiles and hollow cheers, they backed a man they felt to be, in the words of a contemporary journalist, "a Socialist, a foe of Prohibition, a menace to Americanism, common, vuygar and undisciplined."

The candidate chose to ignore the half-hearted quality of the endorsement. In his acceptance speech and in the campaign that followed, LaGuardia came out slugging. "If any man feels timid about this fight," he told the convention, "let him so tell his leader and we'll put someone with a fighting heart in his place. The day of 50-50 politics in this town is over. . . . On January 1, every Tammany Commissioner and his deputy will be out of office."

If the Republicans were hesitant in their backing of LaGuardia, they were loud in their criticism of Walker. In his keynote address, Emory Buckner, who had conducted the Queens sewer probe and been responsible for Borough President Connolly's conviction, asserted that the mayor had only hampered his efforts. "Jimmy, to be sure, did direct his Commissioner of Accounts to investigate the situation," Buckner said. "The result would have been the same as all of Jimmy's investigations—a temporary alibi, a smart jest and what not. It was Al Smith and not Walker who exposed the scandal." In addition, the Republicans for the first time formally named the "prominent Tammany district leader" rumored to have been involved in the milk scandals. Why had this man, Charles L. Kohler of the Tenth A.D., not been questioned during the inquiry, they wanted to know, and why was he now, as Walker's budget director, in "a key position for party plunder"?

LaGuardia, the "Little Flower," was in most respects the complete opposite of Walker. Unlike the dapper mayor, he thought so little of his tailoring that once, before making a speech in the House of Repretatives, he stashed a lamb chop and a beefsteak in the pockets of his rumpled suit so that he could draw them forth to make a point about rising prices. His oratory, which ranged from bombastic denunciations to falsetto digs, was undignified but effective; so was his use of the word "lousy," his favorite adjective. Yet LaGuardia, despite surface appearances, was no clown. A formidable vote-getter, even though running in New York City on anti-Tammany tickets, he had served in Congress continually since 1916 except for one term as

president of the board of aldermen. Unlike Walker, he believed in
the virtue of hard work. As a congressman, he tirelessly pored over
thousands of bills submitted by his colleagues, perusing them for
faulty statistics and outright thievery. When the house was in session,
he was constantly in attendance, not even leaving for lunch. Over
the years, the progressive Fiorello seldom bested the conservatives
who then dominated the Congress, but he proved an effective gadfly.

Though he was born on New York's Lower East Side, LaGuardia,
whose immigrant father became a bandmaster with the Eleventh
Infantry, was reared in army posts in the western states. As a nine-
teen-year-old high-school graduate, he entered the U.S. consular service and from 1901 to 1904 was stationed in Budapest and Trieste.
There he learned French, German, and Italian (which his parents
had not taught him), as well as several Slavic and Croatian dialects.
(Later, when he entered politics in New York, he added Yiddish to his
linguistic skills. "I also know a little English," he was fond of saying.)

Back in America, LaGuardia studied at New York Law School and
was admitted to the bar in 1910. An amusing speaker whose quips
guaranteed a full house, he quickly became a leader of the city's
Italians. In 1914, he was defeated in his first try for Congress, but
two years later was sent to Washington from the Twentieth A.D.
in Harlem. During these years, Fiorello discovered the thrills of
aviation, learning to fly at Mineola, Long Island. When World War I
began, he enlisted in the army air service, was sent overseas, and
rose to the rank of major. Among the slim, dashing American aviators,
with their immaculate uniforms and chivalrous airs, the unkempt
LaGuardia could have passed for an orderly. After the war, though still
in Congress, he was importuned by the Republicans to run for the
aldermanic presidency.

LaGuardia fooled everyone by winning (no Republican having won
city-wide office in years), but he did not enjoy the office. Returning
to Congress, LaGuardia continued his independent ways, loudly
calling for reduction of the military establishment, repeal of Prohibition, and the rights of the working man. Wherever he went, puffing on his foul cigars, he stirred controversy. Now, compaigning for
mayor in 1929 on the Republican-Fusion ticket, he would run true to
form; he would not beat Walker, but he would raise some embarrassing issues.

With Walker, McKee, and Berry the solid choices for city-wide
renomination, Tammany turned its attention to New York county offices. To give the impression of working to solve the Rothstein murder, a new but not necessarily energetic district attorney was needed

to replace Joab Banton; the tiger pounced on one of its sachems, Thomas C. T. Crain, a sixty-nine-year-old supreme court justice more in need of rest and quiet than of prosecuting criminal cases. At the same time, it enlarged the responsibilities of County Clerk Thomas M. Farley, the leader of the Fourteenth A.D. who had converted his clubhouse into a gambling establishment, designating him as the candidate for sheriff—Charles W. Culkin, the incumbent and Walker's old Greenwich Village mentor, opting for retirement. The Crain and Farley nominations are noteworthy, for both men would figure prominently within the next two years in the scandals enveloping the Walker administration. Crain would be castigated for nonfeasance in office, Farley for the huge sums of money in his "little tin box."

Buoyed up by still another victory over the IRT, the mayor was in good humor that August. The company had just admitted to making improper withdrawals from operating revenue during the 1919–29 period and in settlement had made a cash payment to the city of some $6,291,000. "Who could say no?" was Walker's statement upon receiving the check.

To a New York intent on progress, yet sentimental over its past, James J. Walker was the *beau ideal*. His straight dark hair, brushed back tightly to his head, his quizzical blue eyes, his generous mouth— these physical marks were known to all New Yorkers. His clothes were in the latest styles, he whirred through the streets in his high-powered Dusenberg, he cheered the saxophone solo in the newest jazz composition. At the same time, he talked lovingly of the days when the steam engines of the elevated lines puffed their way along the tracks, remembered singing "Sweet Marie," kept faded photos of his mother and father on his City Hall desk. Most New Yorkers of the Roaring Twenties did not know or did not care about the financial irregularities he permitted. Only with the coming of the Depression would they lose patience with their smiling, good-hearted mayor. "One thing about Jimmy," the Irish would say even then, reluctantly and among themselves, "he may steal a dime, but he'll always let you take a penny."

Walker was genuinely incapable of understanding the criticism he was beginning to receive. "There is one trouble with being Mayor," he told a visitor to City Hall in late summer, "and that is that the days are too short. Twenty-four hours are not enough to do a day's work in. It is no wonder that I am occasionally late." Then how, he was asked, did he manage to greet so many celebrities?

"A lot has been said of the times I have been photographed with distinguished visitors. The photographs appear in the papers and when the people see them they fail to realize that it takes but a few seconds to take a picture. . . . People ought to see me at other times. They ought to see me here until 7:30 in the evening."

The mayor drew a denicotinized cigarette from a pigskin case and lit it. "I have been called the Night Mayor of New York," he said. "I made that joke myself. But I want you to know this Night Mayor has been in nightclubs exactly three times since he held office. Quite a record for a playboy, don't you think?" (Walker evidently did not consider the Casino a nightclub.)

"I have gone to many dinners, but what have they been for? Either in honor of some distinguished man or for the benefit of some charity. In either case, I feel it is the duty of the Mayor to attend this kind to function." (Walker had addressed some 250 such dinners in his less than four years in office.)

Before the visitor left, he remarked that Walker had seemed to be having fun as mayor.

"I have had a lot of fun," Jimmy said, "but the trouble is that I have not had as much as I get the credit or the blame for. That's where my kick comes."

In late September, the mayoral campaign began to heat up when LaGuardia revealed that City Magistrate Albert H. Vitale, a prominent Bronx Democrat, had in 1928 received a loan of $19,940 from Arnold Rothstein. District Attorney Banton had made a misstatement, LaGuardia said, when he previously announced he had found "no document indicating any financial transaction between Rothstein and any man in public life." According to the Republican candidate, the late gambler's files contained a copy of a letter attesting that Rothstein, on July 2, 1928, had sent a $19,940 check to Vitale. "Judge Vitale is actively campaigning for Mayor Walker," LaGuardia said. "I now ask the Mayor either to repudiate or support Vitale."

It was not that Fiorello had discovered the whereabouts of the missing Rothstein documents. "The papers that did not reach the Grand Jury," he said, "will never be seen by me—nor by anybody else—you can bet on that." Instead, he had unearthed the one letter left in the files linking Rothstein and a Democratic politician.

Throughout the furor that followed, D. A. Banton, doubtless wishing that Thomas C. T. Crain, the man replacing him, was already in office, would be spectacularly quiet. His only comment about the Rothstein letter was, "I know nothing about it. I never heard of it." Magistrate Vitale, however, talked freely. After characteriizng La-Guardia's charge as "despicable," he freely admitted he had gotten a loan from Rothstein. But he denied there had been "a personal transaction" between him and the gambler. "On June 15, 1928," he said,

"I met a friend of mine, a professional man of high standing whose name I do not care to bring into this controversy because he has since died. I mentioned that I needed ready cash temporarily, and he promised to see what he could do. . . . On either June 17 or 18, I received a letter containing a check for $19,940. Either the letter or the check bore Arnold Rothstein's signature, and that was my first knowledge he was concerned in the transaction. . . . When the note became due on July 2, I drew my personal check, payable to the Rothmere Mortgage Corporation and mailed it to them."

Vitale had needed a short-term loan, he explained, to bolster his stock holdings, which at the time were plunging downward in a market decline. He had not known that his "friend" would get the money from Rothstein, whom, he said, he had met but twice, and then only to exchange a few words.

LaGuardia derided the magistrate's explanation, saying that "If there is one thing we need in this city it is honest magistrates. I am going to clean out the whole bunch of them. The judges of the Magistrates' Courts were never so low as they are today." He was equally caustic about any inquiry Walker might make into the Vitale affair, implying that the Mayor would try to "paint the lily white."

Stung by LaGuardia's criticism and by demands that he suspend the magistrate pending an investigation, Walker responded angrily. "Have you consulted the law?" he said. "Well, let me save you a little trouble. The Mayor appoints a Magistrate but he cannot remove one. Only the Appellate Division can do that. Once a Mayor has appointed a Magistrate—and I did not appoint Vitale—he can do nothing about it."

Members of the appellate division, meanwhile, made it clear they would take no action without a formal request from the City of New York Bar Association. Officers of the association, in turn, were "unwilling to discuss the matter." So the matter temporarily rested. Before the year ended, however, Vitale would figure in still another embarrassing situation. Amid a certain amount of low comedy, it would prove his undoing.

In the first week of October, even while leaders in advertising, the garment and fur trades, and the maritime industry pledged their support to his re-election, Walker appeared in a campaign movie. "The Mayor, with grace and ease many a movie or a stage star might envy," reported the New York *Times*, "played the principal role in a Movietone production of 'Building With Walker,' produced in the open air at Broadway and 47th Street. The Mayor's monologue, which might have been entitled 'My City,' was followed by scenes of subway construction with steam-shovel accompaniment, interspersed with musical interludes by a band." Unimpressed, *The Evening Post* came out for Republican-Fusion candidate LaGuardia. Reacting to a Walker statement that he would "take leadership and advice" from Tammany chieftain Curry, the newspaper declared, "Only supreme self-confidence could have led to so imprudent a declaration. . . . This reduces the Mayoralty fight to its essentials: LaGuardia vs. the Boss of Tammany Hall. We can't see how [anybody] can hesitate to vote against Curry. They may like Walker's personality, but do they like Curry's?"

LaGuardia chose this occasion to lay a second broadside on Walker, stressing the favoritism he had shown Sidney Solomon in the matter of the Casino lease. First he roared that the restaurant's concessions (Belmar shoes, Tecla pearls, Bonwit Teller, taxi and hat-check service) annually took in an amount more than twice the $8,500 rent that Solomon paid the city, adding, "So greedy are the managers of this joy establishment that there is some system of even taking a percentage of the waiters' tips." Then he thundered that the Casino's daily average receipts of $8,000 alone almost equaled the yearly rent. After noting that the mayor visited the establishment at least three times a week, LaGuardia declared, "So great is the interest in [its] success that a certain high official in the city government when he calls at the Casino asks what the income was on the previous day. . . . The Casino is not only a whoopee joint but also a source of great revenue for important Tammany officials." Reached by phone for a comment, Solomon refused to let a reporter read him Fiorello's statement. "It would only make me mad," he said.

That the electorate was paying little attention to these attacks on Walker was indicated on October 25, when he attended ceremonies marking the beginning of work on the Triborough Bridge, which would connect Manhattan, the Bronx, and Queens. While bands played sprightly marches, tugboats paraded up the East River, and army planes roared overhead, the mayor, reported the *Times*, "was sighted afar and from that moment until he had made his way through the crowd and taken his seat in the bandstand, the audience stood and cheered him." Clearly his popularity was as great as ever. Yet, within a few days, America would undergo the catastrophic financial disaster that would create the Depression of the 1930s. Walker's life-style would not seem so amusing in the hard times to come.

Though business conditions were bad in 1929, stock prices had been going up and up, largely because so many ordinary citizens were buying securities on sizable margin. In February, the board of the

Federal Reserve Bank, taking note of this situation, tried to prevent the relending of federal reserve funds by banks to brokers. Though it did not dare raise the rediscount rate (and delay the hoped-for business recovery still further), the FRB forbade the use of its funds for speculation. The fiat had little effect. By summer, stock prices were still soaring, loans to brokers totalled $6 billion (compared to $3.5 billion at the end of 1927), and some 300 million shares of stock were being carried on margin. By early September, when the market reached its peak, many investors were convinced the paper prosperity would never end. General Electric, which just eighteen months before had been selling at 128 3/4, was selling at an adjusted price of 396 1/4. General Motors, which had been at 139 3/4, was at 181 7/8. Radio Corporation had risen from 94 1/2 to 505.

In New York that fall, workmen were tearing down the Waldorf-Astoria Hotel at Fifth Avenue and Thirty-fourth Street, making way for the Empire State Building; the Chrysler Building was rising at Forty-second Street; and John D. Rockefeller, Jr., was making plans for the office complex he called Radio City. The boom in skyscraper construction was never greater, and the male passers-by who looked upward to admire the marvels, their hair brushed straight back with sleek exactitude, dressed much the same: wide-brimmed hats, starched collars, dark suits with matching vests. Women, their hair shingled in back and curled forward over their ears, cultivated the straight-up-and-down look: V-necks, "waistlines" at the hips, skirt lengths just below the knee. Everybody seemed to own an automobile (the higher and more angular, the more prestigious), and radio sets were selling for as much as $135 (the better to hear Rudy Vallee's nasal tones). New Yorkers were humming "Singin' in the Rain," reading *All Quiet on the Western Front*, watching Eddie Cantor in *Whoopee!* Babe Ruth, Bill Tilden, and Bobby Jones were still the biggest names in sport, but their reigns, like the bull market, were about to end.

On October 24, the stock market, which had been sagging the entire month, finally broke. Day after day, the torrent of sell orders continued, as banks demanded their money and brokers called in their margin accounts. Tuesday, October 29, was the single worst day; 16,410,000 shares were traded in the New York Stock Exchange, and prices virtually collapsed. It was not until November 13 that the slide finally stopped. At that time, General Electric had fallen from its adjusted September high of 396 1/4 to 168 1/8, General Motors from 181 7/8 to 36, RCA from 505 to 28. In a grim example of wishful thinking, the public began hearing the song "Happy Days Are Here Again." The years of "Republican" prosperity were over.

On the eve of the November election, LaGuardia wound up his campaign with a final charge against Walker, saying that he "knows who murdered Arnold Rothstein and the police know, but they do not dare to bring the murderers to trial [for fear] they will tell all they know and bring to light a most revolting scandal." Turning his invective on Grover Whalen, Fiorello declared. "It takes more than a silk hat and a pair of spats to make an efficient Police Commissioner."

LaGuardia was a candidate whose time was four years away. When the votes were counted the next night, Walker was re-elected by better than a 2-to-1 margin, an unprecedented victory in a mayoral contest. His vote total was some 865,000, compared to the challenger's 368,000. LaGuardia did not win a single assembly district, even in the heavily Italian sections of the city. Tammany won every major contest but one, re-electing the controller and the aldermanic president and putting into office four of the five borough presidents, sheriffs, county clerks, district attorneys, registrars, supreme court judges, city court justices, county judges, a general sessions judge, municipal court judges, a surrogate, and a congressman. The sole Republican triumph was that of Queens Borough President George U. Harvey. Walker was predictably jubilant. "I hope this will be the last of the timeworn, moth-eaten, imaginary slogan, 'Anti-Tammany,' " he said.

As soon as he knew he had won, Walker paid a call in his official limousine on Betty Compton, who was rehearsing a new play at the Lyric Theater. A policeman was dispatched to bring her out to the car. It had been a stormy, snow-filled November day, and Betty, who was wearing a scanty costume, balked at going out into the cold. The policeman simply wrapped her in a blanket and carried her.

In truth, the mayor had been far more interested that fall in Betty and the play, a Cole Porter musical called *Fifty Million Frenchmen*, than he had been in campaigning. He had practically commuted between New York and Boston during the weeks the show had endured its out-of-town shakedown. On one occasion, he had even gone on-stage during rehearsal and, trying to enlarge Betty's part, instructed the orchestra how it should play one of her numbers. Later, in New York, when Betty complained about the size of her dressing room, Walker got her quarters enlarged by threatening the show's management with violations of the building code. Several weeks after his re-election, the mayor attended the musical's opening, escorting Betty's mother—a patrician-looking, white-haired woman he called "the Duchess." After the performance, the trio went on to a celebratory party at the Casino.

Fifty Million Frenchmen was a financial success despite the $6.60

cost of an orchestra seat in the midst of the market crash; it ran on Broadway for almost a year, grossing some $50,000 a week. The musical, with numbers like "You've Got That Thing," "You Do Something to Me," and "Find Me a Primitive Man," was also an artistic triumph. 'When it comes to lyrics," wrote critic George Jean Nathan, "this Cole Porter is just so far ahead of the other boys in New York that there is just no race at all." The show's book dealt with Americans in Paris, and the settings ranged from the banks of the Seine to the Ritz to Longchamps to Montmartre to Les Halles. William Gaxton, a long-time Walker pal, played Peter Forbes, a wealthy playboy determined to marry Looloo Carroll, a girl from Terre Haute, despite her mother's plan to wed her to a Grand Duke. As a complicating factor, Forbes had made a bet that he could live in Paris for a month without money. Eventually, of course, he won both Looloo and the bet.

Betty Compton's role was that of a young friend of Looloo, and, along with an actor named Jack Thompson, she danced through "You've Got That Thing," "Why Shouldn't I Have You?" and "Pierre, What Did You Do to Me?" Wrote John Mason Brown in the *Post:* "The dancing, which is fast and furious throughout, and especially engaging when Jack Thompson and Betty Compton are at work, comes as an accompaniment to the liveliest music of the season."

A couple of weeks later, Magistrate Vitale figured prominently in his second news story of the year—this one in his capacity as honorary life president of the Tepecano Democratic Club in the Bronx. (Tepecano was the dialectic misspelling by some Italian enthusiasts of the political nickname of General William H. Harrison, hero of the battle of Tippecanoe.) Vitale's club was mostly composed of lawyers who advertised, bail bondsmen who used assumed names, and similar civic-minded individuals. Most people did not realize, however, that some 10 percent of its 300-man membership also had police records. This fact was brought home to New Yorkers when, at about 1:30 A.M. one Sunday morning in mid-December, seven men with revolvers entered the upstairs room of the Roman Gardens, where the club was having a testimonial dinner for Vitale, and robbed the guests of some $5,000 in money and jewelry. A police investigation subsequently showed that seven of the victims had arrests and convictions ranging from burglary to homicide; the most prominent of these was Ciro Terranova, the city's so-called Artichoke King, who had grown wealthy by monopolizing the sale of vegetables in Italian neighborhoods and by extorting tribute from Italian businessmen, gamblers, and contractors. Terranova, who rode in an armored limousine with bulletproof windows, had recently been questioned about the killing of Frankie Marlow, a Broadway racketeer with whom he had been feuding and who, coincidentally, had recently been hustled into an auto and killed. Facing the hold-up men in the Roman Gardens, Terranova was all smiles. "Ain't you fellows ashamed of yourselves to hold up this dinner given to Judge Vitale?" he told the intruders. "We are all paisans ourselves."

Undoubtedly the most inconvenienced Tepecano guest, however, was Detective Arthur Johnson, who was relieved of his service revolver. Commissioner Whalen promptly demoted Johnson to patrolman and suspended him from the force for consorting with known criminals. The kindly Magistrate Vitale then drew up a petition asking that Johnson be restored to his former rank. Retorted Whalen: "When Vitale finds out the character of some of those who attended the banquet, he will probably stop circulating the petition."

At his departmental trial, patrolman Johnson, a twenty-year police veteran, testified he had been invited to the dinner to have some "eats." A band of five pieces had played, "there was singing, there were people making speeches, there was an address by Judge Vitale." When the hold-up men burst into the room, Johnson continued, he had looked at Vitale, who "shook his head at me."

"Did you believe that to be a signal to you?" the patrolman was asked.

"I figured that he meant, 'Don't start anything.' . . ."

"Did you have in mind the safety of the diners?"

"Absolutely."

"Did you feel that if you took any action it might provoke a fusillade of shots?"

"It would have meant a slaughter."

After the robbers fled, Johnson said, he held a hurried conference with Vitale. "I said, 'This is a terrible state of affairs. It is terribly embarrassing. You are a judge and I am a police officer disarmed.'

"Magistrate Vitale told me to keep quiet and 'don't say nothing' and he would try to obtain some information."

Vitale did more than just get "information." Within three hours, he arranged for the return of Johnson's revolver. "Around 4 A.M. Sunday, I was called to the Tepecano Democratic Club and Judge Vitale brought me to an anteroom where there was a desk," Johnson testified. "He pulled out the top right-hand drawer and said, 'There is your gun.' I asked him where he had got the gun and he was unable to advise me, stating that it had come back and that was all he knew about it." Further police inquiries showed that the cash and jewelry, in like manner, had also been returned to the guests.

The day after Christmas, the story of the Vitale dinner took still another turn. Inspector Joseph J. Donovan, drawing on information he had received from police undercover agents, declared that "those in the inner circle at the dinner that night knew two hours before the robbery took place that it was going to [happen] and they were instructed not to harm anybody." Ciro Terranova, who had supposedly signed a "contract" with a Chicago killer for the assassination of Frankie Marlow, had arranged the whole tableau for the purpose of retrieving the incriminating document. "Terranova had agreed to pay the man from Chicago $20,000," said Donovan. "He had paid him $5,000, but was delaying paying him the rest, so much so that the man informed Terranova that if he did not come across quick he would turn the document over to the police. So Terranova, knowing of the dinner that was to be given Judge Vitale, invited his friend from Chicago. . . ." Unlike the money and jewelry, the "contract" was not returned.

Deeply offended by this accusation, Terranova granted a reporter an interview in his $50,000 Pelham Manor home, which he took pains to point out was not the "fortress" the police were fond of calling it. A big Christmas tree glowed warmly through the windows; a religious shrine could be seen on the snow-covered lawn. The house itself, a snug Spanishlike villa, was isolated from its neighbors, but Terranova said this distance gave him the needed repose which he, a quiet, introspective man, required.

Terranova then claimed he was being made a scapegoat in a political feud. "The reason I am being dragged into this thing," he said, "is because of a political fight in the Bronx." He asserted that the faction led by Bronx Boss Flynn, FDR's secretary of state, was vying with Walker and Tammany for control of the city. The Walker faction "tries to harm Mr. Flynn. To do that, they pick on Vitale, one of Mr. Flynn's supporters. To get Vitale, they make a goat out of me." All that he wanted, said Terranova, was peace and quiet. "I am content to be let alone. I am happy at my home with my wife and family."

Hearing of the countercharge, Walker made a typical rejoinder: "Terranova has his animals mixed. He's not a goat. He's a jackass."

Patrolmen Johnson, at the end of his departmental trial, was restored to duty but not to his detective status. Ciro Terranova did not stand trial for either the fake robbery or the Marlow killing, there being only hearsay evidence against him. In the spring of 1930, Vitale would be removed from office by the appellate division, which based its action on his acceptance of the Rothstein loan.

As the last year of the glittering 1920s ended and the grayness of the Depression set in, the members of the board of estimate raised their salaries without a dissenting vote. The mayor's salary was increased from $25,000 to $40,000, the controller's from $25,000 to $35,000, the aldermanic president's from $15,000 to $25,000, and the salaries of the borough presidents from $15,000 to $20,000. Walker declared that his advocacy of the increases was not for himself but for his colleagues. It made little difference to him, he said, whether he made $25,000 or $40,000. "In either case," he joked, "I shall have nothing left at the end of the year." In a financial transaction of a more personal nature, the free-spending Walker accepted $26,500 in bonds from J. A. Sisto, a financier who was interested in municipal legislation that might give his Checker Cab Company an advantage in city taxi operations. The $26,500 ostensibly represented part of the profit from a joint venture by Sisto and Walker into the stock market earlier in the year, although Sisto had risked all the initial capital. The mayor put the bonds in his safe where, like so many "benefices" he accepted from admirers, they did not stay for long. James J. Walker, who lived for the moment, did not yet realize in December of 1929 that his moment in time was beginning to pass.

1930

"Oh Cu Chulainn," said Ferdiad, "what has brought thee out to do battle with me?"

"Come now, Ferdiad," replied Cu Chulainn, "it is you who have come to contend with me at this ford, urged on by the false promises of Ailill and Medab." With that, the heroes picked up their shields, darts, swords, and ivoried spears, and the fighting began. They cast no weapons that did not strike nor blows that did not resound. Yet so skilled was each champion's defense that neither man could bloody the other.

"Let us cease now from this bout, Cu Chulainn," said Ferdiad, "for it is not by such that our decision will come."

"Yea, let us cease," answered Cu Chulainn.

Early on the morrow, the champions resumed their combat at the ford, this time using two long-shields and two heavy, hardsmiting swords. From dawn to twilight they fought, until each was covered with clotted gore from shoulder to thigh.

Again they left off the fight. They parted without a kiss, a blessing, or any sign of friendship. No healing herbs were sent from Cu Chulainn to Ferdiad that night, nor was food or drink brought from Ferdiad to him.

Both champions now were full of heavy thoughts. No longer was either certain that he would be the one to survive. . . .

Some time in January, Walker's constant public appearances with Betty Compton disturbed the stern Irish-American morality of Patrick

209

Cardinal Hayes, head of the New York Archdiocese. In his role as Father Shepherd, he called the mayor to his residence at Madison Avenue and Fiftieth Street, in the shadows of St. Patrick's Cathedral, and warned him that the affair was creating a scandal. The cardinal, hard working and ascetic, was a forceful personage; even Walker's charm could do little to turn aside his blunt accusations. To Tammany's leaders, conscious of the prelate's power among their Catholic constituents, the criticism was cause for worry. Honest graft and a bit of gambling were manly foibles, but fornication and adultery were terrible sins. Walker promised to try to mend his ways, the cardinal harumphed that he owed it to those who believed in him, and the politicians fretted.

Tammany's concern over Cardinal Hayes' displeasure was understandable. Sixty-two years old in early 1930, he presided over perhaps the largest and richest Catholic diocese in the world. Besides Manhattan, the Bronx, and Staten Island, it included Duchess, Orange, Putnam, Rockland, Sullivan, Ulster, and Westchester counties. The see's Catholic population was about 1,250,000, its churches numbered some 450, its priests some 1,500. In a given year, such was the generosity of the immigrant Irish, it contributed more money to the Vatican than the whole of Europe. The Cardinal, who had received his red hat in 1924 from Pope Pius XI, was the first native-born American to rule the diocese. With his thick shock of hair, clear skin, and startlingly blue eyes, he looked in his early forties. Strangers found it difficult to believe they were meeting a Prince of the Church. Once, while traveling through Oklahoma, he and one of his clerics dropped in at a nearby convent, where they hoped to use the chapel to celebrate their masses. "It is Cardinal Hayes," explained the aide to the nun who came to the door. "That one?" she answered doubtfully. "He's too young to be even a Monsignor!"

Patrick Joseph Hayes, both of whose immigrant parents died when he was still a boy, was raised on New York's Lower East Side by his aunt and uncle. While he was still in grade school, his fondness for book learning was interpreted as a vocation. "He got the callin'," said his aunt with conviction. A succession of Catholic schools followed, and in 1892 he was ordained at St. Joseph's Seminary in upstate New York. Shortly thereafter, he was appointed a curate at St. Gabriel's on East Thirty-seventh Street. For young Father Hayes, the post was a fortuitous one. His pastor, Monsignor John Farley, advanced rapidly in the church hierarchy, taking his curate along with him. Between 1897 and 1914, Monsignor Farley rose to auxiliary bishop (Father Hayes becoming his secretary), then archbishop of the New York diocese (his protégé being named Monsignor), and finally cardinal (Hayes becoming auxiliary bishop). In the years before World War I, the work of the two men focused to a large degree on setting up the Catholic school system, from grade schools to colleges. A good education, the prelates perceived, would enable the children of immigrants to escape the tenement ghetto.

In 1918, just as Bishop Hayes was preparing to visit American troops in France, Cardinal Farley died; his protégé took over the administration of the diocese and was soon named archbishop. In the postwar years, Archbishop Hayes saw the necessity of drawing together all the see's social services into one central organization. The result was Catholic Charities. Its first drive for funds, in 1920, raised $1 million, and the sum increased each succeeding year.

As the head of the New York archdiocese, Cardinal Hayes led a frugal life, habitually rising at 6:30 A.M., sleeping on a narrow cot, and never entertaining. He drank little and ate sparingly. Each night he would work in his study until ten, then read his breviary for an hour. If he was feeling frivolous before retiring, he would take a walk around the Central Park reservoir. Despite the lecture he had given Walker, Cardinal Hayes was a kindly man; he did not enjoy being forced to discipline one of his flock. He was certain, however, that the mayor's liaison with Betty Compton was a grievous mistake.

While the mayor did not end his relationship with Betty, he did, in the early part of the year, perform some charitable acts that the cardinal might well have approved. First he took care of his old adversary, Red Mike Hylan, by appointing him a judge in children's court, at a salary of $17,500 a year. Then he made sure that the widow of his long-time friend, former Police Commissioner Warren, was named to a $4,000-a-year job with the sanitation commission.

Another aspect of Walker's humanity could be seen in February, when he reappointed Magistrate Mark Rudich of Brooklyn to a ten-year-term following the jurist's exoneration of misconduct charges. Rudich, acting largely out of pity, had dismissed a case against a woman shoplifter coming before him. The defendant, who already had three convictions, would, if found guilty, have had to be sentenced to life imprisonment under the terms of the Baumes Law. A law-and-order-conscious New York legislature in 1926 had passed this draconian measure, sponsored by Senator Caleb H. Baumes of upstate Newburgh, although it made no distinction among felonies as diverse as shoplifting, armed robbery, and murder. The bar association grievance committee, in clearing Rudich, declared that he had erred in judgment but recommended he be renamed to the bench. "You are a good judge," Walker told him at the swearing-in.

A week later, twenty-nine-year-old Ruth St. Clair, the shoplifter in question, was brought to trial. The evidence was clear-cut, and the jury took only fifteen minutes to find her guilty as a fourth offender. Mrs. St. Clair, the first woman to be convicted under the Baumes Law, heard herself sentenced to life imprisonment. Weeping and hysterical, she was carried from the courtroom.

Though the unemployment resulting from the market crash was just beginning to be felt, it was bad enough in March to touch off the worst riot the city had seen in years. Some 35,000 New Yorkers, attending a protest demonstration staged by the Communist party, jammed into Union Square, where they listened to impassioned speeches under the watchful gaze of Commissioner Whalen and some 1,000 policemen. "The principal idea, of course, was to provoke the police and force them to resort to brutality," Whalen maintained afterward. About 2:00 P.M. the Communist leaders told Whalen they intended to tell the crowd to march on City Hall, so that they could put their case directly to Walker. "You won't accomplish anything by numbers," the commissioner replied. "I am telling you now if you attempt to proceed we will break up the parade." Shortly thereafter, William Z. Foster, the principal Communist spokesman, mounted the speaker's platform and shouted at the crowd, "We asked Whalen if we could go to City Hall. The answer was 'No!' Are we going to take 'No' for an answer?"

Thousands of voices screamed that they were not.

"Then fall in line and proceed," commanded Foster.

With that, the 2,000 Communists in the throng began to form a line of march, hoping to encourage the onlookers to join them. When the parade turned down Broadway toward City Hall, Whalen acted. Hundreds of patrolmen, mounted and on foot, swinging night sticks and blackjacks, rushed into the crowd, hitting out at everyone with whom they came in contact. The attack immediately scattered the demonstrators, knocking many of them off their feet. "Some of the Communists showed fight," wrote an observer. "This only served to spur the police." One demonstrator, shaking his fist at the police, called them "Cossacks, murderous Cossacks!" He was knocked down, kicked, and beaten; even after he staggered to his feet and ran, he was pursued, blows raining down on his head and shoulders.

Within fifteen minutes, the riot was over. Nobody was killed, but a hundred or so persons were injured. Foster and the other Communist leaders, who prudently had left Union Square before the fighting began, were peacefully arrested when they later appeared at City Hall, ostensibly to confer with Walker.

Commissioner Whalen, when not dealing with Communist threats, occupied himself in early 1930 with a host of pressing matters. He called for a speed-up of traffic in the Broadway theater district, banned smoking at police headquarters, and demanded a city ordinance that would require taxi drivers to wear uniforms and peaked caps. Another of his achievements was the creation of the Police Academy, which was installed in a one-time candy factory on Manhattan's East Side; its students were required by Whalen (who admired Cossacks) to purchase royal-blue Russian-style blouses with "Police Academy" embroidered on the breast pocket in bright red letters. The commissioner also busied himself by having police headquarters sandblasted and its huge gold dome regilded and illuminated at night by spotlights of various colors. Whalen had done all that was expected of him by Tammany Hall. He had bustled about, concerning himself with trivia, while the public forgot its concern over Arnold Rothstein's murder. Now it was time, Tammany felt, for a more staid, less flamboyant police commissioner.

In May, Grover Whalen would resign. He would be replaced by Edward P. Mulrooney, who had been a policeman for thirty-four years and held the rank of assistant chief inspector. "Not gifted with any special brilliance or cunning," a contemporary journalist would write of Mulrooney, "he is nevertheless endowed with a natural diplomacy; he has been brought up to take orders and he is personally above reproach. The Cop's Cop apparently is, for Tammany, the right man for the work in hand."

Mulrooney, who joined the force in 1896, was first assigned to the Marine Police. In the summer of 1904, when an excursion boat named *General Slocum* caught fire in the East River, with the loss of almost 1,000 lives, he was one of the heroes of the rescue attempts. He went for three days without sleep and once the blaze was extinguished went down into the blackened hulk and personally removed twenty-nine bodies. Only afterward did he get sick. Mulrooney climbed steadily upward in the department—sergeant, lieutenant, and, in 1923, captain. Three years later, he gained inspector's rank. During this time, he served in almost every branch of the force. The new commissioner had seen mayors come and mayors go. He tried to keep his police responsibilities separate from politics, but long service had taught him that a cop had to show at least minimal consideration for those who saw to his advancement.

At the age of fifty-six, Mulrooney still had the hard body of his youth; his face was heavily lined, his green eyes peered from beneath heavy lids. When he chuckled, two gold teeth could be seen in his smile. He spoke with a strong Lower East Side accent ("thoid" for "third" and "berled" for "boiled"). Extremely taciturn, the commissioner could keep a secret. He had not even told his wife and daughters of his appointment; they had gotten the news from the papers.

In February, bothered by a series of colds, Walker departed with Betty for a two-week vacation in Florida. Previously, the mayor had only to pay $47.50 (each way) for a private car to take him South, the railroads being happy to donate an entire Pullman car to men of influence for the cost of a single ticket. In recent months, however, the Interstate Commerce Commission had decreed that anyone who wished to occupy a whole car would have to pay the equivalent of all the fares. Lacking a "benefactor" to accompany him on this particular trip, the mayor was forced to part with $1,187.50. (Even James F. Eagan, who in addition to being the Tammany secretary was also stationmaster at Pennsylvania Station, could do nothing about the ICC ruling.)

While in Florida, Walker and Betty stayed at Sarasota, the winter home of the circus, where they were the guests of showman John Ringling. As usual, the mayor did some unsuccessful angling. "Where are the fish, Mr. Mayor?" a reporter asked him on his return to New York. "Right where they've been for years," said Walker. Then he rushed to St. Patrick's Cathedral (without Betty, of course), just in time to attend the wedding of Miss Veronica Curry, Boss Curry's daughter.

The strain of trying to keep pace with his twenty-five-year-old mistress was beginning to tell on the forty-eight-year-old mayor, who was also burdened by the knowledge that his younger brother, George, was gravely ill with tuberculosis. Though the mayor had always been a hypochondriac (his medicine chest was filled with pills and potions of dubious value), he was, in late April, so genuinely run down that he was ordered by his physician, Dr. William Schroeder, Jr. (who was also head of the sanitation commission), to stay in bed a week. "Complete physical nervous exhaustion due to overwork," was the way the medical report read. By now Walker was living in the Mayfair Hotel at Park Avenue and Fifty-sixth Street, which was closer to Betty's East 76th Street apartment than the Ritz-Carlton. Immediately after the bed-rest period, he left incognito for Bermuda aboard the steamship *Arcadian*, accompanied once again by Betty.

Despite a weight loss, Walker looked natty on boarding the *Arcadian*, an accomplishment due largely to the efforts of Jeann Friedman, the tailor who earlier had decided that the mayoral trousers should button directly onto the mayoral vests, the better to hang in straight lines. Recently, Friedman had developed two new ensembles for Walker. One, which he called the Hyde Park, featured a plain jacket and vest with vigorously striped trousers, in the same color. The other, the Biaritz (for "lolling"), combined a flannel jacket with tweed knickers. All seventy suits in Walker's wardrobe, courtesy of Friedman, had the same aggressive lapels, the same pinched waists; the trousers uniformly measured ten inches wide at the knee, nine and one-quarter at the bottom, with no break at the instep. Currently the *pièce de résistance* of the Walker wardrobe was a one-button dress topcoat in black, with satin lapels, collar, and cuffs. "When you see a feller put on dress clothes and then a regular topcoat like a gray or maybe a brown, ain't it comical?" Friedman asked.

In the first week in May, Kings County Judge W. Bernard Vause, president of the Brooklyn Democratic Club, was indicted for mail fraud in connection with the failure of the Columbia Finance Corporation. The judge, who had once advocated using the whipping post for criminals, was accused of having lent the prestige of his office to what was actually a bogus corporation and conspiring to cheat tenement dwellers, many of whom did not read or write English, of some $400,000. Vause had tried to work through the corporation's president, Solomon Cruso, accepting money only through intermediaries, but the threat of jail had encouraged Cruso to talk before a federal grand jury, and gradually the real degree of his involvement emerged.

A second charge against Vause, a confidant of Boss McCooey, was that he had accepted $250,000 in legal fees while sitting on the bench in 1926 for negotiating the lease of city piers to the United American Lines. U.S. Attorney Charles H. Tuttle, who uncovered the transaction, pointed out to New York District Attorney Crain that it was illegal for city judges to practice law and demanded that he take action. United American, which with Vause's help had its pier leases approved on June 29, 1926, by the Sinking Fund Commission—of which Walker was chairman—soon afterward sold its three passenger ships to the Hamburg-American Line for some $9 million. Obviously, the acquisition of the piers enabled United American to negotiate a far more profitable deal.

Just as obviously, Vause's pier fees had been shared with Democratic politicians. United American, Tuttle explained, would make its payments to Joseph F. Boyle, an attorney who was employed by the Vause firm at a salary of seventy-five dollars a week. Boyle, in turn, would take the checks made out in his name and deposit them in his own account; then he would draw his own checks, at the direction of the judge, "to the order of such payees as the latter designated." One such designee was "William Jerome," a psuedonym for Vause's brother George, a clerk in his office. Checks made out to "Jerome" were deposited by George Vause in a second account. Then, presumably at the judge's direction, George would make out blank checks and give them to a shadowy figure named "Baxter." Neither Vause brother knew much about this man, or so they testified, but nonetheless they paid him large percentages of the money they had obtained from United America.

"What did Baxter have to do with these piers?" the persistent Tuttle asked.

"I don't know," Vause said. "He was a free agent."

Joseph F. Boyle, the go-between who had started the laundering of the steamship line's payments, was more helpful. "Baxter," he testified, must have been William Baxter, a man who had been an occasional process server in Vause's law office and who was often used as a "dummy" in corporate paperwork. Unfortunately, he had died in 1926, after receiving the last of the blank checks from George Vause. There the trail of money ended.

If Judge Vause was vague as to why he had hired Baxter, officials of the United American Lines were obtuse as to why they had retained the jurist. "They did not know who had recommended him to do work in connection with the leases," said Tuttle. "They did not know what work he did, and they never received from him any reports. Both they and he merely say he was retained to 'get' the leases and he got them."

Vause resigned from the bench in June because of "poor health and limited means." A month later he was convicted of mail fraud (the pier investigation never was pursued by D. A. Crain, no doubt at Tammany's insistence), and given a six-year sentence. In 1932 he finally went to jail.

In a related case, William E. Walsh, chairman of the board of standards and appeals and a good friend of Walker, was indicted that June by both federal and county grand juries. The federal charge, a roundabout one, stated that he had failed to file an income-tax return for 1929 even though he had allegedly accepted a $30,000 bribe from John ("Fishhooks") McCarthy, a Bronx builder, for granting various zoning exceptions. Walsh's defense was that the builder had simply loaned him $30,000 in cash on the basis of an unsecured note; since he intended to pay the money back, there was no income to report. The county charge was that he had accepted a gratuity while holding public office. Specifically, for the last forty months he had occupied a $4,000-a-year apartment, at 25 East Eighty-sixth Street, while paying an annual rental of only $1,500. The reduction had allegedly been obtained through the efforts of the same Fishhooks McCarthy.

Within days of the indictments, Walsh resigned from the board. The federal charge against him, for income-tax evasion, never could be proved; though he was brought to trial on the county charge, he was acquitted on the ground that he had not personally requested the rent reduction. Thereafter, Walsh lived in relatively quiet retirement.

About this time, U.S. Attorney Tuttle began to scrutinize the tax returns of William F. ("Horse Doctor") Doyle, a former veterinarian who had compiled an incredible record of success before the board, over a nine-year period receiving some $2 million in fees from clients for whom he obtained building variances. Doyle, who had been scrupulous in demanding part of his payments by check and the rest in cash, explained the discrepancies between his income and his tax returns by admitting that he had split his fees. But he would not say with whom, on the ground that it might incriminate him. The federal tax case against Doyle came to naught, so Tuttle turned the matter of the fee-splitting over to New York District Attorney Crain, who just let it drop. The veterinarian, who in the past three years had banked some $420,000, retired to Deal, New Jersey, beyond the reach of subpoena, where he hoped he would be forgotten. This was not to be. In the summer of 1931, Judge Seabury would compel him to testify before the legislative committee investigating Walker's administration.

Charles H. Tuttle, the fifty-one-year-old U.S. Attorney now scanning the tax returns of Tammany's henchmen, was described by a contemporary as "a born valedictorian." His family had sailed to America, not on the *Mayflower,* but on the *Planter,* a more prestigious vessel that brought the first Church of England stock to these shores. Since then, generations of Tuttles had specialized in becoming either clergymen or lawyers. Young Tuttle went to Columbia, where he took the Chandler Prize in American history, the James Gordon Prize in English prose, the Bonner Medal in English literature, and a Phi Beta Kappa key. After being admitted to the bar, he practiced skillfully for twenty years with the Manhattan firm of Davies, Auerbach & Cornell, where he wrote and compiled 110 volumes of briefs. In court, the declarations of the spare, hatchet-faced Tuttle bristled with scriptural phrases. Once, while representing Carl Mays, a major-league baseball pitcher, in a salary dispute, he described the athlete as "a baseball Behemoth, whose force is in the muscles of his belly, who moveth his tail like a cedar, whose bones are as tubes of brass."

In middle age, Tuttle heard the call that he might better serve his fellow men if he entered politics. He had been one of the chief strategists in Frank D. Waterman's losing 1925 mayoral campaign against Walker and James W. Wadsworth's losing 1926 senatorial race against Robert Wagner. At this point, the party leaders, feeling that Tuttle should have his confidence restored, got him the U.S. attorney's appointment.

As a federal prosecutor, Tuttle pursued his duties with great zeal, obtaining twice as many convictions as any of his predecessors. While compiling this statistic, he nonetheless managed to discontinue the practice of allowing the spavined and the elderly, for a cash consideration, to take the rap for big bootleggers, and thereby "restored the jails to an amateur basis." Nor did Tuttle, now in public office, forget his moral obligations, blocking the efforts of the Freethinkers' Society to keep public-school children from receiving after-hours religious instruction.

By vigorously investigating such Democratic bagmen as Judge Vause, William E. Walsh, and Horse Doctor Doyle in mid-1930, Tuttle was preparing a public record that would make him the Republican nominee in the race against Governor Roosevelt that fall. Still, he recognized that he could not prosper in politics until he developed less rectitude and more joviality. Wrote journalist Alva Johnson: "A nervous dread still lingers that someone will take advantage of his bonhomie by uttering a coarse word."

$$\approx\!\approx\!\approx$$

On the surface at least, Walker that summer carried on business and pleasure as usual. During July he formally welcomed golfer Bobby Jones to the city after his victories in the British Open and Amateur, saw Allie off on yet another tour of Europe (a month-long trip on which she was accompanied by Mrs. Mastbaum), himself enjoyed a six-day fishing trip in New Hampshire, and even sent the obligatory birthday greeting to Tammany Sachem Voorhis—now one hundred and one. But the Depression was settling into the economy's bones. While the stock exchange's top 100 listings sank to new lows for the year, unemployment in the city rose to 300,000. Citizens who had ignored and even smiled at Walker's irresponsibility, preferring to call it charm, now were beginning to listen to his critics. Socialist Norman Thomas, a perennial adversary of the mayor, was hotly pursuing the issue of corruption in the magistrates' courts. Somehow he had obtained a copy of one judge's daily calendar; it was dated

July 14, 1925—before Walker took office—but no matter; it clearly indicated the influence of Tammany's district leaders with the judiciary. Among the names scribbled by the magistrate on the calendar, next to those many of the defendants coming up for hearings on that date, were "Ahearn," "Hamill," "Healy," "McCooey," "McManus," and "Farley." Such notations, Thomas said, were reminders that the leaders, many of whom were chief clerks in the various courts, wanted leniency or dismissal in these cases. He named eleven magistrates who, he maintained, had been involved in such "fixes."

"I am increasingly of the opinion," said Thomas, "that the chief clerks are the creatures of intrigue and fixing in most courts. They are the connecting links between police, bondsmen, fixers and sometimes magistrates. There should be housecleaning of these clerks." (Just a few months earlier, Boss McCooey had retired as chief clerk of Brooklyn's surrogate court on a $6,800 pension; of course, he retained his county leadership.)

The growing criticism caused Walker, in late July, to summon the heads and principal deputies of the city's thirty-eight departments for a special meeting at City Hall. "There are approximately 125,000 officers and employees of this city," he told the politicians assembled in the board of estimate chamber. "When you read the headlines about various judicial officers who are charged with malfeasance or misfeasance, I think there is much to take courage from in the fact that there have been mentioned from time to time only [a few] individuals."

Despite the mayor's disclaimer, U.S. Attorney Tuttle was unimpressed. In August, he touched off still another scandal in the Walker administration by turning over to District Attorney Crain evidence indicating that former Magistrate George Ewald had bought his appointment. (Ewald had resigned from the bench a few months earlier, after Tuttle had charged him with supplementing his income by selling fraudulent mining stock through the mails—a federal offense.) The U.S. attorney declared that Ewald, who had been appointed to magistrate's court in 1927 by Walker, had obtained the seat as a result of a $10,000 payment to Martin J. Healy, Tammany leader of the nineteenth A.D. and deputy commissioner of plants and structures. When Healy refused to testify in his own behalf, on the ground that it might incriminate him, the mayor suspended his commissioner from office, the first such disciplinary action he had taken against any member of his official family during his five years in office. Healy subsequently admitted taking the $10,000 but insisted that it had been a loan and that it had been given to him by Mrs. Bertha Ewald, the would-be magistrate's wife. It was coincidence, said Healy, that the money had come from Mrs. Ewald; the unsecured, interest-free loan had been innocently negotiated by Thomas P. Tommaney, chief clerk in the Manhattan sheriff's office and a close political associate. Tommaney, who knew Healy needed funds to buy a summer home, had called on Mrs. Ewald, and she had immediately offered him the money.

Although the story was ingenuous, it was to the liking of all concerned. Certainly Ewald, who was sweating out the mail-fraud allegation, had no wish to become involved in bribery and criminal-conspiracy charges. He testified that he knew nothing about any checks his wife drew because he never looked at their joint statements from the bank but "turned [the letters] over to her unopened." Though Mrs. Ewald had a fairly good head for business, he said, she did have a weakness for making unsecured loans. "I remember in 1924 she lent $7,500 to the Kerman Brothers Film Exchange on Seventh Avenue. It was six months before I learned about that." In his own testimony, Walker declared that Healy (whose district, incidentally, embraced the German enclave of Yorkville) had never spoken to him about appointing Ewald; his decision had been based on the strong recommendation the aspiring magistrate, who was of German descent, had received from the Steuben Society—the German-American political and social club. "Ewald did not need any greater support than he had," Walker said, "so if he voluntarily contributed money for that appointment he might just as well have thrown it in a sewer."

The one discordant note in the inquiry was provided by Emmerich J. Boczor, Ewald's one-time secretary. He was the "mystery witness" Tuttle had supplied to D.A. Crain for the purpose of aiding the county investigation. Boczor swore that Dr. Francis M. Schirp, chairman of the Steuben Society's New York political committee, had boasted to him that he and Healy had gotten Ewald his appointment. When the secretary told his employer about the remark, Ewald was frank but bitter. "He didn't tell you that he received $2,000 and Healy $10,000, all turned over from Mrs. Ewald, did he?" Later, said Boczor, the magistrate again admitted that he had bought his office.

"Where were you at the time?"

"In his home, in the dining room."

"And when was it that he said that?"

"Just one year ago."

Two days later, the New York grand jury nonetheless cleared Ewald of bribery. No great stress was placed on Boczor's testimony by D.A. Crain, and, though Dr. Schirp was called for questioning, he was not asked about the secretary's charges. This tepid investigation was not to be the end of the Ewald affair. Public indignation would soon force Governor Roosevelt to ask the appellate division to look into the magistrates' courts. In mid-September, the Ewalds, Healy, and Tommaney would all be indicted, charged with the purchase and sale of public office; they would come to trial toward the end of the year.

On August 25, the very day that the appellate division voted affirmatively to investigate the magistrates' courts in Manhattan and the Bronx, the news that the Honorable Samuel Seabury had been named to head the appellate inquiry into the magistrates' courts all but passed unnoticed. The fifty-seven-year-old Seabury, who had been the unsuccessful Democratic candidate for governor in 1916 and who had once referred to Al Smith as "the best representative of the worst element in the Democratic Party," was in London and could not easily be reached for comment. It remained for Charles C. Burlingham, president of the New York City Bar Association, to say of Seabury (who had written an insightful book about the quality of justice in the lower courts) that the appellate division "could not have selected a better man." Even if Seabury had been in New York, however, his appointment would not have stirred much interest. Once quite active in politics, he had been in retirement from public life for the past fourteen years.

Samuel Seabury was born in 1873, in the rector's house attached to the Church of the Annunciation on West Fourteenth Street. His father, William Jones Seabury, Professor of Canon Law at the General Theological Seminary, was a priest of the church, as his father had been before him. When not singing in the choir, the boy passed his time in the elder Seabury's library, where he could gaze at a portrait of his great-great-grandfather Samuel (a resolute Tory who had been the first Episcopal bishop in the United States), or listen to his father read from his latest monograph ("Suggestions in Aid of Devotion and Godliness"). Samuel went to New York Law School, where he was adjudged so precocious that the authorities, even before his graduation in 1893, eagerly put in use a textbook he had written on corporate law. A few years afterward, he and his father, in a curious confrontation, experienced at firsthand the power of Tammany Hall. William H. Walker, then superintendent of public buildings, decided to condemn St. John's Burial Ground in Greenwich Village, the last resting place of many eminent Protestants—including some Seabury antecedents—and convert it to a public park for his (largely Catholic) constituents. It dismayed Mr. Walker not a bit, incidentally, that the condemnation would enhance the value of his house at 6 St. Luke's Place, just across from the cemetery. Even while the senior

Walker was asking architect Stanford White to design the new park, the two Seaburys found themselves among the disgruntled Episcopalians obliged to disinter their kin.

Young Samuel's politics was progressive, sometimes radically so, In 1897, he strongly supported socialist Henry George, the economist who believed in the elimination of all taxes except a single levy on real estate, for the mayoralty. Though George died just before the election, it is doubtful that he could have won; the masses voted overwhelmingly for Tammany candidate Robert A. Van Wyck. Elected a judge of the city court four years later, at the age of twenty-eight, Seabury quickly asserted himself, firing six Tammany-appointed clerks accused of stealing jury fees. In court, the youthful jurist thought nothing, when the occasion called for it, of reprimanding his seniors. District Attorney William Travers Jerome, a fellow reformer whose work exposing Tammany corruption for the Lexow Committee had made him one of the best-known men in America, once told Seabury he should accept a defense attorney's word on a legal matter because the man was "a gentleman."

"The court does not care to be dictated to by you, Mr. Jerome," said Seabury. "You may immediately leave the courtroom and withdraw from the case." Choking with anger, the usually unflappable Jerome all but ran from the court. "I don't know where I am," he complained.

In 1905, with the help of William Randolph Hearst, Seabury was elected to the New York Supreme Court. Hearst was then in his own progressive period, and his Municipal Ownership League was campaigning aggressively for the rights of the working man. In the higher court, Seabury solidified his reputation for forcefulness. Sometimes, however, it seemed he went too far. In 1914, shortly after being elevated again—this time to the court of appeals—he presided at the second trial of Charles Becker, the corrupt police lieutenant who was accused of the murder of gambler Herman Rosenthal. Here his advice to the jury greatly aided the prosecution. "If an accomplice was corroborated as to *some* material fact, the jury may infer that he says the truth," said Seabury. "A witness does not need to be corroborated in everything." The jury agreed with this dubious logic, and the police lieutenant was sentenced to the electric chair.

Now Seabury encountered a subtle irony. Charles Whitman, the district attorney on the Becker case, in 1916 was given the Republican gubernatorial nomination, largely on the strength of the favorable publicity he had received during the trial. His Democratic opponent was Seabury, who by this time was estranged from the increasingly conservative Hearst and allied with the publisher's perennial adversary, Charles F. Murphy. The candidates were evenly matched that fall, and the race was decided for the Republicans only when Theodore Roosevelt, likewise impressed by Whitman's conviction of Becker, threw his third-party weight to the district attorney. Seabury, who had resigned from the court of appeals to make the race (after serving but two years of a fourteen-year term), must have reflected that the Lord works in wondrous ways.

In the years thereafter, and all through the 1920s, Seabury abstained from active politics and pursued a law career. He began to build a reputation as a "a lawyer's lawyer." According to his biographer, Herbert Mitgang, "Most of the time he was called upon to handle appeals. An attorney in a case would come to his office and ask him to assist by serving 'of counsel.' He listened to the facts, weighed them as if rendering a decision, and then decided if the legal merits were sufficient for him to take on the appeal." For straightening out the $93 million estate of financier Jay Gould, an effort that occupied Seabury and his staff intermittently over a ten-year period, he received a $1 million fee. The judge celebrated, in typically cerebral fashion, by buying a $4,500 grand piano.

Pink of face and strong of jaw, the man who would be Walker's relentless interrogator wore his silver hair parted in the middle; his blond eyebrows bristled over a clear, steady gaze. He wore immaculate but severe clothes, suits in black or gray with white shirts; his only concession to frivolity was a large emerald ring on his left hand. He was never heard to use slang or indulge in a wisecrack, and his presence was such that he could invest the blowing of his nose with theological overtones. He and his wife were mutually devoted but childless. During his fourteen-year hiatus from politics, Seabury took periodic trips to Europe, building up a splendid collection of first editions in the fields of political economy and jurisprudence. In London, when he received the news that he had been chosen to conduct the inquiry into the magistrates' courts, he was reading a newly acquired tome, published in 1631, called *The Just Laywer*. The coincidence was significant. In the months to come, Seabury would see himself as leading the forces of light, Walker the forces of darkness.

As August drew to a close, the mayor was obliged to deny stories that he had been caught in a gambling raid on the Montauk (Long Island) Casino. He had been in a restaurant next to the Casino, he said, but had not been involved in the raid. Deputy Sheriff Max Mittenleifer contradicted him, saying, "As the Mayor was coming out, I hailed him. He said, 'All right, officer, just a minute.' He called me to one side and said he was Mayor Walker. He asked me to let him go to his boat. I did so." Retorted Walker: "If I had been to the Casino and someone had asked me if I were the Mayor, I would not have identified myself." The truth was that Walker and Betty Compton, with a party of friends, had been cruising off Montauk Point at the tip of Long Island. Rough weather had forced them ashore. All that the seasick Walker had wanted was a hot meal, but Betty had insisted on visiting the Casino, which was both restaurant and gambling palace. She was completely absorbed in a card game, with $2,000 worth of chips in front of her, when the raiders arrived. The mayor, more alert, darted into the Casino's kitchen and then made his way out of the building, where he explained who he was to Sheriff Mittenleifer. The furious Betty, however, was taken to Night Court, and it was a few hours before she was released. Back on the yacht with Walker, she demanded to know why he had deserted her.

"Monk," he said, "I knew you'd get out all right. But as for me, Governor Roosevelt has decided to keep the [magistrates' courts] investigation within bounds. It might be a good idea if I didn't tempt fate at this moment by showing up in the hoosegow."

Roosevelt, with a re-election campaign coming up, might well have wanted to tamp down exposure of Tammany's influence in the courts. Events were now moving on their own momentum, however, and no politician or group of politicians could bring them to a halt. In early September, New Yorkers learned that State Supreme Court Justice Joseph Force Crater had been missing for four weeks. Crater, who had been appointed to the bench only the preceding April, had been on vacation with his wife in Belgrade Lakes, Maine. On August 5, he visited New York, dropping in on his official chambers and staying the night at his cooperative apartment at 40 Fifth Avenue. The next morning he went to his chambers again, where he filled several portfolios with his private papers and had them sent to his home. Crater also had the court attendant cash two personal checks—one for $3,000 and one for $2,150—and return the money to him in bills of large denomination. In early evening, the judge, who affected starched choker collars and spats, bought a single ticket for *Dancing Partners,* a new show that had just opened at the Belasco. Then he dropped in at Billy Haas' restaurant, a favorite eating place for show people, on West Forty-fifth Street; there Crater encountered some friends, an attorney and a chorus girl, who invited him to join them. All three left the restaurant together about 9:15 P.M.—well after *Dancing Partners'* curtain time. Crater hailed a passing cab and stepped inside while his friends waved good night. He was never seen again.

Two explanations were offered for Crater's decision to disappear.

One theory was that the judge, one-time president of the Nineteenth A.D.'s Cayuga Democratic Club—the stronghold of Martin J. Healy—had bought his appointment and now feared exposure. Indeed, on May 27, 1930, about six weeks after being named to the bench, Crater withdrew $7,500 in cash from a bank account and sold securities for an additional $15,779. The $23,279 total was suspiciously close to a supreme court justice's $22,500 annual salary, and a year's pay was said to be the minimum fee for political favoritism.

A second motivating factor behind Crater's disappearance may have been his part the year before in the financial juggling of the Libby Hotel on the Lower East Side. When the hotel had gone into bankruptcy, the stockholders being unable to meet the $1,500,000 mortgage, Attorney Crater had been appointed referee to administer the property and supervise bids from interested realtors. On June 27, 1929, despite the fact that the Libby was appraised at $1,200,000, it was sold to the American Mortgage Loan Company, a subsidiary of the American Bond and Mortgage Company, for $75,000. The sale was sanctioned by Supreme Court Justice Alfred Frankenthaler, a close friend of Crater, despite rumors that the city was instituting condemnation proceedings that would pay many times this sum. On August 9, 1929, the city bought the property—in conjunction with a street-widening program—for an astounding $2,850,000. The American Bond and Mortgage Company, and parties unknown, in a few months had made a profit of $2,775,000 out of their $75,000 investment.

As the search for Crater continued, it became clear that the forty-one-year-old judge, a teetotaler in robust health, had not been an entirely faithful husband. One woman, identified only as Lorraine Fay, had been contemplating a $100,000 breach-of-promise suit. Crater was likewise linked with Marie Miller, a nightclub hostess, and Elaine Dawn, a former Ziegfeld girl who worked at the raucous Club Abby, which the judge had often visited, according to Mrs. Crater, "for political reasons." "Sex," the *Evening Graphic* observed, "is the direct reason for nine-tenths of missing persons." Such speculation did nothing to mollify Mrs. Crater, who, still in Maine, declared "the newspapers were making a burlesque" out of the case and refused to come to New York. Then it was learned that she had visited the city briefly back in August, just before the judge's disappearance became public knowledge. A phone check on her Fifth Avenue apartment showed that on August 29 she had twice called Martin Healy in Blue Point, Long Island (at the summer house he had bought with Ewald's "loan"). Testifying before a grand jury, the

Tammany leader explained that Mrs. Crater's calls had been "half-hysterical" pleas for help. He insisted he knew no reason for the judge to disappear voluntarily.

Here the investigation temporarily stalled. In late January of 1931, after the grand jury was discharged, Mrs. Crater would come back to New York, making a discovery that would add still more mystery to the case. While unpacking valises and putting clothing away in various drawers, she came across four manila envelopes in a bedroom bureau. All were addressed to her in the judge's handwriting. One contained some $6,600 in cash, as well as three checks for some $500, another four insurance policies totaling $30,000 (which Mrs. Crater would not be able to collect on until 1937, when her husband was declared legally dead), and a third Crater's will, naming her the beneficiary. The fourth envelope, however, was the most intriguing. It contained a confidential memorandum to his wife, which listed some twenty persons or companies who owed him money, and ended "Am very weary. Love, Joe." The most startling item read: "Libby Hotel—there will be a very large sum due me for services when the city pays the two and three-quarter millions in condemnation. Martin Liffman will attend to it—keep in touch with him." Liffman, the attorney for the American Bond and Mortgage Company that profited so handsomely from the Libby Hotel sale, subsequently denied that he owed Crater anything.

Through all the months and years that followed, Crater would never be found, although his whereabouts were a constant source of conjecture. Perhaps the most bizarre rumor, that Crater did not disappear for political reasons at all but had been murdered, was raised in 1953. The story went that Crater, while still an attorney in 1929, had ostensibly taken a fee of $5,000 to "fix" a forgery charge. The fix had not worked, and the defendant was sent to prison. As Crater got into the taxi upon leaving Haas' restaurant on August 6, friends of the forger supposedly had poked guns into his ribs and kidnaped him. His captors wanted not only their $5,000 back but $20,000 more as recompense. The judge, unable to believe they would dare harm so influential a man as he, laughed at the demands—whereupon his kidnapers shot him twice in the back of the head, decomposed his body in a bathtub of hydrochloric acid, and dumped the remains, tub and all, into the brackish waters of New Jersey's Passaic River.

Toward the end of September, the special state grand jury appointed by Governor Roosevelt to pursue the buying and selling of judgeships summoned Tammany leader Curry and Director of the Budget Charles H. Kohler (the leader of the sixteenth A.D. who

allegedly had been involved in the 1926 milk scandal) to appear before it. The governor had called this grand jury to supersede the
county investigation after D.A. Crain had failed to secure indictments against the Ewalds, District Leader Healy, and Tommaney;
the indictments had been forthcoming, and the quartet was now awaiting trial. Curry remained in the grand jury room only a few minutes,
however, and when he emerged he was red-faced with anger. "I'll
give you a statement," he told reporters. "I came down here prepared
to testify and I was insulted." Though Curry did not elaborate on the
nature of the insult, an equally indignant Kohler, who stalked out of
the room soon afterward, explained in shocked tones that he had
been asked to sign a waiver of immunity. "They asked me to sign
as soon as I got inside," he said. "I told them I was born in this city
and had lived here all my life and my father before me. I came here
to answer questions, not to sign papers."

Hiram C. Todd, the assistant state attorney general in charge of
the inquiry, had been interested in what Curry and Kohler could tell
him about the appointment of Amadeo Bertini to the bench to replace
Francis X. Mancuso, the judge who had been forced to resign in 1929
after the failure of the City Trust Company. "Evidently Mr. Curry
has changed his former policy in which he said he would be willing
to do anything in his power to aid this investigation," Todd said. "As
for Mr. Kohler, he seemed to want to deliver a speech." From Albany,
Governor Roosevelt promptly announced that, if he were re-elected
in the fall, he would ask the legislature to pass a law requiring public
officials to waive immunity in investigations of their official acts. The
Tammany leaders of all twenty-three A.D.'s were then subpoenaed
to appear before the grand jury. Virtually all of them, following
Curry's lead, refused to sign the waivers.

"Why help a political investigation?" said Martin G. McCue, leader
of the Twelfth A.D. and chief clerk in the surrogate's court.

"Were you insulted?" he was asked.

"No," McCue smiled, "not very much."

James J. McCormick, leader of the Twenty-second A.D. and deputy city clerk, was even more forthright. "I wouldn't sign anything
but a check," he said.

Angered, Governor Roosevelt dispatched a letter to Walker demanding that he order all Tammany leaders who held city jobs to
sign the waivers or forfeit their posts. "Whether they are within their
legal rights is not the question," wrote Roosevelt. "Their action as
government servants is contrary to sound public policy." Said Walker
of the governor's statement: "His suggestions will be carried out
promptly." So the public defiance of the Tammany leaders, mitigated

by promises of cooperation, was smoothed over; it would be many weeks, however, before they would be forced to testify, and even then, substituting garrulousness for silence, they would admit nothing.

Toward the end of 1930, national unemployment, which had been in the vicinity of three to four million at the beginning of the year, was rising to the six million mark. Nowhere was there a greater concentration of the homeless and hungry than in New York, the once gay Gotham of only a few months before. The Municipal Lodging House, for example, was sheltering 1,500 people a night and feeding some 4,000; the Salvation Army was ladling out 22,000 bowls of stew daily; and still-rich New Yorkers were contributing substantial sums to the Emergency Employment Committee, which paid heads of families $15 for three days' work in the public parks. Taking note of these conditions, the Communist party on October 16 staged another unemployment demonstration at City Hall, and a group of Communists actually forced their way into a board of estimate meeting.

"When is the ice cream going to be served?" asked Walker, apropos the confusion inside the chamber when Louis Engdahl, a party spokesman, elbowed his way forward and announced he represented the city's unemployed.

"I speak for the noise outside," said Engdahl.

"The chair is not in a frame of mind or in a physical condition to appreciate a good joke today," answered Walker.

"If you are not in condition you might let someone else take your place."

"You can't bully this chair," said Walker, losing his patience.

Engdahl then tried to present a list of demands, which called for free rent, gas, and electricity for the unemployed, free food and clothing for their children, and abolition of all vagrancy laws. He was peremptorily gaveled down.

"Are you prepared to stand aside, because if you are not you are likely to go to jail," said the mayor.

"You have already jailed most of our best leaders," replied Engdahl.

"Yes, and you are not far behind them," said Walker, signaling for the police to remove his adversary.

"I'll see you again, Mr. Mayor," shouted the Communist as he was escorted from the chamber.

"I'll have to be looking from the outside—through a set of bars," Walker shouted back.

Sam Nessin of 16 West Twenty-first Street, another Communist spokesman, then jumped to his feet before the board and demanded that New York do something for the 300,000 unemployed. He suggested that a $7 million increase in the police department budget be diverted to unemployment relief. Nessin did not truly irritate Walker until, referring to the Communist riots in Union Square earlier that year, he declared that working men "were sent to jail by men who paid for their places on the bench—and that's no matter to wisecrack about!"

"And it's nothing to run a temperature about, either," rejoined the mayor.

"Well, I'll run a temperature," said Nessin. "You are a lot of grafting Tammany politicians. I would rather be a member of my working class than one of your grafting officials."

At this point, Walker banged his gavel furiously. "You dirty whelp," he said, "that remark prompts me to come down and thrash the life out of you."

The mayor did not handle Nessin himself, however, but told the police to eject him. Once the Communist was taken out into the corridor, detectives threw him down the building's stairs and, without giving him a chance to regain his feet, showered blows upon him. Again and again, as he was subjected to a hail of punches to the head, face, and body. Nessin desperately tried to rise from the ground. Finally, with blood spurting from his nose, his eyes blackened, and his clothing in shreds, he broke away from the police and made a dash down the City Hall steps. The patrolmen on duty outside the building then beat him with less fervor for a few more minutes. Nessin eventually was arrested on the charge of inciting a riot. Later he was taken to Bellevue, where he was treated for a fractured jaw; his condition was termed "not serious."

In the weeks before the November gubernatorial election, Republican candidate Charles H. Tuttle strove to improve his chances against Governor Roosevelt by stressing Tammany corruption. He accused the Democratic incumbent of avoiding "the fundamental issue of good government," asked repeatedly why Roosevelt had not permitted the special grand jury investigating the Ewald case to extend its inquiry into other judicial areas, and declared that his opponent was already eyeing a presidential nomination and feared disclosure of Democratic graft would block his way to the White House. FDR sidestepped these charges, but Tammany did not. Mayor Walker addressed a traditional rally of the faithful, complete with bands, red torches, and florid speeches, at the new Wigwam in Union Square. "Crime, graft, larceny, thievery are not partisan," speciously declaimed Walker; "they are individual, if they exist at all, because if graft were partisan there would be only one party in the State of New York. . . Day after day, I hear it—'Why don't you go back at them?' is the cry. 'Why don't you call the role of the line of march to jail of influential, important Republicans?' And we answer, 'That is not our system.' It has never been the idea of the Democratic Party to attain success because of the shortcomings of our opponents. Our party, all to its credit, has insisted on winning political victories on its own virtues."

Once the balloting was complete, it was clear that Tammany could still get out the vote. The city ignored both Tuttle's disclosures of municipal graft as a U.S. district attorney and his corruption charges as a gubernatorial candidate, helping to re-elect Roosevelt by giving him a hitherto unheard-of 600,000-vote plurality. Pointing out that the Republican nominee had failed to carry a single assembly district in any one of the five boroughs, Walker saw the results as an "unparalleled vote of confidence" in his administration. James A. Farley, chairman of the State Democratic Committee, viewed the victory in a different light, saying "I do not see how Mr. Roosevelt can escape becoming the next presidential nominee."

Toward the end of 1930, former Magistrate George F. Ewald's alleged buying of office from District Leader Healy was on the court docket again. After Manhattan District Attorney Crain had failed in August to obtain an indictment against Ewald, the case was taken over, as we have seen, by the state. Brought to trial first in November were Healy and his colleague Thomas T. Tommaney, on charges of accepting $10,000 from Ewald and his wife. (Healy and Tommaney by now had resigned their municipal offices as deputy commissioner of plants and structures and chief clerk in the Manhattan sheriff's office, respectively, but they still retained their Tammany leaderships.) There was no question that the $10,000—half in cash and half by check—had passed from the Ewalds to Healy by means of Tommaney; the debate was whether the money was a bribe, as the state maintained, or an interest-free loan, as the Ewalds insisted. Neither was there any question that Tammany was vitally interested in the case. "The witness room in Supreme Court had the air of an anteroom in Tammany Hall," wrote a journalist on one occasion. "Two district leaders, Andrew H. Keating of the 13th and City Clerk Michael Cruise of the 12th, sat around chatting with Tommaney, former chief clerk in Sheriff Thomas Farley's office, and waiting to be called. The sheriff dropped in himself for a moment, and through a mistake in dates Mayor Walker walked over from City Hall and stayed long enough to be photographed."

Hiram C. Todd, the assistant attorney general, first drew from Peter Eckert, Mrs. Ewald's father, the admission that his daughter was an excellent businesswoman. She had been a partner in his prosperous movie-theater operation, Mr. Eckert testified; she kept the firm's books, deposited funds, drew checks—all with an accountant's exactitude.

"What's the interest on $10,000 for five years?" the prosecutor mused. "Roughly, about $3,000. And we're asked to believe that she lent it to [Healy], whom she didn't even know, without a bit of security and without interest. Would an experienced businesswoman do that?"

The defense, which did not call Healy and Tommaney to testify, based its case principally on one point of logic and one witness. Would it have been logical, the defense attorney asked, for an experienced politician like Healy to accept a check from Mrs. Ewald if his dealings with her had been anything but honest? Testifying in Healy and Tommaney's behalf for thirty-five minutes was an unsmiling James J. Walker, who continued to maintain that he had nominated Ewald, a German-American, to the magistrates' court strictly on the recommendation of the Steuben Society, the German-American social club.

After the jury had been out sixteen hours without reaching a verdict, the judge gave them a legal pep talk. "It is true one juror has a perfect right to hold out against all the others, but it is also true that it is the duty of a juror, before taking such a stance, to have a reason for his action," the jurist said. Whatever happened in the jury room that last week in November, it is certain that one or more jurors decided to remain capricious. The first Healy-Tommaney trial ended with no verdict. A second trial, a month later, also resulted in a hung jury. That the selection of these panels was not without Tammany influence was borne out by the fact that many of the prospective jurors had received pre-trial visits from interrogators, falsely representing themselves as being from the district attorney's office, who asked them about their politics and their attitude toward the defendants.

When the Ewalds were brought to trial in January of 1931, Emmerich J. Boczor, the former magistrate's one-time secretary, again repeated his testimony, in a strong German accent, that Ewald had admitted to him having paid for his job. "I say: 'Dr. Schirp [chairman of the Steuben Society's political council] told me in front of your chauffeur that he made you a judge,'" Boczor stated. "He [Ewald] says to me in sarcastic tone: 'He told you so, did he? He told you also that for that job he got $2,000 and $10,000 went to Healy?'"

The defense countered by alleging that Boczor had been shell-shocked, during World War I, while serving with the Austrian navy, no less, and that his unstable mental condition led him inevitably to "biting the hand that fed him."

Walker again testified for the defense, reiterating that Healy and Tommaney had not approached him about Ewald's appointment. "Had you heard at the time of the appointment of Ewald he had paid $10,000 for his job?" Prosecutor Todd asked the mayor. Looking Todd squarely in the eye, and speaking strongly, Walker replied: "I had not, or he wouldn't have been appointed."

The mayor's testimony again carried great weight; this jury once more disagreed on a verdict. Subsequently, all indictments against Healy, Tommaney, and the Ewalds were dismissed.

Late November found referee Samuel Seabury beginning the appellate division's inquiry into the magistrates' courts. These were the city's lowest judicial forums, which dealt with infractions ranging from traffic violations to disturbing the peace, from gambling to prostitution; in theory, each magistrate sat sequentially in all of these courts but, in practice, most tended to specialize. Isidor Kresel, Seabury's special counsel, touched off a bombshell at the first public hearing when he revealed a system of bribery, graft, and corruption in the women's courts that had existed for years. Kresel's methods were simple but painstaking; he would seek out the financial assets of lawyers, judges, and policemen, then ask them to explain their bank balances in terms of their salaries. Usually, they could not do so with any degree of credibility. Bit by bit, after weeks of preparation, Kresel drew from John C. Weston, an assistant district attorney from 1921 to 1929, a startling admission. During this period, Weston had amassed some $90,000, yet he could explain only $70,000, leaving $20,000 unaccounted for.

"Where did you get that?" asked Kresel quietly.

"I got it from the lawyers around the court, around the women's court," said Weston in a resigned tone.

"To put it rather succinctly and boldly, Mr. Weston, this $20,000 is a total of bribes that you took and received as representative of the district attorney's office in that court?"

"I am sorry to say that it is, Counsellor."

Over the years, said Weston, he had received bribes—at the usual

rate of twenty-five dollars a case—from dozens of lawyers, bondsmen, and policemen for aiding in the discharge of 600 vice cases involving 900 defendants. Jefferson Market, the dingy, sprawling, red-
brick building where women's court was held, had until recently
housed butchers, grocers, and other tradesmen in its south wing, while
justice was bought and sold in its north adjunct.

Weston named twenty-one lawyers and a half-dozen each of bondsmen, judges, and policemen who had played a part in framing and
then fixing vice cases. Within a few weeks of being assigned to
women's court in 1921, he said, he had fallen in with the system of
graft; he continued to accept bribes until his resignation in 1929. A
lawyer would say that he could use some help "in having a case
thrown out," and Weston would agree "by my silence and by nodding my head." Then, while the arresting officer was perjuring himself and the magistrate was nodding sleepily on the bench, he would
"not ask any more questions than were absolutely necessary."

"You stood by and allowed the case to go out without making any
effort to get at the true facts?" asked Kresel.

"That is right," the witness agreed.

Following Weston on the witness stand was "Chile" Mapocha
Acuna, a thirty-one-year-old native of Santiago who had emigrated
to this country ten years before. After a series of misadventures, he
found work in Reuben's, on Broadway between Eightieth and Eighty-
first streets, where in the early morning hours he "served sandwiches
to famous actors and actresses." There he made the acquaintance
of members of the vice squad, who were accustomed to cadging free
meals on the premises and who offered him a profitable sideline.
Acuna became one of their "stool pigeons," testifying both in shake-
downs of real prostitutes and in frame-ups of innocent women.

"Tell us," said Kresel, "how you went about gathering evidence in
these cases."

"Well," said Acuna, "we [he and the other pigeons] usually ate
about 1 P.M. and 9 P.M., while the role was being called in the station houses. Then we'd stroll around to the front of the house, where
a detective friend would meet us. If we had any addresses, we gave
them to him, and sometimes he would already have addresses. . . .

"The policeman would give us $5 or $10 in marked bills. Then we
would set our watches together. We would arrange it so I would
have just enough time to give the marked bills to a girl. Then when
the police entered they would go through this little comedy. They
would accuse me of everything they could imagine and I would deny
it all, insisting that the woman was my wife. . . . Then they would
take me into another room and pound on the wall to make it sound as

if they were beating me. Finally I would give them a fictitious name and address. . . . They would always bring the girls in as prisoners. The next day, when the case came to court, the officer would testify that the man in the case had given a fictitious name and could not be found. I was always the unknown man."

"Did you always succeed in getting evidence?" asked Kresel.

"Oh, no," said Acuna, "lots of times there was no evidence."

"But the arrests always were made?"

"Invariably."

"Now this is important," said Kresel. "Tell us whether you informed the arresting officer in those cases that there was no evidence."

"Yes, lots of times," replied Acuna. "They kicked me out and made the arrests anyway."

As the days of testimony went on, dozens of women who felt they had been wrongly accused of prostitution were encouraged to tell their stories. Mrs. Rosa Ricchebuono, sister of two Catholic priests and a nun, was in a housedress scrubbing her kitchen floor when "a strange man came in and made an indecent proposal. I said, 'Get out.' He grabbed me by the wrist and placed me under arrest for flirting with him. I couldn't realize that such a thing could happen to an innocent woman in her own home." Mrs. Ricchebuono's neighbors, hearing the struggle, argued with the police but to no avail; she was charged with prostitution. Mary Palmer, another woman wrongly arrested, was told by a bail bondsman that "$500 would take care of everything. I didn't know what he meant by that. I said, what if the police get up in court and lie? [The bondsman] said, 'Don't worry, if the cops are taken care of, you have nothing to worry about.' We were tried and discharged that day." Angelina Coloneas, a young waitress, told how another stool pigeon, one "Harry the Greek," had gained her confidence by proposing marriage. "He asked me to visit his room and see something he had bought me as a wedding gift. A few minutes later, two policemen rushed in and arrested me on an immorality charge and threw [him] out." The police gave Miss Coloneas the names of a bondsman and lawyer, who "took $800 from me for their services." She was discharged by the magistrate.

At one point in the inquiry, Kresel asked Acuna how much money he was paid for each job.

"Five dollars or ten dollars for each 'collar,' " said the stoolie.

Acuna, who had just been released from the penitentiary, explained that he had fallen out with the police a year before, when they tried to railroad a middle-aged woman into jail. Moved by her pleas, he had dropped his role of the "unknown man" and testified for the defense. The woman had been acquitted, and the police were nettled. Within a few weeks, they arrested Acuna for extortion, asserting he had demanded $250 of a speakeasy owner to provide police protection.

In December, Acuna began to identify the police with whom he had worked. (The Chilean had been assigned a round-the-clock guard of six police lieutenants by Commissioner Mulrooney, who let them know they would never receive their captaincies if the witness met with an accident.) On December 3, the diminutive stoolie walked up and down a double line of burly officers, reaching up on tiptoe from time to time to clap an accusing hand on the shoulders of a man who had employed him. With Mulrooney watching with narrowed eyes, Acuna simultaneously called out each man's name and precinct house. Only once did he falter, when he singled out an officer named Thomas F. Hart and identified him as "William Schmitzges."

"My name is Hart," said the patrolman defiantly.

"Well, you're Schmitzges' partner," said Acuna with a hurt look on his face. "I had you mixed up."

In all, the Chilean identified twenty-eight policemen as having participated in the frame-ups, and before the day was over a furious Commissioner Mulrooney was drawing up departmental charges against his men on a massive scale.

The explanations of the vice squad officers as to how they had accumulated the tens of thousands of dollars in their bank accounts were both colorful and imaginative. Patrolman James Quinlivan, a veteran of eighteen years in the department, was asked to answer for only the last five years. During this period, he had deposited some $31,000 and his wife some $58,000. Ah, said Quinlivan, discussing his own savings, about $10,000 of this money had been won more than twenty years earlier, on a horse called Flora Belle. Quinlivan kept this sum, which grew to $20,000 as a result of a $10,000 inheritance when his father died, in a trunk in his house. Later, on his honeymoon, he had won $3,000 at a track in Maryland, where gambling was legal—bringing his cash reserve up to $23,000. The remaining $8,000 of his in savings had been amassed by card-playing, he hinted, but he refused to be specific about his gambling on the ground that it might incriminate him. Anyway, he had chosen only in recent years to take the total sum out of his trunk and put it in the bank; that was the reason his deposits were so suspiciously large.

Mrs. Quinlivan never did testify about her own $58,000 in savings. She and her children went off, during the inquiry, to visit unknown friends at an unknown site in Pennsylvania. Patrolman Quinlivan had no idea of her whereabouts.

Perhaps the most ingenuous cover-up came from Robert E. Morris, another member of the vice squad, in accounting for a $50,000 sum. Morris declared that $10,000 of it came from gambling (before he entered the department, of course), and that the remaining $40,000 had been given him twenty-one years earlier by his Uncle George, now deceased, whom he had bumped into at Coney Island. It was a fortunate meeting for the police-officer-to-be, for Uncle George peeled forty brand-new $1,000 bills off his roll and handed them to his young nephew.

What was Uncle George's business?

"Well, I know his business," said Morris, "but I don't think it is fair to ask that question if a man was not in a legitimate business . . . he is dead . . . a man should [not] stand here and run down my relative with the lowest."

Why would Uncle George, with a wife and three children of his own, be so generous with young Morris?

"I was always his favorite nephew, he always thought a lot of me," the officer said earnestly.

The exposure of police graft put Walker on the defensive. "We believed conditions were pretty good in New York in comparison with the past until the findings of this investigation," he declared to a committee of civic leaders at City Hall. "But we must not look upon conditions with an eye to the past. We do not want to break down the morale of the department."

With the city's lowest courts so heavily under siege, Chief Magistrate Joseph E. Corrigan found himself unexpectedly very much in the center of a maelstrom. Though he had been named to the leadership of the courts only that spring, when Walker knew he needed someone of unassailable integrity to gloss over the evidence of scandal, Corrigan had been a magistrate for twenty-three years. Among confreres who were not known, generally speaking, either for their legal expertise or their lineage, the rumpled, bald-headed jurist was doubly a rarity: he knew his law and he was listed in the *Social Register*. Indeed, it was a sign of his independence from Tammany that he had toiled those twenty-three years in the magistrates' courts, while clambake orators were pushed into the firmament of general sessions or even the State Supreme Court.

Young Corrigan, whose uncle was an archbishop in the New York archdiocese and whose father was a physician, grew up in monied circumstances. As a collegian, he attended Seton Hall in New Jersey, where he was a small but combative quarterback on the football team. Later, he compiled an impressive record at Columbia Law School, topping off his achievements by founding the *Law Review.* Corrigan went into corporation law, but found it dull; in 1903, at the age of twenty-eight, he wrangled a job as an assistant in the office of William Travers Jerome, the reform-minded district attorney. New York at that time, as at most times, badly needed reforming. Wrote journalist Milton MacKaye: "Its saloons were the most luxurious in the world, its politicians were the most unprincipled, its millionaires were the richest." As an assistant D.A., Corrigan could dance at Tim Sullivan's parties, sup at Jack's, play cards at Canfield's, and, in MacKaye's words, "yet retain his self-respect." In 1907, during Mayor George B. McClellan's feud with Boss Murphy, he was named to the magistrates' courts. On the bench, Corrigan remained tolerant. For the vice squad and its entrapment techniques against prostitutes he reserved a special contempt. One day, meeting a woman on the street who some time before had blackened the eye of a po-liceman testifying against her in Corrigan's court, the magistrate doffed his hat, extended his hand, and said, "I've waited three years to congratulate you for that." Though a nominal member of Tam-many, Corrigan was seen far more often at his exclusive clubs—play-ing cards at the Calumet or squash at the Racquet and Tennis. It was his good fortune, then, when his first ten-year term was up in 1917, that the city had a Fusion mayor, John Purroy Mitchel, who renamed him to the court. By 1927, when Corrigan's abilities had made him the city's best-known magistrate, it would have been unthinkable for Walker not to name him to a third term.

The new chief magistrate lived with his wife and two young daugh-ters at 32 West Tenth Street. At fifty-five, he was spry and fit. He read widely in three languages, played contract bridge superbly, and detested district leaders who tried to tip the scales of justice. Within weeks of his promotion, he took steps to break up the "clubby" atmosphere of the magistrates' courts, shifting nearly all the clerks and attendants from their old courts to new ones. (Corruption was evident, not just in vice cases, but in all the courts. A gambling charge could be fixed, for instance, by bribing a clerk to fill out a form No. 0-14, which "informed" a lazy or venal magistrate that in the clerk's opinion the facts "did not present the basis for a legal complaint." In 1929, when there were 4,838 arrests for bookmaking, 4,677 were dismissed.) Now, in 1930, backed psychologically by the Seabury investigation, Corrigan at long last was able to institute some reforms.

One of the first magistrates to draw criticism during Seabury's in-quiry was Jesse Silbermann, who was revealed to have close ties with

Mark Alter, a lawyer extremely active in women's court cases. Counsel Kresel pointed out that Silbermann had been quick to take the unsupported word of a policeman in finding the aforementioned Mrs. Rosa Ricchebuono, the sister of two priests, guilty of a vice charge, yet equally quick to reject such unsupported evidence when Mrs. Nina Artska, a teacher of ballroom and ballet dancing, came before him on a similar count.

Was the reason for this contradictory behavior, Kresel asked, "because in the Artska case the defendant was represented by your great friend, Mark Alter?"

"Not my great friend, my friend," answered Silbermann.

"And in the Ricchebuono case the defendant was represented by Leo Lefkowitz, a lawyer whom you did not know?" pursued Kresel.

"No!" shouted the jurist.

Mrs. Ricchebuono's arrest had taken place on a Tuesday night in July of 1930, when a vice squad officer walked into her apartment while her husband was at work, roughed her up as the noise of passing Third Avenue El trains all but drowned out her screams, and, despite her neighbors' protestations that she was "a good woman," took her to the precinct house. The case came before Silbermann, with Lefkowitz, a friend of Mr. Ricchebuono, as attorney for the defense. After the arresting officer testified that he had arranged the assignation with the woman at her apartment the previous Saturday night, Lefkowitz produced a witness, a streetcar motorman, who swore that he had taken Mrs. Ricchebuono to do some marketing on the evening in question, and as a result, she could not possibly have been at home. Silbermann, despite the motorman's evidence and a probation officer's favorable report about the defendant, had refused to hear character witnesses and had nonetheless sentenced her to the workhouse.

"In the light of subsequent events, Judge," said Seabury to Silbermann, temporarily interrupting Kresel's examination, "don't you think you were wrong?"

"No, I don't," the witness replied. "I'd do the same thing again."

Silbermann had not been so stern with Nina Artska, who had been arrested on a vice charge in January of 1929. Mrs. Artska testified that a man had entered her studio on West Eighty-fourth Street one afternoon, asked for a dance lesson, and insisted on paying her in advance. Minutes later, the police had pounced on the "stool pigeon," cuffed him about, and taken her to the station house. There the cards of many lawyers had been given her. One of them, she remembered, was that of Mark Alter, Silbermann's friend. Mrs. Artska eventually retained Alter, to whom she paid $250 in advance. On the morning of the hearing he asked her for another $100, saying that "yours is a very difficult case." The frightened dance teacher agreed to pay the extra sum, and when she did come before Silbermann, the charge against her was dismissed.

To drive home the point that Silbermann and Alter had acted in collusion on the Artska case, Kresel brought John Weston, the former prosecutor, back to the stand.

"Did you have any dealings with Alter in the [Artska] case?"

"He gave me $25 as my part."

The Silbermann-Alter connection was even more obvious in the case of Mary Felder, who had been arrested in September of 1925 for shoplifting in Klein's, a large department store on Union Square. Samuel Klein's business, which had a turnover of $25 million annually, was conducted on a self-service basis, with hundreds of women darting from clothes racks to dressing rooms and back again; the frenetic nature of the establishment made it extremely vulnerable to thievery, and the store lost about $100,000 worth of merchandise that way every year. A store detective had spotted Miss Felder, who was trying to walk out wearing a $17.95 dress; she had failed to remove the price tag. Previously, the girl had stuffed her old dress into a package. Taken to Samuel Klein's office, she admitted the theft, saying she had lost her handbag containing her money in the store, while shopping for a dress and, fearing her mother's anger, had decided to make up for the loss. Questioned by the police at the precinct house, she again admitted her guilt and wrote her mother a note, saying she was sorry for what she had done. When the case came before Silbermann, however, with Mark Alter representing the defendant and Prosecutor Weston appearing for the people, the store detective was not called as a witness, and Miss Felder's case was dismissed.

Angered, Klein pressed for another hearing, and soon afterward the case was reopened. To the store owner's consternation and Alter's glee, the presiding magistrate was again Silbermann, who had already expressed the opinion the girl was innocent. Despite the strong testimony of Klein, the store detective, and the arresting officer, charges against the defendant were again dismissed.

Now Kresel, in the magistrates' court inquiry, was asking Silbermann to explain his reasoning in the case.

"The testimony, as I recall it," said the judge, "is that the girl went into Klein's with a pocketbook containing an envelope which had a week's salary in it. While she was trying on a dress, the pocketbook with the money disappeared. She ran through the store shouting that she wanted her pocketbook . . . until she finally reached the front of the store. . . . My recollection is I concluded that she finally ran out.

The reason I discharged her was not that I did not believe the testimony of the people's witnesses . . . but because in her excitement she was not able to form the intent to steal. That's a matter of law."

At this point, Seabury interjected to say that Silbermann was maintaining that the facts of the case could be interpreted in different ways. The jurist agreed.

"But you don't mean to say that as a magistrate you had the power to pass upon a question of fact, do you?" asked Seabury. (The statutes required that in such questions the magistrate had to hand the defendant over for trial in a higher court.)

"No," lamely replied the witness.

For these and similar instances "of unfair and unjudicial conduct," Silbermann would be removed from the bench, by the appellate division, in July of 1931.

Meanwhile, Walker was denying that his administration was trying to slow down the Seabury investigation by refusing to pay its costs. "In the case of the claims of the assistant attorneys," he said, "Controller Berry asked the opinion of the corporation counsel and when the opinion was adverse the controller withdrew payment until such time as a Supreme Court Justice overruled the opinion. Thereupon the controller lost no time in announcing the disputed bills would be promptly approved. . . . Yet the cry instantly was raised in some of the newspapers that the Walker administration was seeking to obstruct the investigation."

Two other magistrates prominent in the news that December, not so much for corruption as for impropriety, were Francis X. McQuade and Louis B. Brodsky. Both men had pursued various business interests while sitting on the bench, apparently in direct conflict with the law (". . . no City magistrate shall engage in any other business but . . . shall devote his whole time . . . to the duties of his office"). When the market crashed in late 1929, their financial interests, which were largely of a speculative nature, had greatly suffered, and attention was drawn to their activities. McQuade, for instance, had used his judicial prestige to endorse the stock of the Ajax-Texas Corporation, "a speculative venture of questionable merit." The company was no longer in existence, and, declared Seabury, "apparently those who invested in its securities have suffered a complete loss." Not a stuffy jurist by any means, McQuade had also invested in a Havana gambling casino and had promoted numerous professional prize fighters. His consuming passion, however, was a long and ultimately fruitless lawsuit he was conducting over the ownership of the New York Giants baseball team. With heady responsibilities like these, it was clear that McQuade, who had been a magistrate for nineteen years, did not always have the time to consult his Blackstone.

On December 9, the morning McQuade was scheduled to testify before Seabury, he announced his resignation. A statement issued in his behalf mentioned the magistrate's lawsuit against the Giants and declared, with a straight face, that since "this action is shortly to come to trial . . . it is a matter of great doubt whether a man while a magistrate should hold an office in a business of this character." Walker went along with the charade. "As Magistrate McQuade explained it to me," he said, "he was legally compelled to give up one or the other. He chose to relinquish the magistracy."

Magistrate Brodsky, who had originally been appointed by Mayor Hylan in 1924 (at the suggestion of James J. Hagan, leader of the Seventh A.D.) to fill out an unexpired term, had been reappointed by Walker in 1929 (on the recommendation of Marshall Ingraham, Hagan's successor) to a full ten-year term. Trying to establish the jurist's close ties with Tammany, Counsel Kresel and Referee Seabury brought up a case several years earlier, in which Brodsky had dismissed charges against twenty-one men accused of gambling in the Seventh A.D. The arresting officer had personally identified the defendants, but Brodsky had not been swayed from his conviction that they were innocent. Why had he thrown out the case, Kresel wanted to know.

"I can't remember," the magistrate said.

Seabury then intervened.

"By the way," he asked, "in what political district was this address where the arrests took place?"

"Why," said the magistrate, smiling and tugging at the end of his pince-nez, "I think it was in my own."

Since becoming a magistrate, Brodsky had engaged in the purchase, sale, rental, and management of real estate totaling some $1 million; he was the president of six corporations, an officer of three others, a director of all nine; yet the Depression had brought about a situation, by his own admission, in which his realty losses "were running into hundreds of thousands of dollars." Even wilder were Brodsky's stock-market speculations. Over the same six-year period, he had kept accounts with eleven brokerage houses, buying and selling $3,517,276 worth of securities and eventually coming up with a $116,-425 loss. Brodsky kept his financial empire going by continual borrowing, drawing funds from one corporation and paying them to another, and by postdating checks.

"The giving of a check postdated is called 'kiting,' isn't it?" asked Kresel.

"Not exactly," hedged the magistrate.

It was Brodsky's relationship with one of his brokerage houses, Weisl & Company, that interested Kresel the most. The magistrate's account there had been guaranteed against loss by Robert H. Loeb, a member of the firm, who had previously appeared before him on charges of disorderly conduct and grand larceny—the result of an altercation with a former lady friend about the ownership of a diamond bracelet. After dismissing the disorderly charge, Brodsky had used his "good offices" to persuade the woman to drop the larceny allegation.

"Was there any money passed?" asked Kresel.

"Not while I was there."

"You simply used your good offices. What did they agree on?"

"Oh, I'm not sure of the amount. Maybe it was about $12,000 . . . the value of the bracelet."

The larceny charge against Loeb was dropped by the complainant in January 1929. Two months afterward Brodsky, by his own account, met the grateful broker on the street.

"We shook hands," said the magistrate. "We talked a while and he said, 'Why don't you open an account with us? I think I can make some money for you.' "

When the market crashed and Brodsky's margin account at Weisl & Company came under pressure, it was Loeb who took the $33,000 loss that resulted, indicating that his regard for the judge's "good offices" could withstand adversity.

At the request of Chief Magistrate Corrigan, the appellate division at year's end suspended Brodsky from his courtroom duties. Strangely enough, the court would in 1931 acquit the magistrate and return him to the bench, saying that his complicated realty and security transactions did not constitute "doing business" in terms of the law. Yet Walker, as Tammany's chief apologist, was finding it harder and harder to remain blasé about the magistrates' courts. Dominated by the district leaders, they had, of course, been rotten long before he took office. But James J. Walker had gone along with the system. For the mayor, the gay piping was fading. The sad tunes would soon be heard.

1931

So close were the blows that Cu Chulainn and Ferdiad struck at the ford that their heads met above their shields and their feet below, their spears bent and curled, the spirits of the glens and the beings of the air screamed with fear.

Then Ferdiad, catching Cu Chulainn off balance, gave him a thrust so that his blade was buried to the hilt in Cu Chulainn's chest. Blood flowed from the warrior's body until the waters ran crimson with the spillage.

Cu Chulainn, knowing he could not endure without help, bethought himself of his friends from the fairy-mound who would protect him when he was hard-pressed. Whereupon Dolb and Indolb arrived to help Cu Chulainn, smiting Ferdiad with unseen blows.

"Not alike is our foster-brothership, O Cu Chulainn," Ferdiad shouted with great anger.

"How so, then?" answered Cu Chulainn.

"Thy friends of the fairy-folk have aided thee, and thou didst not disclose them to me."

"Why complainist thou, O Ferdiad?" baited Cu Chulainn. "Thou hast a horn skin whereby thou can multiply feats of arms upon me, and thou hast not disclosed to me its secrets."

So the fight was joined again. . . .

During the first few weeks of the New Year, New Yorkers were talking about the investigation of judges Brodsky and Silbermann, the mayor was testifying for the defense at the trial of former Judge Ewald and simultaneously calling for a clean judiciary, and the mysterious manila envelopes—ostensibly left behind by Judge Crater—were being found by Ewald's wife. Then, in late January, Walker suffered the ignominy of a dislocated shoulder. Though the press attributed the injury to a bathtub fall, there was speculation that it had occurred at a late-night party. At any rate, the mayor did not appear at City Hall for nine days.

On February 2, the Seabury inquiry received a calculated setback. General counsel Isidor J. Kresel was accused by Max D. Steuer, a lawyer with close Tammany ties who had been conducting a separate investigation into the recent failure of the Bank of United States, with condoning "irregular business practices" while serving as the bank's attorney and sitting on its board. (The closing of the bank, which owed some $161 million to its depositors, was the greatest failure in American banking history.) Public service was a virgin field for Max D., who usually defended miscreants, but in the Bank of United States he had a real issue. For while there was considerable doubt as to Kresel's responsibility for the bank's failure, there was no disputing that the institution's borrowing and lending practices reflected bad or even venal management; the obvious Tammany hope was that Kresel and, more indirectly, Seabury, would themselves be tarred by scandal. Moreover, the bank investigation was giving Max D. an opportunity to settle a sixteen-year-old grudge with Kresel, who had once defended A. L. Erlanger, a wealthy theatrical producer, in a breach of promise suit brought against him by a Steuer client named Edith St. Clair, a musical comedy star. Though Erlanger had been forced to pay up, Steuer had found himself in danger of disbarment for allegedly coaching Miss St. Clair on her lines. Though acquitted, he had always held Kresel to blame for the attack on his ethics.

The Bank of United States, most of whose sixty-one branches were located on the Lower East Side, had a resounding title but no connection at all with the federal government; most of its half-million depositors were lower- and middle-income people, and their accounts represented their life savings. Steuer contended that $112 million of the bank's $400 million in deposits had "disappeared" in the last three months of 1930. While he castigated Bernard K. Marcus, president of the bank, and Saul Singer, executive vice president, for having made a quick profit of $6,600,000 out of the failure, he saved some of his sharpest remarks for Kresel. (It should be mentioned that

Kresel, who had invested $437,000 in the bank's stock, had lost the entire sum.)

The witness-stand exchanges between the two lawyers were continually disputatious. At one point, Steuer brought up an $8 million transaction in which the Bank of United States allegedly paid itself, with its own money, a debt of that amount owed by two of its affiliates, and then had the debt wiped off its books. When Kresel replied that he could not remember the details of the matter, his interrogator marveled at the witness' "amazing lack of recollection."

"I *am* testifying, Mr. Steuer," Kresel said angrily.

"I wish that I could think so," responded Steuer.

Kresel explained that, while he remembered a clerk in his office bringing him the contract involved in the transaction, he had not personally handled the matter. Was the bank better off as a result of the debt shifting, Steuer wanted to know.

"I'm responsible for my clerk," said Kresel. "The bank did not lose a thing."

"Never mind the heroics. You know that you're not criminally responsible for the acts of your clerk."

"What are you doing, trying indictments?"

"I'm just protecting the depositors," Steuer assured him.

On February 10, a Manhattan grand jury returned indictments against Marcus, Singer, and six other bank officers. Among them was Isidor Kresel, who promptly resigned his post as Seabury's special counsel, writing to his chief that he wished to "remove all embarrassment to the important public work you have in hand." Commented Seabury: "Kresel served with an unflagging industry and devotion and he performed with outstanding skill . . . The investigation [of the magistrates' courts] is going right ahead."

Marcus and Singer would be found guilty of violating the state banking laws and given jail sentences. Kresel, as the bank's attorney, would likewise be found guilty, on the ground that he had advised the two men in their misappropriation of funds. When Kresel's case later came up before the court of appeals, his conviction was unanimously reversed, and he was vindicated. At the time of the indictments, however, Steuer and Tammany were filled with pious rectitude.

Born in Austria, Steuer came to this country as a child in the 1870s, traveling in steerage. He grew up on the Lower East Side, where he peddled newspapers, wandered through the streets with a cowbell around his neck selling matches, and worked as a tailor's apprentice. He toiled in the post office while going to City College and somehow put himself through Columbia Law School. Short, squat, and unimpressive looking, except for a notably predatory nose, Steuer at first found it difficult to get clients. Gradually he built up an intriguing record as a courtroom performer, however, and the indicted *cognoscenti* began to recognize his talents.

Out of court, Steuer favored a no-nonsense approach. Called in by a group of attorneys to handle the defense of a monied New Yorker they feared would shortly be indicted, he asked what the charge was. "He has not been charged with anything yet," Max D. was told. "Wait until he's charged with something and then send for me," he advised the attorneys. They happily paid him a $10,000 fee for this advice. The client, incidentally, never was indicted. Another time, Steuer agreed to defend a well-known swindler for a $100,000 fee. "There's a very interesting angle about the case—" the man began. "I don't want to hear about it until I have the money," interrupted Max D. "I'll send the check right over," said the swindler, "but I would like to have you think about—" Said Steuer with finality: "I can't think until I have the money."

This, then, was Steuer, the Tammany lawyer—a fierce, outspoken banty rooster. When his wife telephoned him from the Bank of United States the day before it failed, saying that an official had assured her there was no need to remove her money, Max D. growled, "Did you go there to get money or to have conversation?" Replied the wife: "To get money." Said Steuer: "Then get it." (One of the few occasions he would be bested in repartee was in 1932, when Al Smith faced him and Tammany Boss Curry in a hotel room and said he wanted Herbert Lehman nominated for governor. "The nomination would not be good politics," snapped Steuer. "If Lehman isn't nominated I'll run for mayor and take the town away from you," said Smith. "On what ticket?" asked Curry. "Hell, on the Chinese laundry ticket," Smith replied, putting both Steuer and Curry to rout.)

Samuel Seabury did not allow Kresel's indictment to affect his inquiry into the magistrates' courts. On February 13, Seabury set the stage for still another fantasy-look into a policeman's finances by calling Lieutenant John W. Kenna to the stand. The officer was asked to explain bank deposits of $237,235 that he and his mother, Mrs. Anna Kenna, had made over the previous six years—the period of time he had been a lieutenant, supervising some 1,000 policemen in the Tenderloin, the area on the west side of midtown Manhattan known for its speakeasies, gambling, and prostitution. About $50,000 was in his own name, the rest in hers. Kenna testified that the $50,000 was really his mother's too. He gave her all his pay checks, he said, and she gave other checks and various sums of cash—obtained from rentals—back to him for deposit.

Mrs. Kenna, whose own bank deposits during the same period were some $184,000, subsequently was called to the stand. She testified that her income, from property she owned and from her work as a practical nurse, was $16,500 annually. Doing some fast arithmetic, a Seabury aide named Jacob Schurman showed her that her total income for the six years could only have been $99,000.

"Where," asked Schurman, "did [the rest of] the money come from?"

"I must have had it," Mrs. Kenna replied. "I've saved money all my life. If I earned $10, I saved $9 of it. That's how I've lived."

Schurman assured the witness that she had not had the money six years ago, before her son became a lieutenant in the Tenderloin, her total savings at that time being less than $5,000.

"I must have had it," insisted the witness.

On February 26, the strangulation murder of Vivian Gordon, a woman who had volunteered to testify against the police in a vice case, caused speculation that the corruption uncovered by Seabury might have homicidal repercussions. The thirty-two-year-old, red-haired Miss Gordon, who was found at the foot of an embankment in Van Cortlandt Park in the Bronx, had been choked to death with a clothesline. A few days earlier, she had been scheduled to meet with a Seabury aide to give preliminary testimony on alleged frame-ups of vice cases but had not kept the appointment. The press concluded that she had been silenced by grafting policemen. From headquarters, Commissioner Mulrooney roared that there "would be a black spot on the shield of every patrolman" until her killer was found.

Miss Gordon, who was also known as Benita Bischoff, had been sentenced to the reformatory on a prostitution charge back in 1923; the arresting officer at that time, whose name was currently appearing in the Seabury inquiry testimony, was, by coincidence, on a cruise to Bermuda when she was murdered. The victim's other brushes with the law included extortion and disorderly conduct charges. It was in 1923, too, that she had been divorced by her husband, John Bischoff, who had been given custody of their daughter by the court. At the time of her death, Miss Gordon had been living in an East Thirty-seventh Street apartment from which, according to the superintendent, she was in the habit of departing at nine o'clock each evening and not returning until dawn. She had kept a detailed but cryptic diary, and, after glancing through it, the police officer in charge of investigating the crime dryly observed, "She was evidently a woman of many acquaintances."

After numerous false leads, many of them obtained from Miss Gordon's diaries (she had often thought, with some justification, that many of her associates were out to "get" her), the police finally arrested Harry Stein, a thug who had already served a jail term for strangling and robbing a woman. It is almost certain that the Seabury inquiry had in no way brought about Miss Gordon's killing and that the police were blameless. Stein apparently had assaulted her in a taxi driven by an accomplice and had murdered her for jewelry and a fur coat. The evidence against Stein was impressive. Not only had witnesses seen him trying to sell the victim's jewels and coat within days after the killing, but the accomplice, testifying for the prosecution, confessed to his part in the crime. Amazingly, the jury would vote for Stein's acquittal. (Subsequently, he would be convicted of chloroforming and robbing still a third woman and given a twenty-five-year sentence.)

In early 1931, Betty Compton was seeing less of Jim than she wished. It was not that the twenty-six-year-old dancer had lost her appeal for the mayor, who was nearing fifty, but because, increasingly harried by the Seabury investigation, he was finding it more and more difficult to give her the attention she required. Betty could not stand solitude; her days and nights had to be spent among friends and admirers. Now Walker was canceling dates at the Casino, was sometimes even forgetting to telephone. A combination of poor health and bad temper had forced her to leave *Fifty Million Frenchmen* the year before, so that Betty no longer had even the tenuous discipline of the theater. Pacing about her East Seventy-sixth Street apartment, waiting for calls from Walker, she would pat her hair automatically and put another record on the gramophone. But Betty was not, in the words of a contemporary journalist, "fashioned of passive flesh or ruled by a placid nature." She began to flirt with the movies, at one point spending a few weeks in California before her peripatetic nature (and Walker's insistence) brought her back to New York. She also began to flirt with other men.

On Friday, February 13, Betty was scheduled to take a screen test at the Paramount studio in Astoria, Long Island. Instead, ostensibly because the temperature in the drafty studio was down to forty degrees, she elected to take some dialogue coaching at home from a movie director named Edward C. Dowling. Like any gentleman, Dowling had telephoned before dropping over.

At six that evening, an important political leader reportedly called at City Hall. Tammany had long wanted to break up Betty's affair with the mayor, all the more now that the Seabury hearings were generating so much criticism. At a private conference with Walker, he produced a transcript of the telephone conversation between Betty and Dowling, the result of a wire tap he had arranged. The conversation stunned the mayor, who was convinced, perhaps justifiably, that the dancer was betraying him. After his visitor left, Walker stayed in his office alone for more than an hour. When he did emerge, he dismissed his chauffeur and called a cab. For the next five days he was incommunicado. Later he would say, "I was sick and tired, and hid out on Long Island."

As for Betty, she waited to no avail that Friday night for Jim to take her to the Casino. In some way, she eventually learned about the mayor's visitor and about the tap on her phone. Soon afterward, she took an overdose of sleeping pills and had to be rushed to a private hospital for stomach-pumping. By Monday, February 16, with Walker still at a hideaway on Long Island, she was discharged. A few hours later, perhaps motivated by the belief that it was Walker who had tapped her phone, perhaps by bravado, she married Dowling, a man she barely knew. It was not until the mayor returned to New York on Wednesday, February 18, that he learned of the marriage. On that day, Betty and her new husband, under the name of Mr. and Mrs. Edwards, were steaming to Havana aboard the *Orient*. "This is the finish," muttered a disgusted Walker, but events would prove him wrong.

Walker's public utterances during this phase of the Seabury hearings were calculated to show concern but also, as much as possible, to protect the political system. Speaking to a group of civic leaders at City Hall, the mayor called evidence of police corruption "revolting," but was unwilling to concede that reports were not "exaggerated." A few days later, he belatedly appointed two good men to replace magistrates Henry M. R. Goodman and George W. Simpson, both of whom had resigned under fire when Seabury began to scrutinize their activities. The new appointees, Jonah J. Goldstein and William O. Harris, undeniably would be splendid judges; they were making financial sacrifices to accept the $12,000-a-year posts, and Chief Magistrate Corrigan warmly endorsed their selection. Goldstein had been practicing law with great success for twenty-five years before most state and federal courts; Harris, another attorney of wide experience, had been general counsel for the Allied Chemical and Dye Corporation.

Bondsmen, meanwhile, were being investigated by Seabury with an eye toward explaining their mysterious ability to win freedom for professional criminals on relatively low bail set by considerate judges. On March 10, Jack Greenspan, formerly an agent for the Detroit

Fidelity and Security Company, was called to testify. (As agents for insurance companies, bondsmen were legally allowed to charge 3 percent of the bail money, but many of them established higher under-the-table fees; 2 percent of the legal fee went to the insurance company; 1 percent—or whatever the client could be persuaded to pay —would be retained by the bondsmen.) On the stand, Greenspan was questioned by assistant counsel Jacob Schurman about his relationship with Jack ("Legs") Diamond, the frequently arrested gunman, and Bronx Magistrate Abraham Rosenbluth, whose district leader had seen to it that he was one of Walker's first appointments after taking office in January of 1926. After admitting that he knew both men, Greenspan was shown a two-year-old photo of Diamond in a hospital bed, recuperating from gunshot wounds.

"The picture shows you standing at the bedside of Legs Diamond," said Schurman. "Is that you?"

"Yes," replied the witness.

"Who was the man standing beside you?"

"I don't recall."

"Was it Magistrate Rosenbluth?"

"Yes," lamely answered Greenspan.

By far the most colorful bondsman to testify was Samuel Rothenberg, better known as "Stitch" McCarthy. He had earned his alias thirty-six years before when the original Stitch McCarthy, a reluctant pugilist, refused to enter the ring in a match Rothenberg was promoting. "I collected my boy's end of the take an' I went in there in his place," he later explained. The bony but smallish Rothenberg, who as a Jewish boy in the Lower East Side's Five Points section had been forced to sharpen his footwork to survive the fistic theology of Irish proselytizers, demolished McCarthy's opponent and thereafter assumed the missing man's identity. Subsequently, he opened a poolroom, saloon, and bowling alley on Grand Street, which was patronized by such exotics as Lefty Louie, Gyp the Blood, Whitey Lewis, and Dago Frank, all of whom eventually went to the electric chair for the 1912 killing of gambler Herman Rosenthal. His establishment also attracted personages from more prosaic fields. District Attorney William Travers Jerome liked to bowl in shirtsleeves, and one night he brought in his friend Henry James, who was "the real goods in the book business"; Stitch beat James 290 to 260, with Jerome keeping score. Another time, a young politician named Calvin Coolidge dropped in, took one look at the nude paintings decorating the walls, and fled purselipped into the night.

Soon Stitch, by now a Grand Street fixture, was involved in politics. On one occasion, he ran his bartender for alderman and his pinboy for the state assembly. They campaigned assiduously, riding through the Eighth A.D. ("de Bloody Ate") in dress suits on white horses, handing out free beer and cigars, followed by four supporters playing hand organs. Despite the fact that neither candidate spoke English, they were creating much goodwill. It was at this point that Stitch, suddenly fearful of losing two skilled employees to public service, withdrew his endorsement. He dispatched sandwich-board men throughout the district with signs reading "Don't Vote for Levy and Dulberger. They Are Bums." Neither candidate thereafter had a chance.

It was only in 1923, however, that Stitch went into the bailbond business. His marriage some years before to the former Lilly Marks, "the belle of Willett Street," had been blessed with three children, and the cost of supporting his family made him receptive to new opportunities. Taking note of the large number of Volstead Act violators going in and out of jails, Stitch decided that a bondsman could earn substantial sums even at 1 percent of the bail. Over the next eight years, he provided bail for thousands of "Volsteads," as he called them, without a single default. Sentences being as light as they were for liquor violations, he wasn't taking much of a chance. Stitch's big worry was hold-up men, particularly those who already had three convictions; because of the Baumes Law, which established obligatory life imprisonment for a fourth offense, three-time losers often lammed it.

As bondsmen during the Walker years went, Stitch McCarthy was an honest man. Most of his confreres were not.

In early March, Governor Roosevelt agreed to an investigation of Manhattan District Attorney Crain, the Tammany sachem whose professional conduct had been characterized by the City Club as "incompetent, inefficient and futile." Named to head the inquiry, much to Tammany's chagrin, was Judge Seabury. Commented Mayoral Assistant Charles F. Kerrigan: "The citizens of New York have too much common sense to be disturbed by a group of professional faultfinders and slanderers and their paper organization." One of the charges against Crain was that he had generally failed to obtain convictions or even indictments against those judges, lawyers, bondsmen, and police officers whose illegal activities had been revealed by Seabury. The City Club also argued that he had not prosecuted as strongly as he might have such men as "Horse Doctor" Doyle, District Leader Healy, and former Magistrate Ewald. Still other charges were that his office had not been able to curb "racketeers"—hoodlums who extorted money from legitimate businesses—or public men, such as Judge Mancuso, who had been involved in stock frauds.

A week later, Governor Roosevelt released without comment the

City Affairs Committee's report, which asked him to remove Walker himself from office. Among the charges were:

— That the mayor had "long ignored the shameful conditions existing in the Board of Standards and Appeals"; only the diligence of then federal District Attorney Tuttle had exposed the chicanery of Dr. Doyle and forced the resignation of Chairman Walsh; meanwhile, the mayor had not yet removed Walsh's three colleagues on the Board, "who almost uniformly assented to [his] decisions."

— That the city had been losing $3 million a year by condemnation awards four and five times greater than the value of the property, and that "the Mayor's easy procrastination in handling this whole question . . . was one of many illustrations of his persistent refusal to meet crises in government."

— That Tammany District Leader Charles Kohler, who had been secretary of the health department during a virulent period of corruption and whose activities in that capacity "were such as to disqualify him permanently from the occupying of any public office," was still being retained as the city's powerful director of the budget.

— That the department of hospitals was being used for political payoffs, as proven by the mayor's appointment of such Tammany leaders as James H. Fay of the Anawanda Club to key positions in its hierarchy.

— That the case of Judge Vause, who obtained a $250,000 "slush fund" from the United States Shipping Lines in return for its getting a lease of two city piers, indicated that officials in the Walker administration were receiving pay-offs for such favors, and that "a Mayor ceaselessly alert to the business of safeguarding the interest of the City would have instituted investigations."

— That eight officeholding Tammany district leaders who repeatedly refused to waive immunity before the grand jury investigating former Magistrate Ewald still held their posts, again indicating Walker's "indifference to elementary standards of public office."

— That not only did "at no time the Mayor make the slightest attempt to correct existing conditions in the Magistrates' Courts," but that he "actually sought in every way to obstruct and even block the investigation."

From Palm Springs, California, where he was sunning himself at the estate of attorney Samuel Untermyer on a three-week vacation that would keep him away from New York for most of March, the mayor issued a statement that was uncharacteristically formal. "I shall not make any comment until I return to New York," he said. "To attempt such a thing would cause only useless bickering back and forth across the country without benefiting anyone."

Days later, with the mayor still in California, the Albany law-makers, voting strictly along party lines, narrowly approved the most sweeping inquiry thus far—a city-wide legislative investigation that would look into every nook and cranny of the Walker administration. A nine-member committee was set up, and, once again, Seabury was named to conduct the proceedings. Said Walker tersely: "Let them come." Soon afterward, on his way back to New York, the mayor learned that Betty Compton had separated from Edward Dowling almost immediately after arriving in Havana and that she had now obtained a Mexican divorce. His reaction was noncommittal. Betty might be free, but a worried Walker knew that the investigative subpoena was drawing the noose tighter and tighter around him and Tammany.

Walker arrived in New York on Easter Sunday, the first week of April, and after attending mass at St. Patrick's Cathedral sequestered himself in his suite at the Mayfair. He worked for the next two weeks on his reply to the charges filed with Governor Roosevelt by the City Affairs Committee. One of the few times he surfaced during this period was at a dinner given in his honor by the Jewish Theatrical Guild of America. On the dais with the mayor were such supporters as Samuel Untermyer, Manhattan Borough President Samuel Levy, John F. Curry, John H. McCooey, and Max D. Steuer. In his address, frequently interrupted by loud applause from the 2,000 guests, Walker declared: "I come to you with no brief for myself. I come to you with no apology for my public life. . . . I am guilty of many shortcomings, but when the list is completed there will not be included selfish political ambition." The mayor's emotional words bore little relation to the facts. His audience could only admire his stage presence.

A few days later, Walker issued a rebuttal to the City Affairs Committee allegations. At best his answers were vague, at worst specious. To the criticism of the board of standards and appeals and William F. Walsh, its former chairman, the mayor said that a reorganizational plan was being drawn up, and that Walsh had never been convicted of wrongdoing in a court of law. The charge that the city had been losing $33 million a year in swollen condemnation awards was termed "ridiculous." As for the complaints against Charles Kohler, the Tammany leader who supposedly had skimmed off the milk-scandal graft years before, Walker pointed out that "no investigation has established anything which reflected upon [his] honesty." So the replies went. Even though Governor Roosevelt still refrained from any negative comment, the mayor's defense satisfied none of his critics. Meanwhile, the nine-member legislative committee created to investigate the city government met in New York for the first time. Chaired by State Senator Samuel Hofstadter, a Republican from Manhattan's silk-stocking district, and guided by Seabury, it would begin its public hearings in July and continue them for fourteen months.

That April was the cruelest month to date for Walker. Conscious of his personal popularity, he could not fully understand the attacks on what he represented. Seabury's three-pronged inquiry—of the magistrates' courts, District Attorney Crain, and soon the city government—was mauling the mayor even as it bloodied the Tammany Tiger. Subdued and depressed, Walker had no heart for the moment to resume his affair with Betty. Back in New York, she had been calling him constantly, trying to explain why she had married Dowling. When they did talk, he was pleasant but still cool. At month's end, Betty left with her mother for Europe. She would stay there for almost a year, continuing her calls to Walker via transatlantic cable and running up a phone bill of some $10,000.

During this period, the inquiry into the office of District Attorney Crain was beginning to produce headlines. On April 8, the seventy-year-old Crain testified that, to curb extortion by racketeers in the city's food industries, he had contented himself with bringing together some fifty influential citizens to form a committee that supposedly would "wage war on racketeering." He had thoughtfully provided them with a room where they might receive complaints from harassed food merchants. "I had an appropriate sign made," Crain said, "and directed that it be placed outside the room." The district attorney professed not to understand why merchants might feel they were risking physical injury from hoodlums by making complaints under such public circumstances. Strangely enough, he said, nobody came to the room.

"Then the net result of the committee was nothing, wasn't it?" asked Seabury.

"That is a fair statement," said Crain, who added that the responsibility was not his but the committee's.

John Kirkland Clark, another Seabury aide, then read from a memorandum written by William Morgan, Jr., president of the Middle Atlantic Fisheries Association, which charged that gangsters "shook down" merchants in the Fulton Fish Market to the extent of $25,000 yearly. The memo went on to say that in October 1930, the jobbers who supplied the hotel and restaurant trade had paid a muscleman named Joe ("Socks") Lanza a $5,000 levy. But, Morgan asserted, even though he had provided Crain with a witness, a merchant named John W. Walker who would have testified to this effect, the district attorney had failed to ask questions before a grand jury that might have led to Lanza's indictment.

"Did you ask [Mr. Walker] if he and his fellow dealers had paid any money to Lanza?" said Clark to Crain.

"I did," the district attorney maintained.

"Where?" demanded, Clark, looking at the grand jury minutes.

"In the record."

"Look at it and tell me where it is."

Crain took a look, then, appearing even older and frailer than when he had begun his testimony, admitted, "No, I didn't ask the question."

"Did you subpoena Mr. Walker's books to see if any such payments had been made?" interposed Seabury.

"I issued no subpoenas," said Crain lamely.

Witness Morgan then took the stand to tell about his other dealings with the district attorney's office. As head of the Middle Atlantic Fisheries Association, he said, he had been approached by a member who wanted to buy the gurry, as the waste fish from filet dealers was called, but feared to do so because Lanza, who had an interest in a rendering plant, had a monopoly on the gurry and carted it away without paying anything. Morgan reported, too, that dealers had been forced to buy cans from Lanza, who had still another interest in a can factory, at double their market value. After making these charges to one of Crain's assistants, he had received a letter from the district attorney asking him to produce supporting evidence. But even before he got the letter, Morgan said, its contents were common knowledge in the Fulton Fish Market. When he asked Crain how this could have happened, the district attorney allowed that "one of the copies must have gotten out," but made no effort to find out how.

As witness followed witness in subsequent weeks it was obvious that Crain had been an ineffectual prosecutor. Just as the Tammany sachem had failed to root out the corruption in the magistrates' courts, to convict such organization stalwarts as Walsh, "Horse Doctor" Doyle, Healy, Ewald, and Judge Mancuso, so by his own admission had he been unable to curb serious crime. On the last day of April, Raymond Moley, then a law professor at Columbia and an authority on criminal jurisprudence, testified before Judge Seabury to the effect that Crain had been the city's worst district attorney in the previous twenty-five years. Moley, producing a series of statistical charts that proved his contention beyond a doubt, listed the comparative achievements of Manhattan's last five prosecutors: Crain (1930), Joab H. Banton (1923), and Edward A. Swann (1918)—all Tammany men; Charles Whitman (1913) and William Travers Jerome (1908)—both anti-Tammany. Even though the district attorney's office had jumped substantially in budget and staff through the years and the population of Manhattan had decreased (owing to the establishment of the Bronx as a separate borough), Crain could show only 4.1 convictions for each member of his staff in the area of major crimes; Banton's record had been 4.8 and Swann's 5.7; prosecutors Whitman and Jerome had averaged 10.7 and 16, respectively. "Mr. Crain's record of convictions," commented a reporter covering the hearing, "bore the relationship to Whitman's and Jerome's that the Portuguese army had to that of Germany before the war."

As Professor Moley explained the significance of each of his graphs, Crain slipped lower and lower in his chair, his thin white hands hanging listlessly from the arm rests. Confronted with the evidence of his inability to control crime, he seemed visibly to shrink. Spectators could not help but feel pity for the septagenarian. He had been an honorable supreme court justice for many years, but in allowing himself to be named district attorney by Tammany in the twilight of his career, he had become nothing but a figurehead prosecutor. Crain, like Walker, had shut his eyes to what he did not wish to see.

That summer, Seabury would report to Governor Roosevelt that Crain's ineffectiveness, while obvious, had not been "so gross in character that it requires the removal of the incumbent." Cynics observed at the time that the fact that the district attorney was a prominent Episcopal layman and not an Irish Papist might have made the Protestant Seabury more charitable than usual. Yet, Seabury would explain, Crain had not been guilty of willful wrongdoing, merely of ineptitude. "The fact that the people of the County do not elect the best man to the position is not ground for his removal," the investigator said. "In such cases, the people must suffer the consequences of their conduct." Crain would continue in office.

In the first week of May, a twenty-year-old Irish hoodlum named Francis ("Two-Gun") Crowley shot and killed a policeman in North Merrick, Long Island, thereby touching off a manhunt that resulted in his capture twenty-four hours later in a West Ninetieth Street rooming house—but only after the 100-pound quarry had held off 150 policemen amid shot and shell for more than two hours, while 10,000 spectators gaped from nearby roofs, windows, and sidewalks. The police department's Lewis J. Valentine subsequently wrote: "Undersized, underchinned, underwitted, [Crowley] never developed beyond the mental age of ten and a half. The world would never have known he existed if he had not turned to crime." Raised as an orphan, young Crowley early fell in with thieves; as soon as he learned to drive automobiles, he began to steal them. Between his eighteenth and twentieth birthdays, he was arrested four times for such offenses; the first three charges were dismissed, the fourth brought him a suspended sentence. In February of 1931, Crowley earned the "Two-Gun" sobriquet he so cherished by joining in a free-for-all shooting, in which he wounded two men, in front of American Legion headquarters in the Bronx. A month later, when a detective recognized him, Crowley escaped by wounding the officer. Even the taxi dancers in cheap dance halls were not safe from his temper. With a friend, Rudolf Duringer, he soon afterward shot to death Virginia Brannen, a taxi dancer he believed to be unresponsive to his charms.

It was the Virginia Brannen killing that precipitated Crowley's shooting of the policeman in Long Island. Knowing they were being hunted in the city, he and Duringer stole a car from a Manhattan garage and sought the peace and quiet of North Merrick, where Crowley knew a friendly boardinghouse. There the hoodlum resumed his acquaintance with sixteen-year-old Helen Walsh, who went off with him to park in a lovers' lane. When patrolman Frederick Hirsch of the Nassau County police approached his car and asked to see Crowley's license, his answer was a burst of shots. Seven of them hit the officer, who died instantly. Crowley then sped from the scene, and for a few hours there was speculation that he had also killed Miss Walsh, a girl of "excellent reputation," to keep her from testifying against him. The next day, however, when Crowley and Duringer were traced back to their Manhattan hide-out as a result of an informer's tip, it was learned the girl was alive and with the killer, and that she had accompanied him willingly.

The final shoot-out was a spectacular affair, turning the quiet West Ninetieth Street neighborhood into a noisy battleground. Sensing that he was being surrounded by police in his top-floor apartment, Crowley began firing through the walls. The officers returned the fire with rifles and shotguns and then began to lob tear-gas canisters through the windows; later they chopped a hole in the roof of the brownstone and dropped in still more tear gas. Throughout the barrage, Two-Gun raced from one window to another, from doorway to doorway, firing indiscriminately at a hostile world. He also took time to pen a note, formally addressed "To Whom It May Concern." Wrote Crowley: "I was born on the 31st. She [Miss Walsh] was born on the 13th. I guess it was this that made us mate. When I die put a lily in my hand, let the boys know how they'll look. Underneath my coat will lay a weary kind heart what wouldn't harm anything. I hadn't nothing else to do. That's why I went around bumping off cops. It's the new sensation of the films."

When detectives finally smashed their way into the apartment, the girl was huddled in a corner, and Duringer was under the bed. "I'm shot, I give up," screamed Two-Gun, the only one of the trio standing. (Indeed, he had received four flesh wounds.) He appeared to be weaponless, but a search revealed two pistols inside his trouser legs, their muzzles inside his socks and the butts tucked under his garters.

After a brief trial, Crowley was convicted of murder and given the death penalty. Still in his twentieth year, he died in Sing Sing's electric chair.

The coming of Prohibition, as we have seen, blunted moral sensibilities. Most city dwellers were defiantly against the liquor ban, and most city politicians, eager to pacify the voters, took a lenient view of bootleggers and speakeasies. The ordinary policeman, noting this, saw nothing wrong in accepting "gratuities" to overlook the Volstead Act; soon it was easy for him to accept bribes to permit gambling and prostitution as well, and to rationalize his acts. What complicated the situation further, of course, was the fact that hoodlums who committed major crimes—killings, bank robberies, and the like—were also involved in bootlegging.

Walker understood the police character better than most citizens; in a sense, the force's weaknesses were his weaknesses. It was not surprising, then, that on May 9 the beleaguered mayor led 6,000 of New York's finest in their annual Police Parade up Broadway and along Fifth Avenue. The morning was sun-splashed and clear, the warmest spring day yet; for a man who had been documenting his defense in a stuffy hotel suite these many weeks, it was a fine day to get out in the fresh air. Commissioner Mulrooney, still reeling from disclosures of vice squad corruption, had been eager to have Walker beside him in the line of march. In silk hats and cutaway coats, the two of them stepped off smartly from the Battery as brass bands struck up lively tunes. Up Lower Broadway the mayor came, taking his place under the falling ticker-tape like the Commander Byrds and Gertrude Ederles and Queen Maries who had preceded him. On this day at least, Seabury was forgotten, and Irish Jimmy Walker ruled the city he loved in return. "Hey, Jimmy, how are you?" people kept asking. To all of them, Walker responded with a wave of his silk hat and a wide smile. At Prince Street, a bootblack wearing a hand-me-down cutaway coat danced out of the crowd and up to the mayor's side.

"How are you, Jimmy?" he said.

"All right, Tony," Walker grinned. And then, pointing down at his striped trousers, he added, "I'll give you the pants later."

Near White Street, a woman threw him a sprig of apple blossoms. The mayor's smile grew wider. "I thought they were lilies," he quipped, thinking of the rumors that his political career was nearly at an end. Around Twenty-third Street, a spectactor with a German accent shouted to Walker that on a warm day like this "a glass of beer would taste just right." Yelled back the mayor: "Yes, more than one."

By the time the parade reached Forty-ninth Street, Walker was never so gay. "This is the last lap," he called out.

"Don't hurt yourself," warned another spectator.

"Nothing can hurt me now," replied Jimmy, and indeed it must have seemed to the mayor that the spontaneous applause he had received all along the line of march meant his sins had been forgiven him. In front of St. Patrick's Cathedral, Walker hesitated briefly, then went up the steps to greet Cardinal Hayes, who had so sternly lectured him the year before. He bowed, kissed the prelate's ring, and exchanged a few words with His Eminence before rejoining the parade. At Sixty-second Street, the mayor took his place in the reviewing stand. The mounted headquarters staff, the departmental band, the rifle regiment with bayonets fixed, probationary officers from the academy, a company of Negro policemen, the motor-transport division, the emergency squad, the motorcycle officers—all proudly marched past him. New York would not see another such parade for forty-two years; it would never see another "Jimmy."

One of the last magistrates brought up on charges by Seabury in connection with his investigation of the lower courts was Jean H. Norris, who twelve years before had been named the city's first woman judge, on the authority of Tammany Boss Murphy. (Prior to her appointment, she had been coleader, with George W. Olvany, of the Tenth A.D.) Over the years, the woman judge, who sat for the most part on vice cases, had earned a reputation for giving stern sentences and granting few acquittals. Wrote Milton MacKaye of the New York *Evening Post:* "More than one humble streetwalker, incarcerated in the workhouse for 100 days, was warmed and comforted by the knowledge she had been sentenced by a lady." Not that Magistrate Norris did not have a human side. In earlier hearings, Seabury had already established that, for a $1000 fee, she had once authorized the use of her picture in full judicial robes for an advertisement in which she recommended the use of Fleischmann's yeast. The ad quoted her to the effect that Fleischmann's had greatly alleviated her insomnia, an ailment she had to best at all costs if she were to maintain her strenuous schedule on the bench.

Now, on June 22, Magistrate Norris was on trial before the appellate division for unjudicial conduct with Seabury presenting the evidence. Among the charges was her handling of the case of Mary de Sena, who had come before her accused of prostitution. The defendant had repeatedly been bullied by Magistrate Norris, had been dragged twelve or fourteen feet and forcibly placed on the witness stand, and had peremptorily been found guilty. Later, when Mrs. de Sena's attorney obtained a copy of the official record, he discovered that many passages had been altered or stricken out by the magistrate to conceal her biased comments and behavior. Seabury had obtained a copy of the true record, which the court stenographer fortunately had saved. In one instance, the magistrate's remark, "You know what to do, plead her guilty," had been changed to, "What is it, counsel, do you wish to plead her guilty?" In another instance, the entire episode in which Mrs. de Sena had been dragged to the stand was deleted:

Magistrate to defendant: "Get up."

Attorney: "I will have to call the janitress."

Magistrate, ignoring the attorney's attempt to intercede on behalf of his client: "Take the stand."

Defendant, tearfully, asking the Magistrate to listen to her lawyer: "He is my counsel. I beg your pardon."

Magistrate, harshly: "Will you stop arguing?"

Court Attendant, dragging the defendant toward the stand: "Do as the judge tells you."

Summing up the evidence against Magistrate Norris, Seabury declared that the acts of the Tammany appointee "evince a course of conduct resulting in injustice to defendants, which must have been followed by tragic consequences." The Appellate Division agreed. That summer, voting unanimously, it directed that she be removed from the bench.

July found Commissioner Mulrooney, taking advantage of a new law giving him regulatory power over nightclubs and dance halls, engaged in a clean-up campaign. It had particularly rankled Mulrooney that one of his men, though persent in the Club Abby earlier in the year when Beer Baron Arthur ("Dutch") Schultz had used a jagged bottle to settle a minor underworld dispute, had not reported the incident. (Schultz, whose keg-laden trucks slaked the thirst of the Bronx, Harlem, and the West Side down to Fourteenth Street, was then being harassed by a cold-blooded interloper named Vincent

["Mad Dog"] Coll—more about Coll later—and his nerves must have been tightly strung. It was unusual for Dutch personally to use violence.) At any rate, the contretemps had enraged Mulrooney. Addressing a meeting of 300 nightclub owners at headquarters (many of those attending were mere "fronts"—missing were such nocturnal hosts as Owney Madden, Larry Fay, and "Big Frenchy" de Magne), Mulrooney declared: "The proprietor of a cabaret cannot hope [any longer] to make it a rendezvous for men with criminal records. . . . I know that it has been quite the custom to use them as scenery to dress up the place, and to point them out to customers as Tough Jake or Irish Paddy. But you are not going to do that any more. . . . If you do not keep them out, your license will be revoked." Among the Commissioner's other warnings:

* "You are not going to use ink eradicator to raise $30 [personal] checks to $3,000. That will mean you lose your license."

* The closing was still 3 A.M. "You are not going to dismiss all your patrons and keep the one good party with lots of money, and later on take them out through an alley."

* "You are not going to have any buzzers to be run by a doorman when a member of the department approaches," and "we will not permit closed booths or other contrivances that will prevent immediate inspection by the police."

* To do away with front-men, "We want the photographs and fingerprints of the owner, operator, and manager. They will be in the possession of the police."

* "We will not permit any entertainers or hostesses to mingle with the audience." This stricture, bad news for the Texas Guinans of Gotham, "will be a very rigid regulation."

The police crackdown, which was countenanced by Tammany as another attempt to draw public attention away from the Seabury inquiries, soon faded away. It could not compete with the continuing sage of "Horse Doctor" Doyle, the silver-tongued veterinarian who had earned some $2 million in practice before the Board of Standards and Appeals. Now, on July 21st, Doyle traveled to New York from his home in Deal, New Jersey, to testify before the Joint Legislative Committee about his activities.

"Dr. Doyle," asked Seabury, "did you, in reference to cases pending before the Board of Standards and Appeals, bribe any public official?"

"I refuse to answer on the ground that it might tend to incriminate me."

"Dr. Doyle, did you give away part of the proceeds of these fees to any political leader in the County of New York?"

"I refuse to answer . . ."

Thereupon the legislative committee cited Doyle for contempt; before he could be jailed, however, his attorney obtained a two-day postponement. At 7:30 P.M. on July 22, John F. Curry, head of Tammany Hall, placed a phone call from his suite at the Park Lane Hotel to Justice Henry L. Sherman of the Supreme Court's Appellate Division at his home in Lake Placid, New York. Early the next morning, one of Doyle's attorneys arrived in Lake Placid—300 miles from the city—to plead his client's case, and Judge Sherman coincidentally issued a stay that kept Doyle out of jail—despite the fact that Edward R. Finch, presiding justice of the Appellate Division, was in the city and willing to hear arguments. Just as he had used stays and appeals to avoid jail during the federal inquiry on tax evasion, Doyle was employing these same tactics with Seabury. Just as he had refused to answer tax questions on the ground of self-incrimination, he was not responding to bribery questions on the same ground. But Seabury now knocked this prop out from under Doyle by having the committee grant him immunity from prosecution on bribery or fee-splitting charges. For this continued silence, therefore, the ex-veterinarian late in July finally went to jail.

On August 14, Mr. Doyle, who had maintained what the committee had no right to grant him immunity but had lost his appeal, agreed to retake the stand.

"Will you now [say] whether or not you gave a bribe to any public official, and if so to whom?" asked Seabury.

"The answer is no," said Doyle, his denial amazing in view of the trouble his previous silence had caused him.

"Are you now trifling with the committee?" asked Seabury.

"I am making a serious and truthful answer. . . ."

"Your purpose has not been, has it, to await the ruling of the courts, and then when the courts said you must answer that particular question, to come in and deny it?"

"It has not."

Despite Doyle's dubious testimony and Seabury's extreme skepticism, there was no longer any legal reason to deny him bail. He was discharged on a $20,000 bond after spending but eighteen days in jail and returned to New Jersey, still close-mouthed about his fee-splitting. Months later, the court of appeals would reluctantly approve Doyle's release, saying, "The untruthfulness of [his] answer may be a possible inference, but a necessary one it certainly is not."

On the same day on which he last questioned Doyle, August 15, Seabury brought John F. Curry to the witness stand.

"You are interested in Doyle?" Seabury asked.

"I am interested in any Democrat in the city," said Curry.

"Well, now, when did you first decide to interest yourself in Dr. Doyle?"

"On the evening of Wednesday, July 22nd, I received a telephone call from a reputable lawyer, Alfred J. Talley, who said he would like to secure some judge who would hear an application for a stay in the Doyle case."

"And did you get busy right away trying to find a judge?"

"Absolutely."

Curry insisted that the attorney never told him Doyle was facing jail for refusing to answer questions but instead informed him the veterinarian was testing the authority of the committee to grant immunity.

"And we [Tammany Hall] were glad to take advantage of that," Curry said. "We were waiting for someone to test the [committee's] constitutionality."

The Tammany leader then explained that he had phoned Judge Sherman in Lake Placid, asking him to consider granting Doyle a stay of imprisonment. Afterward, a Doyle attorney had traveled through the night to present his case before the judge, and the stay had been forthcoming.

"If you thought any case was important and affected the interests of the organization of which you are the head," summed up Seabury, "you would not hesitate to try to get a judge to hear [applications]?"

"I would step on the gas whenever it would help the Democratic Party of this city," said Curry forthrightly.

So the episode of Mr. Curry's phone call came to a close—with Seabury stymied and the Tammany boss unperturbed.

≋≋≋

For three months following his appearance in the Police Parade, Walker kept what was for him a low profile in the city. He celebrated his fiftieth birthday in June, granted a newspaper interview in which he talked about the duties of his office but said nothing about his responsibilities, and paid for Allie Walker's stays in Florida, the Midwest and other parts of the country. In July, he watched almost passively while Sachem John Voorhis, nearing his one hundred second birthday and still active, presided at Tammany's 155th Independence Day fete. Meanwhile, the stream of witnesses and wrongdoers, all damaging to the mayor's administration, continued through the Seabury hearings and trials. It was a good time, the mayor thought, to leave New York. On August 8, even as his office was announcing that the $15,000 raise voted him the year before had been donated to ninety-three charities, Walker sailed aboard the *Bremen* for another tour of Europe. He would stay six weeks and take the cures at the spas; his party included George Collins, his confidential secretary; Dudley Field Malone, former collector of the Port of New York, attorney, bon vivant, and close friend; and Dr. William Schroeder, Jr., head of the sanitation commission and Walker's personal physician. On the surface at least, this trip was as carefree as his 1927 European junket. It was also as expensive, for adversity had not made Walker any more frugal.

Landing in Hamburg, the mayor sped by luxury salon car to Berlin, where he indulged in several days of café-hopping. Afterward, in the hope of rejuvenating his liver, he and his party went on to Carlsbad, where he sampled the mineral waters; to Pilsen, where he switched to the more familiar and congenial (if less therapeutic) lager; and next to Vienna, where Walker dined and danced until the early hours. And so his odyssey went.

In Paris at the beginning of September, the mayor gave a talk at the American Club, referring to the Depression and saying he hoped New York's needy could be cared for without a rise in taxes. "A great effort was made last winter by [city] employees in New York. Every one of them took a percentage of his month's salary to supply thousands of families with coal, clothing, and lodging. Yet with all that we were obliged to make an appropriation from our budget of $6 million for unemployment relief." About this time, there were reports from New York that Seabury was interested in the financial affairs of David Maier, another member of the mayor's traveling party, and also in whether the North German Lloyd line, owner of the *Bremen*, had indirectly paid for the group's passage. Maier, who back in 1912 had been the operator of rows of flats used for prostitution and an ostensible "vice-trust magnate," had been sent to Sing Sing for trying to bribe a witness to commit perjury during District Attorney Charles Whitman's exposé of the tie-ins between underworld interests and the police. After thirty-two months in prison, Maier returned to the city, where he strengthened his association with Tammany. He became one of Grover Whalen's official greeters, an officer of the Steuben Society (which had recommended the naming of Ewald to the bench), a friend of judges and magistrates, a dais-sitter at civic banquets, and, lastly, the alleged go-between through whom in 1931 the North German Lloyd line, after years of effort and the payment of $50,000, finally obtained a pier lease. Seabury was convinced, the stories went, that Maier was deeply involved, along with high city officials, in a conspiracy.

While staying at the Crillon in Paris, Walker faced down a group of American correspondents by sending for Maier. When his traveling companion, with great reluctance, entered his suite, the mayor laid his hand on his shoulder and said pointedly, "This is my friend." He described Maier as someone "a million people in my town have honored."

Seabury would call Maier to the witness stand in New York that December. As of now, however, the bare bones of the charges against him were already evident. North German Lloyd, needing a pier for its new ships *Bremen* and *Europa,* had been negotiating for years, not with the dock commissioner or the sinking fund commission—the responsible parties—but with Maier. In a succession of meetings, he had given the Lloyd people his "very good assurances" that he could and would obtain the necessary space. First, of course, a "legal fee" had to be paid. The intermediary suggested by Maier to give "special counsel" to the Lloyd line was William H. Hickin, a prominent Tammany lawyer, and recompense of $50,000 eventually was agreed upon. Overjoyed, the line's resident director, in September 1930, wrote Walker, "I am informed the Sinking Fund Commission [will pass] on our lease. As I feel that the action at this time was largely due to your personal interest, I wish to express my sincerest thanks."

Hickin did not receive the Lloyd line's $50,000 check until June of 1931—a month before Walker left for Eruope. He deposited it in his bank account and shortly thereafter made out two checks to "bearer" for $45,000 and cashed them. What happened to this money would be one of the subjects of Seabury's inquiry.

While Walker was abroad, a vicious gun battle between thugs and police took place in the Bronx and Upper Manhattan, raising anew the public outcry against blatant crimes of violence. Two policemen, three hold-up men, and a child bystander were shot dead during a twelve-mile chase following a payroll robbery, and a dozen more persons were wounded. The pursuit began shortly after two of the hoodlums waylaid the manager of a Bronx fur and dye plant as he was driving the weekly $4,600 payroll to his One Hundred Thirty-third Street office. When patrolman Walter J. Webb, who had been assigned to guard the money, threw open the car door and reached for his revolver, he was killed by a single bullet that pierced his heart. The two robbers grabbed the payroll, pushed the terror-stricken manager out of the auto, and careened off. At One Hundred Forty-ninth Street, they abandoned the car, speeding away in a yellow taxi driven by a confederate. For twenty blocks they raced uptown, pressing the accelerator to the floor and running traffic lights.

When they reached Boston Post Road, they were spotted by motorcycle policeman Edward Churchill. A hail of shots from the hood-lums' taxi almost immediately cut him down; wounded in the stomach and legs, he became the second fatality. An off-duty fireman named Vincent Hyde, who was driving in the vicinity with his family, then picked up the officer's gun and fired at the fleeing cab; he was struck by a bullet in the chest. "I heard shooting, and then a car sped by," Hyde said later from his hospital bed. "A motorcycle policeman drew alongside me. He wasn't ten feet away when I heard him say, 'I got it.' . . . His machine went wild and he fell in the roadway. I jammed on the brakes, hopped out and grabbed his gun."

Speeding along Boston Post Road, the frantic hoodlums fired at anyone in their way. A couple and their four-year-old daughter, driv-ing in their car, all were hit by shots; the child was mortally wounded. Some luckless bystanders were also wounded. At One Hundred Seventy-sixth Street, Detective William Kily and a patrolman, helped by a willing cab driver, took up the chase. The gunmen now turned west, heading across the Bronx toward Manhattan. At One Hundred Sixty-second Street and Park Avenue, two policemen on foot at-tempted to stop their car but were almost instantly wounded and leveled, three more bystanders were hit, and a block further on still another officer was wounded. "Things were pretty slow up to 3:45 P.M.," William Nugent, the cabbie driving the police, said afterward. "I was waiting for a fare when another taxi whizzed past at terrific speed. I decided to follow." Nugent stopped to pick up Detective Kily, who "was standing in the middle of the street with his coat off, pegging a couple of shots" after the bandits. "They were pumping left and right and Kily, who had jumped on my running board, was giving it back to them." At One Hundred Sixty-first Street and Jerome Avenue, "the traffic cop started to dance when the bandits went by. They gave him a full load. He got his gun out and gave it back to them, and then he got in my cab."

Over the Macomb's Avenue Bridge, at the Harlem River and One Hundred Fifty-fifth Street, the chase continued. "I pulled onto the wrong side of the bridge," Nugent related. "All the way across I came weaving through traffic on the wrong side. The boys kept pumping away." Into Manhattan and up Riverside Drive the two taxis roared. "I pushed it down to the floorboard. We must have been doing sixty miles an hour through all that traffic." Whenever Kily and the other officers emptied their revolvers, Nugent would "slow down to give 'em a chance to reload." At Dyckman Street in Washing-ton Heights, one of the most congested parts of the city, "the gun-men's car hit a fruit truck and stopped. The bandits got down on the floor and kept pumping through the doors."

Police and killers now exchanged more than a hundred shots; when the gunsmoke cleared, all three bandits lay dying; each had been hit a dozen or more times.

From London, where he was completing his European tour, Walker offered his own solution for curbing crime. The hoodlum element could be handled, he said, if the law would permit "strong, athletic young cops [to] round up the gangsters in their own districts and beat them up before their own people." Unfortunately, he complained, when the New York police did this, they were charged with assault and battery. With that the mayor went off for a luncheon at 10 Downing Street as the guest of Prime Minister Ramsay MacDonald. There he suggested to MacDonald, who was experiencing his own political difficulties, that what he needed to continue in power were constituents who "vote early and often." MacDonald did not smile, and there was no further talk of politics.

At no time during the European trip did Walker and Betty Compton manage to get together, although each made several abortive phone calls to the other, half-heartedly trying to arrange a rendezvous. Walker was still nettled over Betty's brief marriage to Edward Dowling; she, in turn, could not understand why he did not resign his office, divorce Allie, and live with her in Europe. Their pride still prevented a reconciliation. As for Allie, with whom Walker had not lived since 1928, she waited helplessly in Florida, hoping that Jim would "come to his senses."

Tanned, cheerful, and in good health, Walker arrived back in New York aboard the *Bremen* on September 21; he was met at Quarantine by Charles Kerrigan, his assistant, and Commissioner Mulrooney. Later, when he walked down the gangplank—wearing a visored beret and the red ribbon of the Legion of Honor (both of which he had picked up in France), and carrying a Chinese chow dog—he was greeted on the pier by a covey of politicians and reporters.

"Are you prepared to appear before the Hofstadter Committee at the call of Mr. Seabury?" Walker was asked.

"That's for Mr. Seabury to decide," he replied, flushing.

At noon the next day, Walker arrived at City Hall. He explained to the press, evidently having in mind his promise aboard the *Bremen* that he would be at work "bright and early," that some important papers in his baggage had been mislaid, and the search for them had delayed him. Then he parried all questions about Maier. The mayor also was evasive about the whereabouts of his accountant, Russell T. Sherwood, whom the legislative committee had been seeking for some weeks so as to learn more about Walker's financial affairs. Thereafter he closeted himself in his office, ostensibly to "study the budget."

At a welcome-home dinner that night given him by the Inner Circle, the organization of political reporters, the mayor took an oblique slap at the city investigation. "After I left home," he said, referring to his European trip, "there were sudden discoveries about my short-comings and my failures in office, which did not occur before I left and which seem to have disappeared when I returned." This was blatantly untrue, the charges against Walker having been made six months before, but the newsmen applauded vigorously. In an era when most politicians starched their collars and stuffed their shirts several times daily, most reporters were willing to forgive the ir-reverent mayor anything.

On September 23, Lewis J. Valentine, who had been broken from deputy chief inspector to captain—on Walker's orders—as one of Grover Whalen's first acts as police commissioner, was summoned before the Hofstadter Committee. Since his demotion, which had been allowed to stand by Mulrooney, Valentine had been waiting for the time he would be eligible for retirement—on a pension of $2,500 yearly. His two-story, eight-room house in the Bensonhurst section of Brooklyn was paid for, his children were grown, and he and his wife were looking forward to seeing the part of America outside New York in their Model A Ford sedan. Now the "Honest Cop," a communicant of the church of Our Lady of Guadalupe and a member of its Holy Name Society, was in the public eye again, and many a concerned Tammany leader wondered how much he could tell Sea-bury.

Captain Valentine, resplendent in full-dress uniform, made an im-pressive witness, answering questions quickly and precisely.

"When you assumed command of the Confidential Squad," Seabury asked him, "did you receive any instructions from Commissioner McLaughlin as to the prevalence of gamblers in political clubs?"

"I did," Valentine replied. "[He] informed me there was gam-bling in many clubs, and that it was my particular duty to report to him what the situation was, and to do everything in my power to suppress . . . the professional gamblers."

McLaughlin, the witness added, had been alerted to the gambling by anonymous letters written by women, complaining that men who frequented certain clubs often lost their wages there.

Valentine and his second-in-command, Acting Captain Ezekiel E. Keller, had tried to raid the political clubs, but had run into sub-stantial obstacles. "Where we knew there were a large number of gamblers every day," the witness said, "we tried to get men in—as firemen, railway employees, street cleaners, icemen. . . . In almost every instance we were frustrated and thwarted. . . . [Sometimes] they got as far as the sentinel on the outside, the lookout, and were turned away. . . . In the Perry Club [the Harry C. Perry Club on the Bowery—Perry being chief clerk of the city court] we got a man up to the door leading to the gambling room. He had passed the outside sentinel [but] was refused admission by the inside sentinel."

"I have heard about certain rooms in these clubs being barred by icebox doors," said Seabury.

Valentine answered that Captain Keller, who through extreme diligence had finally managed to break into the Thomas Farley Club on East Sixty-second Street [Farley being sheriff of New York County], had encountered just such barriers.

"What do you mean by an icebox door?" asked Seabury. "Some of us may not recognize it from that description."

"It was the kind of door you would find in a large refrigerator, such as meat markets use," said Valentine. "It was strongly made, and if you attacked it with crowbars or axes it would take you some time to get in."

Seabury next tried to show that the late Joseph Warren, who succeeded McLaughlin as police commissioner, had been forced by Walker to resign because he had continued the raids on the clubs. As everyone knew, Warren's first letter of resignation had been found unacceptable by the mayor—supposedly because the commissioner charged the mayor with political interference. He had then written a second letter, which innocuously stated he was leaving his post to resume his private law practice.

"After the first letter was sent to the mayor," Seabury asked Valentine, "you had a conversation with Commissioner Warren in which you ventured the opinion, in view of what [he] told you were the contents, that the letter would be unacceptable to the Mayor?"

"That is correct."

"Was your prediction verified?"

"That day."

Within a few hours after the letter was sent to City Hall, Valentine explained, Warren received a visit in his office from Francis J. McIntyre, his former law partner and a Walker confidant. The two men talked behind closed doors, then went to the Warren home for dinner.

"Well now, the next day did [Warren] have anything to say to you on the subject?"

"He said he had [talked] with Mrs. Warren and Mr. McIntyre, and that they had prevailed upon him to substitute another letter."

"Was that the occasion when he said the first letter embodied his sincere conviction?"

"He may have said something like that, Judge, but I can't be sure . . . he did tell me, though, that he regretted the necessity for changing it."

Though Valentine bowed out of the committee inquiry at this point, his law-enforcement career would soon experience a rebirth. After Fiorello H. LaGuardia's successful mayoral campaign in 1933, he would be named police commissioner, and the Confidential Squad would be re-formed. Valentine, who had worn a uniform all his adult life but now needed civilian clothes, would buy several expensive suits and a Chesterfield coat at Finchley's. Several days later, wearing the Chesterfield while going down the police line-up at headquarters, the commissioner came across a dapper hoodlum wearing the identical coat. Valentine's face turned red with anger. "That velvet collar should be smeared with blood," he roared to his subordinates. "I don't want these hoodlums coming in here looking as if they stepped out of a barber's chair. From now on, bring 'em in mussed up." The police took pleasure, in the years that followed, in obeying that order.

In early October, Seabury brought Francis J. McIntyre to the stand to describe the role he had played in Commissioner Warren's resignation. McIntyre stated he had gone to City Hall in response to an urgent phone call from Walker.

"The Mayor handed me the letter and asked me to read it," McIntyre said, "I read the letter and I put it down. I said, 'I think it is all right.'"

"That did not end the conversation, did it?" asked Seabury.

"The Mayor immediately said that he did not think it was right, that the letter might be construed that there was some dissatisfaction on the part of the Mayor with the Commissioner which, the Mayor said, 'After all, would probably do [him] no good.'"

"In other words," said Seabury, "the Mayor was solicitious [of] Commissioner Warren?"

"That was one of his attitudes, yes," replied McIntyre.

"Did he say whether he would accept that letter?"

"I said, 'Well, what do you want me to do about it?' And he asked me would I take it up with Mr. Warren."

"Will you tell us, Mr. McIntyre, just what the conversation was you had with Commissioner Warren in his office as soon as you left the Mayor's office?"

"Well, I told Joe what the Mayor had told me about the letter, and told him [the Mayor's] suggestion about resigning on account of his health. To that Joe stood up at his desk and said, 'Absolutely not.'"

"He stood pat?"

"Yes, he stood pat. Subsequently, the subject was dropped. I have a distinct recollection of Joe saying, 'That is final.' "

In the Warren home that evening, McIntyre testified, he told his friend that a second letter of resignation might more graciously explain the commissioner's leave-taking, instead of attributing it to political pressure, by declaring he intended to resume his law practice. After considerable discussion, Warren agreed to write such a letter.

"Didn't Mrs. Warren say," Seabury asked, " 'Why not be pleasant and change it?' "

"She may have said something like that," allowed the witness.

Now Seabury turned his attention to the district leaders whose clubs allegedly were gambling dens. Brought to the stand on Tuesday, October 6, Sheriff Farley was asked to shed some light on how, during the past seven years, he had managed to bank some $396,000 while his wages totaled only $87,000. Like most Tammany leaders, big men or small, the sheriff projected an aura of solidity; even under heavy questioning, such politicians rarely lost their composure; they would answer documented charges with outrageous explanations, yet with great dignity. So ingenuous was Farley's testimony about the source of his income, in fact, that he later became famous as "Tin-Box" Farley.

"You deposited during the year 1925 some $34,824—and during that time, what was your position?" said Seabury, leading the witness along.

"Deputy County Clerk."

"And your salary?"

"I guess $6,500."

"Will you tell the Committee where you could have gotten that sum of money?"

"Monies that I had saved."

"Where did you keep these monies that you had saved?"

"In a big box in a big safe."

"Was [it] fairly full when you withdrew the money?"

"It was full."

"Was this big box that was safely kept in the big safe a tin box?"

"A tin box."

"Sheriff, coming to 1926, did not your total deposits for that year amount to $42,746?"

"That is what I deposited."

"Sheriff, where did you get this money?"

"Monies I saved."

"What is the most money you ever put in that tin box you have?"

"I had as much as $100,000 in it."

"When did you deposit that?"

"From time to time."

In like manner, Seabury questioned Farley about his bank deposits in 1927, 1928, and 1929, always receiving the same reply, that the cash to make the deposits had come from the tin box in his home. Coming to 1930, the committee counsel noted that the sheriff's total deposits had been $65,890 while his salary had been $12,876. How could Farley account for the discrepancy? Seabury wanted to know.

"Well, that came from the good box I had," said Farley, while laughter filled the hearing room.

"Kind of a magic box?" asked Seabury.

"It was a wonderful box," replied the sheriff earnestly.

Soon afterward, State Senator John J. McNaboe, a Democratic member of the committee whose constituency included Farley's Fourteenth A.D., interrupted the questioning in an attempt to make the sheriff's story more credible. Could not the large bank deposits be explained, McNaboe said, by the fact that Farley used his money as a revolving fund, depositing the same money many times in various banks?

"Put it in and take it out," the witness assented.

"What are you worth today?" continued McNaboe.

"About $250,000," said Farley.

"You have told us, Sheriff," resumed Seabury, "of the amounts you drew out of the good box. . . . Now I ask you whether you didn't take other money, other than your salary . . . the proceeds of which you put in the good box?"

"I did not," answered Farley.

About the 3:00 A.M. gambling raid on his clubhouse in 1926 that had been described by Valentine, the sheriff strongly maintained that his supporters had been guilty of no wrongdoing.

"The members that was there was busy packing baseball bats, skipping ropes, and rubber balls, because our May Day outing took place on May 29th—"

"These, Sheriff, were toys for the children?"

"Toys for the children."

"By any chance, did any gambling paraphernalia get mixed up with these childish playthings?"

"They did not."

Farley even denied that his club had ever been fortified with icebox doors.

"The only time I ever did see an icebox door was when I worked in a butcher shop."

"Now, Sheriff," said Seabury, "let me remind you that there are

living souls who took the stand and testified to seeing [such] doors.
Does that refresh your recollection?"

"[Nobody] could say that they had seen icebox doors," blandly
insisted Farley.

In February of 1932, the Tammany sheriff would stand in the
executive chamber of the State Capitol at Albany, on trial before
Governor Roosevelt to determine his fitness to remain in office. Many
people regarded Roosevelt's decision as an indication of the judgment
he could be expected to make on Walker if the mayor should come
before him on similar charges.

≋≋≋

The most feared killer in the city during 1931, while Walker was
being pilloried for his inability to control crime, was twenty-two-year-
old Vincent Coll, who during his beer-running days had been known
as "the Mick" but now was called "Mad Dog." Since childhood, Coll
had been—almost literally—on the sidewalks of New York, supporting
himself through thievery and, later, homicide. At the age of eleven,
he was sent on delinquency charges, to a boys' home. Four years
later, in 1924, Coll was arrested for carrying a revolver and committed
to Elmira Reformatory. Four years after that, having been charged
both with burglary and with assault and robbery, he was sent back
to Elmira as a parole violator. There the prison doctors probed his
psyche. "Typical psychopathic inferior—signs of dementia praecox,"
read their report. "Unable to earn a living—unfit for liberty."

Released in 1929 anyway, Coll hired himself out as a gunman for
beer barons Owney Madden and Dutch Schultz. Four arrests for
robbery and one for carrying a concealed weapon quickly followed,
with the charges being dropped on each occasion; the Dutchman,
who valued the Mick's services, once even put up $10,000 bail for
him. Within a year, Coll began to muscle into the beer racket. When
his former superiors indicated their displeasure, he and his gang resorted to shootings, overturning beer trucks and smashing barrels in
the process. He even kidnaped Big Frenchy de Magne, Madden's
"chief of staff," as he left the Club Argonaut, and passed the time
while waiting for the $37,000 ransom by holding lighted matches to
de Magne's feet. (More concerned about his reputation than about
the physical discomfort, Big Frenchy never would admit to police
that he had been abducted.)

By 1931, Coll was so feared in the underworld that it appeared
he might dethrone New York's leading beer runner, Dutch Schultz

himself. "Coll led a gang into one of the Schultz garages on College Avenue [in the Bronx] and smashed every beer truck and beer rack in the place, doing damage to the extent of $100,000," Lewis J. Valentine recounted afterward. "He led night raids against the Schultz caravans, killing off the drivers and payroll men whenever he found them. [His gang] would wait for Schultz employees in their homes in the dead of night, and kill them in their own bedrooms." Then, during a gang dispute in Harlem, Coll and his men accidentally killed a four-year-old boy with an errant bullet. The shooting outraged the city, and the resultant publicity forced "Mad Dog" to go into hiding.

In October of 1931, despite the subterfuge of dyeing his hair and mustache, Coll was captured by detectives and charged with the child's murder. The key witness against him in court was an ex-convict named George Brecht, whom a trio of policemen had been devotedly guarding for months. Brecht testified that he had seen Coll firing the gun that killed the boy. He was certain of his identification, for he recognized Mad Dog by the dimple on his chin. If Coll had not had Samuel S. Leibowitz as his attorney, he undoubtedly would have been sent to the electric chair. Leibowitz, a mellifluous-voiced product of Brooklyn's public schools who had thus far represented some seventy culprits accused of murder in the first degree, had never lost a capital case.

The problem in the Coll case, as Leibowitz saw it, was how to destroy Brecht's credibility as a witness. He handled the matter astutely. Recognizing that Brecht was nothing more than a petty thief but would be unwilling to admit this low status in court, Leibowitz asked him how he supported himself. Brecht, thinking semifast, replied that he sold Eskimo Pies for a living. Leibowitz then sent out for fourteen of the pies, presenting one each to the judge, the district attorney, and the jurors. While everybody ate the ice-cream snacks, he asked Brecht a series of questions that revealed the witness could not describe the label, did not know the pies' content, and was ignorant of the fact that they had to be packed in dry ice. In the jury's eyes, Brecht lost all credibility, if a man could lie about Eskimo Pies he could lie about anything. Coll was found not guilty. Commented contemporary journalist Alva Johnston: "The able criminal lawyer is the only antidote to the rubber hose and police-fixed evidence. It is almost equally true that the rubber hose and fixed evidence are the only antidote to the able criminal lawyer."

Before Coll could fully resume his homicidal career, Madden, Schultz, and the powers-that-were in the underworld finally agreed to cooperate on a joint project; the elimination of the Mad Dog and his gang. On February 1, 1932, four gunmen forced their way into a Bronx apartment and killed three of Coll's lieutenants. A week later, Walter Winchell wrote in *The Mirror:* "Five planes brought a dozen machine gats from Chicago Friday to combat *The Town Capone.*" Within twenty-four hours, one of the Chicago émigrés walked into a West Twenty-third Street drugstore while Coll was making a phone call, placed the muzzle of a machine gun against the glass, and riddled the gangster from thigh to throat.

Owney Madden, whose penthouse apartment was only a block and a half from the drugstore, had the usual alibi, being with friends at the time of the slaying; he was cleared by the police of all complicity in the crime. Mad Dog Coll's murder was never solved.

Even while Walker was telling a sympathetic audience at a dinner meeting of the Grand Street Boys Association that "Framing is a popular indoor and outdoor sport in New York," Seabury was asking other Democratic district leaders to explain their finances before the legislative committee. Following Sheriff Farley to the witness stand was Kings County Registrar James A. McQuade, the Greenpoint rival of Peter McGuinness who had allegedly permitted gambling in his clubhouse—and greatly profited from it. Over the last six and three-quarter years, McQuade had deposited $547,254.03 in his bank accounts (some $350,000 in cash), while his salary ranged from $9,000 to $12,000 yearly. The registrar—a short, stocky man with a penetrating voice—remained completely self-possessed under Seabury's questioning, paying no visible attention to the frequent outbursts of laughter caused by his testimony.

"Now, bearing in mind what you have told us about not having any other gainful pursuits than your public office," began Seabury, "will you be good enough to tell me where you got the $80,000-odd you deposited in 1925—$55,000 of which was in cash?"

"Money that I borrowed," McQuade genially replied. "If you want me to get to the start of it, I will have to go over the family in its entirety without feeling that I am humiliated in the least or am not humiliating the other thirty-three McQuades. . . .

"I bailed a man out who stole off McQuade Brothers [the family brokerage firm] $260,000, which necessitated the folding up of the firm. After they liquidated, the 33 McQuades was placed on my back, I being the only breadwinner. It was necessary, to keep life in their body, to go out and borrow money. . . .

"I took over their responsibilities. I felt it my duty, being that they were my flesh and blood, part and parcel of me. I am getting along in fairly good shape when my mother, Lord have mercy on her, in 1925 dropped dead. I am going along nicely when my brother, Lord have mercy on him, in 1926 or 1927 dropped dead. He willed me his family, which I am still taking care of, thank God. Two other brothers have been very sick, so much so that when your Committee notified me I was waiting for one of them to die. . . .

"They have 24 children that I am trying to keep fed, clothed and educated, which means that I must borrow money. The extra money that you see in this year or any year has been money that I borrowed. I am not ashamed of it. If the Lord lets me live, I intend to pay it all back. And I borrowed money in 1926, 1927, 1928, and 1929 and in the last month alone, I think, I borrowed $10,000 to keep the roof over their homes."

Seabury expressed skepticism about McQuade's rambling tale.

"I am not interested in what you did with the money," he said. "I am quite ready to assume that you made charitable and benevolent dispositions of [it]. My question is: how, in the year 1925, with your salary of $9,365.40, did you deposit $80,000-odd?"

"I would, for instance, borrow $1,000 off John Brown," McQuade answered. "In two weeks' time John Brown wanted that $1,000 and I would borrow $1,000 off John Jones. Another two weeks or less, he would want that. I would get it off John Smith, so in reality there would be possibly $10,000 deposited for the $1,000 that was actually working."

"I see," said Seabury, "just over and over again using the same $1,000?"

"That is it," said the witness.

"Can you get me the names of the persons from whom you borrowed the money?"

"I can't offhand, Judge. I had troubles enough."

"Have you any data or writing that will enable you to designate these persons?"

"As the money was paid, Judge," said McQuade with great sincerity, "it was off my mind and I thanked God for it and destroyed everything I might have."

When Seabury mentioned that the witness had made cash deposits in 1926 of some $94,000, McQuade again asserted that the sum came from money borrowed for the support of his family.

"I don't know whether I was understood or not, Judge," he said. "Chopped, divided by five, you would get really what I borrowed. . . . If I had time to sit down with you and this Committee from 1925 to date, there wouldn't be over $60,000 involved . . . other than borrowing off Peter to pay Paul, and so on."

"You were offered an opportunity to sit down with us," demurred Seabury, "and you declined it and insisted upon a public hearing, didn't you?"

"That was my misfortune," said McQuade.

"All right," said Seabury, "don't cry when you are getting it."

"You never heard *me* cry," said the witness, sitting upright in his chair. "With all my troubles, I never cried. My name is McQuade."

"That is what I understood it was."

"There are very few McQuades who do any crying," the witness insisted.

"Perhaps you got some of this money by reason of some alliance with professional gamblers?" Seabury suggested.

"Never in my life," replied McQuade.

On October 13, Peter J. McGuinness, the leader of Brooklyn's Fifteenth A.D., was summoned before Seabury. Now an assistant commissioner of public works, Pete made a breezy entrance before the committee. "Good morning, good morning," the bestower of the Benevolent Order of the Pork Chop called out to his hosts as he took the stand.

"I took the state committeemanship away from McQuade in 1924 in a leadership fight," McGuinness explained in response to a question.

"How did you succeed [in view of] all of his large family connections?" asked Seabury, referring to the thirty-three "starving" McQuades.

"Well, Judge," said McGuinness with a wide grin, "I don't think Mr. McQuade has anything on my family."

Queried by Seabury about the 1927 raid on his own clubhouse, Pete frankly admitted he had been called down to Brooklyn's Surrogate Court by Boss McCooey a few weeks before the break-in.

"Mr. McCooey took me in his office," McGuinness testified, his words leaving no doubt about the borough leader's authority. "He said, 'Pete, I want to tell you something. Inspector Valentine has been in here to see me and told me there is professional gambling going on in your club.' I said, 'Mr. McCooey, I don't think so. If that is going on in my club, it is going on without my consent.' 'Well,' he said, 'I want you to go down there and stop it.' I said, 'I will do just as you say, Mr. McCooey.'"

McGuinness told the committee that he had entered the clubhouse that very afternoon through a side door, sat himself down in a quiet corner, and observed the wagering. "They didn't even know I was in the room," he said, referring to the bettors, "until a man appeared at the door and said, 'I want to see Mr. McGuinness.' I said, 'Here I am,' and I jumped up.

"He said, 'Mr. McGuinness, would you be kind enough to give me a letter to the new Maspeth Union Gas tanks, so I can get a job?' I said, 'Come back tonight at 8 o'clock. The stenographer will be here then.'" Pete, who knew everybody in Greenpoint, realized the petitioner was a policeman. As soon as the stranger left, McGuiness testified, "I turned quick on my heels and said, 'Cheese it, here comes cops.' I said [to the members], 'Just take it easy going down them stairs. Just walk out nice and quiet.' They passed out of the building. I said, 'Don't stand in front of the door, go right on about your business.' Then I took the [gamblers] in the office. . . . I told them what Mr. McCooey said, and I said, 'If this thing goes on, you are going to be in a lot of trouble.'"

Though the professional gamblers professed they would mend their ways, the call of the odds was too strong. A few weeks later, with the wagering still going on, the police broke into the club and arrested some 150 members. McGuinness, who was not in the large room where the gambling was taking place but in his private office, was, as we have seen, taken off to jail. Although he was discharged the next morning by a sympathetic magistrate, Pete was greatly disturbed about the incident, and remained so years later.

"My club didn't get nothing, Judge," he testified before Seabury, meaning that he himself had not profited from the operation. "My club didn't get a penny."

Seabury apparently accepted at least this aspect of McGuinness' tale, for he congratulated him on his testimony and ended the interrogation. Wrote a New York *Times* reporter: "The witness was not questioned about his bank accounts, and Mr. Seabury said after the hearing that nothing suspicious was contained in them."

The next day, former police commissioners McLaughlin and Whalen appeared before the committee. Democratic Assemblyman Irwin Steingut of Brooklyn, one of the committee members, immediately asked McLaughlin if, during his fifteen months in office, he had received "the cooperation of the Mayor's office."

"If cooperation was noninterference," hedged the former commissioner, who had a genuine liking for Walker, "I got 100-percent cooperation. I never discussed professional gambling with the Mayor or any other official."

"You were never asked to lay off gambling?"

"Absolutely not."

Now Seabury took over the questioning. "Were you ever asked [by the Mayor] to lay *on* gambling?"

"Judge," said McLaughlin, "I want to be fair. I was never asked to emphasize any part of my police duties."

"You never discussed the gambling situation with the Mayor?"

"I never discussed gambling or anything else with the Mayor that had to do with the performance of my duties."

"Where professional gamblers continuously maintain their operation, they can be discovered by the police within a reasonable time, can they not?" asked Seabury, referring to the raids McLaughlin had ordered against the Democratic clubs.

"Yes."

"And they could not continue unless the police failed to suppress them?"

"That is right."

On the matter of Captain Valentine's Confidential Squad, McLaughlin was his usual forceful self.

"Was [the Squad] a good thing or was it an evil thing and a mistake?" Seabury asked him.

"I don't want to get into controversy with any successor . . . but from my experience the Confidential Squad strengthened the morale rather than demoralized it. You have got to bear in mind that there is no group of men so exposed to temptation [as] the members of the police department. . . . If it wasn't known you had an auditing force in a banking establishment, those entrusted with duties there might not resist temptation. . . . Now that is the kind of constructive Confidential Squad that I aimed at."

Called to the stand next, Grover Whalen—natty in a blue suit but without his customary gardenia—recounted his conversation with Walker on the day he agreed to accept the commissionership. "I never had a detailed discussion with the Mayor about conditions in the Department," he said. "His concern seemed to be entirely with the health of Commissioner Warren and his desire to have him take a holiday and rest. . . ."

"Commissioner, before you entered into the office did you have occasion to discuss with anyone the activities of Captain Valentine?" said Seabury.

"I talked to a man in whom I had great confidence and whom I later appointed to a high command in the Department [this was a reference to Mulrooney], and I came to the conclusion that if I were to have any measure of success in my administration it would depend upon restoring to the force a confidence in the Commissioner . . . and in his belief that the men of the force were honest." Accordingly, he abolished the Confidential Squad.

"Was it your purpose," Seabury asked, "to put Valentine and Keller where their views as to the gambling situation would not be effective?"

"Not at all," the witness replied, "Valentine and Keller meant nothing to me. I handled the situation impersonally."

For some months now, Seabury had been trying to locate and subpoena Russell T. Sherwood, who had shared a safe-deposit box

with Walker all during the mayoral years, had used what was in effect a joint checking account to pay Walker's bills, had established
a brokerage account for the mayor, and through whose hands had
passed since 1926 almost $1 million—of which $720,000 was in cash.
Assets so large, Seabury reasoned, required an explanation. The mild-
mannered, bespectacled Sherwood had gotten acquainted with Walker
while working as a $3,000-a-year accountant with Warren and Mc-
Intyre, the law firm with which the mayor had once been associated.
He began to help Walker with his finances and soon became indis-
pensable. "I haven't seen a checkbook of my own or a stub or can-
celled voucher in six years," the mayor later would admit. When
Sherwood was not making payments for the "yacht" Allie Walker
often rented on her vacations, he was paying the mayor's tailor, accepting blocks of stock, buying letters of credit. In one of his more
Byzantine moves, he opened a brokerage account in March of 1927
with a deposit of $100,000, which he admitted was not his money;
the account never was used for stock trading but simply to accumulate cash; when Sherwood closed it four and a half months later, he
withdrew some $263,000 in cash, which he presumably placed in the
safe-deposit box he shared with Walker. How the over-all $1 million
came to Sherwood-Walker is an intricate story, and one that will never
be fully documented. A "benefactor" like publisher Paul Block might
contribute $50,000 at a clip, while a salesman like William J. Scanlan,
who had just sold the city some street-sweepers, might donate $6,-
000 of his $10,000 commission. By July of 1930, the original safe-
deposit box, located in the vaults of the Chase Company at 115 Broadway, was deemed too small and a larger box was substituted. About
this time, Sherwood—helped by the mayor—secured a $10,000-a-year
job with the Manhattan Trust Company, which soon after hiring him
received substantial deposits from the city for safekeeping.

At Manhattan Trust, Sherwood—according to Frederick C. Harris,
the bank's secretary—proved a valuable, conscientious employee. In
August of 1931, however, when Seabury issued a subpoena for him,
the accountant failed to show up for work. Two days later, Harris
testified, Sherwood visited the bank briefly to claim some personal
property he had left there; the property consisted of two large pack-
ages—"contents unknown"—bound together with a strap. Toward the
end of August, the accountant, who was now hiding from Seabury
in Asbury Park, New Jersey, again conferred with Harris, who again
did not inform the committee of the wanted man's whereabouts. In
early October, the fugitive instructed Harris by letter from Chicago to go to the safe-deposit box he shared with Walker and open
it; naturally, the box was now empty. A week later, when Sherwood

was in Mexico City (where he had gotten married), the two men spoke by telephone. During this period, Harris—clearly the middleman between the accountant and the mayor—dropped in on Walker three times. The reason for the first talk, by the bank officer's testimony, was "to cultivate the acquaintance of the Mayor"; the second time, noticing a crowd in front of City Hall, he had decided to drop in and ask the mayor what the occasion was; the third time, reading in the paper that the mayor was ill, he had paid him a courtesy call at his apartment. Never, Harris claimed, had they discussed the missing man.

By the end of October, Seabury had seen to it that the forty-six-year-old Sherwood was served with a subpoena in Mexico City. When he ignored the order, he was found in contempt and fined $50,000; moreover, he lost his $10,000 bank job. Interviewed by reporters while boarding a St. Louis-bound train with his bride, Sherwood declared, "My stay in Mexico has been solely for the purpose of enjoying my honeymoon. You can bet your lives that Mayor Walker has not been keeping me in Mexico. I am not his employee nor have I ever been so. I am a friend of his."

For more than a year, until the Seabury investigation was long over, Sherwood would demonstrate that friendship by remaining incommunicado to the press through constant travel and the use of assumed names. Although he saw Walker off to Europe in September of 1932, and allegedly passed several hundred thousand dollars in cash to him, the accountant remained outside New York State's jurisdiction for the rest of his life. In 1933, he and his wife settled in East Orange, New Jersey, where—though unemployed—he managed to keep both a $200-a-month apartment and an expensive automobile. As the years went on, however, Sherwood's financial position became increasingly precarious. When a reporter managed to corner him to ask whether Walker hadn't left him "holding the bag," he replied candidly, "I'm afraid we'll have to let that inference stand." In 1954, he received a last financial setback when the New York Court of Appeals ruled that some $37,000 impounded for years in a Sherwood brokerage account should be forfeited to the state—to be applied towards the $50,000 fine still standing against him. Three years later, at the age of seventy-two, Walker's friend and accountant died of cancer.

None of the Seabury revelations about the Democratic machine had the slightest effect on how the city voted in the November, 1931 elections. Tammany Hall and its allies in the other boroughs won every contest for the judiciary and virtually every one for the state assembly and the board of aldermen (one Republican being elected to each body from Manhattan's Fifteenth A.D.—the "silk-stocking" district). Samuel Levy was elected Manhattan's borough president by the largest plurality yet amassed. In Brooklyn, even Registrar Mc-Quade was returned to office, bringing happy smiles to the wan faces of the "33 starving McQuades." Trumpeted Tammany Boss Curry: "It is evident that the electorate realizes that the Democratic party is the instrument to relieve them from economic distress and from Prohibition and its attendant evils." What the elections really showed, of course, was that the Republicans, never popular in the city even in prosperous times, were regarded in hard times with downright loathing.

Not at all discouraged, Seabury continued to press his case against the Walker administration. On November 17, after lengthy verbal sparring with builder Fred F. French, he established that the witness had in 1926 retained the law firm of George Olvany, then Tammany's leader, to seek a variance from the board of standards and appeals for a building at 551 Fifth Avenue. Though French had worked through James F. Donnelly, a partner of Olvany, the attorney ostensibly representing French's interests before the board was not Donnelly but a third party, one John N. Boyle. When the variance was forthcoming, the builder paid Boyle $30,000, and he in turn passed $25,000 on to Donnelly.

"When we were going over the plans," French began his testimony, "my designer informed me that there was a discrepancy in the building laws. Under one clause a certain floor space would be permitted, but under another clause 60,000 feet less of floor space would be permitted."

The builder then had called Donnelly. "I asked him if he had done such cases and he said, 'Yes, many of them,'" French recounted.

"Why did you retain Mr. Boyle after you had already retained Mr. Donnelly?" asked Seabury.

"I told Mr. Boyle that [he] would take charge for me as my representative, that he would pay Mr. Donnelly his fees, and that I would make directly to Mr. Boyle whatever I had to pay, and what is more our fee was to be paid only if we got a favorable decision."

At this juncture, Senator John J. McNaboe broke into the questioning to remark that such contingent fees were common practice. Mc-Naboe, like most of the Democratic members of the legislative committee, was a creature of Tammany; he and his colleagues had sought, all during the months of the inquiry, to harass Seabury and interfere with his development of testimony; when they got too raucous, they would be gaveled down by Republican Chairman Samuel H. Hofstadter, and because they were in the minority they would invariably lose the vote after calling for various points of order.

Senator Hofstadter declared that the issue was not one of contingent fees but whether the public interest was violated when such fees were offered to people who had ties to quasi-judicial bodies in exchange for results before those bodies.

"This great holy idea that is being expressed here is bunk," rejoined McNaboe. "New York City is getting wise to what this Committee is doing."

When Hofstadter rapped for order, McNaboe yelled, "Don't bang your gavel at me."

"Don't be impertinent to counsel," said Hofstadter.

Continuing the questioning, Seabury asked French if his retaining of Donnelly meant that "you made the selection which you thought would be most likely to assist you."

"Yes, sir," replied French. "But not, in my mind at least, because I thought he had influence."

"Did you consider that fact a disqualification in retaining the firm?" asked Seabury, as the spectators roared with laughter.

Now Assemblyman Louis A. Cuvillier, another Democratic member of the committee, interrupted the proceeding. "I think that is an improper question," he told Seabury.

"The objection is out of order," ruled Chairman Hofstadter. "This witness himself referred to the subject first."

French's dealings with the board of standards and appeals on the Fifth Avenue building (which became the headquarters for his extensive realty operations) were so congenial that he did not hesitate subsequently to hire Olvany's law firm to get him a variance, as we have noted, for the $100 million Tudor City project he was erecting at Forty-second Street and the East River. It seemed that the law at that time permitted two of the four apartment towers to be twenty stories high, but the remaining two only fourteen stories.

"So when you look at the buildings, you have an architectural monstrosity," French testified by way of stating his position. "I told Mr. Donnelly that I didn't think in our interests and in the interests of the residents of New York City this ought to be permitted." Besides, the witness added, the smaller apartment towers obviously would bring in fewer rentals, and "I did not want to throw away the stockholders' money."

Despite adverse reports from city engineers, this variance also had been granted. French thereupon paid $75,000 to Frederick J. Flynn, a lawyer hired by Donnelly to put French's case before the board—

both Olvany and Donnelly remaining very much in the background. The intermediary kept only $4,000, passing on the rest of the money to the firm.

On November 19, Seabury dropped another bombshell, revealing publicly for the first time that Olvany's firm, during the five years he had been Tammany's leader and for two years thereafter, had banked more than $5 million in legal fees. Most of the money, he charged, had been earned in practice before the board of standards and appeals. Called to the stand, the tall, athletic-looking Olvany, tanned from a recent Florida vacation, seemed quite fit, showing no trace of the ill health that had reportedly caused his precipitous departure from the Tammany leadership.

"Judge, there is practically no such thing as leader of Tammany Hall," he explained modestly. "The members of the executive committee of the Democratic party of New York County select one of its members to be in charge. Tammany Hall is simply a name."

"You and I couldn't have any difference between us that the leader of the party exercises great political power?"

"There is no argument about it."

"Let me give you a concrete case. Mr. Walsh [William E. Walsh—the former board chairman] was on the stand here a few days ago and he told us [that] you asked him on several occasions to call on you at Tammany Hall, and that you discussed with him certain cases which were pending before the board."

"That is true."

"You think that an effective way of calling the attention of the board to matters that ought to be changed was for the litigant to make his complaint to you?"

"No, except that [a litigant] would come to me and I would try to help him."

Although he conceded that much of his firm's work had been before the board, Olvany declined to give the committee a list of his fees, client by client, for the last seven years. "It would be absolutely an endless task." About the use of intermediaries like Boyle and Flynn to plead cases before the board, and about his firm's insistence on being paid in cash, Olvany said he knew nothing. His was a demeanor that could not be ruffled. Good Samaritans, he seemed to feel, had to expect criticism. He left the courtroom with his dignity—and his bank balance—intact.

On November 20, Walker once again fled New York and the damning headlines generated by the Seabury hearings. He announced he was going to California, at the request of the octogenarian mother of Thomas J. Mooney, a labor agitator who had served fifteen years of a life sentence in San Quentin, to ask the governor for executive clemency for her son. Mooney had been convicted of participating in a San Francisco bomb-throwing in 1916 that had cost ten lives; over the intervening years scores of organizations and individuals, suspecting that the witnesses against him had perjured themselves, had asked that he be pardoned. At a City Hall press conference earlier, Walker had started to read the telegram from Mooney's mother aloud, only to find his eyes filling with tears. "Read it for me," he said, passing the paper to a nearby reporter. "Dear Mr. Walker," the message went. "I am 83 years old. In the name of God and his Blessed Mother will you come out to help my boy? It is my last chance to put my arms around him before I meet my God."

Just before he left by train for the West Coast, Walker was asked by another reporter in Grand Central Station what he thought of the suggestion of one New York newspaper that while in California he might find it convenient to confer with Russell T. Sherwood, who was still traveling throughout the Far West. "Too foolish to call to notice," the mayor snapped. More to his liking was a leaflet he received from a Mooney supporter entitled "Is California Justice Still Alive?" Smiled Walker: "I sincerely hope it is."

Arriving in San Francisco, Walker (whose party included State Senator John Hastings of Equitable bus fame) met with California Governor James Rolph, Jr., and then drove to Mrs. Mooney's home. While sound-cameras whirred and Speed Graphics flashed, he sat down with the aged woman, who was inarticulate with emotion. "I want you to know," he said, "that there is hardly anyone in my city who does not feel that your case is theirs." Finally Mrs. Mooney, eyes glistening, threw her arms around the Mayor's shoulders.

For the next week, the mayor passed the time agreeably while waiting to present his formal case to Governor Rolph. He went to the theater ("The Silent Witness"—with Lionel Atwell), saw a Thanksgiving Day football game (St. Mary's vs. Oregon), and hobnobbed with San Francisco society. Then on December 1, introduced as "James J. Walker of the New York Bar" and severely attired in black morning dress, he spoke for two hours in a packed courtroom before the governor and his legal advisers. In a voice made hoarse by a bad cold, he assailed the character of the two men whose testimony had convicted Mooney, saying they were acknowledged perjurers. To back up this statement, he pointed out that Mooney's trial judge, ten surviving members of the jury, and the district attorney who prosecuted the labor organizer all shared this opinion and now felt that he was innocent of the bomb-throwing and the killings. "What could commend with greater force," he asked the governor, "a case to the pardon power of this state?" Walker next read into the record a letter Mooney had sent him in which the prisoner demanded a pardon as his due, saying he would rather die in jail than accept a mere parole. "Are they the words of a compromiser?" asked the mayor. "Are they the words of a coward? Such a coward as one would have to be to perpetrate that dastardly crime?"

Nonetheless, Walker was not successful in his mission; Mooney would not be pardoned until a later California governor granted him his freedom in 1939.

One of the most amusing stories involving Tammany district leaders and their affinity for hard cash was explored by Seabury in mid-December. Called before the legislative committee was Manhattan Deputy Chief Clerk James J. McCormick, a power in the Twenty-second A.D., who expressed amazement when he was informed that his bank deposits over the last seven years totaled $299,499. While carrying out his municipal duties, McCormick had specialized in performing civil marriages; it was he who, in 1926, had united Ellin Mackay and Irving Berlin in wedlock. Now he admitted, with great good humor, that after performing such ceremonies in his palm-tree decorated office he would accept gifts from thankful bridegrooms that came to some $18,000 yearly.

"They hand me once in a while a ten," he said, "but the fives is more prominent than the rest of them."

"How many twenties come in a day, on the average?" asked Seabury conversationally.

"You would be lucky to get one a week."

"Is it not your practice, Mr. Clerk, when you marry these parties, to open the drawers of your desk—and you have in plain sight of those who are there a $20 bill?"

"Oh, no," said McCormick.

"What right did you think you had to make money from citizens for performing the duty for which the city paid you $8,500 a year?"

"When I first took that position, I was telling some friends about people offering me money. One of them happened to be a lawyer. He said, 'That ain't unlawful, you can accept that.'"

"Thinking it might be graft, you took legal advice on the subject?"

"No," said the witness. "Just a couple of friends at the clubhouse one night. We got talking about it. . . ."

McCormick then complained that his tips from marriages had fallen off as a result of the Depression. "Nowadays, times is getting harder," he said.

"How much have they fallen down?" asked Seabury.

"About 50 percent. Only the colored people get married nowadays."

Before the hearings were adjourned for the Christmas and New Year's holidays, Seabury presented a far less comic case of corruption—one that touched, once again, on Walker himself. The committee counsel brought up the matter of the pier lease that had finally been granted to the North German Lloyd line after years of negotiation with the mayor's friend David Maier, and after the payment of $50,000 as a "legal fee" to a Tammany lawyer, William H. Hickin.

"You felt, did you not, that this was money that was being extorted from you or you would not get the lease?" Seabury asked Edgar W. Hunt, a Lloyd representative.

"I don't like to use such words," said Hunt, flushing.

"I know you don't."

"I advised my company to pay that money because I felt unless we paid it we could not get the lease."

"Now, which was it?" persisted Seabury. "Was it bribery or was it extortion?"

"Well, Judge," said Hunt, "I don't like to characterize it with either word."

Referring to the fact that $45,000 of the $50,000 fee had been converted into cash by Hickin and could not be traced further, Seabury asked whether it was Hunt's understanding that most of the fee was going to be passed on by Hickin to parties unknown.

"The rest was to go someplace else?"

"Exactly, but if you ask me where someplace else, I don't know, Judge."

"You never asked for any detailed explanation?"

"The only thing I was trying to do was get the price fixed as low as possible."

When Hickin, a powerfully built, well-dressed man with an impassive face, was called to the stand, he refused to sign a waiver of immunity, saying that the hearings provided "no representation by counsel and there are insinuations and innuendos that I don't like."

"I don't want to examine you," replied Seabury, discharging him. "I would rather stand on the record."

The last man to give testimony was sixty-one-year-old David Maier, slight and nervous, with grayish hair and mustache; as he answered Seabury's questions, his hands shook visibly. He admitted that he had told representatives of the Lloyd line he could get them a pier lease, but said he had acted for a "particular friend" with great influence in city politics.

"Who was that particular friend?" asked Seabury.

"I would rather that you didn't address me on that, because I would have to bring in a dead man," said Maier piously.

After a minimal prodding, Maier gave the name of his friend as William F. Grell, a German-American politician and former sheriff of New York County who had died a half-dozen years before. Grell's supposed efforts to help the Lloyd line, according to the witness, were triggered by his desire to improve German-American relations after World War I. It was Grell, said Maier, who had suggested hiring Hickin.

"After Hickin came in, your conferences with the gentlemen connected with the Lloyd line were simply as the messenger of Hickin?" said Seabury.

"If you want to put it that way," answered Maier.

"Aren't you deprecating yourself?" rejoined Seabury.

At City Hall that evening, Walker declined to comment on Maier's testimony; what happened to the $45,000 converted into cash by Hickin was never discovered.

1932

Cu Chulainn, anxious to end his fight with Ferdiad at the ford, finally called for a gae bulga, which he affixed to his leg so that it was concealed by the waters in which they fought. This weapon, which gave the wound of a single spear when it entered the body, had thirty barbs when it opened, and could not be drawn out without hacking the flesh all around. Cu Chulainn balanced the gae bulga upon his irresistible right foot, and when Ferdiad raised his shield to ward off a blow from above, Cu thrust the gae upward from below. It cut its way deep into Ferdiad's body, until his every joint and every limb were filled with its barbs.

"Ah, that blow suffices, I am fallen," gasped Ferdiad. "But yet it was unfair of thee to make me fall, not by your hand, but by your foot." And with that Ferdiad sank to the ground and died.

"Ah, Ferdiad," spoke Cu Chulainn, looking down on the fallen hero, "greatly have the men of Erin deceived and abandoned thee, to bring thee to contend and do battle with me!"

In January, the city learned from Seabury that "Tin-Box" Farley, sheriff of New York County, and Charles W. Culkin, his predecessor, had been keeping the interest on public and private funds left in their care and diverting it to their personal use. Culkin, the Greenwich Village district leader who had first sent Walker to the assembly twenty-two years before, was so embarrassed by the disclosure that he set about making plans for his retirement—naturally, on a pension —from his current $8,000-a-year job with the department of finance. During a committee recess on January 8, he was asked if, as rumor had it, he had already filed his retirement papers.

"Do you have to go digging in my private affairs? Haven't I enough on my mind already?"

When a reporter remarked that retiring from public life on a pension was hardly a private matter, Culkin only mumbled, "Go away and let me be."

During his four years as sheriff, from 1926 through 1929, Culkin had banked $25,544 in interest. Like many Tammany leaders, however, he was known to share what he had, or at least a part of it, with needy constituents. He kept a card file of the poorer people in his district and was widely regarded as a generous distributor of bounty, one who was "always good for a touch." By the standards of his cohorts, he had a strong sense of financial responsibility.

When "Tin-Box" Farley was called to the stand by Seabury, his attitude was far more belligerent than Culkin's. His only regret about skimming off the interest, he made it clear, was that he had not gotten all of it. He had learned only recently that his cashier—mistakenly, in the sheriff's view—had shared the interest between him and the various owners of the principal. Though he had banked about $400,000 over the last seven years, Farley was indignant that a few thousand dollars had escaped him.

"The first knowledge I had that there was any discussion about the interest was in the press last week," he told Seabury. "I then asked Mr. Connelly [his cashier], 'What have we been doing with the interest? Did we pay any of it out?' He said, 'We did.' I said, 'From now on, don't pay any out. That interest belongs to me.'"

When Seabury asked whether the sheriff contended he was entitled to the principal, as well as the interest, of any funds entrusted to him for safekeeping, Farley stared at him blankly.

"The witness does not understand what 'principal' means," declared Assemblyman Cuvillier, breaking the silence.

"He is sheriff," said Seabury. "He ought to know that much."

As the difference between "principal" and "interest" was explained to him, Farley leaned forward in his chair, his one inch of forehead between hairline and eyebrows furrowed in concentration. No, he finally allowed, making an ethical distinction, he did not feel he was entitled to "one penny" of the principal.

To the allegation that the sheriff had permitted professional gamblers to use his clubhouse, Seabury now added the charge that Farley had misappropriated some $15,000 in interest. On February 16, the case went to Governor Roosevelt in Albany. Before the hearing in the executive chamber began, Farley—a mammoth figure—circulated affably among the spectators, slapping backs and shaking hands. Then, under direct questioning by the governor, he not only emphatically denied that he had been in league with gamblers but continued to insist that he was entitled to the interest money. His attorney went even further, going back into English history to claim that the sheriff of a county, as the king's representative, had always had title to all money and property under dispute; Farley had acted with great restraint, he maintained, in not keeping the principal.

"That's a new one on me," said Roosevelt, whose Harvard education had not prepared him for such historical irrelevancies.

"Where is the statute that gives [Farley] the right?" demanded Seabury. "We don't have to go back to the common law and trace Farley's kingly powers. It is perfectly clear that the statute today precludes him from using interest. . . ."

When the hearing resumed the next day, Farley's attorney did most of the talking. Trying to explain how the sheriff had deposited hundreds of thousands of dollars in his bank account, he stressed his client's thrift. "He still occupies the same flat at 361 East Sixty-fifth Street in which he had lived for ten years, and before that he paid a rent of [only] $25 a month . . . and the fact is that Mrs. Farley has always insisted on doing the household work herself." Farley's myriad bank dealings, the attorney declared, should be viewed in a manner quite apart from the dealings of ordinary persons. "Don't forget," he told the governor, "that Sheriff Farley's life's work is being a political leader—and political leaders are called upon to handle [large] sums of cash. They are handing it out all the time to needy people. . . ."

By now Farley's confidence had largely disappeared. Asked by Roosevelt if he could be more specific about how his savings and his activities as a sort of neighborhood banker—endorsing notes, cashing checks, making loans to constituents—could have accounted for his bank deposits, the sheriff hung his head and said, "If I could, I would be only too glad. . . ."

A week later, Roosevelt, who was already running hard for the Democratic presidential nomination and certainly did not want to alienate the Tammany machine, made a difficult decision. In the most gentle manner possible, he removed Farley from office. "I do not believe," the governor said, "that a complete explanation has been made by the sheriff as to the total of the deposits. . . ."

In early March, the ex-sheriff would escape criminal punishment for his alleged misdeeds when he was acquitted of the charge of misappropriating $118.74 in official funds. Though he never again served in municipal office, "Tin-Box" Farley long remained a legend—and a source of envy—among Tammany stalwarts.

In early March, Charles S. Hand, who had been a member of the city's three-man sanitation commission since June of 1930, resigned his job, saying that he could no longer "tolerate the insistent and persistent illegal actions" of the commission's chairman, Dr. William Schroeder, Jr. Both men were close friends of Walker, of course, and the open rupture added to his troubles. Hand had been an outstanding political reporter for Pulitzer's *World* and later an $18,000-a-year editor for Hearst's *American;* outspoken and honest, he had been prevailed upon by the mayor in 1928 to become his $10,000-a-year secretary, a post he filled most capably. As the investigative clouds gathered, he had been eased out of that sensitive position by a Tammany that had more and more come to dominate Walker's appointments. The mayor had tried to make the transfer more palatable to Hand by moving him into a $17,500 sanitation commissionership. Dr. Schroeder, a Brooklyn surgeon with Tammany affiliations who had accompanied Walker on his most recent trip to Europe, was far more of an organization man; if Hand was tolerant of Tammany, Schroeder, who earlier in the administration had been commissioner of the patronage-ridden hospital department, could be termed intensely cooperative.

Hand, whose specific responsibility in the sanitation department was street cleaning, had first gone over Schroeder's head to Walker several months before, when he discovered that his chief—despite the adverse reports of city engineers—had approved the purchase of ten "dustless" sweepers at a cost of $105,000. The machines, it turned out, did not raise much dust, but they did not do much sweeping either. (In 1927, $6,000 of the commission from a similar purchase had found its way into the Walker-Sherwood bank accounts.) Though Hand's appeal had been fruitless, he had hung on. What now triggered his resignation was his inability to persuade Walker to countermand a recent order by Dr. Schroeder that took the sixty-one garages and myriad equipment of the street-cleaning unit (a $30 million responsibility) out from Hand's supervision. Schroeder had given the responsibility to a ten-dollar-a-day auto mechanic who reported directly to him—and who ostensibly would raise no objection about what equipment was purchased where, or for how much.

Loyal to Walker throughout, Hand declined to elaborate on

Schroeder's "illegal actions" with the press. "That is a matter I believe the Mayor should explain," he said. "He knows all about it."

While there was no public comment from the mayor on the resignation, Bernard Sachs, chairman of a civic committee concerned with the cleanliness of the streets, declared: "I regret very much Commissioner Hand felt himself forced to resign. There was no question but that he was hampered in his work. . . ."

Through the weeks that followed Hand's leavetaking, Tammany continued to ignore the revelations of corruption; as Governor Roosevelt defeated Al Smith in the New Hampshire presidential primary, the leaders—pausing only long enough to elect a new Grand Sachem to replace John Voorhis, who had died at the age of 102—actually let it be known they thought Walker would make a splendid vice presidential standard-bearer. Certainly the mayor retained New Yorkers' affections, if not their trust. Riding alone in an open car, he gaily led the annual St. Patrick's Day parade down Fifth Avenue while hundreds of thousands—helpless under his charm—lustily cheered their "Shamus." When Walker reached the reviewing stand he promptly doubled back along the line of march to Pennsylvania Station, while bands played "Will You Love Me in December as You Do in May?" —to catch a train for a brief holiday in Hot Springs, Virginia.

Yet Seabury continued to accelerate the legislative inquiry, and Walker, in the seldom-exposed sober recesses of his nature, knew he would soon have to answer some difficult questions. On April 26, the affairs of the Equitable Coach Company, in which the mayor had so interested himself in behalf of State Senator John A. Hastings during the first three years of his administration, began to receive a thorough airing. Calling Charles B. Rose, former vice president of Fageol Motors—a Kent, Ohio, bus manufacturer—to the stand, Seabury established that Rose, Frank R. Fageol, the company's president, and William O'Neil, president of General Tire and Rubber of Akron, Ohio, had been the triumvirate behind the Equitable. The three men had initially put up $120,000 to finance the venture; after gaining the bus franchise for the Equitable, they hoped to supply it with hundreds of buses and thousands of tires yearly—all at a substantial profit. Even while Walker was running for the mayoralty in 1925 and the Equitable was in its "embryonic stage," Rose testified, Senator Hastings had been "in contact with the Mayor."

"Have you any doubt that Hastings' contact continued after Mayor Walker took office?" asked Seabury.

"No," Rose replied.

In testimony a few days later, Seabury elicited from Rose the information that Hastings, without putting up a cent, was to receive one-third of the common stock in the Equitable—a holding equal to that of the bankers who would supposedly finance the company. So important did Rose, Fageol, and O'Neil believe Hastings' influence with "political agencies" to be that the triumvirate (together with J. Allan Smith, Fageol's New York representative) felt they had to be content with the remaining one-third of the stock, even though they had been forced to increase their original $120,000 investment to $280,000. It was estimated by management consultants that the 210,000 common shares of the Equitable would return some $600,000 a year in dividends alone; this meant that Hastings' dividend windfall would have been $200,000 a year, or $2 million over a ten-year period. At the end of that time, his stock would have been worth at least an additional $4,380,000.

Rose, whose recollection of the details of the Equitable matter was abnormally weak, recovered his memory only after Seabury produced documents or asked questions that required cut-and-dried answers. He remembered, for instance, that two days after Walker had pushed the Equitable franchise through the board of estimate in late July of 1927 he had seen his associate O'Neil off to Europe.

"Who else did you see in the stateroom?" said Seabury.

"There were a great many people there," replied Rose.

"Was the Mayor of the City there?" asked Seabury.

"Yes, sir," admitted Rose, to the accompaniment of spectator laughter and the banging of Chairman Hofstadter's gavel.

On May 3, when Seabury called Frank Fageol to the stand, the bus manufacturer (who like most witnesses had refused to sign a waiver of immunity) pooh-poohed the whole idea that the Equitable had sought political influence. Hastings was retained, Fageol said, because he was "an expert on transportation matters."

"You never understood that he had any influence here in New York?"

"What would that have to do with getting the franchise?" asked Fageol innocently.

According to Fageol, what had kept the Equitable, after receiving the franchise, from raising the $20 million necessary to put its buses on the streets of Manhattan, Brooklyn, and Queens was the death of Anson W. Burchard of General Electric. Nobody else could be found to put money into the Equitable, and in early 1929 the transit commission had been forced to declare the franchise nonoperative. Fageol and his associates lost their $280,000, and the only winner, at least in a limited way, had been Hastings. From September of 1925 until the end of 1928 he had drawn, in salary and unpaid "loans," some $60,-

ooo from Fageol Motors and General Tire and Rubber; this was exclusive of his "expenses," which used up the larger portion of the remaining money.

Controller Charles W. Berry, who testified before the committee on May 4, charged bluntly that Walker's insistence on awarding the bus franchise to the Equitable had split the city's Democrats. Conciliatory meetings had to be arranged that were attended by all the Democratic county leaders, together with the members of the Board of Estimate. As we have seen, twelve of the board's sixteen votes were required for the franchise's passage. According to Berry, the mayor (three votes) first gained the support of Richmond (one vote) and the Bronx's McKee and its borough president (four votes) by allowing those boroughs separate bus lines. Then he bought Manhattan's co-operation (two votes) by agreeing that the Equitable's line in that borough would only run crosstown. Finally, still two votes shy of the needed twelve, Walker came to an understanding with Brooklyn (two votes) through a combination of harsh words and soft promises—some $150 million in new subways.

"On the day [of the voting]," testified Berry, "I don't think any-body knew that the vote was going to be taken. I was present at the Board's morning session and attended another meeting that after-noon, and [Deputy Controller Frank J.] Prial sat for me. It had all been settled that [the Bronx] was to get theirs and [Richmond] was to get theirs. I told Prial I did not think I could go along. A few minutes later, Brooklyn President [James] Byrne came to me and said, 'I have changed my mind about my vote.' 'Well,' I said, 'that is your privilege.' "

"You believed the franchise as contemplated was not in the interest of the city?"

"I didn't think it was," said the witness.

Seabury next called William H. Woodin, president of the Ameri-can Car and Foundry Corporation, and Charles E. Mitchell, head of the National City Bank—both of whom had been approached by Walker for Equitable financing, before and after the granting of the franchise. Woodin declared he had considered Hastings "the repre-sentative of the Mayor" and had assigned Charles Hardy, his general counsel, to get from the senator the details of the Equitable's opera-tion.

"Practically nothing was furnished me by Hastings at all," Hardy told Seabury when his turn came to testify. Yet the "ugly rumors" about the bus company's political machinations were so persistent, Hardy continued, that he felt compelled to go to then Tammany Boss Olvany, whose name was being thrown about by Hastings, and advise him that the senator's "loose talking . . . might land someone in the grand jury room." Olvany, the witness said, had observed that his name was not the only one being mentioned, and that there was "safety in numbers." Subsequently, on Hardy's advice, Woodin had kept American Car and Foundry out of the financing.

In early 1928, with General Electric not honoring Anson Burchard's commitment, and men like Woodin refusing to step into the Equitable picture, Walker invited National City's Charles Mitchell to come to City Hall.

"He asked if I would study the situation with the idea of our company doing some public financing for the Equitable," testified Mitchell, "or to go before the public and ask for subscriptions."

After his bank's experts had examined the Equitable and had found it a poor credit risk, Mitchell continued, he had sent Walker a letter to that effect.

All these damning statements proved irritating to Senator Hastings, who on May 10 came uninvited to the committee hearings while Seabury was re-examining Frank Fageol and proceeded, by audibly repeating Seabury's questions and jeering at Fagoel's reluctant replies, to force a recess. The senator thereupon approached Seabury and demanded that he be called as a witness that very day. When the chief counsel replied that he would have to wait several days to testify, the thirty-two-year-old Hastings became enraged, grabbing Seabury by his coat lapels and shaking his fist before the white-haired counsel's pince-nez. "You coward, you political blackmailer!" he screamed. "You're afraid to call me on the stand!" Seabury called for the sergeant-at-arms, pointed at the senator with distaste, and said, "Throw him out!" A policeman came from the back of the room and, with club upraised, seized the bellowing Hastings and pushed him into an anteroom. "No cop will take me anywhere!" the senator shouted as he was propelled through the doorway. "I do not propose to stand idly by," he said later in defense of his conduct, "and have myself daily maligned."

Hastings would not be called to the witness stand for ten days, and Seabury during the interval continued to elicit evidence of how both he and Walker had engaged in questionable financial activities. In one instance, where two large taxi fleets had each sought to gain influence at City Hall, the two men had, in a sense, played one company against the other.

J. A. Sisto, who had a substantial financial interest in the Parmalee Transportation Company, owners of Yellow Taxi, first met Walker in June of 1929. He was introduced to him by John J. McKeon, a

long-time Walker friend and a former associate of the late Jules Mastbaum, the wealthy motion-picture exhibitor who had been the mayor's
earliest "benefactor." According to the slim, impeccably dressed Sisto,
a financier who at the time had just underwritten some Cosden Oil
securities, he talked with Walker in the midst of a convention at the
Ritz-Carlton Hotel in Atlantic City, New Jersey. Several other men
were present in the suite, and one of them idly asked Sisto "if I
didn't think it would be a good thing for Mayor Walker to own some"
—meaning some of the oil stock. So taken was the Parmalee backer
with the idea of largesse that, upon his return to New York, he bought
an additional 1,000 shares of the Cosden Oil securities, with the "mental reservation" that a portion of any profits that accrued would go to
Walker. Buying the stock in the name of a relative who lived in British Guiana, Sisto held onto the shares a few months, then sold out at
the beginning of the 1929 crash for a profit of some $85,000. He now
wanted to honor his mental pledge to the mayor, Sisto testified, but did
not know how to proceed. What complicated this innocent situation
further was the fact that Sisto, in the falling market, was short of cash.
Would Walker be insulted, he asked McKeon, by the gift of some
"good, sound bonds"? Sisto was assured the mayor was an understanding man. He thereupon selected $26,535 worth of bonds, placed
them in an envelope, and gave them to McKeon, who hurried off to
City Hall. The mayor's friend said nothing to Walker of the gift until
the two of them were riding uptown in the official limousine, when he
took the sealed envelope out of his pocket and handed it to Walker,
who placed it in his own pocket.

Testifying before Seabury, Sisto stated that when the mayor later
thanked him for the bonds, he had urged Walker to consider a board
of taxicab control. Such a supervisory city agency, he had told the
mayor, would protect big taxi fleets like Parmalee from independents
and safeguard the "large investments" of the established companies.
Walker had been properly responsive, and, indeed, a suitable control
bill had eventually passed the municipal assembly.

"Can you recall," said Seabury, "whether your conversation with
the Mayor was before he had appointed a commission to study the
taxicab situation?"

"No, I cannot," replied Sisto.

On the same day, Seabury revealed that the Terminal Cab Company, a rival of the Parmalee firm, had put Senator Hastings on its
payroll in October of 1930, at a salary of $18,000 a year, "for his
technical knowledge and his political acquaintanceship." B. M. Seymour, vice president and general manager of the Terminal, testified
that when his company had started operations in New York he had

found the Parmalee "strongly entrenched politically," and as a stranger who did not know his "way about," he turned instinctively to Hastings.

"Did your company have any written agreement with Senator Hastings?" asked Seabury.

"There is no written agreement," responded Seymour.

"Was it Senator Hastings' custom to appear regularly at the office of your corporation?"

"Sometimes we saw each other two or three times a day, and again not for several days."

"Did he have any regular order whereby he would come to the office at 9 and stay until 4 or 5?"

"He decidedly was not a clock puncher," admitted Seymour.

Even as Seabury and Walker were coming closer to their inevitable confrontation, the mayor in mid-May led a noon-to-midnight parade of New Yorkers demanding the legalization of beer. The theme was "Beer for Taxation," and several hundred thousand thirsty fiscal experts—a tenth of them marching and the rest cheering—advocated the repeal of Prohibition as a way to balance the budget, curb unemployment, and encourage investment. In morning coat and striped trousers and carrying a derby, Walker swung down Fifth Avenue from Seventy-ninth Street to continuous bursts of applause. Behind him, dozens of bands blared lively tunes, especially the "Maine Stein Song" and "How Dry I Am." A group of capitalists marched under the banner "Leaders of Industry"—three of them walking (Walter Chrysler, E. F. Hutton, James Moffat) and the rest in hansom cabs. The Lambs Club and the Friars were there, as were the National Vaudeville Artists. Formidable in beards and judicial robes, the actors who played supreme court justices in the long-running musical comedy "Of Thee I Sing" gave the parade their approval, while Walker's actor friends William Gaxton and Victor Moore (who played the president and vice president in the political spoof) waved happily and the girls in the chorus blew kisses from automobiles. Ordinary citizens, many of them carrying the tin pails used to bring beer home from saloons, joined in the fun. Walker led the march across Central Park South and then up Central Park West to Seventy-second Street. Back of him were political notables like John F. Curry and John H. McCooey, a baby in arms with a sign reading "My Daddy Had Beer, Why Can't I?" and various ethnic groups in peasant costumes. With the "day" parade still unfinished, the mayor—returning to the East Side—led the "night" parade down Fifth Avenue. By eight that evening, when he rushed off to attend a dinner of the Anvil Chorus, a Brooklyn newspapermen's club, Walker had worn a hole in the brim of his derby by constantly waving it at admirers.

On the committee front, Seabury next called William J. Scanlan, a salesman of street sweepers, snow loaders, voting machines, and garbage carts, who was so chummy with the mayor that he took his phone calls at City Hall. It was Scanlan who had received a $10,000 commission for selling ten "dustless" sweepers to the city in 1927; two weeks later, his own check for $6,000 somehow found its way into the bank account that Russell T. Sherwood used to pay Walker's bills. In testimony before the committee, Scanlan could not recall why the check was drawn or in whose name, and he asserted that he had recently destroyed all his financial records in a backyard bonfire.

"Anyone else present?" said Seabury.

"I guess my wife and boys might have seen the conflagration."

"No special ceremony?"

"Oh, no," answered Scanlan.

Bringing up the matter of the $6,000 check, Seabury sought to jog the witness's memory.

"After you had drawn the check, where did you deposit it, or to whom did you give it?"

"I assume I must have made it out to cash right at the bank."

"Why do you assume that?"

"If I draw a check as large as that," said Scanlon, "I generally took care of my family. I took care of my mother, my widowed sister and my wife. I am always in debt, and as soon as I get a big check I don't have it twenty-four hours, sometimes, before it is all cashed out.'

"But you see, Mr. Scanlan, this big amount you drew out in one check."

"I am trying to refresh my memory. . . ."

It also developed that Scanlan had, in 1930, divided his commission for some covered wagons with the mayor's brother, Dr. William H. Walker, to whom he gave a total of $2,828. Scanlan contended that Dr. Walker was his physician and that the payments were for medical services.

"The amount you owed him at the time was approximately one-half of your commission?"

"Approximately."

"Is this book that I show you your checkbook? . . . One that survived the fire?"

"Correct."

"I call your attention to stub #842, made to the order of W. H. Walker . . . you notice it says, 'Balance—27 fight tickets?' "

"Yes."

"Did you know that it was never paid for fight tickets at all, but that it was paid as a split in the commission you got on the covered-wagon transaction?"

"It was not."

"Don't you observe that something [on the stub] had been erased? . . . So that at first when you drew this check you had written 'cov. wag.'—indicating covered wagon?"

"Yes."

"Then when you got a subpoena to bring your check books down, you erased the words 'cov. wag.' [and wrote in 'fight tickets']?"

"I don't recall when I did it."

On May 20, Seabury showed to the public that J. Allan Smith, the Equitable's New York representative, had paid with cash for a $10,000 letter of credit that Mayor Walker had used on his 1927 trip to Europe, and that the mayor had been given this letter on August 9, the day before he officially signed the Equitable's bus-franchise contract and sailed on his vacation. The witness Seabury used to tell this incriminating story was, ironically, Senator Hastings, who finally got his chance to testify. The gist of his explanation, as we have seen, was that Smith, to enhance his prestige with Arthur Loasby, then president of the Equitable Trust Company (which had no connection with Equitable Coach), had asked Hastings if he could use the money the mayor and his party had pooled for their vacation to buy a letter of credit from the bank. Hastings had prevailed upon Senator Downing, who was handling the details of the trip, to be cooperative. Smith got the money, bought the letter, and that was that—except that Senator Downing could not corroborate Hastings' story.

"Senator Downing isn't living now, is he?" asked Seabury of the witness.

"You are not suggesting, by indirection, I had anything to do with his death, are you?" demanded Hastings.

"No, no, there was no such suggestion. . . . Who else was present when you got the $10,000 from Senator Downing?"

"Nobody else."

"Did you give any receipt to Senator Downing for the $10,000 that he paid you?"

"I don't know, I may have."

"Have you ever made any effort to find that receipt?"

"I looked for my papers when I came back from California [where he had gone with Walker while the latter was pleading for Tom Mooney's release], and I found that my office had been ransacked. . . . I think the receipt is among my papers that you seized."

"Well, you are mistaken in that," said Seabury mildly.

By the time Walker and his party reached Paris in September of 1927, they had used up the original $10,000 credit, and the mayor put through an additional $3,000 draft against the Equitable Trust Company. During the fall, Arthur Loasby asked repeatedly that his bank be reimbursed for the overdraft, directing his pleas, not to Walker, but to the Equitable's Smith. "Dear Allan," he finally wrote in January of 1928, "That $3,000 matter has never been taken care of. Can't you do something about it?" Shortly afterward, Smith sent Loasby a check for $3,047.50, covering the overdraft plus interest.

Testifying before the committee, Hastings maintained that Senator Downing had made up the overdraft in cash and given it to him piecemeal, and that he had passed the sums on to Smith, who had amassed the full amount and then—still intent on prestige—sent his check on to Loasby.

"And were all these payments made [by Senator Downing] in his office in the Capitol?" Seabury asked.

"No, I met him one time either at Luchow's or at Billy the Oyster Man's, and he gave me some money there one evening to give to Mr. Smith," asserted Hastings.

"Anyone else present?"

"I don't remember."

"When you got the money from Senator Downing, did you deposit it in the bank?"

"Certainly not, I gave it to Mr. Smith."

"And where did you keep it before you delivered it?"

"In my pocket," said Hastings defiantly.

So the interrogation proceeded, while on the streets outside the hearing room newsboys hawked papers with the screaming headline: "Walker Got $10,000 from Bus Backer." To the average New Yorker, however, the mayor's personal guilt was still not evident. Perhaps some Tammany leaders took money, perhaps his friends did, but certainly not Jimmy. He would explain everything, most people felt, when he finally appeared before Seabury.

≈≈≈

As matters now stood, there were at least three incriminating charges against Walker: one, that with the aid of a mysterious brokerage account, myriad bank deposits and checks, and a joint safe-deposit box, he had used Russell T. Sherwood, a modestly paid accountant, to amass some $1 million since 1926; two, that he had conspired with Senator Hastings, who might have made millions of dollars out of the deal, to push the Equitable bus franchise through the board of estimate; and three, that he had pocketed some $26,500 in bonds from taxi entrepreneur J. A. Sisto, sent in a sealed envelope via an intermediary, at a time when Sisto was seeking his cooperation in setting up a taxi control board that would protect his investment.

On May 25, the day the mayor was called to testify before Seabury (he had been served with a subpoena only twenty-four hours before), thousands of New Yorkers thronged the Manhattan County Courthouse, and some 700 of them managed to squeeze their way into a hearing room that ordinarily seated half that number. Representatives of the Committee of One Thousand, the League of Women Voters, and various other civic organizations sat in judgment, while such friends of the mayor as theater magnate A. C. Blumenthal, attorney Dudley Field Malone, and labor leader Joseph R. Ryan rallied to his side. Four women with Park Avenue addresses confessed that they were so afraid of losing their places that they had brought their lunches. The spokesman for a group of burly gentlemen from Chicago declared they had journeyed to Gotham "to help Jimmy out." Society's bluebloods fought their way into the proceedings along with Tammany's Irish, and each faction, in the words of a contemporary journalist, emerged "with a new respect for each other's elbows . . . they had met where the race went to the strong, in the narrow doorway [to the chamber]. . . ."

Chairman Hofstadter entered the courthouse unnoticed, and even Seabury elicited no more than polite applause, but the mayor's arrival, both outside the building and in the hearing room, touched off the crowd's deepest feelings. Cries of "Good luck, Jimmy," "Atta Boy," and "You tell him, Jimmy," greeted the smiling Walker, encouraging him to clasp his hands over his head in the manner of a prize fighter entering the ring. Even after the proceedings began, and Walker had signed a waiver of immunity, the chairman found it most difficult to keep order.

Seabury's first line of questioning focused on the mayor's advocacy of the Equitable bus franchise despite seemingly better contractual offers from several competitors—including one called the Service Bus Company.

"Do you recall that with the application of Service Bus there was a flat five-cent fare with no zoning regulation?" began the chief counsel, comparing this to the Equitable's plans for some ten- and fifteen-cent fares.

"I cannot remember the details of [all] the applications," replied Walker.

"You are not prepared to say, are you, that the application of the Equitable, so far as rate of fare was concerned, was superior to Service Bus?"

"I wouldn't attempt to say in any one feature which franchise was the better," hedged the mayor.

Given this opening, Seabury proceeded to compare the prospective operation of the two companies in one feature after another—with the Equitable invariably emerging a poor second.

"Now, you remember the number of buses included in the Equitable franchise was some 853 against 1,103 for Service Bus?"

"I don't remember it because it wouldn't make a bit of difference," the mayor fenced. "The Board of Estimate [might] approve of any contract that would have, say, a minumum of 1,000 buses. If a company had 5,000, it would probably keep 4,000 in a garage," he added, drawing appreciative laughter.

"The time of commencement of operations is also [important], is it not?"

"Yes, I think so."

"I call your attention to the fact that, as far as the Equitable was concerned, 50 buses per month were stated to be possible following the making of the grant, while with the Service Company 150 buses per month were promised."

"That is a matter of [promises]. Why, the best offer, according to that theory, that the city ever had for bus operation came from a company located on Long Island, and upon investigation it turned out they were in the hay and feed business."

"That brings us to another question. . . . Didn't Service Bus accompany its petition with a certified check for $100,000?"

"Even if they did, $100,000 would not be sufficient to capitalize and maintain—"

"It would be superior to nothing, wouldn't it, Mr. Mayor?"

"Well, a $100,000 check for one man to fulfill a contract might not be as good as J. Pierpont Morgan's mere promise to fulfill."

"But the Equitable didn't have J. P. Morgan's promise, did it?"

"We both know *that*," acknowledged Walker, causing another ripple of laughter.

"The question I am interested in is why, as Mayor of this city, you urged the passage of the Equitable bus franchise."

"Mr. Chairman," said Walker, turning from Seabury and addressing Hofstadter, "I don't believe that your counsel or you have any legal right to inquire into the operations of an Executive's mind or cross-examine him about how he reaches his conclusions. . . . But notwithstanding that, let me tell you why. . . ."

"I will be most happy to have you do so," said Seabury.

"Upon the recommendation of the Board of Transporation—based upon their analysis—[the Equitable] was the best independent company, because it not only offered the initial five-cent fare but something that I had advocated—namely, new blood into the traction interests of this City."

"Do you remember Mr. Delaney [the board of transportation chairman] said that financial responsibility was essential? You agreed with that?"

"Of course I did."

"Did you rely upon the belief that the Equitable would win the support of [General Electric's] Anson W. Burchard?"

"I think someplace you will find in the newspaper files a statement by Mr. Burchard that he was interested."

"Are you not in error, Mr. Mayor, and was not the statement that was published a statement that *you* made in March 1929, when you said the Equitable backer had been Anson W. Burchard?"

"That's not correct."

"Do you remember on March 4, 1929, áfter the matter of the Equitable came back to the Board, making this statement: 'The Board understood that the General Electric Compány was behind [the financing]'?"

"I don't remember what I said at a meeting two years ago."

"When the franchise was granted," continued Seabury, "you knew, did you not, that the only hope the Equitable had to secure financing was that it might sell stock against the franchise?"

"You are testifying and asking me whether I like the testimony," retorted the mayor. "Is this an inquiry or is it a persecution of me? If it is [an inquiry], give me another forum where I will be even with counsel, and then I will make it a personal competition. . . ."

Going on to Hastings' part in the affair, Seabury asked: "Do you know whether an effort was made to ascertain whether Senator Hastings had any stock interest in Equitable Coach?"

"I do not."

Moreover, the mayor asserted, though his friend had often discussed the company's franchise plans with him, he "knew better" than to request favored treatment.

"Well, did you not ask Senator Hastings to appear before Deputy Controller Prial to disclose any interest that he had?"

"There constantly appeared at the Board of Estimate agents of the traction companies, political hopefuls, disappointed politicians," the mayor began. "It was by one of these men that the statement was made that there was a six-hundred-and-some-odd-thousand-dollar slush fund . . . I stopped the meeting [and] made the motion that the matter be repaired to the Controller for a thorough investigation . . . he was given a free hand to make an investigation in his own way."

"Don't you know, Mr. Mayor, that the witnesses went away—Fageol and the others—and that he had no power of subpoena?" asked Seabury.

"I didn't know that . . . I have no recollection of it, in any event."

Here Hofstadter interrupted: "I think it might properly be said that our record indicates that some of these men—Fageol, Rose, perhaps Smith—did testify before the Controller but then refused to come back."

"But they didn't run away," said Walker.

"How do you know they didn't?" demanded Seabury.

"You made a misstatement on the record in a serious matter, and I am calling attention to it," Walker said, fastening on the counsel's minor error.

"Apparently you are making a speech, Mr. Mayor," retorted Seabury.

"Well, they're not so bad. Did you ever listen to one of them?" gibed Walker, while the audience laughed again.

After the luncheon recess, Seabury brought up the mayor's $10,-000 letter of credit.

"Now you know that the ledger card of the bank shows that the letter was obtained by [the Equitable's] J. Allan Smith." said the chief counsel.

"I know it now, I didn't know it at the time," said Walker. "I know it because I have read it in the papers."

"Did you supply any of the funds that were used in obtaining that letter of credit?"

"I did."

"How much?"

"Three thousand dollars [in cash] . . . it was left for Senator Downing by me in the Mayor's office."

"Did you get a receipt from Senator Downing?"

"I did not. I did not ask for one. We weren't that kind of friends."

"Who else did you understand contributed to the letter?"

"Commissioner [William] McCormack, Senator Downing, and I am quite sure Hector Fuller," said the mayor, referring to his traveling companions. "[Fuller] can tell you more about that."

"Senator Downing is dead, isn't he?"

"With great regret to me."

"And Mr. McCormack is also dead?"

"I hope counsel is not going to leave this record with what might be called an inference because these two men are dead. If there is any lack of honesty in my statement, Mr. Fuller is alive, Mrs. Walker is alive. . . ."

"Did Hastings tell you why he was [urging] the letter of credit?"

"He didn't."

"Did he tell you he wanted to increase the prestige of J. Allan Smith?"

"I never heard Smith's name mentioned in connection with it. It was Senator Downing who told me Senator Hastings had asked him, if we were carrying any letters of credit, to let him get them for the prestige that would [accrue] to some friend of his."

"What did Senator Hastings have to do with arranging for the payment of the overdraft?"

"I don't know."

Seabury's next line of questioning, before the day's session ended, was a distinct surprise. It concerned Walker's relationship with publisher Paul Block, a "benefactor" who had given the mayor some $246,692, from which Block had dutifully deducted income-tax payments, between February of 1927 and August of 1929—at a time when the publisher had a substantial interest in a company hopeful of selling tiles to city subway contractors. The money, Walker testified, represented his share of the profits from a joint brokerage account in which Block had done all the investing.

"Did you agree to stand any loss that might arise in the course of trading?"

"I was ready to."

"Was there any understanding that you should?"

"The subject was never discussed."

"What was the method [of withdrawals] that developed?"

"By Mr. Block's determination. When he drew any money from the account he drew a similar amount for me. On a couple of occasions, upon his inquiring whether I needed any money, he drew the amount if the reply was in the affirmative and drew a similar amount for himself—so he told me—to keep the account even."

In 1927, it developed, the mayor had realized $102,500 from the brokerage account; in 1928, $94,165; in 1929, only $50,027.

"Now, what did you do with the cash, Mr. Mayor?"

"Took it home and put it in a safe. Not a vault, not a tin box—a safe in my house."

"Did you deposit [any money] in a bank?"

"None of that money from the Block account was deposited in a bank, but was kept in my home available for Mrs. Walker and myself. . . . These monies were all tax paid, and I never deposited them

in a bank where they might be confused with monies that were not
tax paid."

"[Of the] $102,000 which you received within five months in
1927, can you give the Committee some idea of the disposition that
you made of it?"

"No, I cannot. . . . Where I got the money I am willing to tell
you, but where I spent it, that seems to me to be going just a
little too far."

Interrupted Tammany Senator McNaboe, referring to how Walker
had spent the money: "That is of no interest to us."

"Will the witness speak, please?" ruled Hofstadter.

"It is none of our business what he did with the money!" shouted
McNaboe.

"You must abide by my rulings," declared Hofstadter, whose patience had been monumental in the face of continual interruptions
from Democratic committee members McNaboe, Cuvillier, and Steingut. Walker's determination not to discuss how the money had been
spent became understandable when Seabury brought up a $7,500
check that Walker had uncharacteristically drawn on the Block account in 1929 and then turned over to Betty Compton—although
Seabury did not mention Betty by name.

Developing this point, Seabury asked: "Would you be good
enough to look at these papers and tell me if they represent a letter
of credit and increases that were authorized by you?"

"They were not authorized by me."

"They are payments, however, to the same person to whom the
$7,500 was paid from the Block account which you authorized?"

"Evidently."

"Do you know whether the letters of credit referred to were arranged by Russell T. Sherwood?"

"I don't know," said the mayor, who still maintained that Sherwood
was not, strictly speaking, his agent.

"I call your attention to these [five] certificates. I ask you whether
they are inscribed in the name of Russell T. Sherwood for 100 shares
each?"

"They are."

"I ask you whether these certificates [also] were endorsed to the
person to whom the proceeds of the $7,500 check was paid?"

"They are endorsed to the same name."

"Mr. Mayor, were these transactions carried out through your
authority given to Russell T. Sherwood?"

"The answer is no," said Walker.

Shortly thereafter, with Betty Compton's anonymity—as the "unnamed person" to whom the mayor had been so generous—still protected, the hearing adjourned.

Smiling, affable, and seemingly untouched by Seabury's barbs, Walker unhurriedly made his way through the applauding crowd to his waiting limousine. That night he lashed back at his "critics" before an enthusiastic audience of 18,000 persons gathered at Madison Square Garden for the Police College graduation exercises. Even before he spoke, while he was inspecting the police class, it was obvious that his personal popularity had not suffered. "As he marched, the wave of applause rolled up behind him, higher and higher," a reporter wrote, "to be climaxed with the stamping of feet, hysterical whistling and the shrill cries of women." Face flushed and eyes sparkling, Walker finally took his place on the speaker's dais. There he declared that the Seabury investigations of the magistrates' courts, District Attorney Crain, and his administration had, by eroding police morale, all but turned New York into a lawless city. "Criticism based on individual ambition, criticism arising out of political jealousy, criticism emanating from vindictiveness," he said, "have brought back to the streets of New York something that had not existed for the past 20 years." The specious charge elicited another wave of thunderous applause.

On May 26, when the mayor returned to the courthouse for his second and final day of testimony, Seabury again brought up the Block "beneficence."

"Would you be good enough to state the reason for Mr. Block's donation to you?"

". . . Mr. Block for several years had manifested a very generous friendship for me. It is not an unusual thing. Mr. Block's life has been characterized by generosity."

"Now, among the papers that you have produced, there are no check-stub books or canceled vouchers for any period prior to November 1930, are there?"

"I never kept them myself. I haven't seen a checkbook of my own or a stub or canceled voucher in six years."

Seabury next focused the inquiry on Walker's dealings with J. A. Sisto, who had testified he had been brought together with the mayor by John McKeon.

"I met Mr. Sisto in Atlantic City for the first time in the summer, and it probably was 1929," said Walker, "upon the occasion of the convention of the Paramount-Famous Players Company, where I addressed the banquet. It was after the dinner that we adjourned to some quarters, where there was a broadcast to Admiral Byrd in Little America, and where there were gathered all the executives of Famous Players. That is my recollection of where I first met Mr. Sisto."

"Do you recall in that meeting at Atlantic City anyone making reference to Sisto being interested in Cosden Oil and suggesting you be called in on the transaction?"

"There was reference to the fact that there was a pool in Cosden Oil, and I was invited to participate, and I said I would."

"To what extent?"

"To the extent, when I was told the pool was closed, of $26,000."

"Did you put up any money?"

"No, I didn't."

"Was there any written commitment from you that in the event of a loss you would pay your share?"

"There wasn't, and I don't understand that that is the practice amongst gentlemen. . . ."

"Do you remember, Mr. Mayor, making a statement that you didn't have the money to buy the stock, or words to that effect?"

"That never was said."

Here Seabury quoted previous testimony from Sisto, who had declared Walker had said he "didn't have any money to buy securities."

"Why, I never met the man in my life until I went [to Atlantic City]," the mayor protested. "How did he know whether I had a dollar or not? I certainly never told that to anybody and wouldn't if it were true."

"Do you remember his [subsequently] calling on you at City Hall and expressing his views on regulating competition in the taxicab business?"

"I never discussed them in detail with him."

As a final justification for having accepted the bonds from Sisto, Walker read into the record his subsequent veto of a taxi-fare rise in April of 1930. "If I had signed the ordinance, the [Parmalee's] thousand taxicabs would have taken in, in 365 days, more than $1 million in addition to what they did get," he claimed.

Now Seabury set up another line of questioning. "Do you not recall that Mr. McKeon called on you at City Hall, and rode uptown with you at the end of the day, and that on the way uptown he took a sealed envelope and handed it to you and said it was from Sisto and you put it in your pocket?"

"*No* is the answer to every element in that [question]," said Walker hotly.

"That is my recollection of Mr. McKeon's testimony."

"That did not happen. The bonds were handed to me when I was dressing to go to a banquet somewhere and somewhat hurried so I didn't even look at them."

"How long did you keep the bonds?"

"I didn't keep them. I gave them to Mrs. Walker."

"When?"

"I put them in the safe at home the following day, and she was out of town at the time, but in talking to her over the telephone shortly thereafter, I mentioned that I had put some bonds in the safe for her."

"Well, you remember depositing the coupons [in the bank], do you not?"

"They were deposited."

"Do you know who deposited them?"

"No, but I assume it was done by the law office—probably by Mr. Sherwood, because he transacted any little business [Mrs. Walker] had and took care of her accounts—audited them—and paid bills for her and did other services for her. . . ."

After the luncheon recess, Seabury delved more deeply into Walker's relationship with Sherwood.

"Mr. Mayor, do you know whether after that safe-deposit box was opened in the joint names of yourself and Mr. Sherwood another box, a larger box, was subsequently obtained?"

"I do not."

"There were never any bonds, securities, stock, or cash placed in either of these boxes?"

"I don't know, but there never were any of mine."

"Do you know William J. Scanlan?"

"Slightly."

"There is nothing you can suggest that would throw any light as to why he should have paid $6,000 of a $10,000 commission received under a city contract to Russell T. Sherwood?"

"There is no reason I can think of. . . ."

"Mr. Mayor, how long have you known Sherwood?"

"Approximately fifteen years. I place that by my entrance into the law firm [of McIntyre and Warren]."

"He was in touch with you up until your last trip abroad?"

"Yes."

"Frequent times?"

"He would come to City Hall to bring checks for me to sign, which in the vast majority of cases were for bills for my home."

"I find from a transcript of Sherwood's account in the Central Hanover Bank, between August 27, 1929, and November 5, 1931, checks to the order of Mrs. Nan Walker Burke aggregating $15,-500. . . . Were these payments made by your authority?"

"Among other things I did of a personal nature was to make provisions for my widowed sister, and that varied between $800 and $1,000 a month. It was my custom to give Mr. Sherwood the money in cash. He kept the money and gave her the checks out of his account."

"Now, there were—during the same period I have indicated—checks for the expenses of the yacht, *Mary W.*, that amounted to $6,034.37," said Seabury, continuing to show for the record that Sherwood had, certainly in effect, been Walker's financial agent. "Can you tell me whether they were made on your behalf?"

"They were made at Mrs. Walker's instance, but I accept the responsibility. . . . I would give [Sherwood] money, and he would mail a check for the salary of the captain. . . . These bills never came individually to me, Judge, but [Sherwood] would bring me an account of checks—of the butcher and baker and other things—which Mrs. Walker sent him directly. . . . That was the best way of getting that attended to. . . ."

"You had your own personal account in the Chatham and Phoenix Bank?"

"Yes, that was the bank in which I always deposited my salary check and paid, to a great extent, current expenses. Other expenses, that might be called luxury, came out of the cash, and the cash, as I have testified, was kept apart from that other money because it had been tax paid."

"When did you hear for the first time that [Sherwood] had fled the jurisdiction of the Committee?"

"After I returned from Europe."

"You know, do you not, Mr. Harris, who is connected with the Manhattan Bank [where Sherwood was employed before fleeing the committee's subpoena]?"

"Slightly."

"Harris testified that he telephoned Sherwood at Mexico City on October 11 and that shortly thereafter he called upon you at City Hall. Do you remember that interview?"

"It is quite possible that he may have called . . . I am certain that he never mentioned the name of Sherwood."

After establishing that the records of some half-dozen banks and brokerage houses showed that some $1 million—$720,000 of it in cash—had been handled by Sherwood since 1926, Seabury asked: "Now, Mr. Mayor, can you give the Committee any information as to the source from whence Sherwood derived the money?"

"I think the question is very general," Walker replied. "I don't know anything about his private affairs because he never told me and I never inquired."

The mayor's answer to this crucial question touched off a spirited defense of his character by the Democratic committee members.

"Don't you see, Mr. Mayor," sneered Assemblyman Steingut, "along about 4:30 today counsel must have a headline. We are going to get the headline now."

"Just a minute," said Hofstadter, pounding his gavel.

"It is outrageous on the part of counsel to attempt to introduce this type of evidence," added Steingut. "It is not even decent."

"Stop!" ordered Hofstadter, gaveling furiously.

"I hope he proves [the money] is mine," said Walker to loud laughter. "I will try and collect it."

"Stop! Stop!" ruled the chairman.

"Seven hundred and fifty thousand dollars for this," said Steingut, referring to the ostensible cost of the legislative inquiry, "for the persecution of the Mayor of the City of New York."

"Stop!"

"Why, in the darkest days of Russia nothing like this would ever take place," retorted Steingut the anti-Bolshevist, while uncontrolled laughter filled the room.

"Nobody pays any attention," said Senator McNaboe, "Don't get excited."

"The Mayor says he denied it," added Assemblyman Cuvillier, whose remark caused the loudest laughter of all. "That ends it."

Seabury in conclusion showed through financial record that Sherwood on August 9, 1927, had withdrawn $263,836 from an "investment trustee" brokerage account that he had opened only four and a half months before, with $100,000 that he had admitted was not his money. (He had never used the account to trade but simply to accumulate cash.) At Sherwood's request at the time of the withdrawal, a brokerage house officer had converted the $263,000-odd to cash, mostly in $1,000 bills, at the Federal Reserve Bank. The accountant had departed the broker's premises carrying the money in a bulky package.

"I am trying to follow the reasoning the papers are supposed to get," commented Walker. "Not only did I have the $102,000 that I testified to that I had from Block, but now it develops that I got $260,000-odd the day before I left for Europe on August 10. Yet I had to sell my soul to the Equitable Bus Company to get a $10,000 letter of credit."

While Seabury made no specific reply to this gibe, the mayor's critics later pointed out that the withdrawals before his 1927 European trip may well have gone into the safe-deposit box he shared with Sherwood—a prudent settling of affairs before going on holiday.

As for the $10,000 letter of credit, it served to meet the expenses of the trip.

Be that as it may, the mayor's confrontation with Seabury now was at an end. "I have had my day in court," he told the committee before taking his leave. "It hasn't all been pleasant. If I have irritated the committee and if I have appeared to have been annoyed myself, I ask you to accept my apology. . . ."

As Walker passed through the hearing room's doorway, a dozen female admirers showered him with roses; he stopped, addressed a few quiet words to them, then went down the courthouse steps to his limousine. Today the cheering from the waiting crowd was not quite so loud. The subtle change worried the Tammany leaders not a bit. Even if Governor Roosevelt should remove Walker from office, they boasted, they would run him again, and the people would re-elect him by a larger margin than ever. They may well have been right.

The next day, May 27, Seabury wound up his look into Walker's financial affairs by calling to the stand two of the mayor's closest friends—Parks Commissioner Walter R. Herrick and publisher Paul Block.

In September of 1926, Herrick reluctantly testified, he had been the go-between for Walker in purchasing 350 shares of stock (for $39,000) in the Interstate Trust Company—passing 300 shares on to the mayor and keeping 50 for himself and the broker. This flatly contradicted Walker's previous testimony that he "never bought or caused to be bought" any stock in the Interstate. The reason Seabury made so much of this issue was that the 300 shares, all of which ended up with the backers of the Equitable Bus Company (and were used to help defray promotional expenses), would have established still another link between the mayor and the Equitable.

"What was the substance of the conversation you had with the Mayor [on the Interstate stock]?" Seabury asked Herrick.

"That he would like to get some of the stock," replied the uncomfortable parks commissioner under oath.

"Did the Mayor pay for the stock, the 300 shares?"

"The money came to me from City Hall, Judge."

"Did you understand that it was money sent you by the Mayor?"

"By the Mayor. . . ."

"What did you do with [the shares]?"

"Sent them up to City Hall."

"There is no doubt that your purpose was to send these shares to Mayor Walker?"

"No."

After introducing evidence that the stock certificates later had been distributed among Smith, Fageol, and Hastings, Seabury read from some of Herrick's earlier testimony:

Q. Do you know what the Mayor did with the stock?
A. I remember saying, "Jim, I hope you have got the stock yet." [It had increased markedly in value.] With a laugh, he said, "No, I put it up for collateral, and it is all gone." I said, "That is too bad."

"You have no reason to believe your earlier testimony is incorrect, have you?" said Seabury.

"Not except from the Mayor's testimony that I read yesterday," replied the squirming Herrick.

When Paul Block came to the stand, Seabury immediately brought up the joint brokerage account he had established for Walker—from which the mayor had drawn some $246,000.

"Will you be good enough to tell the Committee why you made this donation to the Mayor?"

"I will tell you," testified Block, "although it sounds a little silly. The Mayor telephoned me one day and asked if I would take a drive with him. It was on a Sunday. I said, 'I have promised my youngster' —who is only ten—'that I would take a walk with him.'

"He said, 'Why don't you have Billy drive with us?' I said, 'Well, that is fine.' I knew that would please Billy. He said he would be up in an hour, and my youngster and I went downstairs—at the time we lived at 74th Street and Fifth Avenue—and we walked up and down in front of the house. Naturally, our minds were on the Mayor, and the youngster said, 'How much salary does the Mayor get?' And I told him, '$25,000'—which was his salary at the time.

"'Does the City give him a house?' [said Billy]. And I said, 'No, they don't.' I recall he said, 'Does it give him an automobile?' And I said, 'Yes, but not to Mrs. Walker.'

"'Well,' this youngster said, 'can he live on what he gets?' And I said, 'Well, I suppose he can, but it probably is a problem.'

"And, Judge, I want you to believe me that it entered my mind then that I was going to try to make a little money for [the Mayor]."

After the account was set up, Walker could tap it for funds as often as he liked. "I never expected to make any such money for the Mayor," Block said defensively. "I thought I could make $30,000 or $40,000 or possibly $50,000. It turned out I couldn't make that little. The boom went on and the stocks went up, and in the first ten months it amounted to $220,000 for each of us. . . ."

About Walker's appearance before Seabury, the New York *Times* editorialized: "Mayor Walker left the witness stand trailing clouds, not of glory, but of mystery. Never were there so many explanations which themselves demand explaining, never so many stories quite incredible as they stood, never so many flat contradictions by [other] witnesess. . . . Has he been all these years so happy-go-lucky about public affairs as well as private, so amazingly careless about money matters, that he could not recall the facts even when they were brought to his attention? . . . A most extraordinary set were constantly in and out of City Hall and consorting with Mayor Walker. According to their standards, anything might happen. . . ." A few days later, *The New Yorker* expressed its feelings about the mayor more irreverently: "He is the logical Chief Executive of this town, [check] stubs or no [check] stubs. He had come by large amounts of money with minimum effort. . . . He had spent it without stint. . . . He had traveled widely in foreign lands. . . . In other words, he's the man we all dream about being."

The last session of the legislative committee, on June 1, dealt with Dr. William H. Walker, the mayor's older brother, who had banked $431,258 in the previous four years and who admitted under questioning that he had earned more than $100,000 of this sum by splitting fees with the four physicians designated by the city to treat municipal employees under the terms of the Workmen's Compensation Act. Moreover, the physicians—Drs. Thomas J. O'Mara, Edward L. Brennan, Harris Feinberg, and Alfred B. Cassassa—had often pursued unusual lines of treatment in their unstinting efforts to heal the injured. A workman who had cut his finger might be fitted out with an expensive abdominal belt, one with a sprained ankle might require X rays—not only of the ankle but of the hand as well. Assemblyman Irwin Steingut asserted that such care was desirable, since one should never underestimate the importance of small injuries. He himself, he announced, had a "bad big toe" he had been trying for years to find a specialist to cure.

"I hope you will consult Dr. Walker, Assemblyman," said Seabury.

Calling Dr. Walker to the stand, Seabury produced two sets of checks—one from the city to Dr. O'Mara, the other from Dr. O'Mara to the witness. The split invariably was 50-50 with the odd penny— if there was one—always going to Dr. Walker, and the total of payments to him from O'Mara alone coming close to $50,000. A stout, phlegmatic man, in every way the physical opposite of the mayor, Dr. Walker admitted receiving the money, but claimed that the fee-splitting resulted, not from city cases, but from other services he had performed for O'Mara. The fact that the city checks had been split so precisely he termed "coincidences."

"What service did you render?" Seabury inquired.

"Any service he required."

"Medical or political?"

"Medical," said Dr. Walker, playing nervously with his spectacles, which finally broke under the pressure of his thumb.

With Dr. Brennan, the second of the physicians treating city employees, Dr. Walker shared a joint bank account into which had gone some $226,000 over the past four years; while allowing that some of this money was fee-splitting for "services rendered," the mayor's brother insisted the bulk of it came from compensation cases he and Brennan handled for a stevedoring company. He also shared a joint bank account with Dr. Feinberg, and from both Drs. Feinberg and Cassassa, he had accepted city checks that simply were endorsed and passed on to him for deposit.

Seabury concluded the examination by showing that Dr. Walker, besides earning $100,000 from fee-splitting, was a medical examiner for the board of education, at $6,500 a year, pocketed numerous fifty dollar fees as an official for various boxing matches, and shared equally with salesman Scanlan in many of the latter's commissions. Echoing Scanlan's earlier testimony, Dr. Walker claimed these payments were for "medical services and fight tickets," but could not explain why the splits should so closely follow Scanlan's receipt of the commissions, nor why they should be so tidy.

June passed slowly for Mayor Walker. Ever peripatetic, he went to Detroit to attend an immensely forgettable conference of U.S. mayors, came back to New York to reiterate in the papers that Seabury had established no grounds by which he could be removed from office, briefly recaptured a bit of earlier glory by presenting a city scroll to aviatrix Amelia Earhart (who had become the first woman to fly alone across the Atlantic). Then on June 22, the inevitable happened: Walker was ordered by Governor Roosevelt to reply to Seabury's formal fifteen-count summary of the charges against him. The preparation of the mayor's written defense would occupy him and his staff for almost a month.

In the meantime, Franklin D. Roosevelt and his strategy board were trying to seize the Democratic presidential nomination. Campaign manager James A. Farley and Bronx Boss Edward J. Flynn (FDR's secretary of state and dispenser of patronage in the city) had arrived in Chicago, the convention site, a week before the proceedings opened in order to lay the groundwork. Though Roosevelt had the pledges of a majority of the delegates, he required a two-thirds advantage for the nomination. Blocking him, principally, were Al Smith, who had the votes of Tammany Hall and its allies as well as the backing of the Democratic machines in Jersey City and Chicago, and John Nance Garner, who had the support of his native Texas and of California—the latter state being kept in line for Garner largely through the efforts of William Randolph Hearst, now directing his publishing empire from San Simeon, California. It was not that Hearst, the old Tammany-hater, had developed any sudden affection for Al Smith—merely that as a convinced isolationist he frowned on FDR's internationalism.

Farley and Flynn, together with FDR advisor Louis Howe, tried to ram their man through in the early sessions by attempting to change the rules so that a simple majority of the delegates would prevail. The howl that went up from smaller states, which invariably used their votes to strike an advantageous patronage position, all but cost Roosevelt the nomination then and there; the two-thirds rule was retained. On the first ballot for the nomination, which did not conclude until nearly 6:30 A.M. on July 1, Walker came onto the convention floor just before the official tally was announced. Somewhat disheveled, having come directly from his bed, he joined the Tammany faction and asked to be recognized.

"Who is the gentleman who addresses the chair?" came the response, while tired politicians stirred with interest.

"Walker, a delegate from New York."

"For what purpose does he address the chair?"

"The delegate was not here when his name was called, and his alternate voted in his stead. The delegate requests permission to cast his own vote."

"The request is granted."

Then came the declaration, typical of the impetuous Walker, that thrilled the convention.

"I desire," he said, "that my vote be cast for Alfred E. Smith."

No matter that Walker was engaging in theatrics. "The thunder of applause that followed," wrote journalist Warren Moscow, "was spontaneous, general and hearty. Mayor Walker was the hero of the moment. Delegates shouted at each other, danced, cheered, [yelled] in less refined terms that he had 'intestinal fortitude.' All were aware that the mayor's future was resting in the hands of Governor Roosevelt." Enthused Smith, from whom Walker had grown progressively more alienated: "Good old Jim! Blood is thicker than water!"

The first ballot failed to put Roosevelt over, as did a second and a third; finally, at 9:15 in the morning, with delegate heads nodding all over the floor, the convention was adjourned until 8:30 that night. From California, Hearst had listened closely to the voting. Now a phone call from Farley assured the publisher that Roosevelt's internationalism had been grossly exaggerated; besides, said Farley, interminable balloting could only erode Roosevelt's strength and might just make Smith the nominee. Hearst pondered this Hobson's Choice, then through an intermediary sent out the word: "Tell Garner that the Chief believes nothing can now save the country but for him to throw his delegates to Roosevelt." In Chicago, meanwhile, Farley was sweetening the taste of defeat for Garner by offering him the vice-presidential nomination. When the convention resumed late on July 1, Texas and California switched their votes from Garner to Roosevelt, breaking the deadlock and ending forever Smith's chances of regaining political power. Then the rush to vote for Roosevelt was on, with only New York, Massachusetts, Rhode Island, New Jersey, and Connecticut declining to leave Smith's side. "Do you intend to support the nominee?" Smith later was asked. "I have no comment to make," he replied, digesting the irony that the Tammany he had labored so diligently to reform had ultimately been his undoing. Back in Albany, a smiling FDR was making plans to fly to the convention the next day to deliver his acceptance speech. "We are ready for action," he said, radiating confidence.

In his formal letter to Governor Roosevelt demanding that the mayor be removed from office, Seabury had asserted that Walker's explanations of "gross improprieties" were "unworthy of credence," and he had detailed, among other charges, the by now well-known stories involving the Sisto bonds, the disappearance of Russell T. Sherwood, the favoring of the Equitable group, the Paul Block "beneficences," and the fee-splitting of the mayor's brother. Now, on July 28, Roosevelt released the text of Walker's reply, which began by saying that the legislative inquiry had been politically inspired. "Not one witness testified," maintained the mayor, "that any act of mine was emphasized by any illegal or dishonest consideration . . . that I had ever sought or received money for any official act . . . that I had ever done anything, by malfeasance, misfeasance, or nonfeasance, affecting injuriously the City of New York." Walker went on to tell Roosevelt: "It was more than a coincidence that all of the matters that were thought to reflect upon the Mayor were held until the later part of May, when my appearance at a public hearing could be staged as a climax, just before the National Conventions."

When the mayor dealt with Seabury's specific points—admittedly

based on circumstantial evidence in many instances—the sheer weight
of the charges made his replies seem flimsy. (Nor did he help restore his credence by mentioning, almost in an aside, that ten of
Seabury's fifteen charges were irrelevant, for the reason that they
concerned events that had taken place during his first term.) About
legislation that might have benefited Sisto, such as a control board
limiting the number of cabs, Walker declared the ordinance had been
pushed, not by him, but by the taxicab commission. About Paul Block,
the publisher who dreamed of subway tiles, the mayor said, "He is a
man of great wealth. He has no need of anything which I as Mayor
could give to him." About the Equitable, he stated that the franchise
had been recommended, not by him, but by the board of transportation, and that as a result the board of estimate had determined "the
best offer had been received from Equitable." About Herrick's testimony regarding his alleged purchase of Interstate Trust Company
securities, he declared that "the apparent inconsistency vanishes, in
view of his uncertainty as to his recollection." As for the letter
of credit, he insisted his European party had paid for it in good faith.
About Sherwood and the $1 million that had been handled by the ac-
countant since 1926, he said, "I know nothing about his personal
affairs. . . . I do know he had [other] clients for whom he did income-
tax work and made reports. Any of them might well be asked the
same questions as were asked me." And so his answers went.

"The Mayor's position," retorted Seabury on August 3, "may be
summarized as a claim of honest intentions based wholly upon un-
recorded mental reservations . . . and a plea that even if the facts
be true they may not be inquired into because they occurred in a
prior term of office." Bringing up the Sisto bonds, the chief counsel
declared that both Sisto and McKeon had testified Walker had said
he could not afford to buy any Cosden oil stock; "It is difficult to
imagine what [interest] they could have had in so testifying if the
testimony were false, for both were interested in enhancing the respectability of the transaction." Seabury next drew attention to
Walker's current claim that in his dealings with Block "he was liable
to bear a share of any loss," although before the committee he had
called the gifts "beneficences." The Equitable inquiry, Seabury went
on, clearly showed that the mayor, once referred to in correspondence
among the backers as "the boy friend," was intimately connected
with Senator Hastings. Even clearer, declared the counsel, was Walker's
connection with Sherwood, from joint safe-deposit box to bond coupons to the Scanlan sweeper check to the "trustee" brokerage account. (For good measure, Seabury totaled up some $75,000 in cash,
plus the purchase of securities and letters of credit, that Sherwood

had paid the "unnamed person"—Betty Compton.) As for Dr. Walker's activities, the counsel said: "No doubt the Mayor would have us believe that it was just an accident that the city doctor in each borough happened to select the Mayor's brother to do him the honor to share his fees."

Summoned before Roosevelt for removal hearings beginning Thursday, August 11, Walker knew that his twenty-three-year-old political life, nurtured in a Tammany clubhouse in Greenwich Village, might well be ending in the executive chamber in Albany. With him was Allie Walker, who, for appearances' sake, he had summoned from her Florida exile; dressed in brown silk and wearing an enormous orchid corsage, her hair concealed by a cloche hat, she was smiling but wan, not fully recovered from a recent abdominal operation. From the very beginning of the sessions, Roosevelt, a grave but courteous figure facing the mayor across a huge desk, let it be known that he was in total control of the unfolding drama. He ruled that Walker would have to answer for the acts of his first administration as well as his second, and he denied Walker's request that each of the hundreds of witnesses who had testified before Seabury be recalled and the mayor be allowed to cross-examine them. "I can't be unlike every human being in the world," protested the mayor emotionally but to no avail, "without an opportunity to look into the faces of my accusers. . . ." Stopping further argument, Roosevelt reminded Walker that he had always had the right to summon witnesses in his own behalf—a right of which he had not availed himself.

The Albany hearings were a complete contrast to the appearance of the mayor before the Hofstadter Committee, when hundreds of sympathizers had jammed into the hearing room. Now only a handful of quiet spectators were permitted to view the proceedings. Roosevelt devoted that first day to reviewing, calmly and scrupulously, the matter of the Sisto bonds. Though no new facts emerged, the governor several times rattled Walker with his questioning.

When the mayor was retelling his story of how he had accepted the $26,500 in bonds without looking at them, thinking they were just his share of a stock pool, Roosevelt seized upon an incongruity. How did you know, he asked of Walker, "how many shares . . . you were getting?"

"I beg your pardon," said the mayor blankly.

The question was repeated.

"I didn't know . . . if I didn't know . . . my understanding was—" Walker stammered, "there were no questions asked . . . if I never heard of [the shares] again it would have been all right with me. . . . I mean there was no definite agreement."

The next day, when the hearings resumed, Roosevelt pressed Walker hard on his dealings with Paul Block and John Hastings. (Allie, worn out by the earlier excitement, did not attend.) When the governor asked Walker why, though he now maintained the $246,-000 from Block was not a gift, he had originally called the money a "beneficence," the mayor offered an apology. "When I used the word "benefice," I didn't think I would be on trial for my selection of English," he said. "If I had been, I probably would have been convicted years ago. . . ." Roosevelt then asked Walker whether he could explain why, even under the theory of a joint account, he had drawn out the first $102,500 in 1927, before the profits had fully accrued—as Block had admitted. "Let me submit," said the mayor, "that while there may be some discrepancies in the testimony . . . [they] had nothing to do with my official conduct. . . . There wasn't a dime of taxpayers' money in [the account]." Remarked FDR thoughtfully: "This is true, but you were getting something that had not yet accrued to you."

When the governor brought up the subject of Senator Hastings and the Equitable, Walker repeated his earlier testimony that he had not known Hastings had a stock interest in the company. Roosevelt then brought up Hastings's statement that he had concealed his relationship with the Equitable "at the specific request of the Mayor," who was anxious that there be "no water, no promotional stock." Walker replied that he could recall no such conversation. With seven of Seabury's fifteen charges disposed of, the governor adjourned the hearings for the weekend and went off to confer at his home in Hyde Park, New York, with vice-presidential candidate Garner. Walker departed for New York, leaving behind Allie, who was too fatigued to make the trip. With Walker on the train going down to the city was real-estate and theater magnate A. C. Blumenthal, and it was at his estate in Larchmont, New York, that the mayor would sequester himself.

Alfred Cleveland Blumenthal, who had attached himself to Walker sometime in 1930, had milked the association for all it was worth. An accomplished celebrity-hunter, ever mindful that the company of the famous would impress bankers and help him raise money for his realty and theater ventures, he was the last of Walker's "benefactors," though his tightness with money symbolized the steady decline in the mayor's fortunes. Blumey's "benefices" usually consisted of nothing but bogus job offers, party invitations, and the company of the girls in his shows; his moral sense, wrote journalist Alva Johnston, "was offended at the idea of disturbing another man's destiny by giving him money." When he did part with a modest sum, he insisted the money be repaid. "I'm not the kind of a mugg that doesn't go after it and get it back again," he admitted.

A diminutive Californian who favored ensembles—suits, ties, shirts, and socks of the same color—Blumenthal had made his original fortune in real estate on the West Coast but went bankrupt at age twenty-nine in the Los Angeles panic of 1924. He explained the misfortune by saying that he had trusted dear friends. Starting anew, Blumenthal between 1925 and 1930 bought and sold more than 1,000 movie theaters and earned more than $4 million in commissions. He did this by convincing the big movie studios that they should own their own picture houses, and he was particularly successful in this regard with William Fox of Twentieth Century Fox. Soon Warner Brothers and Paramount, stampeded by the Blumenthal-Fox tornado, were frantically bidding against them, forcing theater prices up to two and three times their worth. The competition reached its peak in mid-1929 when Blumey, acting for Fox, bought control of Loew's, a $140 million corporation that owned Metro-Goldwyn-Mayer and a nationwide chain of picture houses—earning himself $1,230,000. Alas, when the stock market crashed a few months later, Fox's movie empire broke into smithereens. Blumenthal now proved his versatility by selling the movie mogul out (for another hefty commission). "God will strike you dead for what you did to me," said Fox, giving him the ultimate accolade. (Anticipating the crash, Blumey had previously transferred his own assets into government bonds.)

Along the way, Blumenthal married actress Peggy Fears, a one-time Ziegfeld beauty, and snagged such personages as Charlie Chaplain, Jack Dempsey, Lupe Velez, Lili Damita, Pola Negri, Constance Bennett, and, of course, Walker, to dazzle financiers and keep his name in the papers. During the 1930s, the mayor seemed to show up at Blumey's apartment in the Ambassador Hotel almost weekly just to marry love-struck theatrical couples. Recently, he had even convinced Lenore Ulric, who was starring in a Broadway play for Blumenthal at $1,500 weekly, that she should renounce her contract for a percentage of the gross receipts—which turned out to be only $300 weekly. At his Larchmont estate, Blumey repaid the favor by granting Walker refuge from Seabury and Roosevelt. The guests sunned themselves around the swimming pool, where they frolicked with showgirls, talked big deals, were pummeled by masseurs, watched the latest movies, and reveled in lively blasts of music from concealed organ pipes. Everyone had fun.

When the hearings in Albany resumed on August 15, Parks Commissioner Herrick repudiated his story that Walker had given him the money to buy 300 shares in the Interstate Trust Company—stock that ultimately was used to help finance the Equitable bus scheme. Seated before the governor, he now insisted that he could only say the money was brought by one of his office boys "from City Hall." Pressed by Roosevelt, Herrick admitted that his change in testimony was based upon Walker's denial that he had purchased the securities or had any conversation with him about them. Called next to explain his role in the Sherwood expenditures, the mayor recited the litany that had been found lacking so many times before: Sherwood was little more than a messenger boy for him, seeing to it that his salary checks were deposited in the bank and his household bills were paid.

"Would it be in order," interjected Seabury, who attended the hearings throughout, "if I were to call to your Excellency's attention that there was a letter of credit arranged for by Sherwood—two of them—that amounted to $16,000, and that those letters were made out for the benefit of the person for whom a check—"

"After 14 months of this gentleman with this kind of parading must he be permitted here—" shouted Walker, who had acknowledged that he had authorized a $7,500 payment through Sherwood to his "personal friend," Betty Compton, but insisted that he had nothing to do with the additional $75,000 that Sherwood had subsequently paid out to her.

"Did you know anything about those letters of credit?" said Roosevelt.

"I did not," said Walker, "and I assume also, as counsel might in any effort for fairness, that the same person might have had charge accounts, bought real estate . . . and the assumption [that I had bought them through Sherwood] wouldn't any more follow . . . except for publicity purposes."

Roosevelt stared reflectively at the mayor for a long moment.

"Strike out everything he said after 'I did not,'" he said to the stenographer. "You have got to stick to the issues," he told Walker.

The following day, the subject of Sherwood came up again and again.

"I wish he were here," said Roosevelt pensively at one point, alluding to how the accountant could clear up the conflicting testimony.

"So do I wish he were here," said Walker.

"Did you do anything about it, then, when you found he was in Mexico city?"

"I had no reason to believe that the subpoena would not bring him back."

"Isn't it a curious thing for you, when a man with whom you had a safe-deposit box and who looked after your personal affairs, disappears, and the whole town is looking for him, and he turns up, not to communicate with him?"

"I had no reason to believe he would disobey the subpoena."

"So you just let it ride?"

"I would rather he was here today. Then I wouldn't have to spend so much time on inferences and innuendo."

Allie Walker, meanwhile, had been ordered home to New York and St. Luke's Place by Dr. Schroeder, who had decided she had not fully recovered from her operation. "Mrs. Walker will not have to be operated on again, but she will have to be careful," Walker declared as he saw her off.

On August 17, when John J. Curtin, the mayor's attorney, demanded once more that the hundreds of witnesses who had testified before the Hofstadter Committee be recalled before Roosevelt, the governor modified his earlier stand. He ruled that he would issue subpoenas for the witnesses, but Curtin would have to pay their expenses and be responsible for getting them to Albany. When the attorney protested, Roosevelt cut him short, saying he should experience no trouble in this regard since most of the testimony against Walker had been given—reluctantly—by his friends. A red-faced Curtin, realizing he had been outmaneuvered, had no choice but to abandon his plan to recall the whole parade of witnesses, although he subsequently produced those persons most friendly to the mayor.

The day's highpoint came when the governor asked Walker what he had done about the testimony before the legislative committee two months earlier that the physicians doing city compensation work had split their fees with Dr. William Walker. "Do you consider that a proper, ethical practice?"

Stammered the mayor: "Well, unless I . . . If I . . . if the city was defrauded . . . it would be a matter of serious interest. If, on the other hand, the city was not defrauded and the doctors—because of some arrangements they had between them—were paid off by splitting the check, or as many checks as there were—I don't see anything unethical about that."

"Let me put it this way. If you were a doctor and had to give half your fees to somebody else, wouldn't you try to get more money out of the city?"

"A man who had to give half his salary might do almost anything."

On subsequent days, Attorney Curtin called some selected pro-Walker witnesses to testify before Roosevelt. On August 23, Paul Block declared that the reports he had tried to sell tiles to city subway contractors were gross exaggerations. In 1927, he had put about $140,000 into a company headed by research chemist Robert Beyer, he explained, in the hope that Beyer could develop synthetic tiles; he had not known at the time that Senator Hastings also had an interest in the company. Although Beyer had never developed the tiles on a commercial basis, Block continued, he "came over to my office one day and said he had had an examination made of [the tiles] in some department of the City that does this kind of work, and he was very enthusiastic, because they had given him a fine report, and he said something about how he might now interest the [subway] contractors. I immediately said to him, 'Now that is something that I cannot permit you to do, because it would embarrass me on account of my friendship with the Mayor.'"

"Do you often engage in transactions of that kind?" said Roosevelt wonderingly, referring to the risk of putting $140,000 into Beyer's largely unproven process.

"Often in the years 1927, '28 and '29," replied the publisher.

Block, who had brought his son Billy to the hearings, then reiterated that he had sought no favors from the mayor in return for the $246,000 he had given him.

Since Walker was now saying he would have made good on any loss in the brokerage account, Roosevelt asked Block how he could explain his earlier testimony that he "would not have allowed him" to stand a loss.

"I meant I would have tried to prevent him from standing it. That is really what I meant," said the publisher lamely.

The next day, intent on proving that Walker had indeed paid with cash for the $10,000 letter of credit allegedly bought by the Equitable, Curtin called several witnesses to the stand. One was Hector Fuller, the mayor's English-born and reared scrollreader during the great years of visiting dignitaries. Fuller took a blasé view of the proceedings and once even addressed the governor as "my dear boy"— a lapse that somehow passed unnoticed. He swore that he himself had put $1,000 into the fund, yet admitted he had spent far more than his share, and he stuck to his story even when Martin Conboy, the governor's legal advisor, asked him who had defrayed the $3,000 overdraft.

"I can't imagine," Fuller replied with an English drawl and an air of ennui.

"You were just satisfied to have it paid?"

"Yes, sir," said Fuller.

So the second week of Albany hearings passed. They would have been resumed on Monday, August 29, but for the death the previous day of George Walker at Saranac Lake. George's death came as no surprise to the harassed mayor—he had been informed earlier that the tubercular condition of his brother, who was confined to a clinic at Saranac Lake, was worsening—but, added to the strain of the removal proceedings, it further sapped his strength and combativeness. Nothing was wrong with the mayor organically, Dr. Schroeder announced, but the "combination of recent events" necessitated at least a week of complete rest. Though Roosevelt set Friday, September 2, as the date for resuming the inquiry, it was left unclear whether Walker, suffering from "nervous exhaustion," would comply.

While the mayor was in seclusion, the governor announced he would disregard the objections of Supreme Court Justice Ellis J. Staley to his handling of the hearings. While Justice Staley had denied Walker's plea for a stay, upholding FDR's removal powers, he had criticized the governor for "failing to make Mr. Seabury retell his case before him and . . . holding the Mayor accountable for private business transactions and the official acts of his first term in office." Roosevelt answered each point in turn. First, he asserted that common sense dictated that his most pressing duty in the Walker case was to render a fair decision within a reasonable period of time. He had offered the mayor the right to call witnesses, he said, but to prevent endless procrastination had insisted it was the defense's responsibility to produce them. Walker's right of cross-examination, Roosevelt observed wryly, had been ably exercised by the Democratic members of the legislative committee. Second, he reaffirmed the policy he had laid down as an executive ruling in the case of Sheriff Farley, that the interests of good government required a public official to account for his private income. Third, the governor pointed out that the alleged misdeeds attributed to Walker during his first term had not been public knowledge; therefore his re-election could not be interpreted as a mandate from the voters giving him absolution, and he should be held accountable for any transgressions in either term.

Both the court's refusal to grant a stay and Roosevelt's firmness further depressed the mayor. On Thursday, September 1, a pale and listless Walker attended a solemn requiem mass for his brother in St. Patrick's Cathedral, whose pews were jammed to capacity with 3,000 mourners. Later, he and family members, together with nearly every important Democratic politician in the city, took the last ride with the deceased to Cavalry Cemetery. The funeral cortège included twenty-five cars, five of them piled high with flowers. At the graveside, the mayor's friends were shocked by his appearance. "Jim looks worse than George," whispered FDR Campaign Manager James A. Farley with grim humor. (Despite his ties with Roosevelt, Jim Farley always retained his affection for Walker.) After the burial, the mayor took Nan Burke, his sister, off to one side.

"Nan," he said abruptly, "I'm going to resign."

"When?" she asked, so shocked it was all she could think to say.

"As soon as I leave the meeting at the Plaza," said Walker, referring to an afternoon meeting of Tammany strategists that had been called by Curry.

At 10:40 that night, consulting no one else, Walker resigned from the mayoralty. That his decision had been some time in the making was reflected in his typewritten statement, which was dated August 14. "Three weeks ago I went to Albany with my counsel confident that we would be accorded a fair hearing. . . ." Walker's letter of resignation began. "Day after day during the proceedings, it became more and more apparent that I was being subjected to an extraordinary inquisition . . . I feel that if I further submit I would demean myself as well as the citizens of New York who have twice honored me by electing me Mayor by overwhelming majorities. . . . I have gone about as far as anyone could in answering questions about every act in my life. . . ."

Walker would, he said, seek vindication by running once more for the mayoralty in a special election that fall. In the meantime, Aldermanic President Joseph V. McKee would become the city's acting mayor.

Curry and McCooey were ominously silent in the aftermath of Walker's decision; no admirers of FDR, they instinctively wanted one of their own to vindicate himself; as astute politicians, however, they realized the impossibility of running the discredited Walker on the same ticket with his adversary, who happened to be running for President. Al Smith, who still had not made his own peace with Roosevelt, was more vocal, saying he could not support a man who had "quit under fire."

For the next ten days, Walker avoided public appearances, dividing his time between his Mayfair suite and Blumenthal's Larchmont estate. He had cabled the news of his resignation almost immediately to Betty Compton, who was in Paris, and they had made plans for a reunion abroad.

On August 10, James J. Walker—accompanied by a dog, a valet, and a former secretary, George Collins—sailed for Europe aboard the Italian liner *Conte Grande;* the trip was for his health, he said, and "to get away from desks and telephones." Among the small party seeing him off were Allie, Hector Fuller, Blumenthal, and Dr. Schroeder. No, he told reporters, he didn't want to talk about anything political; he would be back in New York in time for the city's Democratic convention on October 6, and he would speak his mind then. "I really am being shanghaied by a medical man," he said, pointing to Dr. Schroeder. Then he retreated to his cabin.

Even after the ship was well out into the Hudson, Allie remained at the pier, waving him good-bye.

AFTERMATH

Many times man lives and dies
Between his two eternities
That of race and that of soul
And ancient Ireland knew it all.
Whether man die in his bed
Or the rifle knocks him dead
A brief parting from those dear
Is the worst man has to fear. . . .

Cast a cold eye
On life, on death.
Horseman, pass by!

—W. B. Yeats

When he was scheduling his voyage, Walker's original plan had been
to journey up from Italy to the south of France for a reunion with
Betty Compton, whom he had not seen for the past year and a half.
About the time he arrived in Naples, however, his traveling companion, George Collins, fell ill, and Walker decided to stay with him.
He arranged instead for Betty to come to Italy, and they met in
Pompeii. There, reports agree, he told her that he intended to seek
renomination at the city mayoral convention and subsequently to vindicate himself at the polls. After serving out the balance of his term,
he would then divorce Allie, and they could be married. Betty argued bitterly against Walker's political decision. The strain of another

329

campaign, she insisted, would further injure his health; as for Allie, if he did not run for office, he could ask her for a divorce a year sooner. With nothing settled, Betty returned to France, and Walker and Collins soon afterward boarded the Italian liner *Rex* for the trip back to New York—and the convention.

Before steaming out of the Mediterranean, however, the *Rex* developed engine trouble, forcing it to drop anchor at Gibraltar. During the delay, Walker brooded over his future. Finally Betty's arguments converted him to her point of view. Leaving Collins in the care of the ship's physician for the trip homeward, he rejoined his mistress in Paris, where he dawdled away the days while his supporters in New York frantically cabled for word of his intentions. On October 4, only forty-eight hours before the convention, he embarked aboard the *Bremen* for the westward voyage—knowing full well that he would be at sea when Tammany and its allies met to select a new candidate.

In New York, meanwhile, Curry and McCooey had been having their problems. Acting Mayor McKee, aided by a lower-court decision, had been insisting that a special mayoral election was illegal and that he should serve out the balance of Walker's term. Barely a day went by that one newspaper or another did not carry a photo of the handsome, forty-three-year-old McKee, often with his attractive wife and young children, and comment on how good a chief executive he would be. Indeed, during Walker's frequent absences from City Hall over the years, it had been the dutiful, intelligent McKee, sitting in the mayor's chair, who had kept municipal business moving through the board of estimate. At one point Walker himself, noting that McKee had presided over the board far more often than any other aldermanic president, had observed that he was "the logical successor for my job."

Why, then, did Curry and McCooey regard McKee with narrowed gaze and pursed lips? Not for his Irishness and his Catholicism and his exemplary family life—that was all to the good. Not even for his seriousness and his academic degrees (A.B., M.A., LL.B., LL.D.)—those could be tolerated. No, the reason the bosses of Manhattan and Brooklyn disliked McKee was much simpler: the acting mayor was the protégé of Bronx Boss Ed Flynn—then a Roosevelt confidant. "They felt that this might start me on the way to becoming city leader," Flynn said years afterward.

Yet, if Tammany and McCooey felt distaste for McKee, they were finding it increasingly difficult to give silent lip-service to the supposed Walker candidacy; he and FDR on the same ballot would have been mutually destructive, of course, and now the Catholic archdio-

cese was taking a stand, in an oblique way at least, on Walker's private
life. On September 22, Martin G. McCue, who until his death had
been leader of the Twelfth A.D., was eulogized in pointed terms at
a high requiem mass at Manhattan's St. Agnes Church by Monsignor
John P. Chidwick. Besides having been chaplain of the battleship
Maine when it was sunk in Havana harbor, Monsignor Chidwick was
known to be a spokesman for Cardinal Hayes, who often preferred
to have his views expressed indirectly. For a eulogy to be delivered
at a Catholic funeral mass, moreover, was a rare happening in those
days, and it underscored the importance of the prelate's remarks.
Smith, McKee, Berry, Curry, McCooey, and all the Irish district
leaders were present in the church, and room had been made for a
scattering of Italian and Jewish politicians as well, as Monsignor
Chidwick lauded the late McCue's character: "While our friend
was a man of affairs who mingled with the leaders of the city and
state, and on whom popular favor was showered, he was a man beneath it all who had a strong faith and lived his life according to the
teachings of the Catholic Church.

"Would to God," continued the Monsignor, "every man in public
life would understand that he is an example, a model and a guide to
young people who are apt to be drawn to him. Not only in official
life, but in private life, should a man be clean and pure."

McKee and Flynn, better than almost all their political peers,
understood that the Democratic machine would have to reform itself, and reform itself drastically, if Tammany was to preserve its
power on the city and state level. They were not heeded. The year
1932, which saw almost 900,000 New Yorkers on the dole and some
$6 million voted by the board of estimate for the relief of the unem-
ployed, foretold the end of Tammany and its Irish district leaders
as a major political force.

In early October, knowing that the court of appeals would shortly
reverse the earlier ruling and call for a mayoral election, Flynn made
another bid to enhance McKee's candidacy. Although he had been
barred from all formal Democratic meetings, he talked long and hard
with McCooey in private. If McKee were nominated at the October
6 convention, said Flynn, "I would be most happy to retire from
politics." For a while, he was optimistic. "It looked as if we would
succeed in getting a Mayor who had the same popularity as Walker,
but who was without the Walker shortcomings." Ultimately, however,
the Bronx leader's reasonableness was regarded as weakness. While we
do not know how strong a case McCooey made for McKee, the
Democratic nomination in advance of the convention was firmly
denied him.

At the same time, Tammany knew it could not renominate Walker, for Roosevelt had made it clear that he would not speak on the same platform with him. When Curry learned, therefore, that Walker had changed his mind about running again, and that he had arranged to be at sea during the convention to preclude any possibility of an emotional draft, he considered himself most fortunate. Walker's name was put in nomination, when 30,000 Democrats met in Madison Square Garden on October 6, but it was quickly withdrawn when the chairman read a cable from the ex-mayor declining the honor, and all the chants of "We want Jimmy" could not bring it back again. "I cannot see how I could campaign," the wire went, "without daily reminding the public of the unfair nature of the hearings conducted by the Governor. . . . This in my opinion would do the Democratic party no good. Much as I feel aggrieved by the treatment I have received, I am not one of those who think he is bigger than the party. . . . I request that my name be withheld from the convention."

The man Curry personally selected for the mayoral nomination was Surrogate Court Judge John P. O'Brien, a stentorian-voiced Tammanyite whose appearance, even to admirers, seemed all jaw and no neck. As good a husband and father as McKee, and just as diligent in his work habits, O'Brien would—Curry felt—provide the needed contrast with the deposed Walker. In making his decision, the Tammany boss was only acknowledging a long-time political maxim, which Walker himself had followed when he replaced the publicity-conscious Whalen as police commissioner with the taciturn Mulrooney. "When you are making up the bill for a vaudeville show," Walker had said at the time, "you wouldn't have one banjo act followed by another banjo act." Indeed, O'Brien's credentials were impeccable for Curry's purposes: a loving wife and five fine children (the eldest was at Harvard, but that was hushed up); a devout Catholicism, which reminded him to wear his holy medals even when he jogged in a gym suit; a quiet, thirty-year municipal career topped off first by the post of corporation counsel (he was the tireless fellow who got out the injunctions for Mayor Hylan against the "traction interests") and then by the post of surrogate (where he amicably settled many a family fight over wills and trusts).

O'Brien, of course, did have one minor weakness. An indefatigable public speaker before ethnic groups, he occasionally offended, through an excess of enthusiasm, the very people he was trying to flatter. Before a Jewish audience, he might seek rapport by praising "that scientist of scientists, Albert Weinstein." Before a Greek-American group, he might remind his listeners that he was not unaware of their great heritage, for he had both studied and translated the work of their greatest poet—Horace. Before a Harlem audience, he might refer in complimentary terms to Marcus Garvey, who had swindled some $1 million from New York Negroes with his plan to found a Black Empire in Africa.

Educated at Holy Cross College in Worcester, Massachusetts, and Georgetown Law School in Washington, D.C., O'Brien gravitated to New York at the turn of the century. He joined Tammany, sneered whenever anyone mentioned the word "reform," and soon entrenched himself in the corporation counsel's office. There he perfected the technique of sending residents enormous bills for dubious "personal property taxes"; when the anxious citizens rushed to City Hall to protest, he invariably allayed their fears by giving them exemptions; in this way he made many grateful friends for Tammany. Along the way, O'Brien became a Knight of the Equestrian Order of the Holy Sepulchre, president of the Friendly Sons of St. Patrick, and a denouncer of birth control. It was almost foreordained in the political heavens, therefore, that he rise to the positions of corporation counsel and surrogate. Now he was the mayoral nominee. "Join Tammany and work for it," he once declaimed. "Stay loyal. Stay put. Reward will come." Wired Walker from the *Bremen* to the Democratic standard-bearer: "Perfect nomination. Very happy."

In celebration of O'Brien's leadership, Tammany set about embarrassing McKee in earnest. During the rest of October, it stripped the acting mayor of his fiscal powers in the board of estimate, pushed through a budget that ignored his pleas—in view of the Depression—for a drastic reduction in expenditures, and killed his plans to finally put buses on the streets. On November 8, even as a Depression-conscious electorate across the nation gave Roosevelt an overwhelming triumph over Herbert Hoover at the polls ("All you've got to do to be elected," Garner had told FDR, "is stay alive"), John P. O'Brien was voted mayor of New York, against extremely weak Republican opposition. Though Tammany professed great satisfaction in the triumph, there were ominous signs of voter resentment: the Democratic candidate received a bare majority—51 percent—of the two million votes cast, and Joseph McKee received the astounding total of 252,-000 write-in votes from citizens who spelled his name in seventy-eight different ways, from Jo to Jos to Vee to McGee.

All during this period, Walker remained virtually incommunicado, spending much of his time at Blumenthal's Larchmont estate. "I'm still a Democrat," he remarked, "though very still." A few days before the elections, Betty and her mother returned briefly to New York from France, to wind up some business affairs before leaving with

Walker for an indefinite stay in Europe. On November 10, the trio sailed once again, in first-class accommodations aboard the *Conte Grande,* for Italy and the French Riviera. Not a single politician saw them off. Depending on which reports one believes, the ex-mayor left the United States with as little as $2,500—courtesy of Robert Newman, a Hollywood movie producer—or as much as several hundred thousand dollars, delivered to him by the elusive Robert T. Sherwood before his September sailing and now banked abroad. Whatever the truth, Walker would remain in Europe for the next three years, and he would continue to live in the grand manner that had characterized his mayoralty.

As luck would have it, a Hearst reporter named Nat J. Ferber, traveling to Italy on holiday, was on the *Conte Grande* when it sailed. A day or two out at sea, he coaxed the ex-mayor and Betty out of their cabin and listened, over a late round of convivial drinks, as Walker expressed his resentment over the treatment he had received from Al Smith. "Al and I had been on the outs," he ruminated, "but he was one of my own, a mug from Oliver Street. . . . I knew just what I was doing when I cast that vote [at the National Convention] for Smith. Roosevelt wouldn't have been human if he hadn't taken it out on me."

At a conference of Democratic leaders some weeks later, Walker continued, he learned that Smith's ethics did not permit him to repay the favor. "They were all there, McCooey, Curry, Max Steuer, nineteen of them, including Smith and me. We sat at a round table, Smith at my left. . . . One by one the boys rose to say to me, 'Jim—stick! Let that man *toss* you out. We'll nominate you again, and the people will send you back to City Hall.' . . . This speech was made seventeen times. Only one man remained silent, Smith. [I said] 'What does my friend Al say?' . . . Smith rose and looked directly across the table, without even facing me. Speaking out of the corner of his mouth, he snarled, 'You're through. The public don't want you. If you're nominated you'll be licked. You're through.'" As much as anything else, Smith's stand that day started Walker thinking of resigning. The tough Oliver Street kid who had hustled his way up from the Lower East Side and almost—but not quite—made Tammany respectable had finally lost all patience with the smiling Greenwich Village playboy who had let Tammany run wild.

Walker and Betty settled in Nice, where he toyed with the idea of doing his autobiography, tentatively titled "Letters I Forgot to Mail." To publicize the book (which never got out of the talking stage), a film clip was released in newsreel theaters throughout New York in January of 1933 that supposedly showed the ex-mayor hard at work, with Betty taking dictation. "Send this letter to Mr. Frank D. Roosevelt, Executive Mansion, Albany," Walker directed her. "Wait a minute. . . . I guess we better mark that, 'Please Forward.' . . . They'll know where to send it."

" 'Dear Frank,' " he began, as the film clip faded out.

Meanwhile, Walker was telling Allie, via transatlantic phone, that she would have to file for divorce or he would file in France. On March 21 in Florida, greatly agitated, she tearfully did so. "My name is Janet Allen Walker," she told the judge. "My home is 4617 North Bay Road, Miami Beach. I have lived there for four years."

"What do you mean by 'living' in Miami Beach?" she was asked.

"I spend the major portion of my time there," she replied, still crying. "I keep most of my personal effects there, and have since 1928. When I travel I leave my belongings there."

"Do you maintain any other houses?"

"I have lived briefly in other places but have not changed my legal residence. Most of last summer, unfortunately, I spent in the hospital. . . ."

What caused her husband to desert her? the judge asked for the record.

"I don't know," Allie said, weeping bitterly. "He just left."

"I came here four years ago, after a trip to Cuba, because I liked it here," she continued. "He promised to come and visit me . . . but he never has."

"Have you made any efforts at reconciliation?"

"I certainly have. . . . But even this winter, when I begged him to come down here, he refused."

"Has Mr. Walker contributed in the last four years to your living expenses?"

"Oh, yes, he has never been anything but kind in that respect."

"Are you seeking any alimony?"

"I am not," said Allie, lifting her head for the first time during the interrogation.

A few days after her courtroom appearance, the forty-seven-year-old Allie was granted a divorce. Though Walker had taken good care of her financially during their years of separation (in one shop alone, she had spent some $20,000 on clothes; in another $2,500 on shoes), she now received no money from him until his death, when she was bequeathed $10,000 in his will. After the divorce, she and Jim never saw each other again, and never even spoke. Allie herself lived on, lonely and withdrawn, operating a religious bookstore in St. Patrick's Roman Catholic Church in Miami Beach. She died in Florida, at the age of seventy, in 1956.

In April of 1933, wearing neither hat nor spats but with the red ribbon of the Legion of Honor in his lapel, Walker married Betty Compton in a civil ceremony at Cannes, with only her mother and the required witnesses in attendance. He was approaching his fifty-second birthday, she her twenty-ninth. In the eyes of the Catholic Church at the time, the civil marriage meant that he was living in sin with Betty and therefore was not able to receive the Sacraments; but he was not excommunicated from the Church, as he would have been if they have been joined in a non-Catholic religious ceremony. There is evidence that Walker worried before the marriage about his separation from Holy Mother Church, but his anxiety did not deter him from his decision. For the rest of the year, the couple flitted back and forth from Cannes to Paris to northern Italy to London to Betty's birthplace on the Isle of Wight (where Walker told reporters, "What I would like more than anything else in the world is a little farm here"). When the Boswell Sisters, the New York-based radio singers, met him in London, he told Connee Boswell his true feelings: "How I miss the Big Town!"

That November, with the mayoralty again being contested for a full four-year term, New York's voters made clear their disenchantment with Tammany. Amid the largest balloting yet cast in a city election, Republican and Fusion candidate Fiorello H. LaGuardia was swept into office with some 850,000 votes. Although the LaGuardia victory was made possible only by Tammany's pigheadedly clinging to O'Brien, thereby splitting some 1,200,000 votes with McKee—once again denied the nomination by Curry and McCooey and running on the Recovery Party ticket—the vote tally itself was a mandate. Three out of five New Yorkers going to the polls had in effect repudiated Tammany. Commenting on O'Brien's year in office, Bronx Boss Flynn— the prime McKee backer—later wrote: "All the evils that had existed in the Walker regime continued. Quite properly, this situation led to a demand for a housecleaning."

Within six months, Curry was forced to resign, his place being taken by a triumvirate that included Edward J. Ahearn of the Fourth A.D., Nathan Burkan of the Seventeenth, and James J. Hines of the Eleventh. Although the tiger remained an important force in Manhattan politics for decades thereafter, it did not again come close to dominating the city or the state until the mid-1950s—and then only for a brief period before passing into oblivion.

In March of 1934, with his St. Luke's Place home sold for nonpayment of taxes and a half-dozen lawsuits pending against him in the states for expenses that either he or Allie had incurred in previous years, Walker learned that the federal government was filing a case against him for income-tax evasion. "Even in this doubtful position," he said in a statement from London, "I am glad to be on the same list with Mr. Andrew Mellon"—referring to the fact that Mellon, the multi-millionaire secretary of the treasury under Presidents Harding, Coolidge, and Hoover, was also being investigated. Actually, he continued, he welcomed the federal charges "as an opportunity of vindicating my character. I retired as Mayor simply because of my health."

A parade of visitors abroad that summer and fall brought home news of how "Jimmy" looked and acted. An ex-valet named Sam Greenhouse, who had seen him in Surrey, England, told the press the ex-mayor had gained weight; he was rushing new measurements to Jeann Friedman, Walker's tailor, so that new suits could be cut. A New York politician reported that "Jimmy has passed from wise-cracking to wisdom. . . . In the quietude of rural Old England he is reviewing the turbulent years of the past." Walker was watching La-Guardia's municipal reforms with great interest, the pol added, and had observed that "Fiorello has one advantage I didn't have. He is free to select his own aides and associates. I was not." Still other visitors professed to have noticed great changes in the ex-mayor's life habits; afternoon tea-drinking, quiet dinners, and early bedtimes were mentioned time and again.

That summer, too, saw the death in New York of the ex-mayor's older brother, Dr. William H. Walker, in an automobile accident. Now only Walker's widowed sister, Nan Burke, remained alive in his immediate family.

Later that year, the Walkers moved into a house in Surrey, near the village of Dorking; originally built by Betty's mother, it was totally remodeled and refurbished by the actress. One day each week, Walker took the train to London, where he met old cronies, usually American show-business personalities, at the Savoy bar. Yet he seems to have loved the Surrey countryside, and it came as a great shock to him when, while he and Betty were traveling in Spain, the house burned to the ground. Once more he was rootless.

In March of 1935, still unable or unwilling to pay the bills he and Allie had incurred in American shops and a hotel, Walker was served in London's chancery court with a bankruptcy notice. This was his nadir. When he and Betty dropped in about this time on Eddie Cantor, who was staying at the Dorchester, the comedian who years before had caricatured the then-debonair "Jimmy" in the Ziegfeld Follies was alarmed by his appearance. "He was broken, suddenly old," remembered Cantor. "The man who'd been Mr. Broadway! . . . who'd worn New York in his lapel!" A few months later, however,

Walker's fortunes began, if not to rise, at least to stabilize: the U.S. government announced that it was dropping its tax suit against him, and he and Betty began making plans to return from Europe. "Nothing worthwhile will ever develop [in my future]," he wrote a friend, "unless I remove the thought from some subconscious minds that I don't dare, or can't, return to New York."

On October 31, the Walkers arrived in New York aboard the liner *Manhattan*, to be welcomed at the pier by a crowd of 8,000 led by deposed Boss Curry and a mixed bag of politicians. In bowler hat and light gray topcoat, Walker appeared listless and tired, his face had an unhealthy flush, and his knees occasionally trembled. Yet John J. Dunnigan, majority leader of the state senate, ringingly declared: "He could be Mayor again any time he wants to." Walker, however, left no doubt that he had run his last campaign, "I did my very best," he said at a press conference, "and the record must tell the story. I have no vindictiveness, I have no ill feelings. Now I'm through. . . ."

The ex-mayor and Betty went to live in an apartment at 132 East Seventy-second Street, and Walker was as good as his word; he filled his days by hanging out at the Grand Street Boys or dropping in at the Friars, but he engaged in no politics. In March of 1936, the couple, after several weeks of hesitation and much publicity, adopted a six-week-old baby girl they named Mary Ann. A protective Walker declared there would be no child-photos for publication—then or ever. "We are not seeking publicity for ourselves," he said. "We are very happy to have the child and intend to bring her up quietly. She has brought a new happiness into our home." The following year they adopted a baby boy—James J. Walker, Jr. It was in 1937, too, that Walker's remaining friends in city government, to enable him to qualify for a $12,000-a-year pension, tried to name him assistant counsel to the New York Transit Commission. (When he resigned in 1932, at age fifty-one, he had been in public service the requisite number of years for a pension, but he was too young to claim it; now that he had passed his fifty-fifth birthday he would be eligible—if only he could hold a city job for thirty days.) Righteous cries of protest arose from the proponents of good government. The first appointment, made on August 16, was temporarily rescinded by the State Civil Service. By the time Walker was reappointed, on September 28, more than five years had passed since he left city government, thereby killing all prospects of a pension.

During the next four years, Walker led a relatively uneventful life. He made his peace with FDR, with whom he had a private talk in the White House, gradually recovered his natural jauntiness and emerged again as a popular speaker at city banquets, even hailing LaGuardia as "the greatest Mayor New York ever had." LaGuardia soon repaid the compliment, naming Walker labor arbiter of the women's cloak-and-suit industry; the job, which entailed keeping peace between employers and employees, paid $20,000 yearly, plus $5,000 for expenses. Reflected Walker on the endless arguments he heard, "If a man makes good suits, he'll go broke. If he makes bad ones, he'll go to jail." But Betty, still restless and still young, could never suffer tranquility gladly. In March of 1941, she obtained a Florida divorce from a surprised and heartsick Walker, charging extreme cruelty; they were to share equally in the custody of the children. "He would yell and scream and jump up and down and call me everything in the world," she testified. "At times I had to lock myself in a room to escape possible bodily harm." A year later she took her fourth husband, a fortyish, well-to-do consulting engineer named Theodore Knappen, by whom in January of 1944 she had a baby boy—her first natural child.

Seven months later, at the age of forty, Betty was dead of cancer. The night she passed away, Walker phoned Paul Schoenstein, city editor of the *Journal-American,* to ask him to keep her obituary unsullied by gossip about their affair during his mayoral years and to call his opposite numbers on the other papers and ask them to do likewise. The editor said he would do everything he could. "He was trying to hold back the tears," recalled Schoenstein. "He loved her then, and he loved her as long as he lived."

For some fifteen months, in a bizarre attempt to keep the two adopted children and Betty's infant son together (a wish she had expressed in her will), Walker and the widowed Knappen lived together as co-parents—first on the latter's estate in Old Westbury, Long Island, and then at 120 East End Avenue. Finally the two men realized the absurdity of the situation and Knappen left, taking his son with him. Into the $375-a-month East End apartment with Walker and the children moved his sister, Nan Burke, and her two sons, Paul and Luke—now young men. The family menage got along quite well, with the aging ex-mayor spending many hours with his nephews. "Tip your hat, Uncle Jimmy," said Luke, not many years out of law school, when they passed the Bronx County Courthouse on an auto ride one day; "I tried my first case there and won it."

"Tip *your* hat," Walker told him, "I *built* the courthouse!"

The ex-mayor during this period made his peace with the Church, confessing his sins and once more receiving the Sacraments. On the night table next to his bed, besides a prayer book, he kept two other religious books; one he read to himself—*The Mirror of Christ and St. Francis of Assis;* the other he read to his adopted children—*The Six O'clock Saints*. "While it is true—too awfully true—that many acts of my life were in direct denial of the faith in which I believed," he told a Catholic Communion Breakfast, "I can say truthfully that never once did I try to convince myself or others that my acts were anything but what they were. Never once did I attempt to moralize or rationalize. . . . Never once did I deny my faith to square it with my actions. . . . The glamour of other days I have found to be worthless tinsel, and all the allure of the world just so much seduction and deception."

Though time had brought about a spiritual change, Walker remained to all who knew him the symbol of a gayer, carefree era. He spent the 1940s making speeches at charitable banquets, addressing rallies to help the war effort, going to Friday-night boxing matches at Madison Square Garden. In a New York *Times* interview in April of 1945, when Walker was almost sixty-four, S. J. Woolf wrote of him, "Age has not withered New York's Peter Pan, nor have setbacks soured him. The former Night Mayor has become the Toastmaster of the Town, and a complete public dinner now means everything from soup to Walker."

When Woolf, toward the end of the interview, showed an interest in Walker's latest job, as president of Majestic Records, and asked him if he would be putting out a recording of "Will You Love Me in December as You Did in May?" his subject showed that he had not lost his verve.

"I've been hired to plug the company," Walker said, "not sabotage it."

In 1946 Walker's health—always precarious in these last years despite his youthful appearance—greatly worsened; he suffered headaches and often stayed in his darkened bedroom. On November 12, after a speech before the Grand Street Boys Association, Walker returned home in such poor condition that Nan was forced to call his personal physician to the apartment. After several days of nausea and dizziness, he fell into a coma, was given the last rites of the Catholic Church and taken to Doctors Hospital. On November 18, without regaining consciousness, the sixty-five-year-old Walker died of a clot on the brain.

Thousands of persons, most with tears in their eyes and many carrying rosary beads, passed by his coffin at Campbell's Funeral Home, surrounded by a plethora of bouquets and wreaths. Later Walker's spirit was consigned to his God in a solemn high requiem mass at St. Patrick's Cathedral. His body then was taken for burial to Gate of Heaven Cemetery in Westchester. When his modest estate was finally settled, New York learned that the man who had amassed some $1 million in "benefices" during his terms in office was worth only $38,000.

Among the many achievements of his lifetime, Walker had been proudest—in a peculiarly Irish way—of one accomplishment: He had stuck by his friends, no matter what. Little Jimmy Talker, as his first pastor at St. Joseph's Church in Greenwich Village had called the impulsive, likable schoolboy so many years before, could—by his lights—now rest in peace. Perhaps the best epitaph was sounded by restaurateur Toots Shor, in whose place—a hangout for show-business, sports, and political celebrities—Walker had spent many a gregarious evening. "Jimmy! Jimmy!" mused Shor, looking at the body. "When you walked into the room you brightened up the joint!"

The words echoed the feelings of everyone who had ever known Gentleman Jimmy. The city he loved would never see his like again.

BIBLIOGRAPHY

BOOKS

ALLEN, FREDERICK LEWIS. *Only Yesterday*. New York: Harper & Brothers, 1931.

————. *Since Yesterday*. New York: Harper & Brothers, 1940.

ASBURY, HERBERT. *The Gangs of New York*. New York: Alfred A. Knopf, 1927.

————. *The Great Illusion*. New York: Doubleday, 1950.

BAINBRIDGE, JOHN. *The Wonderful World of Toots Shor*. Boston: Houghton Mifflin, 1950.

BEEBE, LUCIUS. *Shoot if You Must*. New York: Appleton-Century, 1943.

BYNES, THOMAS. *Professional Criminals of America*. New York: Chelsea House, 1969 (reprint of 1886 edition).

CANTOR, EDDIE, and DAVID FRIEDMAN. *Ziegfeld*. New York: Alfred H. King, 1934.

CANTOR, EDDIE, with JANE ARDMORE. *Take My Life*. New York: Doubleday, 1961.

CHURCHILL, ALLEN. *The Great White Way*. New York: E. P. Dutton, 1962.

CLARKE, DONALD HENDERSON. *In the Reign of Rothstein*. New York: Vanguard, 1929.

————. *Man of the World*. New York: Vanguard, 1951.

COHEN, LESTER. *The New York Graphic* Radnor, Pa.: Chilton, 1964.

CONNOBLE, ALFRED, and EDWARD SILBERFARB. *Tigers of Tammany*. Holt, Rinehart & Winston, 1967.

CRATER, STELLA, with OSCAR FRALEY. *The Empty Robe*. New York: Doubleday, 1961.

DALEY, ROBERT. *The World Beneath the City*. Philadelphia: Lippincott, 1959.

EWEN, DAVID. *American Musical Theater.* New York: Holt, Rinehart & Winston, 1958.

FARLEY, JAMES A. *Behind the Ballots.* New York: Harcourt, Brace, 1938.

FERBER, NAT J. *I Found Out.* New York: Dial, 1939.

FINEGAN, JAMES EMMET. *Tammany at Bay.* New York: Dodd, Mead, 1933.

FLYNN, EDWARD J. *You're the Boss.* New York: Viking, 1947.

FOWLER, GENE. *Beau James.* New York: Viking, 1949.

————. *The Great Mouthpiece.* New York: Grosset & Dunlap, 1931.

FULLER, HECTOR. *Abroad With Mayor Walker.* Boulder, Colo.: Shields, 1928.

GARRETT, CHARLES. *The LaGuardia Years.* New Brunswick, N.J.: Rutgers University Press, 1961.

GOLDING, LOUIS. *The Bare Knuckle Breed.* New York: A. S. Barnes, 1954.

GREEN, ABEL, and JOE LAURIE JR. *Show Biz.* New York: Henry Holt, 1951.

GRIBETZ, LOUIS J., and JOSEPH KAYE. *Jimmie Walker.* New York: Dial, 1932.

HANDLIN, OSCAR. *Al Smith and His America.* Boston: Atlantic–Little Brown, 1958.

HARLOW, ALVIN F. *Old Bowery Days.* New York: Appleton, 1931.

HEADLEY, JOEL TYLER. *The Great Riots of New York: 1712–1873* (1873). Reprint, New York: Dover, 1971.

JESSEL, GEORGE. *So Help Me.* New York: Random House, 1943.

JOSEPHSON, MATTHEW, and HANNAH JOSEPHSON. *Al Smith: Hero of the Cities.* Boston: Houghton Mifflin, 1969.

KAHN, E. J., JR. *The World of Swope.* New York: Simon & Schuster, 1965.

KATCHER, LEO. *The Big Bankroll.* New York: Harper & Brothers, 1958.

KOBLER, JOHN. *Capone.* New York: G. P. Putnam's Sons, 1971.

KOUWENHOVEN, JOHN A. *The Columbia Historical Portrait of New York.* New York: Doubleday, 1953.

LARDNER, JOHN. *White Hopes and Other Tigers.* Philadelphia: Lippincott, 1947.

LARDNER, REX. *The Legendary Champions.* New York: American Heritage Press, 1972.

LAVINE, EMANUEL H. *"Gimme."* New York: Vanguard, 1931.

LIMPUS, LOWELL. *Honest Cop.* New York: E. P. Dutton, 1939.

LOVAN, ANDY. *Against the Evidence.* New York: Saturday Review Press, 1970.

LYNCH, DENIS TILDEN. *Boss Tweed.* New York: Boni & Liveright, 1927.

————. *Criminals and Politicians.* New York: Macmillan, 1932.

MACKAYE, MILTON. *The Tin Box Parade.* Robert McBride, 1934.

MAXTONE-GRAHAM, JOHN. *The Only Way to Cross.* New York: Macmillan, 1972.

MAYER, MARTIN. *Emory Buckner.* New York: Harper & Row, 1968.

MEYERS, GUSTAVUS. *History of Tammany Hall.* New York: Boni & Liveright, 1917.

MITGANG, HERBERT. *The Man Who Rode the Tiger.* Philadelphia: Lippincott, 1963.

MORRIS, LLOYD. *Incredible New York.* New York: Random House, 1951.

MOSCOW, WARREN. *Politics in the Empire State.* New York: Knopf, 1948.

MOSES, ROBERT. *Public Works.* New York: McGraw-Hill, 1970.

NORTHRUP, WILLIAM B. and JOHN B. NORTHRUP. *The Insolence of Office.* New York: G. P. Putnam's Sons, 1932.

PRINGLE, HENRY F. *Alfred E. Smith.* Macy-Masius, 1927.

REARDON, WILLIAM L. *Plunkitt of Tammany Hall.* (Reprint, 1905.) New York: E. P. Dutton, 1963.

ROTHSTEIN, CAROLYN. *Now I'll Tell.* New York: Vanguard, 1934.

ROVERE, RICHARD H. *The American Establishment.* New York: Harcourt, Brace, 1962.

SHAW, CHARLES G. *Nightlife.* New York: John Day, 1931.

SMITH, ALFRED E. *Up to Now.* New York: Viking, 1929.

STODDARD, THEODORE L. *Master of Manhattan.* New York: Longmans, Green, 1931.

STOKES, I. N. PHELPS. *New York Past and Present.* Plantin, 1939.

SWANBERG, W. A. *Citizen Hearst.* New York: Charles Scribner's Sons, 1961.

VALENTINE, LEWIS J. *Nightstick.* New York: Dial, 1947.

VAN DEVANDER, CHARLES W. *The Big Bosses.* Howell, Soskin, 1944.

WALKER, STANLEY. *Mrs. Astor's Horse.* Frederick A. Stokes, 1935.

―――. *Nightclub Era.* Frederick A. Stokes, 1933.

WARNER, EMILY SMITH. *The Happy Warrior.* New York: Doubleday, 1956.

WERNER, M. R. *Tammany Hall.* New York: Doubleday, Doran, 1928.

WHALEN, GROVER. *Mr. New York.* G. P. Putnam's Sons, 1955.

WILLEMSE, CORNELIUS. *Behind the Green Lights.* New York: Knopf, 1931.

―――. *A Cop Remembers.* New York: E. P. Dutton, 1933.

WOOLLCOTT, ALEXANDER. *The Story of Irving Berlin.* New York: G. P. Putnam's Sons, 1925.

ZINN, HOWARD. *LaGuardia in Congress.* Ithaca, N.Y.: Cornell University Press, 1959. Reprint, New York: W. W. Norton, 1969.

PERIODICALS (bylined articles)

In assembling material for this book, I must acknowledge a special debt to *The New Yorker,* which in the late 1920's and early 1930's was the only periodical giving its readers the magazine profile as we know it today.

ALEXANDER, JACK. "District Leader," *The New Yorker,* July 25, Aug. 1 and 8, 1936.

―――. "Independent Cop," *The New Yorker,* Oct. 3, 10, and 17, 1936.

BARRY, R. "Mr. Murphy, the Politician's Politician," *Outlook,* May 7, 1924.

BEHRMAN, S. N. "Troubadour," *The New Yorker,* May 25, 1929.

BERGER, MEYER. "Bail-Bond Baron," *The New Yorker,* March 25, 1933.

―――. "Lady in Crepe," *The New Yorker,* Oct. 5 and 12, 1935.

BOYER, RICHARD O. "Inquisitor," *The New Yorker,* June 27, 1931.

―――. "Trade of the Journalist," *American Mercury,* January, 1929.

BULLOCK, W. "Hylan," *American Mercury,* April, 1924.

BUSCH, NIVEN, JR. "The Emerald Boss," *The New Yorker,* March 12, 1927.

―――. "Fire Sign," *The New Yorker,* April 20, 1929.

―――. "Headquarters," *The New Yorker,* May 20, 1929.

―――. "Paid Piper," *The New Yorker,* Nov. 27, 1926.

BUSCH, NIVEN, JR., and A. BARR GRAY. "The Cop in the Silk Shirt," *The New Yorker,* Sept. 25, 1926.

CHENERY, W. L. "So This Is Tammany Hall?" *Atlantic,* September, 1924.

COATES, ROBERT M. "The Realtor," *The New Yorker,* June 1, 1929.

CREEL, G. "Boy-Friend," *Collier's,* Aug. 13, 1932.

CROWELL, J. R. "I Choose to Smile," *Saturday Evening Post,* May 24, 1930.

DAVENPORT, W. "Tammany Touch," *Collier's,* Feb. 11, 1933.

HYLAN, J. F. "William Randolph Hearst," *Forum,* June, 1923.

JOHNSTON, ALVA. "Big Jim," *The New Yorker,* Nov. 28, 1931.

——. "Blumey," *The New Yorker,* Feb. 4 and 11, 1933.

——. "Boss Hague, the Bandwagon and Beer," *The New Yorker,* July 16, 1932.

——. "Centenarian," *The New Yorker,* June 22, 1929.

——. "Courtroom Warrior," *The New Yorker,* March 12 and 19, 1932.

——. "The Gilded Copper," *The New Yorker,* Jan. 12, 1929.

——. "Let Freedom Ring," *The New Yorker,* June 4 and 11, 1932.

——. "Little Giant," *The New Yorker,* May 17 and 24, 1930.

——. "My Lawyer," *The New Yorker,* May 16 and 23, 1931.

——. "No More Lawyers," *The New Yorker,* Jan. 9, 1932.

——. "The Scholar in Politics," *The New Yorker,* July 1 and 8, 1933.

——. "Saint in Politics," *The New Yorker,* March 23, 1929.

KAUFMAN, GEORGE S. "Jimmy, the Well-Dressed Mayor," *The Nation,* June 15, 1932.

LIPPMANN, WALTER. "Tammany Hall and Al Smith," *Outlook,* Feb. 1, 1928.

LITTELL, P. "Why Is Mr. Hylan Mayor of New York?" *New Republic,* Sept. 27, 1922.

LYNCH, DENIS TILDEN. "Boss Rule," *Literary Digest,* June 11, 1932.

——. "Friends of the Governor," *North American Review,* October, 1928.

MACADAMS, G. "Governor Smith of New York," *World's Work,* January, 1920.

McGOLDRICK, J. "New Tammany," *American Mercury,* September, 1928.

MACKAYE, MILTON. "Cop's Cop," *The New Yorker,* Oct. 24, 1931.

——. "Good Morning, Judge," *The New Yorker,* Aug. 30, 1930.

——. "The Governor," *The New Yorker,* Aug. 15 and 22, 1931.

——. "St. George of Manhattan," *The New Yorker,* Jan. 30, 1932.

McKELWAY, ST. CLAIR. "Average Cop," *The New Yorker,* Feb. 10, 1934.

MARKEY, MORRIS. "Day in Court," *The New Yorker,* Sept. 25, 1926.

——. "Our Gangs," *The New Yorker,* Oct. 9, 1926.

——. "The Royal Visitor," *The New Yorker,* Oct. 30, 1926.

MATTHEWS, T. S. "Simple Story," *New Republic,* June 13, 1928.

MERZ, C. "Battle of Tammany Tall," *World's Work,* June, 1929.

OLVANY, GEORGE W. "Present-Day Tammany," *Scribner's,* November, 1928.

OLVANY, GEORGE W., and DENIS TILDEN LYNCH. "Tammany Upheld and Condemned," *Current History,* November, 1928.

OWEN, RUSSELL. "Master Ditch Digger," *The New Yorker,* June 4, 1927.

POWELL, HICKMAN. "The Governor," *The New Yorker,* May 2 and 9, 1936.

PRINGLE, HENRY F. "Bringing Up the City Fathers," *The New Yorker,* Sept. 10, 1927.

——. "Italian Table D'Hote," *The New Yorker,* Aug. 31, 1929.

——. "Jimmie Walker," *American Mercury,* November, 1926.

——. "Local Boy Makes Good," *The New Yorker,* Aug. 3, 1929.

——. "Portrait of a Mayor at Large," *Harper's,* February, 1928.

——. "Tammany Hall, Inc.," *Atlantic,* October, 1932.

——. "What's Happening to Tammany?" *Outlook,* May 15, 1929.

——. "Wheels in His Head," *The New Yorker,* Dec. 13, 1927.

RAY, M. B. "Jimmy Walker Tells How to Make a Good Speech," *American Mercury*, April 30, 1931.

RAYMOND, A. "From Playboy to Pietist," *North American Review*, Feb. 25, 1933.

ROSENBAULT, C. J. "New Ways of the Old Tiger," *World's Work*, July, 1924.

ROSS, MALCOLM. "I'd Give My Shirt for Al," *The New Yorker*, June 23, 1928.

SAUNDERS, W. O. "Red Mike or Honest John?" *Collier's*, May 9, 1925.

SAYRE, JOEL. "Big Shot-At," *The New Yorker*, June 13, 1931.

SUGRUE, THOMAS. "Cardinal Sheperd," *The New Yorker*, Feb. 17, 1934.

THOMPSON, C. F. "New York's Jimmie," *The Nation*, Aug. 28, 1929.

————. "Tammany Monster," *Catholic World*, October, 1928.

WARE, F. "Meet the Mayor," *North American Review*, January, 1928.

WERNER, M. R. "Jimmy Walker and Oakley Hall," *New Republic*, May 27, 1931.

WINSLOW, THYRA SAMTER. "Diamond Mae," *The New Yorker*, Nov. 10, 1928.

PERIODICALS (nonbylined articles, listed chronologically)

"When Hearst and Murphy Fall Out," *Literary Digest*, Nov. 15, 1919.

"Mayor Hylan's Boom for Hearst," *Literary Digest*, Dec. 30, 1922.

"Silent Charlie, the Mayor's Mayor," *Literary Digest*, May 17, 1924.

"Plunkitt of Tammany," *Literary Digest*, Jan. 3, 1925.

"Foley, Last of the Old-Time Tammany Bosses," *Literary Digest*, Jan. 31, 1925.

"Smith's Triumph over Hylan and Hearst," *Literary Digest*, Sept. 26, 1925.

"His Honor Jimmy Walker, Mayor of Europe," *Literary Digest*, Oct. 8, 1927.

"Man Who Makes the Tiger Smile," *Literary Digest*, May 11, 1929.

"Mayoralty Circus," *The Nation*, Oct. 23, 1929.

"Silent Men of Tammany," *Outlook*, Oct. 8, 1930.

"Musical Comedy Mayor," *Outlook*, May 20, 1931.

"Roosevelt's Clash With the Tammany Tiger," *Literary Digest*, Sept. 12, 1931.

"Mr. Curry's Favors," *Collier's*, Oct. 24, 1931.

"Walker's Battle for Mooney," *Literary Digest*, Dec. 5, 1931.

"Seabury Strips the Tammany Tiger," *Literary Digest*, Feb. 6, 1932.

"Verdict of the Nation's Press," *Literary Digest*, June 11, 1932.

"Walker, Hot Coal in Roosevelt's Hands," *Literary Digest*, Aug. 13, 1932.

"McKee's Break With Tammany," *Literary Digest*, Nov. 26, 1932.

NEWSPAPERS

Most of the material in this book by far comes from the newspaper stories of the period. I found particularly helpful the New York *American, Evening Post, Times,* and *World.*

INDEX